Religious Ethics

Principles, practice and society

Declan McCay

Colourpoint
Educational

Rewarding Learning

ISBN: 978 1 904242 93 2

First Edition
Second Impression

Layout and design: April Sky Design
Printed by: GPS Colour Graphics Ltd, Belfast

Cover picture: iStockphoto

COLOURPOINT EDUCATIONAL

Colourpoint Educational
An imprint of Colourpoint Creative Ltd
Colourpoint House
Jubilee Business Park
21 Jubilee Road
Newtownards
County Down
Northern Ireland
BT23 4YH

Tel: 028 9182 6339
Fax: 028 9182 1900
E-mail: info@colourpoint.co.uk
Web site: www.colourpoint.co.uk

The author

Declan McCay

Declan McCay has been teaching Religious Studies for nine years, the past eight of which have been at Thornhill College in Derry, where he is currently Head of Year 14.

He has been involved in the examining of A level Ethics with CCEA for the past seven years.

Declan lives in Derry with his wife Shirley and their two children Orlaith and Odhran.

For Shirley, Orlaith and Odhran. I dedicate this book to them.

Contents

Author Preface

This text has been written specifically to assist both teachers and students in meeting the requirements of CCEA's GCE Religious Studies AS and A2 courses on Religious Ethics. The first section of the book covers the AS course (Religious Ethics: Foundations, Principles and Practice) and the second section deals with the A2 course (Ethics and Society). Both sections address CCEA's requirement to explore 'other aspects of human experience' and while various suggestions are made throughout the chapters it is recommended that students also investigate their own links between the taught course and other aspects of human experience.

This book is a collation of a wide range of material available on religious ethics and every effort has been made to acknowledge the sources used in the endnotes following each chapter. The endnotes provide students with references for the many quotations and points of view given throughout the text. An awareness of scholarly views is an important requirement of A level study, in particular at A2 level. However, it is best for students to avoid simply listing views of scholars in a response but to use them to support their point or argument. The summary of key points at the end of each chapter is useful as a revision guide in preparation for examinations.

Thanks are due to a number of people for their help and support during the completion of this book. Thanks to both Donna Finlay at CCEA and Sheila Johnston at Colourpoint Books for giving me the opportunity to write this textbook. Many thanks also go to Rachel Irwin at Colourpoint for her guidance throughout the completion of this book and to Sean Mc Ilroy (Sacred Heart College, Newry) for his assistance. I would also like to thank a number of my colleagues at Thornhill College who have taken time to proof read sections of the book – Tom Mallon, Karen McFadden and Ciara Collins. Special thanks to Teresa Halligan (Head of Religious Studies) for her encouragement and very welcome suggestions on a range of topics. Thanks also to Sarah Kelly, Principal of Thornhill College, for her support throughout this project.

A very special word of thanks to my wife Shirley and my two children Orlaith and Odhran for their support, understanding and patience. I dedicate this book to them.

Chapter 1

Foundations of Christian Ethics

Chapter overview

This chapter aims to explore the following topics:

- An introduction to Ethics
- Old Testament ethical teaching with specific reference to the Decalogue
- Jesus' teaching from the Sermon on the Mount
- The moral teaching of Saint Paul

INTRODUCTION TO ETHICS

THE AUSTRALIAN PHILOSOPHER Peter Singer defines ethics as follows: "Ethics, also called moral philosophy is the discipline concerned with what is morally good and bad, right and wrong. The term is also applied to any system or theory of moral values or principles."[1] Singer's definition explains the fact that ethics is a branch of philosophy which is concerned with the morality of our actions and whether they are right or wrong. This quotation also highlights how the terms 'ethics' and 'morality' are used in the same context and are quite often used interchangeably. However, at this point it is important to differentiate between the exact meanings of the two words.

The word 'ethic' originates from the Greek word *ethikos* from which we derive the word 'ethos' meaning 'custom' or 'character'. Vardy and Grosch comment that ethics refers to "the customary way to behave in society."[2] In other words, the term 'ethic' refers to a set of principles or moral values which help us distinguish between what is considered to be right or wrong behaviour.

The word 'morality' comes from the Latin word *moralis*. While ethics is concerned with customs or values, morality is more concerned with the actual behaviour of the individual or the action rather than the character or the values held by the person who performs the actions.

In terms of morality, our actions can be described as being either moral or immoral.

- The word **moral** refers to an action which is considered right or good. For example, giving money to those who suffer from poverty would be considered as the right, or moral, thing to do because we are doing something positive in an attempt to relieve human suffering. According to the author Mel Thompson, if our actions are moral it means that they "conform to a set of ethical norms."[3]

- If an action is described as being **immoral** then it can be described as being either wrong or bad and is considered to "go against a professed set of norms"[4]. For example, abortion may be considered to be immoral by many Christians living in Northern Ireland today because they consider it to be the destruction of innocent human life and this is contrary to the commandment: *"You shall not murder"* (Exodus 20:13).

Thompson adds a third definition to the two terms already discussed:

- The word **amoral** is described as an "action that is not seen as morally significant by the person performing it."[5] The action is neither good nor bad in terms of morality because it is committed by someone who does not know the difference between right and wrong, for example, an infant or someone who suffers from a severe mental illness.

For Christians today, the Bible is the ultimate source of ethical values, which include the Ten Commandments from the Old Testament and the teachings of Jesus and Paul in the New Testament. The divine command theory asserts that something is good or moral if God commands it and wrong if he has forbidden it. In 1947, the Swiss, Protestant theologian Emil Brunner (1889–1966) commented: "The good consists in always doing what God wills at any particular moment."[6] Therefore, if we follow Jesus' teaching, it is good to love our neighbour because Jesus commanded it in Luke 10:27 and it is wrong or immoral to kill an innocent person because God in the Ten Commandments said: *"You shall not murder"* (Exodus 20:13). On this issue, the theologian Paul Helm comments: "God does issue commands and that these commands are to form the basis of a believer's morality."[7]

However, some philosophers, mainly from a secular background, have argued that murder is an immoral action regardless of what God commands. They claim that human life has intrinsic value and therefore, whether or not we believe in God and his teaching, we have a moral responsibility to preserve human life. From this perspective, morality does not depend on God. This is evident in our society today because many values held by Christians are also held by those who have not had a religious upbringing.

This debate concerning whether or not God is the source of morality, is referred to as the **Euthyphro dilemma**. In an excerpt from Plato's book, *Euthyphro*, Socrates, having a discussion with Euthyphro, asks this question: "Is what is pious loved by the gods because it is pious, or is it pious because it is loved?"[8] Put more simply, Socrates is reflecting on the question: "Is conduct right because the gods command it or do the gods command it because it is right?"[9] Take the example of murder, is murder wrong because God tells us it is wrong or is murder wrong in itself, regardless of what God says about it?

Philosophers who critically reflect on the implications of the divine command theory ask what if God commanded people to kill? Consider the command given by God to Abraham in Genesis 22:2 to *"Take your son, your only son, Isaac, whom you love, and go to the region of Moriah. Sacrifice him there as a burnt offering on one of the mountains I will tell you about."* Both Jews and Christians accept that in this account God was testing Abraham's faith, however, what if he wasn't? Would his request make the sacrifice of children morally acceptable? According to Tyler and Reid, the existentialist Sören Kierkegaard (1813–1855) did not accept the divine command theory. He claimed: "we should not confuse ethics or morality with doing the will of God."[10] Kierkegaard held this opinion because in many cases, God actually commands immoral behaviour. For example, the Old Testament stresses that the death penalty is an adequate punishment for anyone who curses his or her father or mother (Exodus 21:17) and it also permits a man to sell his daughter as a slave (Exodus 21:7).

In contrast to the view held by Kierkegaard, the French Philosopher René Descartes (1596–1650) argued: "whatever God has revealed to us must be accepted as more certain than anything else…we must still put our entire faith in divine authority rather than on our own judgement."[11] Other philosophers have also accepted the point of view that God is the source of morality. For example, Dostoyevsky claimed: "without God, everything is permitted",[12] ie he claimed that if we do not believe in God then we have no reason to act morally and therefore we have no boundaries to set limits on how we behave.

Despite arguments to the contrary, many Christians today still maintain the view that right and wrong can be defined in terms of God's will. However, for others such as atheists and humanists, morality is not a matter of religious faith but based on factors such as conscience and ethical values promoted by secular society. For Christians today, who do accept the divine command theory – that morality does come from God – scripture is of central importance. For the AS Ethics specification the following three areas of scripture must be considered in detail:

1. The Decalogue (The Ten Commandments)
2. Jesus' teaching from the Sermon on the Mount
3. The moral teaching of Saint Paul

Allsop[13] comments that the moral values promoted by scripture make Christian ethics distinctive in a number of ways. He claims that Christian ethical teaching is unique because living our lives according to God's plan for creation is of central importance. He also comments that because human existence extends beyond death, Christians have an incentive to live a virtuous life in order to gain the reward of eternal life. Allsop also claims that Christian ethics are unique because of the view that human life is sacred as humans are created in the image of God. Finally, according to Allsop:

"the fourth distinctive moral emphasis will be the importance given to love". Love is certainly one word which summarises the entire Christian ethic. This is illustrated through the moral teaching of Saint Paul found in his epistles and the ethical teaching of Jesus and the Decalogue, which all highlight the importance of love of God and neighbour. If Christians can achieve this standard of truly loving God and neighbour, then they can claim to live a morally decent life and will be rewarded with eternal life.

OLD TESTAMENT ETHICAL TEACHING WITH SPECIFIC REFERENCE TO THE DECALOGUE

The word 'Decalogue' is the Greek term for the Ten Commandments, which literally means 'ten words'. The term dates back to the time of the early Church but is still used by Christians today to refer to the Ten Commandments given to Moses by *Yahweh* (the Jewish or Hebrew name for God) on Mount Sinai. The theologian John Drane comments that the number ten is significant: "The fact that there are Ten Commandments is certainly not accidental, but is a learning device so that they could be counted off on the fingers of both hands as they were repeated."[14]

Before we consider the individual commandments and the moral significance of each, it is important to note that Christians today do not structure the Ten Commandments in the same way. The Reformed Churches generally follow one method of dividing the Commandments, while Catholics and Lutherans follow another. Consider the following tables which indicate the differences in how the commandments are numbered:

Table 1 – Division of the Decalogue according to the Reformed Churches (with the exception of Lutherans)

Reference in Exodus	God's Command
1st Commandment 20:2–3	*I am the LORD your God, who brought you out of Egypt, out of the land of slavery. You shall have no other gods before me.*
2nd Commandment 20:4–6	*You shall not make for yourself an idol in the form of anything in heaven above or on the earth beneath or in the waters below. You shall not bow down to them or worship them; for I, the LORD your God, am a jealous God, punishing the children for the sin of the fathers to the third and fourth generation of those who hate me, but showing love to a thousand {generations} of those who love me and keep my commandments.*
3rd Commandment 20:7	*You shall not misuse the name of the LORD your God, for the LORD will not hold anyone guiltless who misuses his name.*

4th Commandment 20:8–11	*Remember the Sabbath day by keeping it holy. Six days you shall labour and do all your work, but the seventh day is a Sabbath to the LORD your God. On it you shall not do any work, neither you, nor your son or daughter, nor your manservant or maidservant, nor your animals, nor the alien within your gates. For in six days the LORD made the heavens and the earth, the sea, and all that is in them, but he rested on the seventh day. Therefore the LORD blessed the Sabbath day and made it holy.*
5th Commandment 20:12	*Honour your father and your mother, so that you may live long in the land the LORD your God is giving you.*
6th Commandment 20:13	*You shall not murder.*
7th Commandment 20:14	*You shall not commit adultery.*
8th Commandment 20:15	*You shall not steal.*
9th Commandment 20:16	*You shall not bear false testimony against your neighbour.*
10th Commandment 20:17	*You shall not covet your neighbour's house. You shall not covet your neighbour's wife, or his manservant or maidservant, his ox or donkey, or anything that belongs to your neighbour.*

Table 2 – Division of the Decalogue according to the Roman Catholic Church and Lutherans

Reference in Exodus.	God's Command
1st Commandment 20:2–6	*I am the LORD your God, who brought you out of Egypt, out of the land of slavery. You shall have no other gods before me.* *You shall not make for yourself an idol in the form of anything in heaven above or on the earth beneath or in the waters below. You shall not bow down to them or worship them; for I, the LORD your God, am a jealous God, punishing the children for the sin of the fathers to the third and fourth generation of those who hate me, but showing love to a thousand {generations} of those who love me and keep my commandments.*

2nd Commandment 20:7	*You shall not misuse the name of the LORD your God, for the LORD will not hold anyone guiltless who misuses his name.*
3rd Commandment 20:8–11	*Remember the Sabbath day by keeping it holy. Six days you shall labour and do all your work, but the seventh day is a Sabbath to the LORD your God. On it you shall not do any work, neither you, nor your son or daughter, nor your manservant or maidservant, nor your animals, nor the alien within your gates. For in six days the LORD made the heavens and the earth, the sea, and all that is in them, but he rested on the seventh day. Therefore the LORD blessed the Sabbath day and made it holy.*
4th Commandment 20:12	*Honour your father and your mother, so that you may live long in the land the LORD your God is giving you.*
5th Commandment 20:13	*You shall not murder.*
6th Commandment 20:14	*You shall not commit adultery.*
7th Commandment 20:15	*You shall not steal.*
8th Commandment 20:16	*You shall not bear false testimony against your neighbour.*
9th Commandment 20:17a	*You shall not covet your neighbour's wife.*
10th Commandment 20:17b	*You shall not covet your neighbour's house, or his manservant or maidservant, his ox or donkey, or anything that belongs to your neighbour.*

Regardless of how Christians today choose to divide or number the stipulations, at the time that the Decalogue was given by *Yahweh* to the Israelites, it was considered to be part of the covenant or agreement which set the Jews apart from other nations. A covenant was a binding contract and in this case, God agreed to treat the Israelites as his favoured nation, if they agreed to love him and follow his commandments. According to Barton: "God promised to keep his side of the bargain, to continue the blessings which he had begun...whilst Israel, for its part, was under an obligation to maintain the contract by loyalty to God, exclusive worship of him, and obedience to his commandments."[15]

One aspect of this covenant relationship was the issue of holiness which is fully developed in the book of Leviticus. God commands the Israelites: *"Be holy because I, the*

Lord your God, am Holy" (Leviticus 19:2). TD Alexander comments that the Decalogue "sets out how the people must live in order to be a holy nation."[16] The Jews had a unique relationship with God, for example, Exodus 19:5 informs us: *"Now if you obey me fully and keep my covenant, then out of all nations you will be my treasured possession."* As the reference suggests, obedience was a very important aspect of the covenant. From the relationship between *Yahweh* and the Israelites it is evident that God is the dominant party who "establishes the terms of the covenant relationship" while the Israelites are the submissive party who must "be obedient to those terms."[17] Israelites however, are free to accept or to reject the terms of the covenant. They do accept and agree to obey the laws given by *Yahweh* and claim: *"We will do everything the Lord has said"* (Exodus 19:8).

The importance of this covenant in comparison to previous agreements made with Noah (Genesis 6:18) and Abraham (Genesis 15) is that this one, which is referred to as the Sinai Covenant, is not with one person as was the case in the previous two, but with a whole nation. The permanence of the commandments which form part of this covenant is illustrated by the fact that *"the finger of God"* (Exodus 31:18) has scribed them on stone tablets.

In Exodus 20:2–17 the commandments appear to be presented in order of importance and if this is the case then the laws dealing with the Israelites' relationship with God are the priority. According to Tyler, this order is important because "if man's relationship with God is right then his relationship with others will be right."[18]

The book of Exodus informs us that before God delivered the Ten Commandments, the Israelites stood waiting at the foot of Mount Sinai and *"there was thunder and lightning, with a thick cloud over the mountain, and a very loud trumpet blast. Everyone in the camp trembled. Then Moses led the people out of the camp to meet with God, and they stood at the foot of the mountain"* (Exodus 19:16–17) and then God *"spoke these words"* (Exodus 20:1).

What follows is a brief discussion of the moral significance of the commandments, which according to Allsop, are "identified by Christians as containing the central moral principles which God wants human beings to observe."[19]

The Decalogue

I am the LORD your God, who brought you out of Egypt, out of the land of slavery. You shall have no other gods before me.

According to TD Alexander, this first commandment stresses that "sole allegiance to the Lord lies at the very heart of the covenant relationship."[20] The fact that the Israelites were requested to be monotheistic highlights that the Decalogue aims to set them apart from other polytheistic nations. Huesman comments that belief in and worship of "one God was intended to distinguish Israel from her neighbours, who all boasted a host of heavenly deities."[21] If this commandment was not adhered to then the punishment for such disobedience was death, according to Numbers 25:1–18 and Deuteronomy 13:1–18. The punishments were so severe because the Israelites were expected to remain faithful to *Yahweh*, to show appreciation for his love and his intervention which enabled them to escape from slavery in Egypt. The Shema, found in Deuteronomy 6:4–5, illustrates the extent to which the Israelites must love God in return for the love he has shown them: *"Hear, O Israel. The Lord our God is one Lord. Love the Lord your God with all your heart, and with all your soul and with all your strength."*

You shall not make for yourself an idol…You shall not bow down to them or worship them.

In order to set the Israelites apart from other nations, it was also important that they did not have images of false gods. In Exodus 32, we are informed that this commandment was broken when the Israelites worshipped the golden calf. Once again, the punishment for such a breach of the rules of this covenant was severe: *"And the LORD struck the people with a plague because of what they did with the calf Aaron had made"* (Exodus 32:35).

You shall not misuse the name of the LORD your God.

The purpose of this stipulation was to insist that the name of God was treated with respect at all times. The Biblical commentator Houston states: "it is quite clear that the improper use of the name *Yahweh* is prohibited."[22] The use of the name of the Lord must therefore be reserved for praising and glorifying God. Blasphemy was the sin of misusing God's name and in order to avoid this sin the Jews completely avoided saying the Lord's name. If *Yahweh* appeared in a text, the reader would not say it but would replace it with the word 'Adonai' meaning 'Lord'.[23]

Remember the Sabbath day by keeping it holy.

In Genesis 2:3 we are informed: *"And God blessed the seventh day and made it holy, because on it he rested from all the work of creating that he had done."* According to this commandment, the Jews were not permitted to work on this sacred day but were to use the time to worship God. The Biblical critic Huesman comments that this commandment has a "humanitarian motive"[24] in that it permits family members, slaves, animals and the *"alien within your gates"* to have a day free from any work. However, Houston argues: "the primary emphasis is on the special character of the day, determined by *Yahweh* in the beginning, rather than on the need of the people to rest."[25]

Honour your father and your mother.

In Exodus 21:15 and 17 the punishment for breaking this commandment is death:
- *"Anyone who attacks his father or his mother must be put to death"* (v15).

- *"Anyone who curses his father or mother must be put to death"* (v17).

This commandment and the punishments for not keeping it listed elsewhere in the Book of the Covenant,[26] highlight the importance of respect for family, which is a value that forms the foundation of a good society, especially a hierarchical one, which was the case in ancient Israel. TD Alexander stresses that the importance of this commandment was because "any attempt to undermine their authority was an attack on the basic authority structure within the local community."[27]

You shall not murder.

Genesis 1:27 states: *"So God created man in his own image"* and the implication of this is that human life is sacred. According to Huesman, this commandment was intended to "protect the very sacredness of human life by forbidding murder."[28] Elsewhere in the Pentateuch (the name given to the first five books of the Old Testament) we are informed that the punishment for murder is death. In Genesis 9:6 we are told: *"Whoever sheds the blood of man, by a man shall his blood be shed."* However, this commandment does not prohibit "judicial executions for capital offences or legitimate deaths resulting from war."[29]

 TASK

A moral absolute is a "moral command or prohibition that's true for all time, in all places and in all situations."[30] It is a rule which can never be broken, regardless of the consequences. Is *"You shall not murder"* an acceptable moral absolute or are there circumstances in which it is morally acceptable to take a person's life? Discuss with specific reference to abortion, euthanasia, war and capital punishment.

You shall not commit adultery.

Through this commandment, the Decalogue promotes the importance of marriage by prohibiting sexual intercourse between a married woman and a man who was not her husband.[31] Again the seriousness of this commandment is stated elsewhere in the Pentateuch: *"If a man commits adultery with another man's wife—with the wife of his neighbour – both the adulterer and the adulteress must be put to death"* (Leviticus 20:10).

You shall not steal.

This commandment promotes respect for the property which belongs to others and therefore prohibits theft. The commandment can be understood as a request to be thankful for what we have in life but it can also encourage us to share with those who have less than us. The commandment can be interpreted as informing us of our moral responsibility to help those who are suffering from the effects of poverty. The early

Church Father, Saint John Chrysostom (347–407) commented: "not to enable the poor to share in our goods is to steal from them and deprive them of life."[32]

You shall not bear false testimony against your neighbour.

The importance of telling the truth is stressed in this commandment and in general terms this commandment refers to "any situation in which untrue words are used to harm another individual."[33] According to Houston, this commandment referred specifically to the testimony of an individual before the Jewish courts.[34] Take for example the law in Deuteronomy 19:18–19 which states: *"The judges must make a thorough investigation, and if the witness proves to be a liar, giving false testimony against his brother, then do to him as he intended to do to his brother. You must purge the evil from among you."*

You shall not covet your neighbour's house, or his manservant or maidservant, his ox or donkey, or anything that belongs to your neighbour.

The final commands are concerned with the inner feelings or thoughts which may lead to actions which have already been forbidden by the previous commandments, condemning adultery and theft. As this stipulation indicates, our internal thoughts or desires to have something that is not ours are as important as our actions in terms of morality.

Some laws in the Pentateuch are casuistic in nature, as they state the law or rule and then the equivalent punishment. Casuistic laws often follow the pattern: "If you… then…" Consider the example from Exodus 21:17: *"Anyone who curses his father or mother must be put to death."* However, the Ten Commandments are apodictic in form, following the pattern: *"You shall not…"* Punishments for breaking the commandments are not listed as actual words of God because at the time they were given it was not even considered that these commands would be broken – they are moral absolutes and are therefore considered to be universal laws, never to be broken under any circumstances. The universal nature of the commandments is illustrated by Christians today who still follow the Ten Commandments while not attaching the same degree of importance to other rules which are not considered to be universal, for example, the food laws in Leviticus. Drane comments that the commandments "in some respects form a charter of fundamental human rights…they are not technically laws at all, for they contain no mention of penalties for those who break them. Rather they are like a policy statement – a bill of rights – showing how relationships between God and humankind were to be viewed."[35]

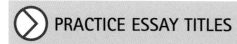 **PRACTICE ESSAY TITLES**

Question adapted from CCEA Summer 2003 AS 6

(a) Give an account of the teaching of the Decalogue. (35)

Your response could make reference to the following points:
- The Decalogue is part of the covenant between God and the Jewish people which sets the Israelites apart from other nations
- A knowledge and understanding of the ethical implications of each of the commandments
- The importance of the Decalogue can be understood by the apodictic statements – breaking the laws are not considered

Question adapted from CCEA Summer 2003 AS 6

(b) Explore the view that the Decalogue forms the basis of Christian ethics. Justify your answer. (15)

Your response could make reference to the following points:
- There are moral values contained within the Decalogue which are still relevant for Christians today, for example *"You shall not murder"* promotes the sacredness of human life and can be applied to issues such as abortion, euthanasia, etc
- Jesus' teaching and the moral teaching of Paul also form the basis of Christian morality – make reference to some specific teachings to develop your response

 OTHER ASPECTS OF HUMAN EXPERIENCE

Section B of the AS Religious Ethics paper, like all the other modules in AS Religious Studies, contains questions which assess 'other aspects of human experience'. In this section of the course it is necessary to investigate material which is not delivered through the taught course but which is linked in content. For this first suggestion concerning 'other aspects of human experience' consider the views of Peter Singer, who claims that the Ten Commandments are no longer relevant for society today.

The Australian philosopher, Peter Singer, whose definition of ethics was used at the outset of this chapter, follows a secular approach to ethics and believes that the moral values presented in the Decalogue and in the whole of the Old Testament, are no longer relevant for the society in which we live today. The left column of the table overleaf contains a summary of what Singer believes to be the key Biblical commandments. They are not directly taken from the Decalogue but are five principles which Singer feels summarise the moral values presented throughout the Old Testament. The information contained in the right column outlines Singer's "new ethical approach" where he has made an attempt at "rewriting the commandments."[36]

 **...continued**

Biblical Commandments	Singer's New Commandments
Treat all human life as having equal worth	Recognise the fact that the worth of human life varies
Never intentionally take innocent human life	Take responsibility for the consequences of your decisions
Never take your own life and always try to prevent others from taking theirs	Respect a person's desire to live or to die
Be fruitful and multiply	Bring children into the world only if they are wanted
Treat all human life as being more precious than non-human life	Do not discriminate on the basis of species

The implications of Singer's views are far reaching in their impact on human experience. As the table above indicates, Singer claims:

- Not all human life is equal. He claims that those who are not rational or self conscious are not 'persons'. For example, infants and those with severe mental disabilities are not to be treated as equal to a person who is fully aware of their environment.
- We should not follow moral absolutes such as *"You shall not murder"*. Singer rejects a rule based approach to ethics and instead promotes an approach which is only concerned with the consequences of our actions.
- Both euthanasia and suicide are morally acceptable because we must respect a person's desire to live or to die.
- Contraception, abortion and in some cases infanticide are morally acceptable if the parents do not wish to have children.
- While not all human life "is of equal worth"[37] Singer does claim that animals who are 'persons' deserve to be treated on a par with humans. If we fail to do this then we are guilty of 'speciesism', which in terms of morality is as bad as racism or sexism according to Singer.

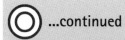 **...continued**

Consider the following questions. Write down your answers and then discuss your thoughts with your class.

1. With reference to Singer's new commandments, which of the five do you consider to be more appropriate for society today compared to the commandments or rules from the Old Testament?

2. Are there any biblical commandments which you feel are still necessary in order to have a moral society today?

3. If we follow Singer's approach to ethics, would the overall impact on human experience be a positive or a negative one? Justify your answer.

From the time the Law was given to Moses, the understanding of the moral implications of the Decalogue and the Mosaic Law in general was developed by the Jews over the following centuries. Their interpretation evolved and became very legalistic, to the extent that the correct observance of the law became more important than anything else, even human need. The author Gordon Reid comments that their interpretation became so legalistic that "the spirit of the law became lost in a mass of regulations."[38] This "mass of regulations" became known as the oral law and was eventually written down to form the Mishnah and the Talmud, which were considered as sacred writings by the Pharisees.

As a result of the legalistic interpretation of the law, the prophets constantly attempted to call the Jewish people back to the real demand of the covenant. As the prophet Jeremiah said, the true attitude towards the law was that Israelites should live as though the covenant was written on their hearts (Jeremiah 31:31–34). The prophet Micah also called the Jews to be more faithful to the demands of the covenant: "*And what does the LORD require of you? To act justly and to love mercy and to walk humbly with your God*" (Micah 6:8).

Jesus came into conflict with the Jewish authorities regarding their interpretation of the Mosaic Law. With specific reference to the Sabbath, for example, there are several occasions when Jesus was in conflict with the Pharisees concerning proper Sabbath observance. In Luke 6:6–11 Jesus healed a man with a withered hand on the Sabbath, which the Pharisees claimed was not permitted by the Mosaic Law. However, in verse 9, Jesus comments: "*I ask you, which is lawful on the Sabbath: to do good or to do evil, to save life or to destroy it?*" and in Mark 2:27 Jesus states: "*The Sabbath was made for man, not man for the Sabbath.*" While the Gospels inform us that Jesus respected the Mosaic Law, it is evident that he opposed a legalistic interpretation of it and when he was asked which of the commandments were the greatest; he ignored the Ten Commandments but instead responded that love was the most important aspect of our relationship with God and our neighbours (Mark 12:29–31).

In the Sermon on the Mount, Jesus gives a new, deeper meaning to the Decalogue and Old Testament teaching in general. In Jesus' own words we are told: *"Do not think that I have come to abolish the Law or the prophets; I have not come to abolish them but to fulfil them"* (Matthew 5:17). On the theme of covenant, Christians today believe that Jesus is the New Covenant: "which superseded the covenant inaugurated centuries earlier at Sinai."[39] Jesus himself indicates this at the Last Supper when he comments: *"This cup is the new covenant in my blood, which is poured out for you"* (Luke 22:20). The old covenant was written on stone tablets, but according to Paul in 2 Corinthians 3:6, the new covenant sealed by the death of Jesus "puts his laws in the hearts and minds of believers."[40]

JESUS' TEACHING FROM THE SERMON ON THE MOUNT

In Jesus' Sermon on the Mount, recorded in Matthew's Gospel, we find "the most extended example of ethical teaching ascribed to Jesus."[41] In this sermon, Matthew presents Jesus as the "New Moses"[42] who provides his listeners with the true interpretation of the Law, the way God intended the Law to be understood and observed when it was originally given to Moses. In the Sermon on the Mount, Jesus sets even higher standards of morality compared to those set out in the Old Testament and on this issue, Stanton comments: "Matthew's Christian community is urged to adopt higher standards of ethical behaviour than those of the majority from whom they have separated."[43] Drane highlights the point: "Jesus' teaching was not a law but an ethic of freedom. Consequently, Jesus did not burden his followers with rules and regulations, but gave them principles and guidelines by which to structure their lives."[44]

In order to make it very clear that Jesus' teaching supersedes that found in the Old Testament, Matthew makes several parallels between Jesus and Moses. For example, just as Moses received the Law from *Yahweh* on Mount Sinai, Jesus delivers the New Law on a mount (Matthew 5:1), whereas Luke's version is referred to as the Sermon on the Plain, which takes place on level ground. Matthew clearly highlights the superiority of Jesus to Moses and goes to great lengths to illustrate that while Moses was a great Old Testament figure, Jesus is the Messiah as foretold by the Old Testament. According to Stanton, Matthew's Gospel contains "ten quite distinctive 'fulfilment quotations'"[45] which aim to prove that Jesus' words and deeds are the fulfilment of Old Testament prophecy.

 TASK

Below are references to three of the ten fulfilment quotations contained in Matthew's gospel. Look up the references and outline what they say about Jesus as the fulfilment of Old Testament prophecy:

- Matthew 2:15   • Matthew 8:17   • Matthew 27:9

Barclay[46] claims that one of Matthew's "main interests is the fulfilment of prophecy" and as Matthew's audience was a Jewish one, it was very important to prove that Jesus was the Messiah promised by the Old Testament. Barclay comments that for "a Jew the surest way to prove that Jesus was the Messiah was to demonstrate that he fulfilled the prophecies of the Old Testament."[47] The relevance of this with regard to the Sermon on the Mount is clear – if Jesus is to provide us with the new and proper interpretation of the Mosaic Law, Matthew wants to make it obvious to his readers that Jesus has the divine authority to make the necessary changes. At the conclusion of the sermon (7:29), Matthew refers to how Jesus *"taught as one who had authority."*

Jenkins comments: "some of the most challenging of Jesus' teachings are to be found in the Sermon on the Mount, which focus on the ethical conduct in our daily life."[48]

The contents of the Sermon can be outlined in the following sections:

Reference	Section
5:1–2	Introduction
5:3–12	Beatitudes
5:13–16	Teaching on Salt and Light
5:17–48	Jesus Attitude to the Law
6:1–18	Three Ways to be good
6:19–7:29	Other Teachings from the Sermon

 TASK

Read Matthew's Sermon on the Mount. Summarise the ethical teaching contained in the Sermon under the headings outlined above.

The Beatitudes – Matthew 5:3–12

The word 'Beatitude' comes from the Latin word *beatitudo* which means 'blessed' or 'happy'. In this section of the Sermon on the Mount, Jesus describes eight types of people who will be happy or blessed in the next life. The moral significance of the Beatitudes cannot be overstated. Allsop comments that the Beatitudes are "Jesus' version of the Ten Commandments."[49] Beswick agrees with this point and comments: "The Beatitudes are to the Sermon on the Mount what the Ten Commandments are to the Old Law. They both form the basic principles on which their respective laws are founded."[50] The Beatitudes contain values which Christians today must attempt to reflect if they are to live a moral life. Jenkins comments that the Beatitudes "emphasise the spirit in which the children of the Kingdom should live."[51] What follows is a discussion of the meaning of each of the eight Beatitudes.

1. Blessed are the poor in spirit, for theirs is the Kingdom of Heaven.

Luke's Gospel contains only four Beatitudes and scholars claim that his version of this Beatitude may be the original. Luke simply states that *"the poor"* are blessed (Luke 6:20). However, Matthew's Beatitude refers to the *"poor in spirit"*. Matthew's intention in spiritualising this Beatitude may be to highlight that it is not material poverty which is being blessed by Jesus but rather in this instance, Jesus is blessing those who are humble, ie the person who knows that they are totally helpless without God in their lives. The poor in spirit referred to do not rely on themselves or material goods but put total trust in God. Barclay summarises the meaning of this Beatitude when he states: "The man who is poor in spirit is the man who has realised that things mean nothing, and that God means everything."[52]

2. Blessed are those who mourn, for they will be comforted.

Some biblical critics argue that it may be incorrect to suggest that this Beatitude simply refers to those who mourn the loss of a loved one. Barclay for example, argues that the true identity of the people blessed by this Beatitude are those who mourn for the sins they have committed. He comments that this Beatitude could be reworded in the following way: "Blessed is the man who is desperately sorry for his own sin and his own unworthiness."[53] Alternatively scholars such as Allison believe that this Beatitude blesses those who mourn over the evil in the world. Allison comments: "Those who mourn are not…sorry for their sins so much as they are aggrieved that…the wicked prosper."[54] Put another way, they mourn over the extent of evil present in the world today. As a result, those who endure this mourning will be comforted by God in the next life.

3. Blessed are the meek, for they will inherit the earth.

This Beatitude can be understood to refer to the person who is gentle in spirit, or the person who is aware of his or her own weaknesses or lack of power and depend totally on God. The interpretation is very similar to that of the first Beatitude. Guy[55] comments that there are parallels between this Beatitude and Psalm 37:11, which states: *"the meek will inherit the land."* This Beatitude refers to those without power on earth but as a reward for their dependence on God, they will be given power in the Kingdom of God at the final judgment.

4. Blessed are those who hunger and thirst for righteousness, for they will be filled.

Luke's version of this Beatitude refers to those who *"are hungry now"* (Luke 6:21) as being blessed, whereas Matthew's version does not bless those who are physically hungry but instead blesses: *"those who hunger and thirst for righteousness"* or as Stanton puts it: "those who are hungry to do God's will."[56] Barclay described this Beatitude as "The most demanding, and indeed the most frightening of them all" because it demands that our desire for goodness should be as intense as "a person dying of starvation wants food, as much as a man dying of thirst wants water."[57]

5. Blessed are the merciful, for they will be shown mercy.

The concept of mercy runs consistently through the New Testament and the message from this Beatitude is quite simply that if we show mercy to others, God will show mercy to us in return. The Lord's Prayer, which is also recorded in the Sermon on the Mount (Matthew 6:9–13), highlights this: *"forgive us our debts, as we also have forgiven our debtors."* McKenzie comments that this Beatitude informs us that "the reward of compassion is to receive compassion."[58]

6. Blessed are the pure in heart, for they will see God.

According to Barclay, this Beatitude "demands that every man who reads it should stop, and think, and examine himself"[59] because it outlines the fact that the motive for all that we do must be pure. He believes our actions must be for the right reasons and not for personal gain. Allison develops this meaning by explaining that *"pure in heart"* refers to "harmony between inward thought and outward deed; it involves singleness of intention, that intention being the doing of God's will."[60]

7. Blessed are the peacemakers, for they will be called sons of God.

This Beatitude refers to those who actively do God's work on earth. According to Barclay: "there are people in whose life bitterness cannot live, people who bridge the gulfs and heal the breaches and sweeten the bitterness. Such people are doing a godlike work...the man who divides men is doing the devil's work; the man who unites men is doing God's work."[61]

8. Blessed are those who are persecuted because of righteousness, for theirs is the Kingdom of Heaven. Blessed are you when people insult you, persecute you and falsely say all kinds of evil against you because of me. Rejoice and be glad, because great is your reward in heaven.

This Beatitude refers to those who are persecuted for the sake of good or on the account of their faith in Jesus. Such people will be compensated in heaven.

 TASK

Having read the section on the Beatitudes, produce a spider diagram in response to the following:

Outline your knowledge and understanding of the moral teaching contained in the Beatitudes.

OTHER ASPECTS OF HUMAN EXPERIENCE

Investigate how Christians faced persecution in the early Church. You may wish to focus on the persecutions under:

- Nero
- Domitian
- Diocletian

You could also consider how Christians today face persecution in various countries throughout the world. One example is the plight of Montagnard Christians in Vietnam. Use the Human Rights Watch website (www.hrw.org) to help with your search.

Teaching on Salt and Light – Matthew 5:13–16

In the section of the Sermon which follows the Beatitudes, Jesus teaches that Christian disciples must be like salt and light.

- Salt improves the quality of food and at the time of Jesus it was used to preserve food. Harrington comments: "when Jesus compares his followers to salt he says that they improve the quality of human existence and preserve it from destruction."[62]
- Guy claims that light "is a common metaphor for a good influence"[63], therefore this teaching implies that Christians today must be a positive influence on the world around them. They must live their lives following the example of Christ and must never hide their faith from the view of others, in the same way that no one buys a lamp and hides it (v14).

Jesus' Attitude to the Law – Matthew 5:17–48

In Matthew 5:17, Jesus is reported to have said: *"Do not think that I have come to abolish the Law or the Prophets. I have not come to abolish them but to fulfil them."*

Jesus is indicating that the laws of the Old Testament are still relevant and still have value. However, Jesus does give the Old Testament Law a much deeper meaning. Jesus has not come to do away with the Law but in the Sermon on the Mount, he does provide Christians with the full, intended or true meaning of the Mosaic Law. Harrington comments: "Jesus came to reveal the true meaning of the Old Testament, to express what the Law and the prophets wished to say, and thus bring it to fulfillment."[64] Jesus considers six areas of Old Testament law and reinterprets them. He contrasts the Old Testament teaching with his own teaching on how God's laws should be followed. Because of this contrast in teaching, this section is referred to as 'The Antitheses'. Each of the six examples follows the same pattern. Jesus introduces the old law with the comment: *"'you have heard that it was said...'"* and he develops his own interpretation using the words *'but I say to you...'"*

1. Murder

"You have heard that it was said to the people long ago, 'Do not murder, and anyone who murders will be subject to judgment.' But I tell you that anyone who is angry with his brother will be subject to judgment."

Jesus said that we must not merely avoid the act of murder but also avoid the anger that can lead to murder. Jesus takes the Mosaic Law a step further and claims that we cannot have the desire in our hearts to do harm to another person. McKenzie comments: "anger, the passion that impels to murder, is as guilty an action as murder itself."[65] For Jesus, moral living is concerned with inner attitudes as much as it is with actions. Jenkins comments: "It is not how people act that is all-important – inner intention and attitude are crucial too."[66] Barclay makes the point even clearer when he claims: "It is not enough not to commit a sin; the only thing that is enough is not to wish to commit it."[67]

2. Adultery

"You have heard that it was said, 'Do not commit adultery.' But I tell you that anyone who looks at a woman lustfully has already committed adultery with her in his heart."

Again Jesus' teaching transcends that found in the Old Testament. In this case he says lust is wrong because it is the "root cause of adultery"[68] and therefore must be avoided. It is important to note that Jesus does not condemn sexual attraction to another person. As Barclay states, Jesus does not refer to the "natural, normal desire, which is part of human instinct and human nature"[69] but does refer to lust or a powerful desire which may lead to immoral sexual behaviour. The steps Jesus recommends that we take to avoid such sin (v29 *"tear your eye out"*; v30 *"cut off your hand"*) are obviously an exaggeration to stress the importance of his teaching in this area.

3. Divorce

"It has been said, 'Anyone who divorces his wife must give her a certificate of divorce.' But I tell you that anyone who divorces his wife, except for marital unfaithfulness, causes her to become an adulteress, and anyone who marries the divorced woman commits adultery."

At the time of Jesus, the Jews allowed a man to divorce his wife for almost any reason. Jewish Law, according to Deuteronomy 24:1, permitted divorce if a man's wife had been 'indecent'. There were two rabbinical schools of thought as to how 'indecent' should be interpreted. Rabbi Shammai claimed divorce was allowed only as a result of an act of unfaithfulness. However, Rabbi Hillel claimed a man could divorce his wife if he found something about her he did not like. This included "causes as trivial as inferior cooking"[70] or even if "she went in public with her head uncovered."[71] In any case, if a man wanted to divorce his wife, she had to be given a written notice of divorce, according to the book of Deuteronomy. For a fuller discussion of divorce, see chapter 4 pages 129–137.

Religious Ethics

According to Jesus' teaching in Mark's Gospel (10:2–12), divorce was not permitted under any circumstances. Matthew's account is different in that it adds the phrase *"except for marital unfaithfulness"*. This addition is referred to as the 'exception clause' and most scholars today agree that this was added by Matthew in order to "satisfy his Jewish-Christian readers, who would have been horrified at the prospect of staying married to an unfaithful partner."[72] Therefore, while elsewhere in this section Jesus' teaching exceeds the demands of the Old Testament, in the case of divorce, Matthew's Jesus agrees with the Old Testament acceptance of divorce and the views of the Rabbi Shammai.

4. Vows

"Again, you have heard that it was said to the people long ago, 'Do not break your oath, but keep the oaths you have made to the Lord.' But I tell you, Do not swear at all…Simply let your 'Yes' be 'Yes', and your 'No', 'No'; anything beyond this comes from the evil one."

For Jews at the time of Jesus, making an oath meant referring to God's name or swearing 'by heaven' when making a promise to God. Jesus' reference to the Old Testament teaching *'You must not break your oath'* is a summary of not one, but various Old Testament passages:

- *"'Do not swear falsely by my name and so profane the name of your God. I am the LORD"* (Leviticus 19:12).
- *"If you make a vow to the Lord your God, do not be slow to pay it"* (Deuteronomy 23:21).
- *"You shall not misuse the name of the LORD your God"* (Exodus 20:7).

Jesus claims that one does not need to swear or make oaths because one's word should be good enough. According to Harrington, Jesus recommends that people should "simply be honest and straightforward in their speech."[73]

5. Revenge

"You have heard that it was said, 'Eye for eye, and tooth for tooth.' But I tell you, Do not resist an evil person. If someone strikes you on the right cheek, turn to him the other also."

In the Old Testament, the concept of *Lex talionis* or eye for eye permitted revenge in an attempt to limit punishment. For example, if a man knocked out your tooth you could knock his out but were not permitted any additional form of revenge. Only a judge could pass this punishment and this was another way of ensuring that violence was limited. But Jesus tells his listeners to offer no resistance to the actions of enemies. They should forgive rather than seek revenge. Jesus once again transcends what is embedded in the Old Law by urging his listeners to forego retaliation. Jesus says people should be compassionate and forgiving rather than bearing grudges and seeking revenge. This teaching to turn the other cheek is described by Barclay as "the characteristic ethic of the Christian life, and the conduct which should distinguish the Christian from other men."[74]

24

6. Love of Enemies

"You have heard that it was said, 'Love your neighbour and hate your enemy.' But I tell you: Love your enemies and pray for those who persecute you."

In Leviticus 19:18, the Jews were instructed to *"Love your neighbour as yourself"* and this was interpreted as simply referring to their fellow Jews. The Old Testament does not mention the command to 'hate your enemy' but Guy comments that this attitude "was a popular addition which many of Jesus' contemporaries would support."[75] Jesus' words demand that Christians love all people, not only members of their own community or religious group. The Greek word for love used here is *agape*, which can be defined as having a genuine concern for the well being of others. There is no expectation to love an enemy in the same way as a family member or close friend but *agape* demands that even an enemy is regarded with "unconquerable benevolence and goodwill which will seek nothing but his highest good."[76]

 TASK

Summarise Jesus' teaching in a table similar to the one below:

Topic	Old Testament: You have heard that it was said...	New Testament: But I say to you...
Murder		
Adultery		
Divorce		
Vows		
Revenge		
Love of enemies		

Three ways to be good – Matthew 6:1–18

For Jewish people at the time of Jesus, there were three important aspects of religious life – almsgiving, prayer and fasting. This section of Jesus' Sermon warns his listeners not to practice their faith in full view of others. If they receive praise on earth for what they do now, in this life, they will not get rewarded in heaven. What troubled Jesus was that some Jews, or as Jesus calls them, the 'hypocrites', performed these tasks for the wrong motives. They took a short term view and as a result, Jesus claimed that they received their reward in their lifetime from men, rather than at the final judgment from their Father in Heaven. Overall, the content of this section reflects Jesus' teaching in the sixth Beatitude: *"Blessed are the pure in heart."*

Almsgiving 6:1–4

Almsgiving refers to the practice of giving assistance to those in need. According to Guy, almsgiving "was regularly practised by the Jews, who were very generous towards less fortunate members of their community."[77] Jesus warns against making a public show and looking for praise when giving alms to the poor. By seeking attention and praise the real significance of the act is defeated by behaving in a way which is similar to that of the hypocrites. Harrington comments that at the time of Jesus, the word hypocrites could refer to actors on stage, but in this context it refers to people who are "phonies"[78] because their reasons for giving to the poor are not genuine. However, those who do give alms for the right reasons will be rewarded by God.

Praying 6:5–15

At the time of Jesus the Jews prayed three times a day. They were requested to stop what they were doing, wherever they where and engage in prayer at the required time. Jesus teaches people to avoid being like the hypocrites when praying; they pray *"to be seen by men"* (6:5). Jesus advises his followers to avoid an outward show of prayer. Sincerity of heart is much more important. According to Harrington: "prayer offered to win human praise is not prayer at all…God will reward only genuine prayer offered in sincerity to him."[79] In this section of the Sermon, Jesus instructed the people on how to pray and the Lord's Prayer is given as a model.

Fasting 6:16–18

At the time of Jesus, Jews fasted twice a week, on Mondays and Thursdays. When Jesus' followers fast, they must not be like the hypocrites who *"disfigure their faces to show men they are fasting"* (6:16). According to Guy, this was common practice among the Jews at the time of Jesus: "To show everyone that they were observing this practice, the pious used to leave their faces unwashed and their hair and beards untended."[80] Instead of this, Jesus followers must not allow their fasting to be seen by others and they will be rewarded by the Father.

Other teachings from the Sermon – Matthew 6:19–7:29

True Treasures 6:19–21

Jesus teaches that people should not build up treasures on earth but that they must concentrate on building up treasures in heaven which will last for eternity. So rather than focus life on achieving the highest paid job or having a big house and many material goods, people should focus on loving God and their neighbour and helping those in need. If they achieve this, then they build up treasures in heaven that can be enjoyed for eternity, where rust and moths cannot destroy them and where thieves cannot steal them (6:19).

The Light of the Body 6:22–23

In this section, Jesus is indicating that the eye is the window by which light gets into the whole body. The light which gets into the body depends on the state of the eye through which it enters and Jesus adds: *"If your eyes are good, your whole body will be full of light...But if your eyes are bad, your whole body will be full of darkness"* (6:22–23). In other words, those whose vision is not fully focused on obedience to God will leave their souls in darkness. However, if the eye is sound the body will be filled with light and the soul will be enriched.

God and Money 6:24

Jesus informs us that one cannot be a slave to both God and 'mammon'. Mammon refers to wealth in general and includes both money and material possessions. There is a choice to be made between God and earthly wealth, and as McKenzie puts it: "the disciple cannot have a divided loyalty."[81]

Trust in God 6:25–34

As the previous verses indicate, trust must be placed in God alone. God will provide for all needs. Jesus points out that God provides enough for the birds and flowers and because humans are more important in the eyes of God, he will provide for them too. Therefore there is no need to worry about food and clothing. According to Jesus, people should worry about the matters of today not tomorrow (6:34).

Judging Others 7:1–6

The followers of Jesus are warned to avoid condemning other people. If they condemn other people, God will condemn them: *"Do not judge, or you too will be judged"* (7:1). Jesus tells us we must first reflect on our own state of perfection, before thinking about passing judgment on another person – we must focus on our greater faults or the *"log"* in our own eye before we pick out the minor faults or *"spec"* in our neighbour's eye (7:3–5).

Asking God in Prayer 7:7–12

Jesus informs us that one can pray with confidence to God, knowing that if a request is made *"it will be given"* (7:7). In 7:11 this message is developed. Jesus says: *"how much more will your Father in heaven give good gifts to those who ask him."*

The 'Golden Rule' (7:12) says: *"do to others what you would have them do to you."* Barclay comments: "with this commandment, the Sermon on the Mount reaches its summit."[82] This teaching is not unique to Jesus however. For example the Rabbi Hillel, whose views on divorce have already been mentioned, outlines this teaching in a negative format: "That which is despicable to you, do not do to your fellow, this is the whole Torah, and the rest is commentary, go and learn it."[83]

The right and wrong ways 7:13–27

The Sermon concludes with a series of examples of people faced with choices. These examples relate to the decision to follow Jesus' teaching contained in the Sermon or to ignore it. The examples given include the two gates (7:13–14); two types of trees and their fruit (7:15–20); two types of followers and preachers (7:21–23) and two types of hearers of Jesus' teaching (7:24–27). In the final example, the man who built his house on solid foundations is compared to the person who acts on the teachings of Jesus, as opposed to only listening to it. So when the storm came, the building did not collapse. Likewise, if Jesus' teaching is put into practice, the storm will be survived and eternal life will be experienced. The other house built on earth and sand could not withstand the wind and rain and collapsed. This is compared to a *"foolish man"* who hears the words of Jesus but does not act upon them; he will not see past the storm, he will not inherit eternal life.

Conclusion 7:28–29

The Sermon ends with recognition of the authority of Jesus. As McKenzie comments: "Jesus has a commission from the Father to teach – a commission the scribes do not have."[84]

◎ OTHER ASPECTS OF HUMAN EXPERIENCE – PRACTICE ESSAY TITLES

a) With reference to other aspects of human experience, critically evaluate the suggestion that the Sermon on the Mount is irrelevant today. Justify your answer. (15)

Your response could make reference to the following points:

- Jesus requests that his followers show mercy to those who have offended them and even tells them to love their enemies. How can we expect people who have endured terrible suffering to apply such principles? For example, could we expect the parents of brutally murdered children to resist anger and not seek revenge but actually forgive their murderer? It could be argued that in the Sermon on the Mount, Jesus sets a moral standard that is too high for anyone to achieve.
- The human experience of those who suffer from domestic violence at the hands of their spouse will not find Jesus' teaching on divorce relevant to their lives. Should such victims not be given the chance to divorce their aggressive partner and make a new start with someone else if they wish? Is this not the lesser of two evils or

should these people be labelled adulterers if they have another relationship?

- Jesus promotes the idea of pacifism in the Sermon. Does that mean that Christians can never engage in war and that they must turn the other cheek to evil dictators such as Hitler and Saddam Hussein? Again, it has been argued that in this context, Jesus' teaching does not seem to promote the 'greater good' for society and therefore is irrelevant for society today.

- However, consider the work of peacemakers such as Martin Luther King and Nelson Mandela, who have applied Jesus' principles of non-retaliation and who have achieved moral victories with regard to human rights issues.

- It has also been possible for people to apply Jesus' teaching on forgiveness to those who have caused great suffering and pain. For example, Gordon Wilson forgave those who killed his daughter in the Enniskillen bomb. In South Africa, those involved in the Truth and Reconciliation committee led by Archbishop Desmond Tutu, have also experienced reconciliation.

- The sermon asks for the giving of alms to those in need and to put God before money or material goods. In Northern Ireland today, this teaching is still relevant to Christians when considering the affluence of so many people in contrast to the poverty others have to endure. While money is donated to charities to alleviate the suffering of those living in poverty in Northern Ireland and in developing countries, there is still so much that needs to be done. It can be argued that if a greater number of people considered Jesus' teaching, a greater number of the world's population could have a more positive experience of life.

b) Using your own research into some of the above examples of other aspects of human experience, do you think Jesus' teaching is irrelevant for society today?

THE MORAL TEACHING OF SAINT PAUL

The teaching of Saint Paul makes a significant contribution to the moral values held by Christians today. In his letters, which make up almost one third of the New Testament, Paul teaches about issues such as the following:

1. The community ethic
2. Freedom from the Law
3. Teaching on love
4. Teaching on marriage and sexual ethics
5. The role of the state

Before considering Paul's ethical teaching, it is helpful to look at a brief overview of his life. Most of the biographical information on Paul comes from his own letters, in particular his letter to the Galatians and his first letter to the Corinthians. However, Luke also gives us some details of Paul's life and missionary activities in the Acts of the

Apostles, and it is a widely held view that Luke accompanied Paul on several occasions throughout his missionary journeys.

In the Acts of the Apostles, we are given some information on the early life of Saint Paul. Before Paul's conversion to Christianity, he went by the name of Saul, and we are told by Luke that he was a strict Jew and was a Pharisee (Acts 23:6). Luke also tells us that Saul was born in Tarsus, in the Roman province of Cilicia (Acts 22:3) and in addition to his Roman citizenship he was heavily influenced by his Greek or Hellenistic background. In Acts we are also told that Saul was very well educated, and we are specifically informed that he was educated by Gamaliel in Jerusalem (Acts 22:3). In his own words: *"I was advancing in Judaism beyond many Jews of my own age and was extremely zealous for the traditions of my fathers"* (Galatians 1:14).

His zeal for Judaism meant that he was involved in the persecution of the first Christians, hence his presence at the stoning of Stephen as recorded in Acts 8:1. In the immediate aftermath of Stephen's death, we are informed that *"Saul began to destroy the church. Going from house to house, he dragged off men and women and put them in prison"* (Acts 8:3). On one occasion, his intention was to visit Damascus in order to bring Christians back to Jerusalem *"as prisoners"* (Acts 9:2). However, on his journey, the risen Christ appeared to him and asked: *"Saul, Saul, why do you persecute me?"* (Acts 9:4) This whole experience, which is outlined in detail in Acts 9, led to the conversion of Saul. Under the guidance of the Holy Spirit, Saul, who we are now told was *"also called Paul"* (Acts 13:9), went on missionary journeys with his companions travelling through modern day Cyprus, Turkey and Greece. Together they converted both Jews and Gentiles to the Christian faith.

A major controversy in the early church was the question of whether or not to accept Gentile converts to Christianity without them first having to agree to follow the Mosaic Law and become circumcised. As strict Jews themselves, the leaders of the Church in Jerusalem believed that this was necessary. However, as a result of their experiences among the Gentiles, Paul and his companions believed that Gentiles did not have to observe the requirements of the Law of Moses before they converted to Christianity. As Tyler and Reid put it, Paul believed that the Gentiles should "not be unnecessarily burdened with obedience to the Law of Moses...it was of no value either way whether a Christian was circumcised or not."[85]

In a very strong letter to the Galatians, Paul argues that all people are justified by faith in Jesus, not through observance of the Torah (Galatians 2:16). Despite the best attempts to resolve this conflict at the Council of Jerusalem, recorded in Acts 15 and Galatians 2, there seems to have been no resolution to this division in the early Church and when Paul returned to Jerusalem after his three missionary journeys he is accused of being *"the man who teaches all men everywhere against our people and our law and this place. And besides, he has brought Greeks into the temple area and defiled this holy place"* (Acts 21:28). A riot developed on the streets of Jerusalem and Paul was arrested (21:33). As he is about to be *"flogged and questioned"* (Acts 22:24) by the Romans, Paul asks: *"Is it legal for you to flog a Roman citizen who hasn't even been found guilty?"* (22:25) So Paul is held in custody as the Roman authorities in Jerusalem dare not punish a fellow Roman citizen before a fair trial has taken place.

The Jews, on the other hand, could not contain their desire for revenge and a group of *"the Jews formed a conspiracy and bound themselves with an oath not to eat or drink until they had killed Paul"* (Acts 23:12). For his own safety, Paul is taken from Jerusalem to Caesarea where he is held in custody under the Roman governor Felix for a period of two years (Acts 24:23–27). At the end of this period, Festus replaced Felix and in an attempt to win the favour of the Jews, he decided to send Paul to face a trial in Jerusalem (Acts 25:9). Paul, feeling that he could not receive a fair trial in Jerusalem demanded a trial before the Roman Emperor, Caesar (25:10). Festus replied to Paul's request: *"You have appealed to Caesar. To Caesar you will go!"* (Acts 25:12)

From Caesarea, Paul set sail for Rome under the guard of Roman soldiers, but on the way they were shipwrecked off the island of Malta and they remained on the island for three months before they finally set sail for Rome again. Acts ends with Paul under house arrest in Rome awaiting his trial before Caesar (Acts 28:30). We are not informed of the outcome of the trial, possibly because the author wants to "end on a high note."[86] However, it is believed that Paul "met a martyr's death...during the persecution of Rome's Christians by the Emperor Nero in AD64."[87]

The community ethic

According to Jenkins, Paul's "ethic is a community ethic."[88] For example, he encourages the Galatians to live in harmony with one another and he urges them to *"Carry each other's burdens"* (Galatians 6:2) and encourages them to *"do good to all"* (Galatians 6:10). His community ethic is clearly expressed in 3:28 when he comments: *"There is neither Jew nor Greek, slave nor free, male nor female, for you are all one in Christ Jesus."* In Pilch's commentary on Paul's letter to the Galatians, he comments that this verse clearly highlights that "Differences are not important, so don't bother about them."[89]

 OTHER ASPECTS OF HUMAN EXPERIENCE

In his commentary on Galatians, Guthrie comments that Paul's message for Christians today is: "In Christ there are neither Europeans or Asiatics, Africans or Chinese, or any other racial groups as such. In Christ there is a new bond which leaps over colour, culture, and customs...it is because in Christ everyone appears the same."[90]

For many people today however, racism and the quest to be treated with equality is a very real aspect of their experience of life. In his famous 'I have a dream' speech made on the 28 August 1963, Martin Luther King's words reflected the words of Paul when he said:

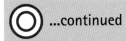 **...continued**

"When we allow freedom to ring, when we let it ring from every village and every hamlet, from every state and every city, we will be able to speed up that day when all of God's children, black men and white men, Jews and Gentiles, Protestants and Catholics, will be able to join hands and sing in the words of the old Negro spiritual, 'Free at last! Free at last! Thank God Almighty, we are free at last!'"[91]

Research the life and work of Martin Luther King with specific reference to how he fought to promote equality for all people living in America, regardless of the colour of their skin.

In addition to his letter to the Galatians, Paul also develops his community ethic in his first letter to the Corinthians. He has heard reports from *"Chloe's household"* (1 Corinthians 1:11) that there are divisions among the Christians living in Corinth. Paul makes the following request to the Corinthians: *"I appeal to you, brothers, in the name of our Lord Jesus Christ, that all of you agree with one another so that there may be no divisions among you and that you may be perfectly united in mind and thought"* (1:10). The Corinthians have created divisions among themselves concerning who converted them to Christianity. Some of them claimed that they *"belong to Paul"*, while others associated themselves with Cephas (Peter) or Apollos, and others linked themselves directly to Christ (1 Corinthians 1:12). Paul is very upset with the fact that they fail to live in harmony with one another and "to Paul it is inconceivable that Christians be divided."[92] In an attempt to unite them he asks them: *"Is Christ divided?"* (1 Corinthians 1:13) Of course the response is 'no', therefore they must not be divided either in order to reflect Christ.

 OTHER ASPECTS OF HUMAN EXPERIENCE

In Northern Ireland there are many Christian Churches. The largest four are the Presbyterian Church, the Methodist Church, the Roman Catholic Church and the Church of Ireland. Ecumenism refers to the attempt made by members of the Christian faith to unite the various Christian denominations, through focusing on what they have in common, rather than on their differences.

Using the internet, explore the work undertaken by the ecumenical movement in Northern Ireland in order to unite Christianity and bring all denominations closer together.

The issue of Christian unity is also developed in chapter eleven of Paul's first letter to the Corinthians. When the Corinthian community gathered to celebrate the Lord's Supper, we are informed by Paul that their meetings *"do more harm than good"* (1 Corinthians 11:17). In this case, the divisions are not based on who converted them to Christianity, but on their social status. As they celebrated the Lord's Supper, Paul comments: *"for as you eat, each of you goes ahead without waiting for anybody else. One remains hungry, another gets drunk"* (1 Corinthians 11:21).

In 1 Corinthians 12:12–31 Paul develops his community ethic by using the image of the body to represent both the "unity and diversity of the community."[93] Paul states that each one of us has one body which consists of many parts. He adds: *"If one part suffers, every part suffers with it; if one part is honoured, every part rejoices with it"* (1 Corinthians 12:26). He then proceeds to apply this to the Corinthian community: *"Now you are the body of Christ, and each one of you is a part of it"* (1Corinthians 12:27). Paul develops the idea that all members of the community must be treated with respect and equality and that they must appreciate that every person has a positive contribution to make to the community. He comments: *"those parts of the body that seem to be weaker are indispensable"* (1 Corinthians 12:22). In this section of 1 Corinthians, Paul insists that no one living in the Christian community should be treated as anything less than a member of the body of Christ.

Freedom from the Law

In his letter to the Galatians, Paul develops the idea that Christians are free from the strict requirements of the Mosaic Law. In Galatians 2:16 he comments: *"a man is not justified by observing the law, but by faith in Jesus Christ."* He develops this point by reflecting on the relevance of Jesus' death for Christians: *"for if righteousness could be gained through the law, Christ died for nothing"* (Galatians 2:21). Paul claims that the Law had a short term role and it was like the custodian of a child, whose task it was to ensure the child's moral and physical development was sufficient to prepare him for adulthood. When the child reached an age of maturity, the custodian was no longer needed.[94] Likewise, the Law was to prepare the people for the coming of Jesus. Now that Jesus had arrived the Law was no longer required, and as Paul himself says: *"Now that faith has come, we are no longer under the supervision of the law"* (Galatians 2:25).

For Paul only one thing can justify or save people and that is *"faith in Jesus Christ"* (Galatians 2:16). The Gentiles too are justified through faith in Christ (Galatians 3:8) and for Paul, Gentiles were not expected to convert to Judaism before they became Christian. Similar to the views held by Jesus, Paul opposes legalism and in Galatians 5:14 he comments: *"The entire law is summed up in a single command: 'Love your neighbour as yourself.'"* For Paul, if we truly love our neighbour, we will not need the law.

However Paul made it very clear that, because they are free from the slavery of the Law (Galatians 5:1) it does not mean that Christians are free to act in any way they please. Paul informs the Galatians that freedom brings moral responsibilities towards their neighbour; therefore he does not favour an antinomian approach to moral living because he does feel that moral principles are important. In Galatians 5:16–25, he outlines the qualities necessary in order to live a morally acceptable life. He contrasts 'living in the spirit' with 'living in the flesh'. If people live in the flesh, which refers to how they may behave according to their human nature, and they refuse to accept God's sovereignty, they will engage in the following types of behaviour: immorality, impurity, licentiousness, idolatry, sorcery, hatreds, rivalry, jealousy, outbursts of fury, selfishness, dissentions, factions, drinking bouts, orgies and the like. According to Paul: *"Those who live like this will not inherit the Kingdom of God"* (Galatians 5:21).

However, in living life in the spirit of God then Christians will reflect the following qualities, which are referred to as the 'fruits' of the Holy Spirit – love, joy, peace, patience, kindness, generosity, faithfulness, gentleness and self control.[95] According to Paul, those who live in the spirit will *"reap eternal life"* (Galatians 6:8) and according to Osiek, this means that "You get what you pay for."[96] Barclay develops this point and argues that for Paul, ethics has an eschatological dimension: "The Christian ethic is an ethic which goes beyond this world and beyond time."[97]

As Galatians 5:22–23 suggests, the fruits of the Holy Spirit are of central importance with regard to a Christian's moral outlook on life. Throughout the Pauline epistles, the importance of the Holy Spirit in the lives of Christians is stressed. Paul believed that the risen Christ was working among the Christian communities through the Holy Spirit. In Galatians 5:25, Paul comments: *"Since we live by the Spirit, let us keep in step with the Spirit."* According to Drane, Paul emphasised that "standards of Christian morality are to be produced, not by sets of rules and regulations imposed from outside, but by the power of the Holy Spirit working within the believer."[98]

 PRACTICE ESSAY TITLE

Question adapted from CCEA Summer 2002 AS 6

To what extent is Christian behaviour more than a matter of simply obeying rules. Justify your answer. (15)

Your response could make reference to the following points:
- The value of rules found in scripture eg *do not murder*
- The opposition to legalism as reflected by the example of both Jesus and Paul
- The idea that rules must be broken in certain circumstances where human need is more important

Teaching on love

Agape or unconditional love was central to the moral teaching of Jesus. In Mark 12:29–31, Jesus comments that love of God and neighbour are the most important commandments. Paul's teaching also reflects this idea. In Romans 13:9–10 he says: *"The commandments…are summed up in this one rule: 'Love your neighbour as yourself.' Love does no harm to its neighbour. Therefore love is the fulfilment of the law."* Barclay comments: "It is basic to the ethic of Paul, as it is to the ethic of the whole New Testament, that the Christian ethic is an ethic of love."[99]

According to Jenkins: "The kernel of Paul's moral advice is faith working itself out in love; expressed in the beautiful passage on *agape* in 1 Corinthians 13."[100] The following quote is taken from 1 Corinthians 13:1–3 and expresses the importance Paul attaches to *agape*:

"If I speak in the tongues of men and of angels, but have not love, I am only a resounding gong or a clanging cymbal. If I have the gift of prophecy and can fathom all mysteries and all knowledge, and if I have a faith that can move mountains, but have not love, I am nothing. If I give all I possess to the poor and surrender my body to the flames, but have not love, I gain nothing."

In the following section of 1 Corinthians 13, Paul clearly defines his understanding of the true meaning of love:

"Love is patient, love is kind. It does not envy, it does not boast, it is not proud. It is not rude, it is not self-seeking, it is not easily angered, it keeps no record of wrongs. Love does not delight in evil but rejoices with the truth. It always protects, always trusts, always hopes, always perseveres. Love never fails" (1 Corinthians 13:4–8).

The Anglican minister, Joseph Fletcher (1905–1991) based his ethical theory, referred to as situation ethics, on the principle of love as expounded by both Jesus and Paul. Fletcher taught that when Christians face an ethical dilemma, they have a moral duty to follow the most loving course of action. The next chapter on ethical theory develops Fletcher's theory and applies it to modern ethical issues.

Teaching on marriage and sexual ethics

In his first letter to the Corinthians, Paul gives an outline of his views on the importance of marriage and sexual morality. In 1 Corinthians 5:1, he comments: *"It is actually reported that there is sexual immorality among you, and of a kind that does not occur even among pagans."* He proceeds to discuss a case of incest in the Corinthian community and refers to *"a man living with his father's wife"* – the assumption being that she was the man's step-mother. Paul's anger is directed at the Corinthian community, who have taken no action against the man involved in this act. Paul comments: *"Shouldn't you rather have been filled with grief and have put out of your fellowship the man who did this?"* (1 Corinthians 5:2) Paul continues that they should *"hand this man over to Satan, so that the sinful nature may be destroyed and his spirit saved on the day of the Lord"* (1 Corinthians 5:5). Paul demands that the man is excommunicated because *"a little yeast works through the whole batch of dough"* (5:6). Getty comments that Paul stresses that "Christians must rid the community of the corruption and wickedness that contaminates it."[101]

The issue of sexual ethics also features in chapter six of the letter to the Corinthians. At the time of Paul, in the first century AD, the Corinthians were well known for their sexual immorality and Kugelman comments that they "had a reputation for debauchery and licentiousness" so much so that "the expression 'Corinthian girl' was a euphemism for a prostitute."[102] Paul's experience of the Corinthian immorality was certainly no different and he encourages them to refrain from pagan practices and to:

> *"Flee from sexual immorality. All other sins a man commits are outside his body, but he who sins sexually sins against his own body. Do you not know that your body is a temple of the Holy Spirit, who is in you, whom you have received from God? You are not your own; you were bought at a price. Therefore honour God with your body"* (1 Corinthians 6:18–20).

He also informs the Corinthians: *"Neither the sexually immoral nor idolaters nor adulterers nor male prostitutes nor homosexual offenders nor thieves nor the greedy nor drunkards nor slanderers nor swindlers will inherit the kingdom of God"* (6:9–10). His teaching on the issue of homosexuality is also addressed in his letter to the Romans, where he states: *"In the same way the men also abandoned natural relations with women and were inflamed with lust for one another. Men committed indecent acts with other men, and received in themselves the due penalty for their perversion"* (Romans 1:27). It is safe to say that Paul demanded a higher moral standard of the Corinthians. Through their baptism they have been sanctified[103] and as a result they must behave in a different manner to that of their pagan neighbours, a manner which reflects their status as Christians.

In chapter seven of 1 Corinthians, Paul deals with the topic of marriage. According to Paul, he has heard that the Corinthians have claimed: *"It is good for a man not to marry"* (7:1), therefore some of them believed that marriage had "no place in the eschatological Kingdom of God."[104] Paul agrees and claims that celibacy is the ideal way to serve God, and he encourages the Corinthians: *"I wish all men were as I am"* (7:7) *"But if they cannot control themselves, they should marry, for it is better to marry than to burn with passion"* (7:9). He goes on to encourage those who are already married to remain faithful to their partner, and here Paul reflects the teaching of Jesus on the permanence of marriage: *"To the married I give this command (not I, but the Lord): A wife must not separate from her husband. But if she does, she must remain unmarried or else be reconciled to her husband. And a husband must not divorce his wife"* (7:10–11).

In the next paragraph of the epistle (letter), Paul deals with the issue of marriage between believers and non-believers. In 1 Corinthians 7:12–16, Paul teaches that if a Christian man or a woman is married to an unbeliever and if they are happy they must remain together. However, if the unbeliever wants to separate then Paul says that they should be permitted to do so. This is referred to as the 'Pauline Privilege' because when the unbeliever leaves the Christian, the Christian is free to divorce their spouse and marry again.

In the final section on marriage, Paul addresses the unmarried and the widows in the Corinthian community. In 7:26–28, he basically tells them to remain as they are. Paul's teaching in the passage reflects the fact that he felt that the Parousia (the Greek term used to refer to the second coming of Christ) is imminent, that they would not have to wait long until the return of Jesus as judge of all humanity. Paul himself writes: *"for this world in its present form is passing away"* (7:31) and that *"time is short"* (7:29).

In addition to Paul's teaching on marriage, he also "demonstrates a special concern for household ethics."[105] Four key points are developed by Paul concerning the relationships within a family unit in his letter to the Colossians (3:18–21):

- "Wives, submit to your husbands, as is fitting in the Lord."
- "Husbands, love your wives and do not be harsh with them."
- "Children, obey your parents in everything, for this pleases the Lord."
- "Fathers, do not embitter your children, or they will become discouraged."

 TASK

Prepare a response to the following questions, making use of as many relevant examples as possible on both sides of the debate:

Question adapted from CCEA Summer 2008 AS 6

a) Explore the view that the moral teaching of Paul is more demanding than that of Jesus.

b) Comment on the claim that Paul's moral teaching is no longer relevant for Christians today.

The role of the state

In Chapter 13 of Paul's letter to the Romans, he tells his audience that they must be obedient to the state authorities, because they have been given authority from God. Pilch comments: "some Christians believed that they were already citizens of another world…and therefore did not have to obey civil authority. Paul feared the anarchy that would result from such an outlook and therefore felt obliged to discourage it."[106] In 13:1–2 Paul states: *"Everyone must submit himself to the governing authorities, for there is no authority except that which God has established. The authorities that exist have been established by God."* If Christians oppose the authority of the state then they *"will bring judgement upon themselves."* Christians are informed: *"this is also why you pay taxes, for the authorities are God's servants"* (13:6). Once again, the teaching of Paul reflects that of Christ, who when questioned by the Pharisees concerning the payment of taxes claimed that we should *"Give to Caesar what is Caesar's and to God what is God's"* (Mark 12:17).

OTHER ASPECTS OF HUMAN EXPERIENCE

Allsop comments: "Christians who lived under the Third Reich in Germany found themselves torn between that respect for the state which Paul urged and their commitment to justice, peace and righteousness in public affairs."[107]

In light of this quotation, research the human experience of those living under Hitler's regime. You may also wish to consider the human experience of those living under the rule of Saddam Hussein in Iraq or Robert Mugabe in Zimbabwe. Critically reflect on how relevant Paul's teaching on obedience to the state is for society today.

 TASK

Using the headings presented in the following diagram, outline your knowledge of the similarities between the moral teaching of Jesus and Paul. Use the information presented in this chapter to develop your notes.

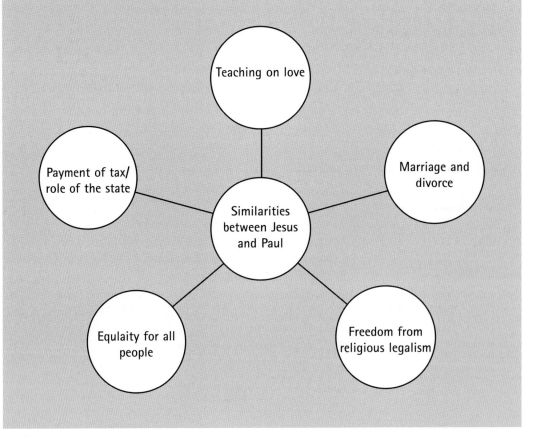

Paul's moral teaching deals with a range of issues including the importance of the community, living a life free from religious legalism but which reflects the love of Christ. His views on sexual morality are very strong and while he prefers that people remain celibate, marriage is acceptable.

Overall, the central drive of Paul's ethical teaching is that Christians should imitate Christ in all that they do. In Philippians 2:5 Christians are told: *"Your attitude should be the same as that of Christ Jesus"* and in Ephesians 5:1 Christians are requested to *"be imitators of God."* Genesis 1:27 asserts that humans are created in the image of God and Paul feels that because of this it is our responsibility to act in a way which reflects the divine image. In 1 Corinthians 11:1, Paul asks that Christians imitate both himself and Jesus: *"Follow my example, as I follow the example of Christ."* It is therefore the Christian responsibility to imitate Jesus and Paul in order to be good role models for others in society.

 PRACTICE ESSAY TITLES

Question adapted from CCEA Summer 2008 AS 6

a) Give an account of the key features of Paul's moral teaching. (35)

Your response could make reference to the following points:

- Background to the life of Saint Paul
- The community ethic
- Freedom from the Law
- Teaching on love
- Teaching on marriage and sexual ethics
- The role of the state
- The call to imitate Christ

Question from CCEA January 2007 AS 6

b) Explore the claim that the key moral obligation for Paul was Jesus' command to love. Justify your answer. (15)

Your response could make reference to the following points:

- Examples of how Paul's teaching on love reflects Jesus' teaching
- Both Jesus and Paul considered love as being more important than laws
- Development of the significance of Paul's command to imitate Christ

◯↷ CHAPTER SUMMARY

Introduction to ethics
- The distinction between ethics and morality
- Definition of terms such as moral, immoral and amoral
- A consideration of the claim that God is the source of morality with reference to concepts such as the divine command theory and the Euthyphro dilemma

Old Testament ethical teaching with specific reference to the Decalogue
- The Decalogue formed part of the Covenant between God and the Israelites
- The ethical values promoted by the individual commandments
- The Ten Commandments as apodictic statements
- Jesus' attitude towards the Old Testament Law

Jesus' teaching from the Sermon on the Mount
- The idea of Jesus as the fulfilment of Old Testament prophecy
- The significance of the Beatitudes
- Jesus' attitude towards the Law – the Antitheses
- Other moral teaching from the Sermon eg the Golden Rule

The moral teaching of Saint Paul
- Background to the life of Saint Paul
- The community ethic
- Freedom from the Law
- Teaching on love
- Teaching on marriage and sexual ethics
- The role of the state
- The call to imitate Christ

Endnotes

1 Singer, P, *Encyclopaedia Britannica,* Chicago, 1985, p627

2 Vardy, P & Grosch, P, *Puzzle of Ethics*, Harper Collins, London, 1999, p4

3 Thompson, M, *Ethical Theory*, Hodder & Stoughton, London, 1999, p28

4 *ibid*, p28

5 *ibid*, p27

6 Quote taken from Bowie, R, *Ethical Studies*, Nelson Thornes, Cheltenham, 2004, p124

7 Vardy & Grosch, *op cit*, p8

8 Quote taken from Bowie, *op cit*, p124

9 Jenkins, J, *Ethics and Religion*, Heinemann, Oxford, 1999, p. 24

10 Tyler, S & Reid, G, *Religious Studies*, Philip Allan Updates, Oxfordshire, 2002, p154

11 Descartes, R, Principles of Philosophy, 1644. Quote taken from Jenkins, J, *Ethics and Religion – Second Edition*, Heinemann, Oxford, 2003, p54

12 Quote taken from Bowie, *op cit*, p126

13 Allsop, P, *Religious Ethics*, Christian Theology Trust, Liverpool, 2000, p40

14 Drane, J, *Introducing the Old Testament*, Lion Publishing, Oxford, 2000, p289

15 Barton, J, 'Old Testament Theology' in Rogerson, J, (Ed) *Beginning Old Testament Study*, SPCK, London 1992, p97

16 Alexander, TD, *From Paradise to Promised Land: An Introduction to the Main Themes of the Pentateuch*, Paternoster Press, Carlisle, 1995, p82

17 Tyler, SK, *Religious Studies*, Philip Allan Updates, Oxfordshire, 2000, p8

18 *ibid*, p24

19 Allsop, *op cit*, p42

20 Alexander, *op cit*, p84

21 Huesman, J, *Exodus*, The Jerome Biblical Commentary, Geoffrey Chapman, London, 1970, p57

22 Houston, W, *Exodus*, The Oxford Bible Commentary, Oxford University Press, Oxford, 2007, p81

23 Huesman, *op cit*, p57

24 *ibid*, p57

25 Houston, *op cit*, p81

26 The Book of the Covenant is a term taken from Exodus 24:7 and refers to the entire collection of legal and moral material contained within Exodus 20:22–23:33, which according to Exodus 24:4 was written by Moses.

27 Alexander, *op cit*, p85

28 Huesman, *op cit*, p57

29 Alexander, *op cit*, p85

30 Bowie, *op cit*, p12

31 Houston, *op cit*, p82

32 *Catechism of the Catholic Church*, Veritas, Dublin, 1994, 2446

33 Alexander, *op cit*, p86

34 Houston, *op cit*, p82

35 Drane, *op cit*, p289

36 Singer, P, *Rethinking Life and Death*, Oxford University Press, Oxford, 1994, p189–206

37 *ibid*, p202–203

38 Reid, G, *Biblical Studies*, Philip Allan Updates, Oxfordshire, 2001, p77

39 Alexander, *op cit*, p94

40 *ibid*, p95

41 Allsop, *op cit*, p45

42 *ibid*, p45; McKenzie, J, *The Gospel According to Matthew*, The Jerome Biblical Commentary, Geoffrey Chapman, London, 1970, p69; Tyler & Reid, *op cit*, p292.
All three sources refer to Jesus as the 'New Moses' in the context of Matthew's presentation of him in the sermon.

43 Stanton, G, *The Gospels and Jesus*, Oxford University Press, Oxford, 1993, p69

44 Drane, *op cit*, p166

45 Stanton, *op cit*, p72

46 Barclay, W, *The Gospels and Acts Vol 1*, SCM Press, London, 1993, p151

47 *ibid*, p161

48 Jenkins, *op cit*, p35

49 Allsop, *op cit*, p45

50 Beswick, F, *The Sermon On The Mount*, First and Best in Education, Northants, 1998, p2

51 Jenkins, *op cit*, p36

52 Barclay, W, *The Gospel Of Matthew*, The New Daily Study Bible, Westminster John Knox Press, 1975, p92

53 *ibid*, p95

54 Allison, D, *Matthew*, The Oxford Bible Commentary, Oxford University Press, Oxford, 2007, p853

55 Guy, HA, *The Gospel of Matthew*, Macmillan Education, London, 1977, p46

56 Stanton, *op cit*, p71

57 Barclay, *The Gospel Of Matthew*, *op cit*, p100

58 McKenzie, J, *The Gospel According to Matthew*, The Jerome Biblical Commentary, Geoffrey Chapman, London, 1970, p70

59 Barclay, *The Gospel Of Matthew*, *op cit*, p105

60 Allison, *op cit*, p853

61 Barclay, *The Gospel Of Matthew*, *op cit*, p110

62 Harington, D, *The Gospel According to Matthew*, Collegeville Bible Commentary, Liturgical Press, 1991, p29

63 Guy, *op cit*, p47

64 Harington, *op cit*, p29

65 McKenzie, *op cit*, p71

66 Jenkins, *op cit*, 1999, p36

67 Barclay, *The Gospel Of Matthew*, *op cit*, p136

68 Harrington, *op cit*, p31

69 Barclay, *The Gospel Of Matthew*, *op cit*, p147

70 McKenzie, *op cit*, p72

71 Barclay, *The Gospel Of Matthew*, *op cit*, p152

72 Tyler & Reid, *op cit*, p182

73 Harrington, *op cit*, p32

74 Barclay, *The Gospel Of Matthew*, *op cit*, p163

75 Guy, *op cit*, p52

76 Barclay, *The Gospel Of Matthew*, *op cit*, p174

77 Guy, *op cit*, p53

78 Harrington, *op cit*, p33

79 *ibid*, p34–35

80 Guy, *op cit*, p55

81 McKenzie, *op cit*, p74

82 Barclay, *The Gospel Of Matthew*, *op cit*, p213

83 'Hillel and the Golden Rule', Jewish Virtual Library, www.jewishvirtuallibrary.org, accessed 28 February 2009

84 McKenzie, *op cit*, p76

85 Tyler & Reid, *op cit*, p436

86 Kurz, W, *The Acts of the Apostles*, Collegeville Bible Commentary, Liturgical Press, Minnesota, 1991, p106

87 Tyler & Reid, *op cit*, p432

88 Jenkins, *op cit*, p37

89 Pilch, J, *Galatians and Romans*, Collegeville Bible Commentary, Liturgical Press, Minnesota, 1991, p19

90 Guthrie, D, *Galatians*, Marshall, Morgan & Scott, London, 1992, p110–111

91 King, ML, 'The I Have A Dream Speech', 28 August 1963, US Constitution online, www.usconstitution.net, accessed 22 January 2009

92 Getty, MA, *First & Second Corinthians*, Collegeville Bible Commentary, Liturgical Press, Minnesota, 1991, p18

93 *ibid*, p57

94 Pilch, *op cit*, p19

95 Galatians 5:22–23

96 Osiek, C, *Galatians*, Veritas, Dublin, 1980, p81

97 Barclay, W, *Ethics in a Permissive Society*, Fontana, 1971

98 Drane, *op cit*, p340

99 Barclay, *op cit*, *Ethics in a Permissive Society*

100 Jenkins, *op cit*, p37

101 Getty, *op cit*, p28

102 Kugelman, R, *The First Letter to the Corinthians*, The Jerome Biblical Commentary, Geoffrey Chapman, London, 1970, p254

103 1 Corinthians 6:11

104 Getty, *op cit*, p33

105 Tyler, *op cit*, p71

106 Pilch, *op cit*, p63

107 Allsop, *op cit*, p48

Chapter 2

Ethical Theories

Chapter overview

This chapter aims to explore the following ethical theories:

- Natural moral law
- Utilitarianism
- Situation ethics

ETHICAL THEORIES CAN BE either religious or secular in nature. They consist of general moral principles or values which can be applied to specific ethical issues such as abortion and euthanasia. These principles advise society, or those following the theory, of the correct way to behave regarding such issues. Before analysing the three ethical theories listed above, it is important to outline some of the key terms referred to throughout this chapter, terms which are central to a study of ethical theory. The terms are teleological ethics, deontological ethics, ethical relativism and moral absolutism.

It is important to note that there are a number of ways to approach the study of ethics,[1] for example, descriptive ethics simply describes the way in which people behave and "examines what we do and the background influences on us. It does not examine issues of right and wrong."[2] However, normative ethics is the term used when the study of ethics is concerned with the examination of right and wrong or moral and immoral behaviour. According to Bowie, normative ethics is concerned with "how people ought to act, how moral choices should be made and how the rules apply."[3] Within normative ethics, there are two main ethical systems or two ways in which we approach the issue of how to behave morally.[4] The two approaches are the teleological approach and the deontological approach.

The teleological approach is based on the consequences of our actions. If our actions produce a positive outcome, then what we have done can be considered moral. However, if our actions produce a negative result, then our behaviour is considered immoral. Consider the following basic examples:

- If I donate money to Oxfam, the consequences of my actions are positive because they will help those suffering from absolute poverty, therefore it is good to give money to charity.
- However, if I illegally dump rubbish in the countryside, the consequences of my actions are negative if the environment will be polluted, therefore it is wrong to dump rubbish in the countryside.

It is important to note that our actions are not judged as right or wrong in themselves, in other words, our actions are not considered to be intrinsically good or bad. The focus of the teleological approach is always on the consequences of our actions. Therefore, following the teleological approach to ethics, the end justifies the means. To use another example, the means, or the action of abortion can be justified if the end or outcome is a positive one for the mother. Teleological theories are not theories which are based on following strict moral rules which can never be broken.

Utilitarianism and Situation Ethics are examples of teleological theories and both theories can be described as relativist theories. Relativism "holds that there are no absolute universal standards"[5] but that moral behaviour will vary from person to person (moral relativism) or from society to society (cultural relativism).

The deontological approach to ethics is based on the morality of our actions. Unlike the teleological approach, the deontological approach does not take the consequences of our actions into consideration at all. As Bowie puts it "the important thing isn't the result or consequence of the action, but the action itself."[6] Therefore, according to the deontological approach, our actions are intrinsically right or wrong and as a result, this approach is based on following rules which can never be broken under any circumstances. Therefore, following this approach, the end does not justify the means. Consider the following examples which use rules outlined in the Decalogue:

- Abortion is immoral in all cases because it is contrary to the command *"You shall not murder."*
- Telling the truth is considered moral because God commanded: *"You shall not give false testimony against your neighbour."*

As the above examples suggest, the deontological approach to ethics is linked to moral absolutism. Moral absolutism refers to rules which govern our moral behaviour and can never be broken. Thompson defines absolutism as "moral principles that hold true for all people in all situations."[7] Natural law and Kantian Ethics are examples of deontological ethical theories which outline moral absolutes that must be followed. If we fail to follow these moral absolutes then it is considered that we fail to act morally.

TASKS

Consider the following points of view on the euthanasia debate and discuss the questions that follow.

> Euthanasia is immoral because killing is intrinsically evil. Killing is always wrong, in all circumstances, regardless of the motives or the consequences.

> Some people may consider euthanasia to be wrong but that doesn't make it wrong for everyone. If a person decides that they no longer wish to suffer then it's their choice whether they live or die.

1. Which approach to morality, absolutism or relativism, is the best for society today in relation to the euthanasia debate?
2. Should we follow moral absolutes surrounding the prohibition of abortion, IVF, contraception and divorce?

Before considering each of the ethical theories in turn, it is important to be aware of the following information for each theory:

1. Origin and development of the theory
2. Key principles associated with the theory
3. Examples of application of the theory to ethical issues
4. An evaluation of the theory
5. Links between the theory and other aspects of human experience

NATURAL MORAL LAW

Natural law is an ethical theory which considers something to be moral if it fulfils God's plan for creation. In simpler terms, natural law asserts that people act morally if they behave as God wants them to behave. At this point it is very important to clarify that natural law is not simply about "trying to act in a way that mimics nature"[8] but it is about humans acting in a way that is in accordance with God's plan for them. In addition to being a religious theory, natural law can also be described as a deontological theory as it focuses on the morality of our actions as opposed to the consequences of our actions. Natural law consists of moral absolutes – rules that cannot be broken under any circumstances.

Natural law was fully developed by Thomas Aquinas in the thirteenth century, although Vardy and Grosch comment: "the natural law approach to morality has a long history"[9] as the concept originated long before the time of Aquinas.

Origin and development of natural law

The concept of natural law can be traced back to the time of the Greek philosopher Aristotle (384–322 BC). In his work *Nicomachaen Ethics*, Aristotle claimed that everything has a purpose. If things achieve their purpose then they are to be considered good whereas if they do not fulfil their purpose they are bad. An example which is often used to illustrate this point is: "A good knife is one that cuts well: that's what it's designed to do."[10] While Aristotle didn't fully develop the natural law approach as far as moral behaviour was concerned, he did claim that the natural way for humans to behave in order to fulfil their purpose was a universal standard of behaviour, as it applied to all people. In *Nicomachaen Ethics*, he argued: "that which is natural is unchangeable and has the same power everywhere, just as fire burns both here and in Persia."[11]

The Stoics were a group of ancient Greek philosophers who further developed the concept of natural law. They believed: "there was a fundamental design and purpose to the universe (the logos), and that one's morality ought to be based on aligning oneself with it."[12] In other words, if we want to behave morally then we must fulfil our purpose, which for the Stoics was to "fit in with the overall plan of the universe"[13] rather than acting in a way which was influenced by thoughts of personal gain or happiness.

The Roman lawyer Cicero (106–43BC) also developed the concept of natural law. In his work *On the Republic,* he argued: "True law is right reason in agreement with nature; it is of universal application, unchanging and everlasting…And there will not be different laws at Rome and at Athens, or different laws now and in the future, but one eternal and unchangeable law will be valid for all nations and all times."[14] Therefore, for Cicero, natural law referred to universal standards of behaviour which were applicable to all people at all times.

The individual who fully developed natural law into an ethical theory was Thomas Aquinas (1224–1274). Aquinas was born at Aquino, an Italian town situated between Naples and Rome. While he was a student at university in Naples, Aquinas entered the Dominican Order. By 1256 he had become a Professor of Theology and he taught in both Rome and Paris. His great works are called *Summa Contra Gentiles* and *Summa Theologica,* although he died before the latter was completed. Aquinas was summoned by Pope Gregory X to participate in the Council of Lyons in 1274, but he died on his journey.[15]

Aquinas made an attempt to apply the ideas of Aristotle and Cicero to human behaviour. He claimed that because every human is created by God, then our purpose is to live life according to God's plan for us. In other words, humans must behave in the way God wants us to behave. According to Aquinas, the laws God has set out for humanity to follow form the basis of natural law. In *Summa Theologica*, he commented: "Law is nothing else than an ordination of reason for the common good promulgated by the one who is in charge of the community".[16] That person in charge of the community is God, therefore to behave morally, we must follow the rules laid down by God. Tyler and Reid comment: "Aquinas maintains that there is a moral code towards which human beings naturally incline, and this he calls natural moral law."[17] Therefore, for Aquinas, like Aristotle and Cicero before him, natural law is a universal theory and this point is developed by Aquinas himself in *Summa Theologica*: "Natural law is the same for all men...there is a single standard of truth and right for everyone...which is known for everyone."[18] Aquinas felt that he had a scriptural basis for his argument that natural law was universal as in Romans 2:14–15, Saint Paul states: *"Gentiles, who do not have the law, do by nature things required by the law...they show that the requirements of the law are written on their hearts."*

Therefore, as mentioned above, Aquinas believed that God has a purpose or plan for creation. He wants humans to act in a specific way and that is why he provided us with rules which govern how he wants us to behave. These rules form the basis of Aquinas' natural law theory – if we behave according to the rules we act morally, however, if we disobey God's rules we behave immorally.

Natural law is therefore a deontological theory because it is based on rules that cannot be broken. It does not take the consequences of our actions into consideration. The rewards for living according to God's plan and being obedient to the moral absolutes laid down by natural law are that people "may reach their eternal destiny with God."[19]

Key principles associated with natural law

There are a number of key principles associated with the natural law theory. These principles consist of the following:

1. Primary and secondary precepts
2. The role of human reason
3. Apparent goods
4. Interior and exterior acts
5. Double effect

1. Primary and secondary precepts

According to Vardy and Grosch: "the starting point for all advocates of natural law is to work out the purpose of human life"[20] and Aquinas felt that God's overall purpose for human life was to live, reproduce, learn, have an ordered society and worship God.[21] These purposes for human life are referred to as the primary precepts and if humans follow the precepts or rules, then it is believed that they behave in a way that is pleasing to God. However, if they do not follow them and do not reproduce or worship God, for example, then they are thought to behave in a way that is morally unacceptable.

Secondary precepts are rules that follow from obedience to the primary precepts. Bowie explains: "secondary precepts are rulings about things that we should or shouldn't do because they uphold or fail to uphold the primary precept."[22] For example, as one of the primary precepts is to reproduce, a secondary precept or rule would be that sexual intercourse must lead to the possibility of having a child or that both contraception and homosexuality are immoral because of the fact that they do not lead to the possibility of new life being created.

2. The role of human reason

Thompson defines human reason as the ability of humans to "direct themselves and therefore take responsibility for knowing and doing what God intends for them."[23] Reason is therefore believed to be our in-built sense of right and wrong, our personal guide to what is considered to be proper behaviour. For Aquinas, our ability as humans to reason enables us to work out what God's plan for us really is. Aquinas himself stated: "To disparage the dictate of reason is equivalent to condemning the command of God."[24] Because scripture does not tell us how to behave in every situation, human reason is needed to supplement scripture, in order to help us when making moral decisions. As Vardy and Grosch comment: "God makes human beings with a certain nature and this nature enables human beings to use their reason and their experience to understand what is right."[25] The role of reason in ethical decision making implies that natural law is linked to a universal standard of behaviour. Thompson comments: "Since natural law is based on reason, it is in principle discoverable by anyone, whether religious or not. For the same reason, it is universal, rather than limited to any one religion or culture."[26]

Aquinas claimed that "reason alone"[27] could help all people arrive at the natural or cardinal virtues which are:

- prudence, which means that we should be careful and not reckless in how we behave;
- temperance, which refers to doing things in moderation and having self-control;
- fortitude, which refers to the ability to have courage when bearing pain;
- justice, which implies that we must be fair to all people.

These virtues should inform peoples' ability to reason and therefore assist them in the process of making moral decisions. Aquinas considered these virtues to be opposite, in terms of morality, from the seven deadly sins (also known as the capital vices); which are pride, avarice (a greed to own things for the sake of it), lust, envy, gluttony (a greed for food), anger and sloth. Other examples of natural virtues according to Aquinas are the Ten Commandments and Paul's teaching in 1 Corinthians 13:13 on the importance of *"faith, hope and love."* Aquinas argued that these attitudes could inform or develop our reason and that "the greater extent to which these are developed by the individual, the greater will be the obedience to natural law."[28]

3. Apparent goods

The concept of apparent goods is a fundamental part of the natural law theory. As outlined in the section above, Aquinas based his theory on the idea that reason can be used to inform humans on how to act morally. However, human experience has shown beyond any doubt that our ability as humans to use reason when making moral decisions is not perfect, or as Gill comments: "humans are fallible in their use of practical reason."[29] For instance, sometimes people fail to use their reason properly and as a result act immorally. For example, human reason did not prevent Hitler from giving orders to murder six million Jews in Nazi concentration camps during the Holocaust. In more recent times, human reason did not prevent the murder of 800,000 people during the Rwandan genocide in 1994. If reason is supposed to act as our moral guide, why do such things happen?

Aquinas' response to this kind of question was that humans act immorally because they seek an apparent good as opposed to what is a real good. Vardy and Grosch explain: "if a person does something that is morally wrong, he or she will do this because they consider this to be a good although the possibility of the individual being mistaken certainly exists."[30] They use the example of Hitler and Stalin to develop their point: "Hitler and Stalin did not seek to do evil – they sought what they thought were goods but they were mistaken – they strove for apparent rather than real goods."[31]

Aquinas himself commented that "No evil can be desirable, either by natural appetite or by conscious will. It is sought indirectly, namely because it is the consequence of some good."[32] Aquinas argued that if our human reason was fully developed, everyone would have the ability to differentiate between real and apparent goods.

4. Interior and exterior acts

In the development of the natural law theory, Aquinas made a distinction between interior and exterior acts. He felt that the internal intention and the external act were as important as each other in terms of morality. He claimed that we should not behave in a good way for the wrong reasons. For example, we should not give to charity simply to attract praise, and likewise "to help an old lady across the road to impress someone is wrong."[33] Note the similarities between Aquinas' teaching and Jesus' teaching on prayer, fasting and almsgiving from the Sermon on the Mount (Matthew 6:1–4).

Aquinas also felt that it was important to consider the fact that "good intentions don't always lead to good actions."[34] For example, a person may steal money to help someone who is seriously in need. However, according to Aquinas, this action of stealing can never be justified despite the good intention. Therefore, as far as natural law is concerned, the end can never justify the means as it is a deontological theory which focuses on our actions alone and does not consider the consequences of our behaviour.

5. Double effect

The final principle associated with natural law to be considered is the concept of double effect. As stated previously, natural law is a deontological theory which judges the morality of our actions as opposed to the teleological theories which consider the consequences of our actions. The idea of double effect encourages followers of natural law to focus only on the primary intention of our actions, rather than any secondary side effects our actions may have. Thompson comments that the doctrine of double effect implies: "if my primary intention was good, I should not be blamed for any secondary effects that result."[35]

The example of a doctor giving pain killing drugs to a patient further illustrates the meaning of double effect. The primary intention of administering the medication is to treat the pain that the patient is enduring, to reduce the patient's suffering. The side effect of the high doses of morphine administered by the doctor may result in shortening the patient's life, but because this is not the primary intention, giving the medication is not considered to be immoral according to natural law.

Examples of applying natural law

Natural law is an ethical theory which can be applied to all kinds of moral dilemmas. The application of moral principles to specific issues is referred to as casuistry. According to Thompson: "Casuistry is the term used...generally for any system that starts with fixed principles and then applies them logically to individual situations."[36] This process is still used by the Roman Catholic Church today who still follows the natural law approach to morality.

One of the most straightforward examples of natural law's application to modern ethical issues is its relevance to sexual ethics. Chapter 4 specifically deals with the topic of sexual ethics so a brief discussion will suffice at this point.

- Aquinas believed that one of God's purposes for the human race was to *"Be fruitful and increase in number"* (Genesis 1:28). Therefore, Aquinas claimed that one of the primary precepts was that humans should reproduce.
- In order to follow this principle, every sexual act must be open to the possibility of conceiving a child. If humans live according to this principle, then on this issue at least, they can claim to live as God intended.
- Any sexual act which does not have the possibility of reproduction as an end result is considered immoral according to natural law. Therefore the use of contraception is immoral for this reason, as are homosexual relationships. This is why, for Roman Catholics, the use of contraception and homosexual relationships are intrinsically wrong. These prohibitions are absolute and can not be broken under any circumstances.

At this point it could be debated that because Roman Catholic priests are not allowed to marry (they must remain celibate), they do not produce offspring. Is this also not opposed to natural law? Aquinas himself was a priest and had taken a vow of celibacy.

He argued that the majority of the population should focus on reproduction, but he added that it was the responsibility of a number of people to remain celibate and focus on the religious and spiritual needs of the Christian community: "so sufficient progress is made if some only attend to generation, while others give themselves to the contemplation of divine things."[37]

 TASK

Consider some other ethical issues faced by society today, for example, abortion, euthanasia, divorce, fertility treatment, designer babies, war, etc. Using the primary precepts, discuss whether the issues are morally acceptable to those who follow a natural law approach to ethical decision making.

An evaluation of the natural law theory

As an ethical theory, natural law has a number of strengths. Firstly, it allows Christians today, using their human reason to guide them, to live as God intends them to live. This is the view of the Roman Catholic Church which was expressed by Pope Leo XIII in the 1890s:

"The natural law is written and engraved in the soul of each and every man, because it is human reason ordaining him to do good and forbidding him to sin...but this command of human reason would not have the force of law if it were not the voice and interpreter of a higher reason to which our spirit and our freedom must be submitted."[38]

Secondly, because natural law is an absolutist theory, it provides Christians with the knowledge and certainty of rules which can never be broken. It is a very simplistic theory as it tells people how to behave regardless of the consequences of our actions. In times of uncertainty in Christians' lives, natural law can provide clear guidelines or a solid set of rules which must always be followed.

Thirdly, because human reason forms the basis of this approach to morality, it can be argued that natural law is a universal ethical theory which can be used by all people whether they are Christian or not. Thompson supports this idea when he comments: "Since natural law is based on reason, it is in principle discoverable by anyone...For the same reason, it is universal, rather than limited to any one religion or culture."[39]

However, there are a number of criticisms of the natural law theory. For example, Protestant denominations do not follow this approach to morality because it "gives to humankind a moral status independent of God's grace."[40] Following the teaching of Luther, the Protestant Churches argue that salvation comes from the grace of God alone and not through the deeds or works of humans, no matter how good those deeds are. Luther himself commented: "A Christian man living in this faith has no need of a teacher of good works."[41] Therefore for Luther there is no need for a legalistic theory such as natural law; all that is needed is faith in Jesus "and this faith soon brings along with it love, peace, joy and hope."[42]

While the Roman Catholic Church still accepts the natural law approach to morality, many other Christian denominations today follow Luther's teaching and argue that Aquinas' theory is too legalistic and does not give enough flexibility addressing moral problems. Many Christians today argue that Jesus was opposed to such a legalistic approach to morality, and Christians must reflect the example of Jesus. According to Bowie, Jesus "debated sharply with the moral legalists of his time, the Pharisees."[43] For example, the Pharisees would not permit the healing of a woman on the Sabbath because it broke a moral rule. The Pharisees claimed: *"There are six days for work. So come and be healed on those days, not on the Sabbath"* (Luke 13:14). However, Jesus had no problem putting human need before rules: *"I ask you, which is lawful on the Sabbath: to do good or to do evil, to save life or to destroy it?"* (Luke 6:9) As discussed in Chapter 1, Paul also believed that Christians were free from the legalism of the Mosaic Law. While Catholics follow natural law and maintain that rules prohibiting contraception, divorce and abortion are absolute and can never be broken, other Christians are more flexible in their approach to such issues and in some circumstances permit the use of contraception, divorce and in extreme cases even abortion.

The claim that natural law is a universal theory has encountered much criticism. We have already considered the view that because natural law depends on human reason, it can be applied to all people whether they are Christian or not. Aquinas' theory of natural law makes the assumption that because of human reason, all humans have common standards. However, natural law is not a universal theory as it does not take cultural relativism into consideration. For example, natural law prohibits murder, yet "at one time Eskimos killed members of their families who would not make it through the winter"[44] and they had no moral problem with this. It must also be noted that atheists cannot effectively apply natural law to ethical issues. If people do not believe in God then they cannot be expected to follow God's plan for creation. Vardy and Grosch comment: "This raises the obvious question of those people who do not accept the existence of God and it might seem that their ends or aims would be different from the believer."[45] In this case the foundations on which natural law is based do not appear to be solid.

Natural law has been criticised because it is a deontological theory, setting moral standards that are absolute. According to Clarke: "the claim that there is some fixed law of nature...is open to question."[46] Clarke uses the example of homosexuality, where many people are attracted to others of the same sex which seems natural to them, yet homosexuality is condemned by natural law. Vardy and Grosch comment: "Recent scientific studies have shown that homosexual tendencies may well be genetic."[47] If this were the case, and people are born either heterosexual or homosexual, then homosexuality should not be condemned by natural law.

The natural law theory has been criticised because it puts too much emphasis on the role of human reason to help solve moral dilemmas. As previously mentioned, reason has not prevented evil acts from taking place. Allsop argues that while "human minds planned the relief of the starving in Ethiopia in 1986" humans also "planned the Holocaust between 1941 and 1945."[48]

The concept of the naturalistic fallacy, a principle often used by philosophers, for example, David Hume (1711–1776), has been used to argue against the natural law theory. The naturalistic fallacy is "the attempt to derive an 'ought' from an 'is'",[49] ie it argues that simply because something 'is' happening it doesn't mean that morally it 'ought' to happen. With regard to the criticism of natural law, it could be argued that simply because something 'is' a command from God does not mean that we 'ought' to obey it. According to Tyler: "Aquinas committed the naturalistic fallacy".[50] Jenkins uses an example to develop the criticism of natural law further, claiming that the purpose of sex, according to God, is to reproduce, "but that does not necessarily mean that people ought to have sex only for this purpose."[51]

OTHER ASPECTS OF HUMAN EXPERIENCE

Natural law has been criticised for being too legalistic because it lacks flexibility when dealing with difficult individual cases. In many ways, society today has rejected moral absolutism in favour of relativism. For example, despite the absolutist teaching of the Catholic Church on the issues of divorce and contraception, many Catholics take a more relativist approach to such issues and apply Church teaching to their circumstances but quite often will act against Church teaching to suit their individual needs.

In this context, it is useful to discuss the concept of proportionalism, which is a more flexible approach to ethics and was developed by Bernard Hoose.[52] According to Vardy and Grosch: "Proportionalism holds that there are certain moral rules and that it can never be right to go against these rules unless there is a proportionate reason which would justify it."[53] Therefore, proportionalism would concede that abortion or the use of contraception "*may* be morally good in certain circumstances."[54] Proportionalism was condemned by the Catholic Church in the 1993 document *Veritas Splendour*.[55]

Below are two examples of human experience which, for many people today, highlight the need for a more flexible approach to morality compared to that permitted by natural law:

- Throughout the world, almost 39 million people are living with HIV.[56] Despite knowing that the use of condoms can prevent the spread of HIV, the Catholic Church, following natural law, have maintained an absolutist position on the issue. Pope Benedict XVI has commented that the spread of Aids could be combated through "fidelity and abstinence."[57] However, it is evident that within the Catholic Church there has been an attempt to apply proportionalism to this issue to prevent the spread of AIDS. Cardinal Carlo

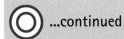 **...continued**

Martini, a former Archbishop of Milan and a very prominent leader within the Catholic Church, has argued that the use of condoms by couples where one had HIV/AIDS was "a lesser evil"[58] because it would prevent the spread of the killer disease.

- In Nicaragua, mainly a Roman Catholic country, abortion laws are very strict. In 2003, a nine year old girl, Rosa, who became pregnant after she was raped, was permitted to have a legal abortion by a panel of doctors and when the girl's parents gave their consent, the abortion was carried out. They felt that having the baby would threaten Rosa's life. However in response to the abortion, the Catholic Church maintained an absolutist approach to the issue and "excommunicated the parents and the doctors who carried out the procedure."[59]

 PRACTICE ESSAY TITLES

(a) Outline the main features of the Natural Law approach to moral decision making. (35)

Your response could make reference to the following points:

- The origins of the theory from Aristotle to Aquinas.
- The deontological nature of the theory.
- Development of key principles associated with the theory such as primary and secondary precepts, reason, apparent goods, etc.
- Examples of application of the theory to ethical issues.

Question adapted from CCEA Summer 2006 A2 6

(b) Explore the view that the natural law approach to moral decision making has much to offer today. (15)

Your response could make reference to the following points:

- For many people the approach has strengths:
  - It is a simplistic and universal guide to morality.
  - It provides us with clear guidelines on a number of issues. For example, contraception, homosexuality, abortion, etc.
- However also has weaknesses:
  - It is too legalistic and does not have the flexibility to deal with individual cases. Use examples to develop your response.
  - It is not a universal theory.
  - It puts too much emphasis on the role of human reason.
  - The theory commits the naturalistic fallacy.

◉ OTHER ASPECTS OF HUMAN EXPERIENCE

The German philosopher, Immanuel Kant (1724–1804), developed a deontological ethical theory which is referred to as Kantian ethics. Kantian ethics is not on the AS or A2 Ethics specification, but it is useful to be aware of the views of Kant when evaluating specific ethical issues throughout this course.

Kantian ethics is a deontological theory based on the concept of duty. It claims it is our duty to obey the moral law, and this moral law is absolute. While Kant agreed with Aquinas regarding human reason's role in moral decision making, he did not accept that the moral law consists of following God's plan for creation. For Kant, the moral law consisted of following the categorical imperative.

The categorical imperative is a principle which aims to help people work out what behaviour is morally acceptable and what behaviour is not. Kant explains the categorical imperative: "There is...only one categorical imperative. It is: Act only according to that maxim by which you can at the same time will that it should become a universal law."[60] Kant believed that the rules (or maxim) we should follow throughout our lives must be rules which can be applied universally to all people, at all times. As Bowie summarises: "If an action is right for me, it's right for everyone. If it's wrong for one person, then it's wrong for all people."[61] For example, following the categorical imperative, it can be argued that telling the truth is an important universal law because if a rule permitting telling lies is universalised "people would no longer believe each other...there would be chaos and people would quickly learn not to trust anybody."[62] Therefore, according to Kantian ethics, lying is always wrong.

Kant also provided us with another principle called the practical imperative: "So act that you treat humanity, both in your own person and in the person of every other human being, never merely as a means, but always at the same time as an end."[63] In this second principle, Kant outlines the view that it is never acceptable to treat a human being as a means to an end, ie it is immoral to exploit another human being. Vary and Grosch comment: "This principle enshrines the idea of the equality of each and every human being irrespective of class, colour, race, sex, age or circumstance."[64]

UTILITARIANISM

Utilitarianism is an ethical theory which "can best be summed up by the phrase: 'the greatest happiness for the greatest number.'"[65] In terms of morality, those who follow utilitarianism believe that our actions are moral if they create happiness for the greatest number of people, whereas our actions are immoral if they create unhappiness for the greatest number.

The word utilitarianism comes from the Latin word *utilis*, meaning useful, from which our word utility is derived. Therefore, utilitarianism can also be referred to as the theory of utility and encourages us to act in a way that is useful or beneficial for the whole of society.

Unlike natural law, which is an absolutist and deontological theory, based on religious principles, utilitarianism is a teleological, secular theory which judges morality on the basis of the consequences of our actions, rather than our actions themselves. Therefore for the utilitarian, the end justifies the means. Utilitarianism can also be described as a relativist theory because what utilitarians consider to be moral can vary for different people at different times, depending on the circumstances.

Origin and development of utilitarianism

Similar to natural law, utilitarianism can be traced back to ancient Greek philosophers. Aristotle believed that good conduct promoted happiness in society and Epicurus (341–270 BC) developed this idea by claiming that a good life consisted of the maximum amount of pleasure and the least amount of pain.

However, it is the English philosopher Jeremy Bentham (1748–1832) who is considered to be the founder of utilitarianism. As a young boy, Bentham was a very bright student who learnt Latin at the age of three and graduated with a degree from Oxford at the age of sixteen.[66] In his adult life, Bentham was heavily involved in both ethics and politics and produced two very influential pieces of work which outlined his views on political and ethical issues. His first publication was called *A Fragment On Government* (1776) and his second was called *Principles of Morals and Legislation* (1789). His views, outlined in both works, led to reform within a number of British institutions during the eighteenth century, including how criminals were treated in prisons and the reform of the Houses of Parliament. His ethical theory still has a significant influence on a number of philosophers today, including Peter Singer.

Bentham was not the only person responsible for the development of utilitarianism. A friend of Bentham, James Mill, had a son called John Stuart Mill (1806–1873), also a child genius, who was greatly influenced by Bentham's views. Mill himself produced a number of influential pieces of work including *On Liberty* (1859) and *Utilitarianism* (1861). In both of these works, Mill fully develops Bentham's theory of utility, setting a higher standard of morality than Bentham's approach. As was the case with Bentham, Mill was also very much involved in politics and became an MP between 1865 and 1868.[67]

Key principles associated with utilitarianism

There are a number of key principles associated with utilitarianism, which consist of the following:

1. Bentham's views with specific reference to the hedonic calculus
2. Mill's views with specific reference to the 'higher pleasures'
3. The distinction between act and rule utilitarianism
4. Preference utilitarianism

1. Bentham's views with specific reference to the hedonic calculus

Bentham believed that humans are motivated by a desire to experience as much pleasure as possible in their lives and to avoid experiences of pain. He wrote: "nature has placed mankind under the governance of two sovereign masters, pain and pleasure."[68] Bentham then related this point to the issue of morality, claiming that it was good to promote happiness and bad to cause pain or unhappiness. Thus Bentham explains his principle of utility as follows: "By utility is meant that property of any object, whereby it tends to produce benefit, advantage, pleasure, good or happiness or to prevent the happening of mischief, pain, evil or unhappiness to the party whose interest is considered."[69] So for Bentham, the utility or usefulness of an action determined whether or not it was right or wrong. According to Bowie, Bentham believed: "Good is the maximisation of pleasure and the minimisation of pain."[70]

Bentham provided the means of measuring the amount of pleasure our actions would create and this is referred to as the hedonic calculus (*Hedone* is the Greek word for pleasure). Bentham intended that the hedonic calculus would be used if we were faced with a moral dilemma, where we could use the hedonic calculus to calculate which course of action would promote the greatest amount of happiness.

According to Bentham, there are seven factors which are used to measure the pleasure generated by our actions:

1. Intensity – How intense will the pleasure be?
2. Duration – How long will the pleasure last?
3. Certainty – How sure or certain are we that we will experience pleasure?
4. Extent – How many people will experience the pleasure?
5. Remoteness – How soon will it be before we experience the pleasure?
6. Richness – Will the experience lead to even more pleasure in the future?
7. Purity – Will the experience of the pleasure be totally free from pain.

According to Bowie the hedonic calculus works as follows: "The balance of pleasures and pains is compared with those of other options and the best result determined. The action that leads to the best consequence is the morally correct one to pursue."[71]

TASKS

Apply the hedonic calculus to the following examples:

1. "Suppose you are a doctor driving to one of your patients, a young mother about to give birth. However, she is in great pain and difficulty and it looks as though she will need a Caesarean section. It is late at night and you come across a car accident down a country road. Two cars are involved and both drivers are injured and unconscious. You discover through trying to establish identities that one of them is the young pregnant woman's husband. The other is an elderly man. You don't quite know the extent of any internal injuries and are of the opinion that without immediate medical help one of them if not both may die. You are faced now with the moral decision of who to help first:

   • The young mother about to give birth?
   • The young woman's husband?
   • The elderly gentleman?"[72]

2. "You are a surgeon with the money for one transplant operation, but there are four patients who would benefit from the donor organ. They are a brilliant scientist working on a cure for cancer, a fifteen-year-old girl, a father of two small children, and a single mother with one child. To whom would you give the operation?"[73]

Bentham's hedonic calculus has faced considerable criticism because it is so speculative. For example, how can we possibly predict the intensity of the happiness that an action will create? How can we ever know the duration of the happiness that we will experience as a result of our actions?

The hedonic calculus is also criticised because the happiness that it attempts to measure is "based on a quantitative measure."[74] It only measures the quantity of pleasure, rather than the quality of pleasure. All students have probably heard their teachers say: "it's not about how much you write but it's the quality of your work that matters". This is similar to what Bentham's calculus is criticised for – too much attention is attached to quantity as opposed to quality. For example, by following the hedonic calculus, it would be possible "to justify the torture of a single prisoner by a group of sadistic prison guards, since the greater number outweighed the pain felt by the one prisoner and the quality of their happiness was not an issue."[75] Bowie adds that following the hedonic calculus could "justify any act if...the result generates the most happiness."[76]

2. Mill's views with specific reference to the 'higher pleasures'

John Stuart Mill agreed with the utilitarian principle of the greatest happiness for the greatest number of people. However, he was very much aware of problems associated with Bentham's approach to utilitarianism, in particular the issue regarding quantity and quality of pleasures. According to Vardy and Grosch: "he wanted, therefore, to define pleasure a little more carefully, and this involved shifting the emphasis from quantity to quality"[77] because he felt that the idea of simply focusing on quantity of pleasures was a philosophy "fit for swine."[78]

Mill believed that there were different levels of pleasure and that "those associated with the mind, such as literary and artistic pursuits are more valuable than purely physical ones, such as eating and drinking."[79] For Mill, the higher pleasures demanded more sophistication, whereas the lower pleasures were no more than basic animal instincts. Mill explained: "It is better to be a human being dissatisfied than a pig satisfied; better to be Socrates dissatisfied than a fool satisfied."[80] Therefore, with regard to the issue involving the sadistic prison guards torturing the prisoner, Mill would argue that the quality of the pleasure gained by the guards could not make such an act moral.

In addition to his contribution to the concept of higher and lower pleasures, Mill also added the harm principle to Bentham's theory in order to protect an individual from suffering at the hands of the majority. Mill commented: "The only purpose for which power can be rightfully exercised over any member of a civilised community, against his own will, is to prevent harm to others."[81]

Mill felt that Bentham's theory was antinomian, an approach to morality which does not consider rules to be important, and that it was necessary to have some rules – firstly, to promote the greatest amount of happiness at all times and secondly, to ensure that all members of society were protected and respected. For example, regarding the moral issue of telling the truth, Mill believed that a rule was necessary to direct all people to tell the truth as in the long term this would secure the greatest amount of happiness for the greatest number. He argued that it may sometimes seem necessary to lie, but he felt that breaking this rule would ultimately lead to unhappiness because "nobody would ever be able to trust anybody to be telling the truth."[82]

It must be stressed, however, that Mill was not a moral absolutist when it came to following rules. He agrees that in certain circumstances it is acceptable to lie, for example, if the consequences of telling the truth are worse than the consequences of telling a lie. According to Thompson, Mill gave two examples of when it may be acceptable to lie.

1. It is acceptable to lie to someone who intends to use our information to further evil purposes.
2. It is acceptable to lie to someone who is dangerously ill about their health if we are afraid that the news will cause him or her additional harm.[83]

3. The distinction between act and rule utilitarianism

Because he agreed with the importance of rules within utilitarianism, Mill's approach to utilitarianism is referred to as rule utilitarianism. Vardy and Grosch define this approach as one which "should first frame general principles or rules, and from these can be derived specific acts which are not permitted."[84]

Some scholars have divided rule utilitarianism into two different categories – strong rule utilitarianism insists that the rules created using utilitarian principles should never be broken under any circumstances, while weak rule utilitarianism argues that in some cases the greatest amount of happiness may be promoted through breaking the rule. Therefore weak rule utilitarianism follows Mill's approach to telling the truth because there are sometimes exceptions to the rule. RM Hare used the following example to illustrate a possible weakness associated with strong rule utilitarianism: Suppose a gunman is chasing someone who hides in your shop. The gunman enters and asks you where the person is. If you followed strong rule utilitarianism then you have to tell the truth because it is morally unacceptable to break a rule, despite the fact that the end result will not promote the greatest happiness for the greatest amount.[85]

While rule utilitarianism is associated with Mill, act utilitarianism or classical utilitarianism is associated with Bentham. According to Bowie: "Act utilitarianism maintains that, whenever possible, the principle of utility must be directly applied for each individual situation."[86] Although act utilitarianism does have greater flexibility than rule utilitarianism, in its strictest form it can have severe consequences for individuals. Consider the following example:

> "An act utilitarian goes out to see a film. On the way to the cinema, she sees someone collecting money for charity. She gives her money to the collector instead of buying the ticket and then goes home. A week passes and she sets out to the cinema again. She meets the collector again, hands over her money and again returns home. In each case, giving up her money to help the greatest number generates the greatest happiness."[87]

Therefore, as this example suggests, it is necessary to have at least some rules which protect innocent people from torture and to ensure that all people are entitled to spend some money on themselves.

4. Preference utilitarianism

RM Hare (1919–2002) "argued for what may be termed preference utilitarianism"[88] in his book, *The Language of Morals* (1973). Preference utilitarianism considers the happiness of those directly involved in the issue rather than society in general. According to Thompson, this approach "takes into account the preferences of the individuals involved, except where those preferences come into direct conflict with the preferences of others."[89] For Hare, "the right thing to do, therefore, is to maximise the chances that everyone's preferences will be satisfied."[90]

Examples of application of utilitarianism

Utilitarianism is an ethical theory which is still used today and can easily be applied to a range of ethical issues. Consider the issues of contraception and homosexuality already discussed in relation to the natural law approach to ethics.

- For utilitarians, contraception is morally acceptable for couples who are happy without children or who already have children and want to limit their family size to have a higher standard of living for existing children, in order to promote the greatest amount of happiness. Utilitarians would also have no problem with people who have a hedonistic approach to sexual relationships and who use contraceptives to prevent the spread of sexually transmitted infections.
- Utilitarians would consider the issue of two consenting adults who are happily involved in a same sex relationship with each other as being moral. This is in contrast to the natural law approach which considers this behaviour to be immoral.

Utilitarianism is described as a practical theory that can be applied to many aspects of society today. For example, on a large scale it can be used to govern a democratic country and on a smaller scale, it can be used to assist the health service in spending a limited budget. Bowie comments: "one could envisage the benefits of using utilitarianism in the management of hospitals, where fixed budgets must be best used to alleviate the suffering of the many."[91]

 TASK

Consider some other ethical issues faced by society today, for example, abortion, euthanasia, divorce, fertility treatment, designer babies, war, etc. Discuss whether the issues are morally acceptable to those who follow the utilitarian approach to morality.

An evaluation of the utilitarianism theory

As an ethical theory which helps people judge whether something is moral or immoral, utilitarianism is arguably based on sound principles. Any theory which attempts to promote the greatest amount of happiness for the greatest number of people in society could be considered to be beneficial. For the utilitarian, the majority is always of central importance, therefore utilitarianism "doesn't support individual pursuits that are at the expense of the majority."[92]

Utilitarianism is a very simplistic theory "based on clear principles".[93] It is argued that utilitarianism is universally more acceptable than natural law because it does not depend on religious beliefs. As Thompson comments, utilitarianism does not "require the acceptance of any prior beliefs about the nature of the world or of religion, and its moral discussions can therefore be appreciated across different religions and cultures."[94]

Utilitarianism has been used to solve ethical issues in the past. Clarke comments:

"The principle of utility has probably provided the greatest impetus to modern social reforms in the UK, such as the Divorce and Abortion Acts of the 1960s. These were reforms that reflected a typical utilitarian concern with maximising certain freedoms in order to minimise certain social evils."[95]

However, there are a number of criticisms of the utilitarian approach to morality. While it does attempt to secure the greatest amount of happiness for the greatest number, it fails to recognise the importance of personal relationships. If a utilitarian was forced to choose between rescuing a scientist who possessed a cure for cancer or his wife from a fire, he is morally obligated to rescue the scientist because of the number of lives he or she would ultimately save. In reality, it is more likely that we would follow our instincts and do what is most important for us personally, and save our spouse.

Utilitarianism has been criticised for putting emphasis only on the consequences of our actions and failing to take the motives for our actions into consideration. Nina Rosenstand used the example of a neighbour who went to her friend's house to turn on the furnace to warm the house for her friend's return from holiday. The boiler exploded however and the house burnt to the ground. Despite the fact that the motives were good, according to utilitarianism only the consequences matter and therefore the neighbour should be punished for her actions.[96]

Utilitarianism also demands that we predict the consequences of our actions so we can decide to act in a way which produces the greatest amount of happiness for the greatest number. However, according to Tyler: "consequences in advance of an action are hypothetical and cannot be judged with certainty, even if actions of similar kinds in the past have produced good outcomes."[97]

A criticism which is unique to act utilitarianism is that it can morally justify discrimination against minorities. According to Bowie, it can justify "horrendous acts as being for the pleasure of the many",[98] such as the persecution and extermination of the Jews because the greater population were brainwashed into thinking that this was pleasurable. John Rawls developed this criticism of utilitarianism. He believed: "utilitarianism does not take seriously the distinction between persons...rights of individuals are set aside for some greater good."[99]

Utilitarian morality is independent of God and this of course is not acceptable to Christians for whom God is the ultimate source of morality. Although there are parallels between the views of Mill who aimed to protect all members of society and the teaching of Jesus in the Golden Rule: *"Do to others what you would have them do to you."*[100] Thompson, for example comments that Mill believed that the Golden Rule was the "ideal perfection of utilitarian morality."[101] However, despite such parallels, utilitarianism is an unacceptable ethical theory for Christians because "it makes no reference to divine law or obedience to a divine commander."[102]

TASKS

a) Using the information from this chapter on both natural law and utilitarianism, in small groups create two spider diagrams comparing the theories.

Diagram 1. Outline the strengths of following natural law in opposition to utilitarianism.
Diagram 2. Outline the strengths of following utilitarianism in opposition to natural law.

b) In your opinion, which theory is the most suitable for society today? Explain your answer.

 OTHER ASPECTS OF HUMAN EXPERIENCE

Peter Singer is a modern day utilitarian, whose views are in many ways similar to those promoted by RM Hare's preference utilitarianism. Singer himself says: "I am inclined to hold a utilitarian position" and in his book *Practical Ethics* he considers how "utilitarianism would deal with a number of controversial problems."[103] In this context, there will be some focus on issues regarded as 'other aspects of human experience' because they are not on the AS taught course.

(i) Infanticide

Singer argues that if society can permit abortion then there should not be a moral problem with the acceptance of infanticide. He states: "If the foetus does not have the same claim to life as a person, it appears that the newborn baby does not either."[104] Therefore, on utilitarian grounds, if parents are not happy with their child for reasons such as severe disability, they should be allowed to have the child killed in a humane way: "Thus infanticide can only be equated with abortion when those closest to the child do not want it to live."[105]

(ii) Animal Rights

In his version of utilitarianism, Singer includes animals who he considers to be 'persons', therefore when he reflects on the greatest amount of happiness for the greatest number, the happiness of some animals are included in this calculation. He is totally opposed to the suffering of animals and claims that if we inflict suffering upon them we are guilty of speciesism. He even claims that some animals are more important than human infants: "There are many nonhuman animals whose rationality, self-consciousness, awareness, capacity to feel and so on, exceed that of a human baby a week or a month old."[106]

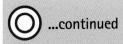 **...continued**

(iii) Environmental Ethics

As a utilitarian, Singer believes that it is our moral responsibility to preserve the environment for future generations in order to maximise happiness for the greatest number both now and in the future. Therefore, if our actions result in the consequences of environmental pollution, we are acting immorally according to Singer. He stresses the fact that we must "preserve intact the amount of wilderness that exists now" so that "future generations will at least have the choice of getting up from their computer games and going to see a world that has not been created by human beings."[107]

(iv) World Poverty

In his attempt to live by the principle of the greatest happiness for the greatest number, Singer donates 20% of his income to Oxfam, because he feels that this money can bring greater happiness to those suffering from absolute poverty than it can to him and his family. He claims that it is our moral obligation to "help those in absolute poverty that is no less strong than obligation to rescue a drowning child from a pond."[108] Singer's view is that if we ignore a drowning child in a pond we are in some ways responsible for their death because we could have helped but did not do so. Similarly, if we ignore those suffering from absolute poverty, we are responsible for their death because we can help but refuse to do so.

PRACTICE ESSAY TITLES

Question adapted from CCEA Summer 2002 A2 6

(a) Explain the utilitarian approach to moral decision making. (35)

Your response could make reference to the following points:
- The origins of the theory from Greek philosophers to Bentham and Mill
- A discussion of utilitarianism as a teleological theory
- A discussion of the key principles associated with the theory such as the hedonic calculus, higher pleasures, act, rule and preference utilitarianism
- Examples of applying the theory to ethical issues

Question adapted from CCEA Summer 2003 A2 6

(b) Examine and discuss the claim that moral rules are necessary for decision making. (15)

Your response could make reference to the following points, using relevant examples where necessary:
- Moral rules provide clear guidelines on acceptable standards of behaviour
- Some rules are universal – they apply to all people at all times
- However, rules can lead to inflexibility and many cases need to be considered on an individual basis

SITUATION ETHICS

Situation ethics is an ethical theory which maintains that something is moral if it follows the most loving course of action. It was developed by an Anglican theologian, Joseph Fletcher (1905–1991), who was a professor of Social Ethics at the Episcopal Theological School in Massachusetts from 1944.[109] His theory was heavily influenced by New Testament teaching and situation ethics is therefore a religious theory. However, unlike another religious theory, natural law, situation ethics follows the teleological approach to ethics therefore it is not based on rules which govern our every action, instead situation ethics is based on the morality of the consequences of our actions.

Situation ethics is a relativist theory because an action may be considered moral under one set of circumstances, but immoral under another. For example, a situationist may accept therapeutic abortion on the grounds that it prevents the mother and unborn child from suffering in the long term. However, if an abortion is carried out because a mother "wants to be slim for a planned holiday",[110] it is not the most loving course of action and therefore in this set of circumstances, abortion is considered to be immoral.

Therefore as far as situation ethics is concerned, there are no fixed rules, no moral absolutes – there is "only one duty and that is to love."[111] In Fletcher's book *Situation Ethics,* he informs us that "Christian situation ethics has only one norm or principle or law that is binding and unexceptionable, always good and right regardless of the circumstances. That is love."[112]

At this point it is important to note the definition of love that Fletcher had in mind when developing his theory. In Greek philosophy four types of love were identified:[113]

- *Philios* was considered to be the love that friends have for each other.
- *Storge* is the instinctive love that a mother will have for her child.
- *Eros* is the word that describes the sexual attraction or love that a couple have for each other.
- *Agape* is a self-giving, unconditional love which promotes tolerance and respect for all people. Paul's teaching on love from 1 Corinthians 13 forms the basis of the Christian definition of agapeism. It is this definition of love that Fletcher had in mind when developing his theory.

Origin and development of situation ethics

As already mentioned in the introduction to situation ethics, Joseph Fletcher was responsible for the development of the theory which was formally outlined in his book *Situation Ethics*, published in 1966. He felt that there were only three general approaches to ethics:[114]

1. The legalistic approach
2. The antinomian or lawless approach
3. The situational approach

While he did accept the role of human reason in moral decision making, he felt that the approach to morality which followed natural law was too legalistic and that on some occasions rules had to take second place to human need. In this area he was heavily influenced by Jesus' criticism of the Pharisees' legalism in the Gospels. Vardy and Grosch comment that because Jesus "attacked the Pharisees' insistence on following the Torah or Jewish Law – Christians cannot and should not lay down any law. When they do, they become more like the Pharisees."[115]

To develop the idea that rules should sometimes take second place, Fletcher's book included a conversation one of his friends had with a taxi driver about American politics:

- The driver said: "I and my father and grandfather before him, and their fathers, have always been straight-ticket Republicans."
- Fletcher's friend replied: "Ah, I take it that you will vote Republican as well?"
- The driver replied: "No, there are times when a man has to push his principles aside and do the right thing."[116]

Therefore, if a rule has to be broken in order to follow the most loving course of action, it is morally acceptable to break that rule. Fletcher comments that "the situationist follows a moral law or violates it according to love's need."[117]

However, Fletcher also rejected an antinomian approach to morality. This approach literally means that there are no laws or guiding principles and ethical decisions are simply about what makes us happy as individuals. He felt that those who took a purely hedonistic approach to moral issues have too much moral freedom. Therefore, Fletcher attempted to develop a theory which was in between both legalism and antinomianism. "Fletcher maintained that there was a middle way between legalism and antinomianism and this lay in the application of *agape*, the love that Jesus commanded."[118]

Fletcher had significant biblical support for his ethical theory. Consider the following references:

- In Luke 10:27, Jesus tells an expert in the Law that the greatest commandment is *"Love the Lord your God with all your heart and with all your soul and with all your strength and with all your mind; and Love your neighbour as yourself."*
- John 15:12–13 also highlights the importance of love for Christians. According

to Jesus: *"My command is this: Love each other as I have loved you. Greater love has no one than this, that he lay down his life for his friends."*

- The importance Paul attaches to the role of love in the lives of Christians has already been discussed in chapter 1, for example, Romans 13:10 states: *"Love does no harm to its neighbour. Therefore love is the fulfilment of the law."*
- In 1 John 4:7–8, the role of love in the life of a Christian is also developed: *"Dear friends, let us love one another, for love comes from God. Everyone who loves has been born of God and knows God. Whoever does not love does not know God, because God is love."*

Despite his role in developing the theory, it is important to note that Fletcher "did not pioneer the basic ideas of situation ethics, which had a longer history."[119] Augustine of Hippo (354–430) took a situational approach to the defence of the city of Hippo when it was under attack from the barbarians. He argued that following the commandment not to kill would lead to the destruction of Hippo, therefore Augustine believed that the most loving thing to do was to kill those attacking the city in self defence to protect themselves and Hippo.[120]

In the twentieth century, a number of theologians began to develop the concept of situation ethics. In 1951, just over a decade before Fletcher's *Situation Ethics* was published, Paul Tillich (1886–1968) commented: "The law of love is the ultimate law."[121] Previous to this, William Temple (1881–1944), former Archbishop of Canterbury, wrote in 1923: "There is only one ultimate and invariable duty, and its formula is 'Thou shalt love thy neighbour as thyself.'"[122] Fletcher's publication of *Situation Ethics* in 1966 was, however, the first formal development of the theory.

Key principles associated with situation ethics

There are several key principles associated with situation ethics:

1. Fletcher's opposition to casuistry
2. Four working principles
3. Six fundamental principles

1. Fletcher's opposition to casuistry

While Aquinas felt that it was acceptable to begin with fixed moral principles and apply them to individual situations, Fletcher, however, felt that it was unacceptable to take a casuistic (defined on page 50) approach to morality. In *Situation Ethics* "he opposed a deductive method of ethical reasoning; that is, he felt that it was unwise to start from fixed rules and then deduce from them what should be done in any particular situation."[123]

For Fletcher, the only rule or principle was to do what love required. In this regard, situation ethics is similar to utilitarianism, as both are:

"based on a single principle which enables humans to enter every situation armed with the experience and precedents of past situations, but willing to lay them aside if the principle of love is better served by so doing and will enable us better to bring about the greatest good."[124]

Fletcher himself agreed that there were similarities with utilitarianism:

"It becomes plain that as the love ethic searches for a social policy it must form a coalition with utilitarianism...Observe that this is a genuine coalition, even though it shapes 'the good' of the utilitarians, replacing their pleasure principle with *agape*. In the coalition the hedonic calculus becomes the agapeic calculus, the greatest amount of neighbour welfare for the greatest number of neighbours possible."[125]

As with Mill's view of rule utilitarianism, Fletcher "conceded that rules could help to inform a person's decision."[126] Fletcher himself states: "It is necessary to insist that situation ethics is willing to make full and respectful use of principles, to be treated as maxims but not as laws or precepts...principles or maxims or general rules are **illuminators**. But they are not **directors**."[127] Fletcher believed that rules should act as guidelines, guidelines which we are not obligated to follow. In other words "where love demanded that a conventional moral rule should be set aside, it was right to do so."[128]

In 1963, Tillich also developed this concept that rules were important for the situationist. In *Morality and Beyond*, he argued that if there were no rules, everyone would have to "work out time and again what was the right thing for them to do, and that in practical terms this would be impossible."[129] Therefore, Tillich was opposed to the concept of reinventing the wheel because if a moral rule has proven to have had a positive impact on human experience, we should follow it when we are required to.

Consider the following example which is used by Fletcher in *Situation Ethics* to illustrate why he was opposed to a casuistic approach to morality:

"In 1962 a patient in a state mental hospital raped a fellow patient, an unmarried girl ill with a radical schizophrenic psychosis. The victim's father, learning what had happened, charged the hospital with culpable negligence and requested that an abortion to end the unwanted pregnancy be performed at once, in an early stage of the embryo. The staff and administrators of the hospital refused to do so, on the ground that the criminal law forbids all abortion except 'therapeutic' ones when the mother's life is at stake."[130]

While the legalistic approach opposes abortion because all killing is wrong, Fletcher argued that the situational approach to this case would certainly favour an abortion as the most loving course of action.

2. Four working principles

Before Fletcher fully explains his theory, he outlines four working principles or four presuppositions to his theory. His theory depends on the following four assumptions:

(i) Pragmatism

Fletcher insists that any ethical theory must be practical. It must have the ability to effectively solve moral problems or to put it very simply, it must work. Vardy and Grosch reflect: "What is the aim towards which it must work? Fletcher claims that the norm or end by which the success or failure of any thought or action is to be judged is love."[131]

(ii) Relativism

Situation ethics is a relativist theory and Fletcher develops the idea that for the situationist, there are no moral absolutes. He comments: "The situationist avoids words like 'never' and 'perfect' and 'always' and 'complete' as he avoids the plague, as he avoids 'absolutely'".[132] As previously discussed, Fletcher agrees that rules are necessary and insists that relativism does not "imply that anything goes."[133] As Fletcher himself stated, situation ethics "relativises the absolute, it does not absolute the relative!"[134]

(iii) Positivism

This presupposition implies that faith in Jesus is voluntary, and freely chosen. Once a person decides to follow Christ they can then make *agape* the most important standard in their lives. Fletcher felt: "a person has to see for themselves that this is the most important thing of all."[135]

(iv) Personalism

While legalistic approaches to morality put rules and regulations before people, Fletcher argues that situation ethics puts people first. This reflects Jesus' attitude to the Sabbath, for example, when he comments in Mark 2:27: "The Sabbath was made for man, not man for the Sabbath." Situation ethics demands that people are treated as being more important than anything else.

3. Six fundamental principles

Once Fletcher outlines the four presuppositions or assumptions, he then proceeds to outline six fundamental principles which form the basis of his theory:

(i) "Only one thing is intrinsically good; namely love: nothing else at all."[136]

Aquinas' natural law asserts that actions are good or bad in themselves, regardless of the consequences. However Fletcher believed that actions are not intrinsically good or bad and therefore "actions are good if they help human beings and they are bad if they hurt people."[137]

(ii) "The ruling norm of Christian decision is love: nothing else."[138]

Fletcher argued that Christians are not governed by laws either from scripture or from natural law. Only the principle of love should govern how Christians should act. This follows from the teaching of Jesus and Paul who broke Old Testament laws when love demanded it. For example, in John 8:3–11, the Pharisees bring a woman who was *"caught in adultery"* and according to the Mosaic Law they were commanded to *"stone such women"*. Jesus replied, *"If any one of you is without sin, let him be the first to throw a stone at her"*, implying that it is acceptable for Christians to reject a legalistic approach to morality and to address ethical issues by following the most loving course of action.

(iii) "Love and justice are the same, for justice is love distributed, nothing else."[139]

Justice refers to the idea that all people should be treated fairly. According to Bowie, Fletcher felt that "Love and justice can't be separated from each other…justice is love at work in the whole community, for the whole community."[140]

(iv) "Love wills the neighbour's good, whether we like him or not."[141]

Fletcher maintained that Christian love or *agape* "is a self-giving love" which "does not depend on being loved in return."[142] Vardy and Grosch comment: "real Christian love, desires the good of the other, not one's own good."[143]

(v) "Only the end justifies the means, nothing else."[144]

This principle suggests that it is not our actions which matter, but the consequences of our actions. Situation ethics is therefore a teleological theory. Situation ethics would permit euthanasia in some cases because the end result, which is the death of the patient, can be justified because the person no longer has to suffer. For someone who no longer wants to live a life full of pain, this action could be considered as being the most loving thing to do.

(vi) "Love's decisions are made situationally, not prescriptively."[145]

By using the word 'prescriptively', Fletcher is referring to rules which prescribe the course of action to follow or tell us what should be done in certain circumstances. Fletcher makes it clear that situation ethics is not a deontological theory and asserts: "whether something is right or wrong depends on the situation."[146] This principle can be understood to promote personal autonomy because individuals are not subjected to moral absolutes but have the "liberty to make judgements and decisions about their own lives."[147]

Examples of applying situation ethics

With regard to the topic of sexual ethics in general, Fletcher says: "Jesus said nothing about birth control, large or small families, childlessness, homosexuality…Whether any form of sex is good or evil depends on whether love is fully served."[148] Fletcher felt that it was not immoral to have sexual relationships outside marriage or same sex relationships unless the people involved "hurt themselves, their partners or others."[149]

Followers of situation ethics will deal with each situation as it arises. If we were to ask them 'Is abortion moral?' they would respond 'It all depends' because a concrete situation is needed. Vardy and Grosch reflect on the morality of someone who has sex with another person for money. "The situationist will say 'It all depends'. If the money is to be used to buy a new dress the situation is different from if the money is to be used to stop the woman's family from dying of starvation."[150] Fletcher himself puts it this way: "The situationist never says, 'Almsgiving is a good thing. Period!' His decisions are hypothetical not categorical. Only the commandment to love is categorically good."[151]

Therefore, in order to apply situation ethics to moral dilemmas, each situation must be analysed and the most loving course of action carefully decided. In his appendix to *Situation Ethics* Fletcher gives four examples to discuss:[152]

1. A woman was talking to Fletcher while sitting beside him on a plane to New York. She told him that she had been asked to serve the intelligence services by going to a European city to lure an enemy spy into an adulterous relationship. This would then allow the enemy agent to be blackmailed into collaboration. She had been assured that no other plan would serve the purpose. In her discussion she cited Paul's description of the body as the temple of the Holy Spirit which should not be abused through unloving sexual relationships. She also cited Paul's teaching in Romans where he asserts that governing powers are given authority by God. She did not know what to do because either way she was breaking a New Testament rule. What is the most loving course of action?

2. Fletcher next discusses a case from the Second World War. A German family was split up at the end of the war. The husband was in a British POW camp in Wales while his wife was in prison in the Ukraine and the children were scattered all over Berlin. On his release, the husband found his children and discovered the whereabouts of his wife who was still in prison. She became aware of his efforts to find her but was told by the camp commandant that the rules only allowed them to release her for two reasons. First, if she was so ill she would have to be moved to a Russian prison hospital or second, if she became pregnant she would be returned to Germany as a liability. She chose this course of action with the help of a friendly guard. On her return home she was greeted by all members of her family even when she explained how she got released. The child was loved more than all the rest because he had done more for them than anybody. Did love justify this action?

3. The third case used by Fletcher is the case of Jim, an engineer who was diagnosed with stomach cancer. Without treatment he would live only for six

months. Surgery was not possible, but if he gave up work and took pills costing $40 for every three days he could live for three years. His life insurance was worth $100,000 and this was all he had to leave his wife and five children. However, it had to be renewed in seven months time. The man had a very important decision to make. He could either decide to borrow money, take the pills and live past the renewal date although his insurance would be cancelled and when he died his family would be in debt. His alternative was to refuse the pills and die while the insurance was still valid and leave his family $100,000. What should he do?

4. Fletcher finally considered the decision to drop the atomic bombs on Hiroshima and Nagasaki in 1945 which killed about 152,000 people. Some members of the advisory committee wanted to give the Japanese a warning by demonstrating the weapon on uninhabited land first to give them the chance to surrender. However, other members of the committee felt that the Japanese were blind to defeat and would continue fighting indefinitely with millions of lives lost. The committee decided to use the bombs as soon as possible on military and civilian targets without any prior warning. Was this a loving decision?

 TASK

In small groups discuss each of Fletcher's four situations. In each case, what do you think is the most loving course of action? Compare your answers with the rest of the class.

An evaluation of the situation ethics theory

Situation ethics is "an alternative Christian ethic that is consistent with the Gospel representation of Jesus",[153] more consistent some would argue than the natural law approach. Jesus rejected legalism and situation ethics does exactly the same. According to Vardy and Grosch: "situation ethics can provide a corrective to taking the natural law approach too far."[154]

As with all relativist theories, situation ethics is a flexible theory which allows people to deal with situations as they arise, rather than always having to follow rules which may not be appropriate to the situation they find themselves in. Situation ethics gives the individual the autonomy to make their own decision based on the most loving course of action for them. Therefore, it is a simplistic theory, uncomplicated by concepts such as primary and secondary precepts or the doctrine of double effect.

Many Christians claim that situation ethics is a sound theory because it is based on love – not a self love, but love of others. At all times, those who follow the theory are expected to put themselves last and others first because true *agape* "seeks the wellbeing of others."[155] However, opponents of situation ethics argue that the theory is too individualistic. This becomes more significant when one considers the different ways in which people define love. For example, depending on what individuals consider love to mean, the theory has the potential to justify "adultery, murder and even genocide in the interests of love."[156] In addition, because the limited importance of rules to guide people in their moral decisions, Vardy and Grosch comment: "it is far from easy in some situations to decide what love requires."[157] It is also highly likely that when we have to decide on the right course of action to follow, selfish motives can easily influence our decisions as "people interpret situations according to their own point of view."[158]

By promoting an ethical approach which is not based on following rules, situation ethics "can lead to crossing boundary lines that are dangerous to cross."[159] For example, if euthanasia is morally acceptable in some circumstances, then because of the slippery slope effect, there might be a gradual decline in moral standards. This could result in the abuse of euthanasia, which may eventually lead to allowing someone to die when it is not the most loving course of action. For example, the person may have become a burden for their families to care for. For this reason, Clarke asserts: "situation ethics is seriously flawed because, in principle, it allows us to ignore the traditional rules of moral wisdom."[160]

As with utilitarianism, situation ethics' weakness is that moral decision making is based on speculating about the consequences of our actions. Vardy and Grosch comment: "it is not easy to determine the consequences of our actions and this the situationist needs to do."[161]

The Catholic Church condemned the concept of situation ethics in 1952, fourteen years before Fletcher's book was published. Pope Pius XII said that it was "an individualistic and subjective appeal to the concrete circumstances of actions to justify decisions in opposition to the natural law or God's revealed will."[162]

 TASKS

Clarke concludes his outline of situation ethics by claiming that Fletcher's theory is "a recipe for moral confusion."[163]

a) What do you think he meant by this comment? Do you agree with his comment? Justify your answer.

b) Compare and contrast the situational approach to morality with the natural law approach. If there could only be one Christian approach to morality from these two, which one would you choose and why?

OTHER ASPECTS OF HUMAN EXPERIENCE

With reference to other aspects of human experience, explore the view that in any age, moral absolutes are necessary.

Included below are a few ideas to help you to develop your response:

Earlier in this chapter other aspects of human experience were considered which suggested that the natural law approach to morality was too inflexible. It was proposed that more flexibility was needed on the issue of contraception with regard to combating the spread of HIV and on the issue of abortion for the nine year old victim of rape.

Now consider the opinion that human experience has shown that some moral absolutes are necessary. It could be suggested that all people would agree that the protection of children is absolute and there can be no exceptions to this rule. The United Nations Convention on the Rights of the Child recognises this and claim that children "should grow up in a family environment, in an atmosphere of happiness, love and understanding."[164]

However, children's rights are abused and the experience of life for many children is a terrible one. For example, according to LASCO, the Latin American Street Children Organisation: "40 million children in Latin America are living on the streets – each minute that passes, three children die of malnutrition."[165]

- Research other ways in which children are not treated with love and understanding.
- Are there any other moral absolutes which are necessary to ensure that the human experience of all people is a positive one?

 PRACTICE ESSAY TITLES

Question adapted from CCEA Specimen Paper 2009 AS 6

(a) Explain the approach of situation ethics to moral decision-making. (35)

Your response could make reference to the following points:
- Origins of the theory in New Testament teaching and development by Fletcher in the 1960s
- The central role of love in the theory and the rejection of legalistic approaches to morality
- The teleological nature of the theory
- Development of key principles associated with the theory, such as the rejection of casuistry, the four working principles and the six fundamental principles
- Examples of application of the theory to ethical issues

Question from CCEA Summer 2007 A2 6

(b) Comment on the claim that for the Christian, 'the end does not justify the means'. (15)

Your response could make reference to the following points:

- Develop the argument that for some Christians the end does not justify the means using examples throughout:
  - Natural law views our behaviour as intrinsically right or wrong regardless of the consequences
  - Moral absolutes are sometimes necessary to protect all people
- Develop the argument that for some Christians, however, the end does justify the means. Use examples throughout:
  - Situation ethics is a more flexible approach to ethics where the end does justify the means
  - The example of Jesus illustrates that it is acceptable for Christians to allow the end to justify the means

CHAPTER SUMMARY

- Descriptive ethics describes how people behave whereas normative ethics is concerned with the examination of right and wrong behaviour. Within normative ethics there are two different approaches – teleological and deontological.
- Teleological ethics refers to theories which focus on the consequences of our actions rather than the actions themselves. Teleological theories are linked to the relativist approach to ethics, which maintains that morality varies from person to person or society to society. Utilitarianism and situation ethics are teleological theories.
- Deontological ethics refers to theories which focus only on our actions, not the consequences of our actions. Deontological theories are linked to the absolutist approach to ethics, which maintains that morality is based on rules which can never be broken regardless of the circumstances. Natural law and Kantian ethics are deontological theories.

Natural moral law

- The theory originated at the time of Aristotle and was fully developed by Aquinas
- Key principles associated with natural law include the primary and secondary precepts, the role of human reason, the difference between real and apparent goods, the idea of interior and exterior acts and the concept of double effect

- Application of the theory to issues such as contraception and homosexuality
- Strengths and weaknesses of the theory

Utilitarianism

- The theory originated at the time of Aristotle and Epicurus and was fully developed by Bentham and Mill
- Key principles associated with utilitarianism include Bentham's hedonic calculus, Mill's focus on the higher pleasures and the distinction between act, rule and preference utilitarianism
- Application of the theory to issues such as contraception and homosexuality
- Strengths and weaknesses of the theory

Situation ethics

- The theory was developed by Joseph Fletcher
- Key principles associated with situation ethics include opposition to casuistry, the four working principles and the six fundamental principles
- Application of the theory to issues such as contraception and homosexuality
- Strengths and weaknesses of the theory

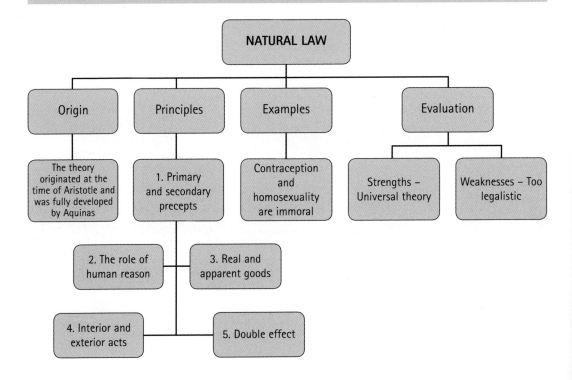

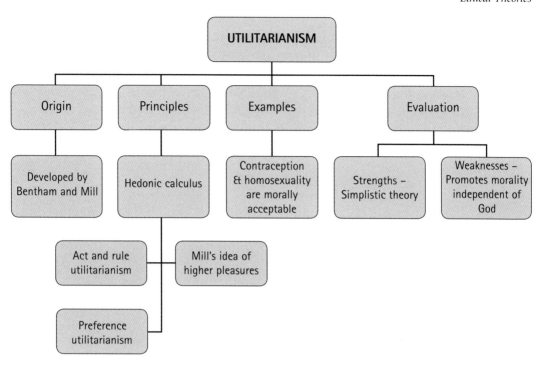

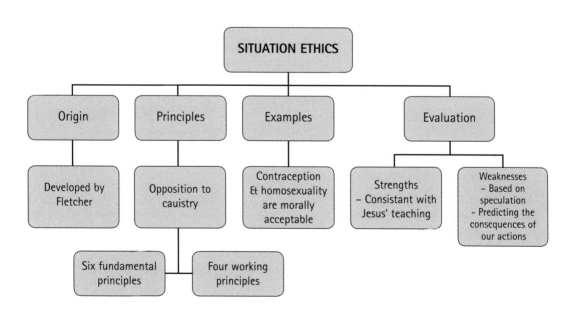

Endnotes

1 For a more detailed discussion see Thompson, M, *Ethical Theory*, Hodder & Stoughton, London, 1999, p1–4

2 Thompson, M, *An Introduction to Philosophy and Ethics*, Hodder & Stoughton, London, 2003, p121

3 Bowie, R, *Ethical Studies*, Nelson Thornes, Cheltenham, 2004, p6

4 *ibid*

5 Tyler, S & Reid, G, *Religious Studies*, Philip Allan Updates, Oxfordshire, 2002, p137

6 Bowie, *op cit*, p37

7 Thompson, *An Introduction to Philosophy and Ethics, op cit*, p132

8 Thompson, *ibid*, p141

9 Vardy, P & Grosch, P, *Puzzle of Ethics*, Harper Collins, London, 1999, p36

10 Thompson, *Teach Yourself Ethics*, Hodder & Stoughton, London, 1994, p56

11 Aristotle, *Nicomachaen Ethics*. Quote taken from Bowie, R, *Ethical Studies*, Nelson Thornes, Cheltenham, 2004, p24

12 Thompson, *An Introduction to Philosophy and Ethics, op cit*, p139

13 *Ibid*, p139

14 Cicero, *On the Republic*. Quote taken from Bowie, *op cit*, p24

15 *ibid*, p32

16 Aquinas, *Summa Theologica*. Quote taken from Bowie, *op cit*, p25

17 Tyler & Reid, *op cit*, p140

18 Aquinas, *Summa Theologica*. Quote taken from Bowie, *op cit*, p26

19 Bowie, *op cit*, p26

20 Vardy & Grosch, *op cit*, p37

21 *ibid*, p37

22 Bowie, *op cit*, p28

23 Thompson, M, *Ethical Theory*, Hodder & Stoughton, London, 1999, p60

24 Aquinas, *Summa Theologica*. Quote taken from Bowie, *op cit*, p26

25 Vardy, & Grosch, *op cit*, p38

26 Thompson, *An Introduction to Philosophy and Ethics, op cit*, p140

27 Vardy & Grosch, *op cit*, p37

28 *ibid*, p37

29 Gill, R, *A Textbook of Christian Ethics*, T&T Clarke Ltd, Edinburgh, 2002, p77

30 Vardy & Grosch, *op cit*, p38

31 *ibid*, p39

32 Aquinas, *Summa Theologica*. Quote taken from Bowie, *op cit*, p26

33 Bowie, *op cit*, p27

34 *ibid*, p27

35 Thompson, *An Introduction to Philosophy and Ethics, op cit*, p141

36 Thompson, M, *Ethical Theory, op cit*, p62

37 Aquinas, *Summa Theologica*. Quote taken from Vardy, & Grosch, *op cit*, p43

38 *Catechism of the Catholic Church*, Veritas, Dublin, 1994, 1954

39 Thompson, *An Introduction to Philosophy and Ethics, op cit*, p140

40 Thompson, *Ethical Theory, op cit*, 1999, p63

41 Luther, *Treatise on Good Works*. Quote taken from Gill, *op cit*, p93

42 *ibid*, p92

43 Bowie, *op cit*, p30

44 Bowie, *op cit*, p29

45 Vardy & Grosch, *op cit*, p40

46 Clarke, P, *Examining Philosophy and Ethics*, Nelson Thornes, Cheltenham, 2002, p136

47 Vardy & Grosch, *op cit*, p46

48 Allsop, P, *Religious Ethics*, Christian Theology Trust, Liverpool, 2000, p27

49 Thompson, *Ethical Theory, op cit*, p22

50 Tyler, S, *Religious Studies*, Philip Allan Updates, Oxfordshire, 2001, p76

51 Jenkins, J, *Ethics and Religion*, Heinemann, Oxford, 1999, p27

52 Hoose, B, *Proportionalism: The American Debate and its European Roots*, Georgetown University Press, Washington, 1987

53 Vardy & Grosch, *op cit*, p48

54 *ibid*, p50

55 *ibid*, p51

56 'The Global Spread of HIV', BBC News, www.bbc.co.uk, accessed 26 January 2009

57 'Pope Rejects Condoms for Africa', BBC News, www.bbc.co.uk, accessed 10 June 2005

58 'Cardinal Backs Limited Condom Use', BBC News, www.bbc.co.uk, accessed 21 April 2004

59 'Abortion Ruling Splits Nicaragua', BBC News, www.bbc.co.uk, accessed 4 March 2003

60 Kant, *Groundwork for the Metaphysics of Morals.* Quote taken from Bowie, *op cit*, p58

61 Bowie, *op cit*, p58

62 Jenkins, *Ethics and Religion*, *op cit*, p44

63 Kant, *The Metaphysics of Morals.* Quote taken from Bowie, *op cit*, p58

64 Vardy & Grosch, *op cit*, p58

65 *ibid*, p63

66 *ibid*, p65

67 Daniel, D, M, *Mill's Utilitarianism,* SCM Press, London, 2006, p1

68 Bentham, *Principles of Morals and Legislation.* Quote taken from Bowie, *op cit*, p39

69 Bentham, *Principles of Morals and Legislation.* Quote taken from Thompson, *Ethical Theory, op cit*, p74

70 Bowie, *op cit*, p39

71 *ibid*, p40

72 Vardy & Grosch, *op cit*, p65–66

73 Jenkins, J, *Ethics and Religion – Second Edition,* Heinemann, Oxford, 2003, p89

74 Vardy & Grosch, *op cit*, p67

75 Tyler, S, *Religious Studies*, Philip Allan Updates, Oxfordshire, 2001, p39

76 Bowie, R, *Ethical Studies,* Nelson Thornes, Cheltenham, 2004, p43

77 Vardy & Grosch, *op cit*, p67

78 Tyler, *op cit*, p38

79 Daniel, *op cit*, p2

80 Mill, JS, *Utilitarianism.* Quote taken from Bowie, *op cit*, p58

81 Mill, JS, *On Liberty,* Cambridge University Press, Cambridge, 1989, p68

82 Thompson, *Ethical Theory, op cit*, p76

83 *ibid*, p76

84 Vardy & Grosch, *op cit*, p70

85 Example adapted from Bowie, *op cit*, p44

86 Bowie, *op cit*, p43

87 *ibid*, p43

88 Thompson, *Ethical Theory, op cit*, p77

89 *ibid*, p77

90 Thompson, *An Introduction to Philosophy and Ethics, op cit*, p146

91 Bowie, *op cit*, p45

92 *ibid*, p45

93 Thompson, *An Introduction to Philosophy and Ethics, op cit*, p147

94 *ibid*, p147

95 Clarke, *op cit*, p127

96 Tyler, *op cit*, p38

97 *ibid*, p39

98 Bowie, *op cit*, p46

99 Thompson, *Ethical Theory, op cit*, p82

100 Matthew 7:12

101 Thompson, *An Introduction to Philosophy and Ethics, op cit*, p145

102 Tyler, *Religious Studies, op cit*, p40

103 Singer, P, *Practical Ethics*, Cambridge University Press, Cambridge, 1993, p14–15

104 *ibid*, p169

105 *ibid*, p173

106 *ibid*, p169

107 *ibid*, p272

108 *ibid*, p230

109 Gill, *op cit*, p100

110 Vardy & Grosch, *op cit*, p156

111 Jenkins, *op cit*, p101

112 Fletcher, J, *Situation Ethics – The New Morality,* Westminster John Knox Press, Louisville, 1966, p30

113 Jenkins, *Ethics and Religion – Second Edition, op cit*, p108

114 Vardy & Grosch, *op cit*, p124

115 *ibid*, p126

116 Fletcher, *op cit*, p13

117 *ibid*, p26

118 Tyler & Reid, *op cit*, p148

119 Vardy & Grosch, *op cit*, p123

[120] Jenkins, *Ethics and Religion – Second Edition, op cit*, p103

[121] Vardy & Grosch, *op cit*, p123

[122] Quote taken from Bowie, *op cit*, p100

[123] Thompson, *Ethical Theory, op cit*, p114

[124] Tyler & Reid, *op cit*, p148

[125] Fletcher, *op cit*, p95

[126] Thompson, *Ethical Theory*, Hodder & Stoughton, London, 1999, p114

[127] Fletcher, *op cit*, p31

[128] Thompson, *Ethical Theory, op cit*, p114

[129] *ibid*, p115

[130] Fletcher, *op cit*, p37

[131] Vardy & Grosch, *op cit*, p123

[132] Fletcher, *op cit*, p43–44

[133] Vardy & Grosch, *op cit*, p125

[134] Fletcher, *op cit*, p45

[135] *ibid*, p126

[136] Fletcher, *op cit*, p57

[137] Vardy & Grosch, *op cit*, p127

[138] Fletcher, *op cit*, p69

[139] *ibid*, p87

[140] Bowie, *op cit*, p104

[141] Fletcher, *op cit*, p103

[142] Vardy & Grosch, *op cit*, p128

[143] *ibid*, p128

[144] Fletcher, *op cit*, p120

[145] *ibid*, p134

[146] Bowie, *op cit*, p104

[147] Jenkins, *Ethics and Religion – Second Edition, op cit*, p103

[148] Fletcher, *op cit*, p139

[149] Bowie, *op cit*, p104

[150] Vardy & Grosch, *op cit*, p130

[151] Fletcher, *op cit*, p26

[152] *ibid*, p163–168

[153] Bowie, *op cit*, p105

[154] Vardy & Grosch, *op cit*, p132

[155] Tyler & Reid, *op cit*, p149

[156] *ibid*, p150

[157] Vardy & Grosch, *op cit*, p131

[158] Jenkins, *Ethics and Religion – Second Edition, op cit*, p105

[159] Vardy & Grosch, *op cit*, p131

[160] Clarke, *op cit*, p133

[161] Vardy & Grosch, *op cit*, p131

[162] *ibid*, p130

[163] Clarke, *op cit*, p133

[164] 'Convention on the Rights of the Child', United Nations Human Rights, www.unhchr.ch, accessed 28 December 2008

[165] Latin American Street Children Organisation, www.lasco.ie, accessed 22 January 2009

Chapter 3

Bioethics

Chapter overview

This chapter aims to explore the following topics:

- The issue of the sanctity of life and the concept of personhood
- The ethical issues surrounding the topic of abortion
- The ethical issues surrounding the topic of human infertility with specific reference to new reproductive technologies

What is bioethics?

IN RECENT YEARS, PARTICULARLY since 1978 with the birth of the first 'test tube' baby Louise Brown, there have been huge advances in medicine and biological sciences with developments such as IVF, surrogacy, saviour siblings and even the cloning of animals. Bioethics analyses such advances in technology and reflects on the moral controversies surrounding them. Wyatt defines bioethics as "Ethical reflection on medical practice".[1] One of the most recent bioethical issues to be debated was the request by UK scientists to have permission to place human nuclei into animal eggs and create 'hybrid' embryos because of the shortage of human embryos available for research. Scientists claimed that the creation of human-animal embryos would assist them with their study of disease. This would help them to find cures and also to advance in other areas such as the treatment of infertility. Despite controversy surrounding the issue, and opposition from religious leaders, the BBC reported in May 2008 that a team of scientists at Newcastle University had successfully produced the hybrid embryos.[2]

Of central importance to the study of bioethics is the understanding of two issues. Our views on both issues will determine our attitude to the topic of bioethics in general. The two issues are:

- sanctity of life
- personhood

For example, someone who believes that life begins at the moment of conception and that it is sacred because it was created by God in his own image, will have a different approach to bioethical issues to someone who does not believe in God and does not accept that a foetus deserves to be treated as a person in the same way that an adult is treated.

SANCTITY OF LIFE

The word 'sanctity' refers to something that is sacred or holy and many people believe that human life is sacred. They maintain that human life has intrinsic value, or value in itself, because it has been created by God and because of this, humans have a responsibility to respect and protect all human life at all times. However, others argue that the 'quality of life' concept is more important than the 'sanctity of life' principle. This approach, held by people from both religious and secular backgrounds, asserts that humans are autonomous beings and have the ability to choose between life and death in certain circumstances. For instance, Peter Singer, a secular philosopher comments that if "the choice was between the sanctity of life ethic and the quality of life ethic, the decision has been made unequivocally in favour of the latter."[3]

The Bible includes a number of references which imply that human life is sacred. For example, in the two accounts of creation recorded in Genesis 1 and 2, we are informed that human life is the high point of God's creation. In the first creation account we are told that God said: *"Let us make man in our image, in our likeness, and let them rule..."* (Genesis 1:26). Wyatt comments that this reference implies that "Human beings are unique in all the vast array of creation because they alone of all the creatures are made in God's image."[4] Humans, reflecting this divine image, possess certain qualities which set us apart from other things created by God, qualities such as "rationality, creativity and spirituality, for instance."[5] In the second account of creation in Genesis 2, we are informed that God is responsible for the creation of human life: *"the Lord God formed the man from the dust in the ground and breathed into his nostrils the breath of life, and the man became a living being"* (Genesis 2:7). Therefore, as both references indicate, the concept of the sanctity of life is evident from the very beginning of the Old Testament.

Elsewhere in the Old Testament the concept of the sanctity of life is also developed. Job 10:8–12, for example, highlights that God is the author of life and therefore life is sacred. Job reflects on the following idea:

"Your hands shaped me and made me...
You moulded me like clay...
You gave me life and showed me kindness."

The prophet Jeremiah similarly develops the idea that life is sacrosanct because it is created by God. Jeremiah 10:23 implies that because God alone gives life, he is the only one who can take it: *"A man's life is not his own; it is not for man to direct his steps."*

The New Testament also refers to the sanctity of life and this is clearly expressed by Paul in 1 Corinthians 6:19: *"Do you not know that your body is a temple of the Holy Spirit"*? In Matthew's Gospel, Jesus is recorded as having said that we should not worry about food or clothes because God will provide for our needs, just as he provides for the birds. Jesus then adds: *"Are you not much more valuable than they?"* (Matthew 6:26) This implies that humans have a unique relationship with God and because of this many Christians believe that human life is sacred.

The biblical view on the sanctity of life can be further developed when we consider that the command not to take life is consistent (with the exception of war and capital punishment, which were very much part of the culture at that time) throughout both the Old and New Testaments. The commandment from Exodus 20:13: *"You shall not murder"* is developed by God's words in Genesis 9:6: *"Whoever sheds the blood of man, by man shall his blood be shed; for in the image of God has God made man."*

Christian views on sanctity of life

The main Christian denominations' views on the sanctity of life reflect the views from scripture which are expressed above. For example, at the 1998 Lambeth Conference, the Anglican Communion declared: "life is God-given and has intrinsic sanctity, significance and worth."[6]

The Presbyterian Church in Ireland also supports this idea of the sanctity of life. In a booklet produced by their Board of Social Witness they outline the following:

"God is creator of life and He is sovereign. We are made in God's image and are unique. All human beings, regardless of age or disability, have infinite worth in His sight because they are made in His image. Being human requires us to be in relationship with other people who are necessarily different from ourselves. Human diversity is part of His sovereign design."[7]

The Roman Catholic Church similarly promotes the sanctity of life. The *Catechism of the Catholic Church* states: "Human life is sacred because from its beginning it involves the creative action of God and it remains for ever in a special relationship with the creator, who is its sole end."[8]

Secular views on sanctity of life

Some philosophers from a secular background do not accept that human life is sacrosanct. They may be of the opinion that if a person's quality of life is so poor that they feel their life is no longer worth living, they should have the autonomy to decide to end their own life. Or in the case of an embryo, parents should be able to abort to prevent the unnecessary suffering of a child who may be born with severe disabilities.

The legal philosopher Ronald Dworkin holds this view and in his book, *Life's Dominion*, he outlines his belief that all people should have the right to decide for themselves whether they live or die. Dworkin explains the importance of personal autonomy in the following quote: "Freedom is the cardinal, absolute requirement of self-respect: no-one treats life as having any intrinsic objective importance unless he insists on leading that life himself, not being ushered along it by others."[9]

Peter Singer also dismisses the Judaeo-Christian view on the sanctity of life. In his book, *Rethinking Life and Death*, he argues: "The traditional religious view that all human life is sacrosanct is simply not able to cope with the array of modern medical dilemmas."[10] As briefly discussed in Chapter 1, Singer believes that the "worth of human life varies", that we should "respect a person's desire to live or die" and "bring children into the world only if they are wanted."[11]

Therefore, if the secular views of Dworkin and Singer are accepted and applied to bioethics, issues such as abortion and euthanasia can be considered morally acceptable because they do not believe in the sanctity of life. For them, the quality of life is of greater significance.

PERSONHOOD

The issue of personhood also informs opinion on bioethical issues. We must reflect on the question: when does a life, deserving protection as a human being, really begin and at what point do we attribute moral status to a human being? In their book, *The Puzzle of Ethics*, Vardy and Grosch ask the question: "Are all human beings persons?" They respond by claiming: "a baby born without a brain may be human because it is made up of human tissue but it would not be regarded as a person."[12]

Vardy and Grosch differentiate between a human being and a person, but what is the difference? For some there is no difference whatsoever and from the moment of conception the pre-embryo is considered to be a person. However, others do not consider all humans to have the qualities of a person, qualities such as rationality, self consciousness and creativity. For example, the baby born without a brain, referred to by Vardy and Grosch, will never be rational or self conscious, neither will someone in a PVS (persistent vegetative state). So while both are human beings, some philosophers would argue that they cannot be considered to be persons and therefore they are not entitled to the same rights or protection as humans who are persons.

Therefore the question of when a human becomes a person is very relevant to the topic of bioethics. Take for example the issue of abortion, which will be discussed in the next section of this chapter. Stott comments: "It is our evaluation of the foetus which will largely determine our attitude to abortion."[13] If we believe that a foetus is a person from conception, we may consider abortion to be immoral as it is the equivalent of murder. However, if we believe that the foetus is not a person, we are more likely to accept abortion in certain circumstances.

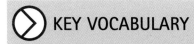 KEY VOCABULARY

It is important to outline the meaning of some key terms related to the development of the unborn child in the womb, which shall be used throughout this chapter:

Pre-embryo – this is the stage of development between conception and 14 days after conception.

Embryo – this is the stage of development from 14 days after conception to 8 weeks after conception.

Foetus – this is the stage of development from 8 weeks until birth.[14]

Biblical teaching on personhood

As previously discussed, teaching from scripture implies that each and every human being has been created in the image of God and therefore has intrinsic value. Biblical teaching also implies that an unborn child in the womb is a person in the eyes of God. Because of this many Christians feel that a human being must be treated with respect from the moment of conception. Wyatt comments: "The biblical narrative insists that God's creative activity does not commence at the moment of birth. Instead, God is intimately involved in the hidden and mysterious process of foetal development within the womb."[15] This is illustrated by Psalm 139:13–14:

"For you created my inmost being;
You knit me together in my mother's womb.
I praise you because I am fearfully
and wonderfully made."

Other Old Testament references which imply that life is sacred from the moment of conception include:

- Job 31:15 – *"Did not he who made me in the womb make them?"*
- Isaiah 49:5 – *"And now the Lord says – he who formed me in the womb to be his servant...for I am honoured in the eyes of the Lord."*
- Jeremiah 1:5 – *"Before I formed you in the womb I know you, before you were born I set you apart."*

In the New Testament, Luke's account of the visitation, when Mary visits Elizabeth, is also used to support the claim that life in the womb has intrinsic value. Luke writes: *"When Elizabeth heard Mary's greeting, the baby leaped in her womb and Elizabeth was filled with the Holy Spirit. In a loud voice she exclaimed...As soon as the sound of your greeting reached my ears, the baby in my womb leaped for joy."*[16] Stott comments that for Luke, the unborn child is as important as a child that has been born because in the context of the visitation, Luke uses the Greek word *brephos* to describe the unborn child. He uses the same word to describe a newborn baby (2:12 & 16) and the children who are blessed by Jesus in 18:15.[17]

Therefore, the biblical material implies that not only is human life blessed by God, but that this life is sacred even in the womb. Wyatt argues: "The consistent witness of the biblical material is that the foetus is part of the human drama, a hidden actor on the human stage; one whom God is creating in secret, calling into existence and into relationship with himself."[18]

Christian views on personhood

As a result of the biblical material, most Christians today believe that from conception the newly created person deserves the full respect and protection accorded to all human beings. According to Wilcockson, the view of John Calvin (1509–64) outlined in the following quote "is representative of both Protestant and Roman Catholic Churches."[19] Calvin commented: "The foetus, though enclosed in the womb of the mother, is already a human being...it ought to be deemed more atrocious to destroy a foetus in the womb before it has come to light."[20]

Stott comments that most Protestant denominations agree that the moment of conception marks the beginning of personhood because "there is no point between conception and death at which we can say: 'After that point I was a person, but before it I was not.'"[21]

The *Catechism of the Catholic Church* also states:

"Human life must be respected and protected absolutely from the moment of conception. From the first moment of his existence, a human being must be recognised as having the rights of a person – among which is the inviolable right of every innocent being to life."[22]

However, this view has been held only since the seventeenth century and prior to this the Catholic Church followed the teaching of Augustine and Aquinas who themselves had been influenced by the Greek philosopher Aristotle.

Aristotle (384–322 BC) made a distinction between the different stages of the embryo's development. He claimed that at the first stage of development, the embryo had a vegetative state which then became an animal-like state. The second stage was when the embryo became a foetus, a recognisable human being which had a rational or intellectual soul.[23] Augustine (354–430) adapted this idea and taught that personhood began at the moment of ensoulment, which is when God implanted the soul in the individual person. Augustine believed that this occurred 46 days after conception.

Aquinas (1224–1274) attempted to develop Aristotle and Augustine's views further. He maintained that the souls of boys were implanted forty days after conception, while souls of girls were implanted 90 days after conception. According to Vardy and Grosch: "This led to the idea that abortion was not a problem provided it was carried out before the soul was implanted."[24] Aquinas agreed with the views of Aristotle, that before ensoulment there was a vegetative soul and an animal soul. He believed that both were then discarded before the foetus became a person, at the time when the human soul was implanted by God.[25]

Christians no longer accept that ensoulment or 'quickening', when the mother first feels the foetus move in the womb,[26] marks the beginning of personhood. For example, Wyatt comments: "Today, vast improvements in scientific information have made the distinction obsolete. There is no stage in foetal development which represents a biological discontinuity and which might be interpreted as the transition from an animal to a human form."[27]

So while there appears to be no doubt about the fact that ensoulment does not mark the beginning of personhood, some Christians also maintain that neither does the life of a human person begin at the moment of conception. They claim: "the embryo or early foetus cannot be regarded as a human individual and does not become worthy of respect and protection until later in pregnancy."[28] This is partly because more than "50% of all embryos created naturally fail to implant and are lost as early miscarriages and on many occasions, the mother will not have known that she was pregnant."[29] Therefore, they believe that it is not acceptable to attach the rights of a person to something that might not exist beyond a few days or weeks. Another reason why some Christians reject the moment of conception as the point marking the beginning of personhood is discussed by Stott: "Some Christians decline to attribute personhood to the newly conceived embryo because as yet it has no brain to sustain either self-supervision or conscious relationships."[30]

As an alternative, some Christians have labelled the embryo or early foetus as a potential person, which therefore deserves to be treated with a significant degree of respect because of what it will become in the future. This view has been developed by Gareth Jones in his book *Brave New People* when he commented: "The foetus is on its way to becoming an actual person and, by the later stages of foetal development, may have most of the characteristics of personhood."[31] In his book *Mere Morality*, Lewis Smedes also supported the view that the foetus was a potential person and commented that the foetus was a "deep ontological ambiguity – the ambiguity of not being something yet and at the same time having the makings of what it will be."[32]

Wilcockson proposes the strengths of referring to the foetus as a potential person. Firstly, it makes abortion always wrong because we could kill someone who could have had the potential to become another Mozart, a great scientist or a charismatic statesman. Secondly, it "avoids the difficulty of deciding when to assign a soul to a clump of cells or a full-blown personality at birth."[33] However, this position has come under much criticism. Some philosophers argue that if we acknowledge that the 'clump of cells' soon after conception is a potential person, why not go further and claim that the sperm and egg also have the potential to create life and therefore it is also immoral to destroy them.[34] Singer provides further examples criticising the view that it is wrong to kill a potential human being. He comments: "To pull out a sprouting acorn is not the same as cutting down a venerable oak. To drop a live chicken into a pot of boiling water would be much worse than doing the same to an egg."[35] Singer adds: "we should not accept that a potential person should have the rights of a person."[36]

As a result of this debate concerning potential persons, Stott argues: "It is the language of 'potentiality' in relation to the embryo which has confused us."[37] He concludes that the view he thinks "should be held by all Christians...looks back to conception or fusion as the decisive moment when a human being begins."[38]

Secular views on personhood

Generally Christians agree that the moment of conception is the time from which the unborn child deserves to be treated with the respect and protection due to any other human being. However, those from a secular background may not accept conception as the starting point for personhood. What are the other options? Wilcockson[39] outlines several possible points during foetal development which could indicate the beginning of an unborn child's life as a person:

1. Syngamy
2. Implantation
3. Formation of the primitive streak
4. Brain activity
5. Viability
6. Birth

1. Syngamy

Syngamy is the name for the process which takes place in the immediate 24 hours after conception, during which time the two sets of genetic material are conjoined.[40] Some people believe that the pre-embryo can be considered a person when this process is complete rather than at the moment of conception. While Singer does not agree that the pre-embryo should be treated as a person from this point, he argues: "there is no 'moment' of conception. Conception in human beings is a process that lasts about twenty-four hours...it seems reasonable to say that conception is a process that is not complete until syngamy has taken place."[41]

2. Implantation

Implantation of the pre-embryo in the lining of the womb occurs up to one week after conception. Wilcockson comments that this is a "morally symbolic moment when the foetus forms a relationship with the mother as a person."[42] What is also significant is that there is now a 60% chance of the pre-embryo developing into a full-term baby, whereas before this point there was only a 30% chance of a successful pregnancy.[43] Stott adds: "It is true both that implantation is an indispensable stage in the development of the foetus, and that the greatest number of spontaneous abortions take place before this moment."[44]

3. Primitive streak

The primitive streak forms on the embryonic cells about fourteen days after conception and it acts like a line of symmetry, ensuring that the pre-embryo fully develops into an embryo and foetus as it should. After this primitive streak has formed, there is no further possibility of the fertilised egg splitting to form identical twins. Therefore the significance of this stage of development is that an individual can now be said to exist from this point onwards. Singer explains why it is unacceptable to even consider the cells to be a person before this point: "If we think of an embryo as an individual from conception – let's call her Marion – then what happens to Marion when the embryo splits? Are the newly formed twins Marion and a new twin, say, Ruth? Or are they two new twins, say, Ruth and Esther?" He adds "As long as twinning is still a possibility, the cluster of cells does not constitute an individual organism."[45]

The Warnock report

Mary Warnock and her team led an inquiry into fertilisation and embryology (The Warnock Committee) in 1986. They decided that from this point, fourteen days after fertilisation, the embryo needed greater protection and some degree of moral status was attributed to it at this stage of development. Therefore if embryos are being used for experimentation, the committee recommended that they must be destroyed on or before the fourteenth day after fertilisation. This recommendation became law when the findings of the Warnock Committee laid the foundations for the Human Fertilisation and Embryology Act of 1990. Below are two recommendations from the Warnock report which are relevant to the discussion at this point:

- **Recommendation 12** – No live human embryo derived from *in vitro* fertilisation, whether frozen or unfrozen, may be kept alive, if not transferred to a woman beyond fourteen days after fertilisation, nor may it be used as a research subject beyond fourteen days after fertilisation. This fourteen day period does not include any time during which the embryo may have been frozen.
- **Recommendation 42** – The embryo of the human species should be afforded some protection in law.[46]

However, after the publication of the Warnock report in 1984, the Catholic bishops of Great Britain submitted their response in opposition to the recommendations of the report to the Secretary of State. In this response, they argue:

"the inquiry's formal recommendations afford quite inadequate protection to the human embryo…such research damages and kills actual human beings…for the first time in the history of our civilisation, deliberate killing of the harmless is to be made not merely permissible but actually obligatory."[47]

OTHER ASPECTS OF HUMAN EXPERIENCE

Fourteen days after conception is the last point at which there is a possibility of having identical twins. In some rare cases, such identical twins are conjoined. In November 2008, conjoined twins, Faith and Hope Williams were born in England. They were joined at the chest and doctors operated on the pair for eleven hours in an attempt to separate them. Hope died during the operation. Faith survived the operation but died a few weeks later, on Christmas day 2008. Reflect on the moral issues associated with such a case.

a) Where the doctors right in their attempt to separate the twins?
b) Should they have allowed the twins to continue living until their natural end?
c) Should the mother have had an abortion in order to prevent the unnecessary suffering?

4. Brain activity

Some argue that the point at which the foetus should be given the rights of a person is when it begins to experience brain activity. Similar to the way in which the end of brain activity can be used to justify the end of a person's life – when someone is brain dead – brain activity can be used to indicate when life begins. However, it is difficult to say with certainty when brain activity does actually begin. After 54 days "spasmodic brain activity occurs"[48] but it is not until 32 weeks that the foetus has continuous brain function. The significance of brain function is that it may indicate some degree of consciousness and therefore the ability to feel pain. Singer comments that studies have found evidence for some brain activity as early as the seventh week of the pregnancy and as a result of this brain activity "it has been suggested that the foetus could be capable of feeling pain at this early stage of pregnancy."[49]

5. Viability

Viability refers to the point from which the foetus could live outside the mother's womb. Those who claim that this point of foetal development marks the beginning of personhood argue that if the foetus can survive outside the womb then it deserves to be treated with respect and therefore must be protected from this point onwards. As technology has advanced, a foetus can now survive from between 22 to 24 weeks into the pregnancy and abortion laws in many countries have used this as their upper limit so that abortions are not permitted after this time with the exception of a foetus which will have a severe disability when born. In the UK the upper limit for abortion was 28 weeks in 1967 but this was reduced to 24 weeks by the Human Fertilisation and Embryology Act of 1990. However, Stott does not agree with using viability to determine personhood because it makes "the moral status of the foetus…dependant on the state of medical technology."[50] Singer develops this line of reasoning and uses the following example to illustrate his point: "Suppose that a woman who is twenty-five weeks pregnant is living in Melbourne, a city with excellent intensive care units for premature babies, but she then travels to a remote part of the desert west of Alice Springs, three days from the nearest airstrip. Are we to believe that the foetus inside her was a living human being when she was in Melbourne, but not when she was in the desert?"[51]

6. Birth

The moment of birth is often used in many countries to mark the point where the child has moral status. As Wilcockson states: "legislation in many countries allows abortion up to the moment of birth but regards the deliberate killing of the baby after birth as murder."[52] Singer comments that it is true that "we are less disturbed at the destruction of a foetus we have never seen than at the death of a being we can all see, hear and cuddle."[53] Mary Anne Warren argues: "birth, rather than some earlier point, marks the beginning of true moral status."[54] However, Scott claims this argument could be discredited because: "there is no fundamental difference between the unborn and the newly born."[55] The baby is the same inside the womb as he or she is outside – nothing has changed. If we follow this way of thinking, a baby born prematurely would be considered to be a person while a more developed foetus in the womb is not. Singer comments: "It seems peculiar to hold that we may not kill the premature infant, but may kill the more developed foetus. The location of a being – inside or outside the womb – should not make that much difference to the wrongness of killing it."[56]

Some philosophers, including Singer, argue that it is not until a point after birth that the infant deserves to be treated as a person, because even at birth the infant does not display the characteristics of a person. In *Practical Ethics,* Singer claims that in order to be a person, one must be rational (ability to reason) and self-conscious (awareness of what is happening to you).[57] He argues that infants possess neither and cannot be considered to be persons. However, Singer takes the discussion even further by claiming that 'non-human animals' such as chimpanzees and dolphins are rational and self-conscious, therefore they should be considered as being persons and have moral status. Look at the following from *Practical Ethics:*

"One cannot plausibly argue that a foetus is either rational or self-conscious... For on any fair comparison of morally relevant characteristics, like rationality, self-consciousness, awareness, autonomy, pleasure and pain, and so on, the calf, the pig and the much derided chicken come out well ahead of the foetus at any stage of pregnancy."

"A newborn baby cannot have a right to life...A newborn baby is not an autonomous being, capable of making choices...In all this the newborn baby is on the same footing as the foetus...The killing of a newborn infant is not comparable with the killing of an older child or adult...There should be at least some circumstances in which a full legal right to life comes into force not at birth, but only a short time after birth – perhaps a month."[58]

As illustrated in the above quote from *Practical Ethics*, Singer believes that an infant deserves moral status about a month after birth. He is not the only philosopher to maintain this view. Michael Tooley argues that an 'entity' such as an infant which "lacks a consciousness of itself as a continuing subject of mental states does not have a right to life."[59]

Despite the secular views held by Singer and Tooley, the majority of Christians believe that the most convincing time for the true beginning of life is the moment of conception. From this point a new and unique person has been created, "which is distinct from both parents, and the child's sex, size and shape, colour of skin, hair and eyes, temperament and intelligence are already determined."[60]

 TASK

In groups, consider each of the suggestions put forward regarding when life truly begins.

Draw a table similar to the one below and indicate which suggestions you are willing to accept and which you feel must be rejected. Discuss your findings with the rest of the class and fully explain your decisions.

When does life begin?	Accept	Reject
Conception		
Syngamy		
Implantation		
Formation of primitive streak		
Brain activity		
Ensoulment or quickening		
Viability		
Birth		
One month after birth		

ABORTION

Abortion is defined as the intentional destruction of a foetus in the womb. The abortion debate continues to attract attention. In October 2008, pro-life groups rallied outside Stormont to protest against the attempt to extend the provisions of the 1967 Abortion Act to Northern Ireland.

TASK

Before the arguments for and against abortion are addressed in any more detail, have a class discussion or debate on whether, in your opinion, abortion should be legalised in Northern Ireland. Fully explain your point of view.

The pro-life movement argues that all human life is sacred and since life begins at the moment of conception, abortion is murder. The pro-choice movement, on the other hand, has a more liberal attitude towards the issue of abortion. While it would be incorrect to say that people who consider themselves to be pro-choice are pro-abortion, the pro-choice movement argue that the rights of the mother and the reproductive freedom of women are more important than the rights of the unborn child.

Consider the following information that outlines the number of abortions performed in England and Wales during a number of individual years since the introduction of the Abortion Act of 1967:[61]

Year	Number of abortions in England and Wales per year
1968	23,641
1978	141,558
1988	183,798
1998	187,402
2007	205,598

Stott considers the amount of abortions taking place on a worldwide scale and comments: "today the estimate is that as many as 55,000,000 abortions take place each year, which means that more than one abortion occurs every second."[62]

The law on abortion

In the UK prior to 1967, abortion was illegal under the 1861 Offences Against the Persons Act and under this legislation the maximum punishment for anyone involved in illegal abortions was "penal servitude for life."[63]

In 1929, The Infant Life (Preservation) Act made a more specific reference to the issue of abortion and it made it an offence to "destroy the life of a child capable of being born alive."[64] The Act also made an exception and permitted abortion in the case of a pregnancy which, if it were allowed to continue, would jeopardise the mother's life.

The next significant point in the development of abortion legislation was in 1938 when Aleck Bourne, a gynaecologist, was prosecuted for performing an abortion on a fourteen year old girl who had been raped by several off-duty British soldiers. Bourne won the case and the judge argued that the girl's mental health needed to be taken into consideration in addition to her physical health, to prevent her from becoming a "physical and mental wreck."[65] The outcome of this case resulted in a steady increase in abortions carried out by doctors over the subsequent years. However, this number was insignificant in comparison to the large number of illegal abortions being performed in 'back street' abortion clinics. The women who had these illegal abortions risked serious infections, infertility and even death due to the poor standards of hygiene.[66] It was to prevent back street abortions that David Steel MP introduced a bill in 1966 to reform abortion law, which was passed in 1967.

For an abortion to be a legal one, according to the Abortion Act of 1967, two doctors must agree that one of the following conditions is met.[67]

A	The continuance of the pregnancy would involve **risk to the life** of the pregnant woman greater than if the pregnancy were terminated.
B	The termination is necessary to **prevent grave permanent injury to the physical or mental health** of the pregnant woman.
C	The continuation of the pregnancy would involve **risk**, greater than if the pregnancy were terminated, **of injury to the physical or mental health** of the pregnant woman.
D	The continuance of the pregnancy would involve **risk**, greater than if the pregnancy were terminated, **of injury to the physical or mental health of any existing children** of the family of the pregnant woman.
E	There is substantial **risk** that if the child were born it would suffer from such physical or mental abnormalities as to be **seriously handicapped**.

The 1967 Act permitted abortion for women up to 28 weeks into their pregnancy. However, the Human Fertilisation and Embryology Act of 1990 reduced the gestational age for an abortion from 28 weeks to 24 weeks for grounds C and D because more recent advances in technology can now give a foetus born prematurely after 24 weeks gestation a greater chance of survival. However, the Act also clarified that abortion for the other conditions (grounds A, B and E) could "now be carried out at any gestational age, up to and including term."[68]

Those who passed the Abortion Act did not intend to permit abortion on demand but to allow those women who were desperate to have an abortion, the women who would turn to back street abortion clinics, to have one legally. These might be rape victims or mothers carrying severely disabled children. Steel commented: "it is not the intention of the promoters of the bill to leave a wide-open door for abortion on request."[69] However, experience of forty years of the Abortion Act has shown that it could be argued that women living in England and Wales effectively have abortion on demand because the "wording of the bill was capable of remarkably elastic interpretation."[70] For example, of the 205,598 abortions in 2007, 98% were on grounds C while only 1% on grounds D and 1% on grounds E.[71] Therefore, as the figures suggest, very few women have abortions because their life is at risk or because they do not want to have a disabled child.

The Abortion Act of 1967 was not applied to Northern Ireland because at that time the government at Stormont had the option to decide whether or not to accept it and they decided not to. When direct rule returned to Westminster in 1972, the act was still not extended to Northern Ireland. Therefore, the law concerning abortion in Northern Ireland remains the same as it was in England and Wales prior to the Abortion Act of 1967. It is based on the 1861 Offences Against the Persons Act and the 1929 The Infant Life (Preservation) Act and therefore abortion is only permitted if continuation of the pregnancy would jeopardise the mother's life. Another attempt to extend the Abortion Act to include Northern Ireland failed in October 2008.

At the time of writing, abortion also remains illegal in the Republic of Ireland. An abortion can be performed only if there is a threat to the mother's life. Due to a number of cases in recent years, this also includes mothers who threaten that they will commit suicide unless they can have an abortion. If someone living on the island of Ireland faces an unwanted pregnancy, or if there is evidence of foetal abnormality, they do have the option of going to England or Wales to have an abortion. Abortion statistics for England and Wales in 2007 show that "there were 7,100 abortions for non-residents carried out in hospitals and clinics in England and Wales".[72] However, the exact number of these non-residents who came from Ireland is not clear.

Biblical teaching on abortion

Biblical teaching on the sanctity of life and personhood, already considered at the beginning of this chapter, is also relevant to the abortion debate. The biblical material implies that abortion is morally unacceptable because from the moment of conception a human being has been created in God's image and for this reason, human life is sacred. Only one other biblical reference is directly relevant to the abortion debate and this can be found in Exodus 21:22–25:

> "If men who are fighting hit a pregnant woman and she gives birth prematurely but there is no serious injury, the offender must be fined whatever the woman's husband demands and the court allows. But if there is serious injury, you are to take life for life, eye for eye, tooth for tooth, hand for hand, foot for foot, burn for burn, wound for wound, bruise for bruise."

Due to the nature of the penalty imposed for the death of the foetus, Stott comments that the lives of the "mother and child are valued equally."[73] Stott argues that abortion is immoral in terms of biblical teaching in general. He comments: "the Bible has much to say about God's concern for the defenceless, and the most defenceless of all people are unborn children. They are speechless to plead their own cause and helpless to protect their own life."[74]

 TASKS

a) Using the information from the previous sections of this chapter, create a spider diagram summarising the most important biblical references that can be related to the topic of abortion.

b) With reference to the quote from Stott above create a spider diagram which outlines any biblical references you are familiar with that highlight God's concern for the weak and defenceless.

Christian views on abortion

In ancient Greek and Roman society, abortion was widely used. Both Plato and Aristotle considered abortion to be morally acceptable.

- In his work, *Republic*, Plato agreed that abortion was acceptable for women over forty years old, probably because of maternal death from child bearing and the increased chances of foetal abnormality.
- In *Politics*, Aristotle accepted both abortion and infanticide if the child was 'deformed' in any way, or if the family size of a couple was already big enough and they did not want any additional children.[75]

However, the early Christians rejected the views on abortion accepted by the Graeco-Roman culture in which they lived. The early Christian writer Clement of Alexandria (AD150–215), for example, commented that those who "use abortive drugs which expel the matter completely dead, abort at the same time their human feelings."[76] The practice of abortion was consistently condemned by Christians until the time of Aquinas in the thirteenth century and his flexibility on the issue was due to his views on ensoulment, outlined previously. He believed that we should give moral status only to a foetus from the moment of ensoulment onwards, which was forty days for boys and ninety days for girls. Vardy and Grosch comment: "Aquinas maintained that if you hit a pregnant woman and she aborted then you had not committed murder if the foetus was earlier than 90 or 40 days."[77]

In the seventeenth century, the Roman Catholic Church "affirmed that ensoulment took place from the moment of conception"[78] and by 1869 Pope Pius IX maintained that the only grounds for abortion was to prevent the death of the mother and that abortion could occur only if it was a side effect of treating the mother. As outlined in chapter two, this principle is referred to as the doctrine of double effect because in a situation such as this "the main purpose is not the abortion, rather it is a by-product of the main purpose"[79] which is to help the mother survive.

Today, the Catholic Church continues to follow natural law, maintaining an absolutist stance in opposition to abortion, with the exception of abortion as a side effect of treating the mother. The Catholic Church claims that abortion is intrinsically evil, regardless of the circumstances because all human life must be respected. The *Catechism of the Catholic Church* states: "Formal cooperation in an abortion constitutes a great offence. The Church attaches the canonical penalty of excommunication to this crime against human life."[80]

The views of other Christian denominations are similar to those held by the Catholic Church as they maintain that all life must be respected and protected from the moment of conception. However, some do accept the fact that in some cases abortion may be the lesser of two evils.

For example, in 1993, the Church of England Board of Social Responsibility produced a report entitled *Abortion and the Church*. In this report they maintained that the mother's life and health were of primary importance. The report commented that the Church of England:

"see abortion, the termination of that life by the act of man, as a great moral evil...circumstances exist where the character or location of the pregnancy renders the foetus a serious threat to the life or health of the mother, in such circumstances the foetus could be regarded as an 'aggressor' on the mother. The mother would be entitled to seek protection against the threat to her life and health which the foetal life represented...the undoubted evil of abortion would in this situation represent the lesser of two evils."[81]

The Methodist Church in Ireland has also published its views on the issue of abortion and their position is similar to that of the Anglican Communion outlined above. They state:

"We believe that abortion on demand is wrong. However, we believe that termination of pregnancy is a permissible, though by no means easy or certain, choice in very specific circumstances, ie where the mother's life is at risk; where there is risk of grave injury to the physical or mental health of the mother; when the pregnancy is the result of rape or incest; when there is a gross abnormality of the foetus."[82]

The quote from *Methodist Belief* outlined above refers to what are considered to be the three 'hard cases' in the abortion debate,[83] cases which many people from both a Christian and secular background feel make abortion the lesser of two evils.

1. The case of rape
2. Severe disability of the foetus
3. The mother's life or health is at risk

1. The case of rape

As previously mentioned, the 1938 case involving Dr Aleck Bourne (page 94) permitted abortion when pregnancy was the result of rape because of the mental state of the young mother. Many agree that this level of compassion should be shown to all victims of rape who become pregnant and they should be morally permitted to have an abortion without question because the pregnancy and birth of the child could further traumatise them. Dealing with rape is difficult enough in itself, therefore if a woman finds out that she is carrying a rapist's child she should have the option of an abortion available to her.

To recall Fletcher's example in chapter 2 (page 68) of the girl with schizophrenia who was raped, the situationist would claim that in some situations, the most loving course of action is to allow the victim to have an abortion. It could be argued that because the child was not conceived by an act of love and because the child may not be loved when he or she is born, abortion is morally permissible. The child could be a daily reminder of the ordeal to the mother or the mother may blame the child for the actions of the father. Fletcher thus argues: "no unwanted and unintended baby should ever be born."[84]

However, from a natural law perspective, even on the grounds of rape, abortion is morally unacceptable. Absolutists who oppose abortion maintain that it is immoral in all cases – it is murder. Pro-life campaigners argue in favour of the rights of the child and state that the foetus has done nothing to deserve death "...if anyone is to blame, it is the rapist not the foetus."[85] An alternative to abortion in this case could be to continue with the pregnancy and then have the baby adopted.[86] It has also been argued that the abortion could cause further psychological damage to the victim of rape. Wyatt puts it like this – an abortion is "the perpetration of yet another assault on a woman who has already suffered terribly."[87]

2. Severe disability of the foetus

For many people from both religious and secular backgrounds, the quality of life principle sways them in favour of abortion in certain circumstances. If, during a pre-natal scan, a diagnosis is made that a child will be born into a life of "appalling and uncontrollable suffering and progressive deterioration which are heart-breaking to watch",[88] many believe that the moral thing to do is to allow the mother to have an abortion. In such a case it can be seen as the lesser of two evils as it prevents a life of pain and suffering for both the child and the parents.

Wyatt disagrees, commenting: "nearly always there is a better alternative to the unwanted or abnormal pregnancy than abortion."[89] It has been argued that the Christian response should be one of caring and support, not killing. By aborting the unborn disabled, society promotes a message that it no longer values the contribution disabled people can make to the community. Wyatt cites the example of Christy Nolan, winner of the 1987 Whitbread Book of the Year. This profoundly disabled man typed his book using a pointer attached to his forehead. He could not speak so his mother read his acceptance speech at the awards ceremony. He had written the following words:

> "Tonight a crippled man is taking his place on the world literary stage. Tonight is my night for laughing, for crying tears of joy…Tonight is the happiest night of my life. Imagine what I would have missed if the doctors had not revived me on that September day long ago…rather than give a baby a chance of life, man treads upon his brother and silences him before he can draw one breath of this world's fresh air."[90]

Wyatt claims that the abortion of a foetus which will be born disabled is a form of "social discrimination against them".[91] He comments: "In Hitler's Germany, even before the final solution to the Jewish 'problem', the Nazis were exterminating wholesale the mentally retarded. In this country the weeding-out process is done before birth, and only with the parent's consent."[92] He believes we must respect all life and if we do not, then our society is no better than it was under the Third Reich in Nazi Germany.

Consider the implications of the doctors and the parents of disabled children deciding who lives and who does not. Christians believe that human beings have no right to 'play God'. For them, each and every individual is born with God-given gifts and talents, and as every second passes, abortion denies the world of this potential. Who are we to decide for someone else that their life is not worth living? Stott recalls a speech made by Alison Davies at an anti-abortion rally in 1983. She was wheelchair bound and despite suffering from spina bifida she was very "glad to be alive." She said: "I can think of few concepts more terrifying than saying that people are better off dead, and may therefore be killed for their own good."[93]

Stott uses another example to support the view that we have no right to play God. On this occasion he quotes Maurice Baring, who told the story of one doctor who asked another for his opinion on the termination of a pregnancy:

> "'The father was syphilitic, the mother tuberculous. Of the four children born the first was blind, the second died, the third was deaf and dumb, and the fourth also tuberculous. What would you have done?' The other doctor replied 'I would have ended the pregnancy' to which he was met with the comment from the first doctor 'Then you would have murdered Beethoven.'"[94]

Stott believes that for Christians, abortion should only be used in the case of anencephaly, which is failure of the brain to develop, where there is no possibility of survival after birth. Apart from this exception, abortion should "not be extended to other – even severe – abnormalities."[95]

3. The mother's life or health is at risk

As has been previously discussed, all Christian denominations accept therapeutic abortions on the grounds that it is better for an unborn foetus to die than to cause the death of the foetus and the mother if the pregnancy were to continue. Following the doctrine of double effect, the Catholic Church permits the treatment of the mother because the death of the foetus is considered to be a side effect of the treatment, not the intended effect. Other Christian denominations such as the Anglican Communion and the Methodist Church also permit therapeutic abortions but extend their acceptance of abortion to include threats to the mother's health in addition to her life.

In reality, very few abortions need to be carried out to save the mother's life. In 2007 not one of the 205,000 abortions performed in the UK was to save the life of the mother. Stott comments: "With the availability of modern obstetric and paediatric practices…the necessity of abortion virtually never arises."[96] Wyatt adds that in many cases abortions are not even necessary to save the life of the mother because "it may be possible to delay termination of the pregnancy until the twenty-fourth or twenty-fifth week, when the foetus can then be delivered and offered a reasonable chance of survival with neonatal intensive care."[97]

 PRACTICE ESSAY TITLES

Question adapted from CCEA Summer 2001 AS 6

To what extent is the practice of abortion incompatible with Christian teaching? (15)

Your response could make reference to the following points:
- Abortion is incompatible with Christian teaching on the sanctity of life
- Abortion is not compatible with Roman Catholic teaching with the exception of therapeutic abortion
- However some Christians also believe that abortion in the case of rape or severe disability is compatible with Christian teaching, for example, Joseph Fletcher

Secular views on abortion

While some people from a secular background also use the arguments for abortion previously addressed, there are a number of other arguments advocating abortion which stem from secular rather than religious opinion. These include the importance of the mother's right to choose and the slippery slope argument opposing abortion.

1. The mother's choice

On opposing sides of the abortion debate, the pro-life organisation defends the rights of the unborn child, while the pro-choice campaigners argue that the rights of the mother are of primary importance. There are various reasons not mentioned previously as to why a mother may want to have the option of abortion. Such reasons include:

- the mother is a student and the pregnancy would interfere with her education and career
- the mother feels that she is too young to face the responsibilities of having children
- the mother feels that she is not financially secure enough to support a child

Regardless of the reasons behind this decision, feminists in particular argue that all women are entitled to the same degree of reproductive freedom as men. Vardy and Grosch outline the feminist position on abortion as follows: "Permitting abortion is seen by many feminists as a way of emancipating women from a form of slavery to their bodies – a slavery that is often used by men to 'keep them in their place.'"[98]

In 1971, Judith Jarvis Thomson produced her famous work entitled *A Defence of Abortion*, in which she argues in favour of abortion, particularly on the grounds of rape. Thomson compares a woman who finds herself pregnant to the following example:

"Let me ask you to imagine this. You wake up in the morning and find yourself back to back in bed with an unconscious violinist. He has been found to have a fatal kidney ailment, and the Society of Music Lovers has canvassed all the available medical records and found that you alone have the right blood type to help. They have therefore kidnapped you, and last night the violinist's circulatory system was plugged into yours, so that your kidneys can be used to extract poisons from his blood as well as your own…To unplug you would be to kill him. But never mind, it's only for nine months. By then he will have recovered from his ailment, and can safely be unplugged from you."[99]

According to Thomson, while the woman is within her rights to agree to the request to remain connected to the violinist for nine months, she is under no obligation to do so. It is also within her rights to individual autonomy to request that the violinist is unplugged even if he dies as a result and the same should be true with pregnancy. The woman's rights to life and ownership of her body are of greater significance than the right to life held by the foetus. The reference to the kidnapping makes this case directly relevant to abortion on the grounds of rape, where the mother has been forced into sexual intercourse which has resulted in pregnancy. As Singer comments: "A woman pregnant through rape finds herself, through no choice of her own, linked to a foetus in much the same way as the person is linked to the violinist."[100] However, Thomson's example is also applicable to supporting abortion beyond cases of rape because the rights of the mother are always paramount.

Towards the end of *A Defence of Abortion* Thomson comments: "While I do argue that abortion is not impermissible, I do not argue that it is always permissible."[101] She comments that her argument supports a "desperately frightened fourteen-year-old schoolgirl, pregnant due to rape" but that in other cases "It would be indecent in the woman to request an abortion, and indecent in a doctor to perform it, if she is in her seventh month, and wants the abortion just to avoid the nuisance of postponing a trip abroad."[102]

While many feminists argue that liberal abortion laws have a positive impact on the rights of women, others argue that abortion has the opposite effect. For example, Wyatt comments: "The tragic irony is that abortion on request…was hailed by feminists as empowering women and liberating them from patriarchal oppression. In fact it has become a means for others, principally men, to exploit and manipulate pregnant women."[103] Wyatt cites the example of feminist lawyer Catharine MacKinnon, who argues that liberal abortion laws "allow men to use women sexually with no fear of any consequence of paternity."[104] However, many men today feel that the current abortion laws should be changed so that their right to protect the life of their child is taken into consideration by preventing the mother of their child from having an abortion without their consent.

While abortion is a choice for many women throughout the world today, it is important to note the emotional effects experienced by a woman following an abortion. Wyatt claims: "Most women experience immediate feelings of relief, but subsequent distress and remorse seem to be common, particularly around the time that the baby should have been born, and in subsequent pregnancies."[105] Stott adds that the effects of abortion on women include "higher rates of depression, self-harm, psychiatric hospitalisation and suicide, as well as a significantly increased incidence of premature labour in subsequent pregnancies."[106]

2. The slippery slope argument

The slippery slope argument is used in ethics generally to imply that once we agree that an action is morally permissible in limited situations, then standards will eventually fall, leading to the action being considered acceptable in a wider range of situations. Warburton describes the slippery slope as being:

"a type of argument which relies on the premise that if you make a small move in a particular direction it may then be extremely difficult or even impossible to prevent a much more substantial move in the same direction…the acceptance of one relatively innocuous practice will inevitably lead to the legitimation of highly undesirable practices."[107]

Abortion statistics can be used to illustrate this point clearly. The 1967 Abortion Act intended to permit abortion only in very limited circumstances. However, within a relatively short period of time, this law has been virtually ignored. For example, in 2007, 98% of abortions were for social reasons such as a woman facing an unplanned pregnancy who wanted to put her career first, or women who felt that they were too young or too old to cope with a child at this stage of their lives. Approximately 200,000 abortions were carried out in 2007 which were not to save the life of a mother, save her from the constant reminder of rape or to prevent the suffering of a disabled infant, the very reasons why the Abortion Act was introduced in 1967.

Therefore many women opt for an abortion because it is an option available to them. Wyatt summarises his view on the effect of the slippery slope: "The reality of the current situation in the UK is that abortion is available for most women on request. The apparent intention of the 1967 Act is being widely flouted."[108] Human experience has therefore shown that the slippery slope argument may apply to abortion. Recall the words of David Steel when he said: "it is not the intention of the promoters of the bill to leave a wide-open door for abortion on request." Despite this view, not long after the Abortion Act's introduction, almost any woman who wanted an abortion in the UK could have one. According to Singer, attitudes towards abortion in Russia have become so liberal that "abortion is widely used by married women as an alternative to contraception."[109]

Application of ethical theory

Kant's practical imperative asserts that we should never treat human beings as a means to an end, but as an end in themselves. Therefore, if we consider the unborn child to have moral status, then abortion is immoral. As Kant's theory is based on rules which are absolute, then if practicing them, abortions can never be permitted regardless of the circumstances.

Utilitarianism on the other hand considers abortion to be morally acceptable if it results in the greatest amount of happiness for the greatest number. The loss of the child's life is outweighed by the happiness of the parents who wanted the abortion and possibly the happiness of existing children, depending on the circumstances. For example, the addition of a severely disabled child to a family will probably mean that parents will have less time to spend with their existing children. As a utilitarian who believes that the happiness of the foetus is irrelevant because it is not a person, Singer argues that abortion is morally acceptable if the parents feel that it is the best option for them.

 # OTHER ASPECTS OF HUMAN EXPERIENCE

Infanticide

Infanticide is defined as the murder of children. It was considered morally acceptable at the time of Plato and Aristotle when unwanted newborn infants were abandoned and left to die. Wyatt comments that at this time, "Like abortion, the intentional killing of malformed or unwanted newborn babies, by exposure, strangling or drowning, for instance, was widespread."[110]

Singer maintains that a foetus or a newborn baby cannot be considered to be a person: "If the foetus does not have the same claim to life as a person, it appears that the newborn baby does not either."[111] Therefore for Singer, abortion and infanticide are both morally acceptable. In *Practical Ethics* he comments: "We should certainly put very strict conditions on permissible infanticide...infanticide can only be equated with abortion when those closest to the child do not want it to live...

...continued

killing an infant whose parents do not want it dead is, of course, an utterly different manner."[112]

To develop his argument, he specifically focuses on the cases of newborn infants with severe disabilities, and whose parents regret the birth of the child so much that they do not want it to live. Singer makes the "realistic assumption" that no other couples would want to adopt the child.[113] He uses the example of children born with severe cases of spina bifida, children who are "permanently paralysed from the waist down and lack control of bowels and bladder. Often excess fluid accumulates in the brain...which can result in intellectual disabilities."[114] He adds that doctors who work with children suffering from such pain and discomfort believe that their lives are so miserable that it is wrong to use surgery to keep them alive and that if the parents do not want the child "it is better that the child should be helped to die without further suffering."[115] As a utilitarian, the happiness of the parents is of primary importance to Singer, who makes it very clear that the life of the child should only be taken if the parents make that decision. In conclusion, Singer comments: "Nevertheless the main point is clear: killing a disabled infant is not morally equivalent to killing a person. Very often it is not wrong at all."[116]

In *Abortion and Infanticide*, Michael Tooley agrees with the views of Singer. He believes "that a newborn baby does not possess the concept of a continuing self, any more than a newborn kitten possesses such a concept. If so, infanticide during a time interval shortly after birth must be morally acceptable."[117]

Infanticide has been one of the major side effects of the Chinese One Child Policy. The policy was introduced by the Chinese government in 1979 in an attempt to limit population growth in the country. As a result, families were permitted to have only one child and had to pay fines if more than one child was born into the family. With only one child per family, many people in China felt that having a male child would ensure social and economic stability for them. Therefore Chinese women did not want to give birth to females so abortion, infanticide and abandonment of females became a major feature of this policy.

 TASK

Research the ethical issues surrounding China's One Child Policy and the impact it has had on the human experience of people living in China under this policy.

It is morally acceptable for society to take responsibility for the needs of women who face a crisis pregnancy and provide them with an alternative to back street abortions or causing greater harm to themselves using folk remedies.[118] However, the Abortion Act of 1967 has not been an adequate solution for many people from both religious and secular backgrounds because they believe it has led to abortion on demand. Over 200,000 unborn children are aborted each year in the UK for social reasons and very few abortions are performed for the 'hard cases'. Using medical technology in this way opposes Christian teaching and contradicts the Hippocratic Oath, dating from the fifth century BC, traditionally taken by doctors: "I will neither give a deadly drug to anybody if asked for it, nor will I make a suggestion to this effect...I will not give to a woman an abortive remedy."[119] The oath was updated in 1948 to include the promise "I will maintain the utmost respect for human life from the time of conception."[120]

The Christian approach generally is that abortion is immoral and while there are denominational differences concerning exceptional circumstances, all denominations agree that the life of the unborn child is a sacred life, created in the image of God.

 OTHER ASPECTS OF HUMAN EXPERIENCE

Wyatt believes that pregnancy crisis centres, such as Care for Life, can provide a great source of comfort for women facing an unwanted pregnancy and claims that they are "a wonderful, authentically Christian response"[121] to the issue. Each centre provides "free pregnancy testing, skilled counselling, clear information on all the options available, practical support and time to explore all the conflicting emotions and long-term implications which an unplanned pregnancy brings."[122]

 TASK

Investigate the help that is available to young people in Northern Ireland who face a crisis pregnancy.

 PRACTICE ESSAY TITLES

Question adapted from CCEA Summer 2007 AS 6

(a) Give an account of the ethical arguments for and against abortion. (35)

Your response could make reference to the following points:

- Religious views in opposition to abortion with reference to the sanctity of life argument and the idea that life begins at conception.

...continued

- Development of denominational views on abortion highlighting that some denominations permit abortion under certain circumstances.
- Secular views on abortion including reference to the concept of personhood and the rights of the mother to choose.

Question adapted from CCEA January 2005 AS 6

(b) Comment on the view that sometimes abortion is the lesser of two evils. (15)

Your response could make reference to the following points:
- Abortion can be the lesser of two evils depending on the circumstances. Develop your response with reference to situation ethics and utilitarianism.
- Abortion can also be the lesser of two evils in the case of a woman who is the victim of rape, whose life is at risk if the pregnancy continues or whose child will be born severely disabled.
- Others believe that abortion can never be the lesser of two evils regardless of the circumstances. Develop your response considering the natural law perspective.

HUMAN INFERTILITY

Infertility, which is the diminished or total inability of a couple to conceive, affects between 10% and 15% of couples in the western world.[123] Modern advances in the treatment of infertility were pioneered by Patrick Steptoe and Robert Edwards through their development of IVF treatment, which led to the birth of Louise Brown, the first test tube baby, on 25 July 1978. Since then, the treatment of infertility has developed even further and medical advances such as surrogacy, Pre-implantation Genetic Diagnosis (PGD) and even the possibility of cloning, bring with them their own set of ethical issues.

It is important to note that for each of the areas of fertility treatment there is no direct biblical teaching. However, biblical teaching on the sanctity of life and personhood is still relevant to debate on the morality of fertility treatment.

1. IVF

In vitro is a Latin term for 'in glass' and *in vitro* fertilisation or IVF refers to the procedure where the egg from a female is fertilised by sperm from her partner or a donor in a petri dish or test tube. At the very beginning of this process of fertility treatment, before fertilisation can occur, women must take hormones which "induce superovulation"[124] and this means that instead of producing only one egg during each monthly cycle, the ovaries are stimulated to produce up to ten, or even more eggs. The woman's eggs are then harvested and are stored until fertilised by either her partner's sperm or the sperm from a donor. The pre-embryo is then checked for any abnormalities and if it is found to be healthy it is implanted into the mother's womb and it is hoped that pregnancy will continue as normal. Those who do have a successful pregnancy through IVF treatment may have their remaining or spare pre-embryos frozen and these can be used for a second pregnancy at a later date if the couple wish.

IVF is a legal method of fertility treatment throughout the UK. Consider the following information provided by the Human Fertilisation and Embryology Authority (HFEA) which illustrates the number of women who receive this method of fertility treatment in the UK and the success rate of IVF treatment:

Year	2004	2005	2006
Number of cycles of IVF treatment	40,164	41,932	44,275
Number of patients undergoing IVF treatment	30,861	32,626	34,855
Number of babies born through IVF treatment	8,251 successful births – giving rise to 10,242 babies	9,058 successful births – giving rise to 11,262 babies	10,242 successful births – giving rise to 12,596 babies
Live birth rate per cycle started	20.5%	21.6%	23.1%

HFEA Facts & Figures 2006 – Fertility Problems and Treatment, www.hfea.gov.uk, accessed 22 January 2009

The first two rows of the table indicate that during each year there are more cycles of IVF treatment than there are women undergoing treatment. This is due to the fact that many women undergo more than one cycle of IVF treatment per year. It is also important to note that the figures presented in the third row of the table indicate that there are more babies born each year than there are successful births. This is because a successful birth can refer to the birth of a single baby or twins or triplets. Many births which are the result of IVF treatment will involve multiple births because quite often more than one embryo will be implanted in the mother's womb in an attempt to ensure higher success rates of IVF. However, it is illegal to implant more than three pre-embryos into the mother's womb at any one time. As indicated by the final row in the table, the overall success rate of IVF is under 25% between the period 2004 and 2006.

Christian views on IVF

The biblical concept of the sanctity of life has led many Christians to conclude that IVF treatment is immoral. This is primarily because the spare embryos referred to above are destroyed or used for research if they are not required by the couple at a later date. Tyler and Reid refer to this as the problem of 'doomed embryos'.[125] If we maintain that life begins at conception, the point at which our genetic identity is fixed, then many Christians believe that this process involves the destruction of innocent human life.

 OTHER ASPECTS OF HUMAN EXPERIENCE

Embryo research

In 1990 the HFEA permitted research on human pre-embryos, both "spare embryos following IVF, and also on embryos specially created for the purpose of research."[126] This research is permitted for a number of reasons including the promotion of advances in infertility treatment, increased knowledge about the causes of miscarriage and developing more effective methods of contraception.[127] As previously stated, the HFEA have insisted that the pre-embryo must be destroyed within fourteen days after fertilisation. Obviously, the time that the pre-embryo has spent frozen does not count towards this fourteen day period.

On utilitarian grounds, such experimentation can be morally justified because the outcome of this research can lead to the greatest amount of happiness for the greatest number. However, others argue that research on embryos has already contributed to the slippery slope. In the 1990s, for example, due to the shortage of embryos for research, scientists requested to use the eggs from aborted foetuses to increase their supply of research material. Vardy and Grosch outline that "all a woman's eggs are present in her body by the time she is a fifteen week foetus"[128] and due to the amount of abortions each year in the UK, there was no shortage of eggs. In 1994 a law was passed in the UK prohibiting the use of eggs from aborted foetuses. However, in 2008 scientists were permitted to use human/animal or 'hybrid' embryos for research purposes.

According to Wyatt, the creation of embryos for the purpose of experimentation "caused considerable controversy at the time"[129] and in response to opposition, Mary Warnock commented: "we must be allowed to take risks when we pursue knowledge."[130] The utilitarian view is that human embryos may be used for research which may help find cures for serious illnesses. In your opinion is this acceptable or should all life be respected from the moment of conception?

A second reason why some Christians may oppose IVF is linked to the implanting of three embryos into the womb in order to ensure a higher success rate. However, if more than one embryo does implant in the lining of the womb, sometimes the pregnant mothers have a selective abortion because they do not want to give birth to more than one or two children. Once again, the sanctity of life argument implies that this practice is immoral and raises the issue of doctors and parents playing God.

◎ OTHER ASPECTS OF HUMAN EXPERIENCE

In 1996, Mandy Allwood became pregnant with eight foetuses after having hormone injections to increase her fertility. She was advised to have selective abortions in order to improve the chances of survival of at least some of the foetuses. Mandy refused to have selective abortions and twenty-one weeks into the pregnancy she went into premature labour and all eight unborn babies died.[131]

The Roman Catholic Church is opposed to IVF because it is contrary to natural law. Catholics believe that sexual intercourse must have both unitive and procreative purposes and therefore it is immoral for reproduction to occur without sexual intercourse. Wilcockson explains: "the process of creating life is not just a biological one, but one which requires the intimacy and love of two individuals to create another human being who is loved and wanted."[132] The *Catechism of the Catholic Church* states that techniques such as IVF are "morally unacceptable. They dissociate the sexual act from the procreative act. The act which brings the child into existence is no longer an act by which two persons give themselves to one another, but one that entrusts the life and identity of the embryo into the power of doctors."[133] The issue of donor eggs or sperm which is sometimes necessary in the treatment of infertility is also considered to be morally unacceptable according to Roman Catholic teaching. The alternative to reproductive technology, according to the *Catechism of the Catholic Church* is "adopting abandoned children or performing demanding services for others."[134]

The Anglican theologian Joseph Fletcher, responsible for the development of situation ethics, felt that IVF was morally acceptable because a child was being born into a loving relationship – in Fletcher's opinion the end clearly justifies the means. Wyatt agrees and claims that IVF enables the couple to "express their love physically, in the form of a child which is genetically their own." However, he continues: "IVF may be acceptable for a married couple provided that no spare embryos are created."[135] The Church of England General Synod in 1997 commented that the welfare of the child is of primary importance: "children are a gift from God in creation and that the welfare of any child created by third party donation of eggs or sperm is of overriding importance."[136] The Church of Ireland have also discussed the issue of IVF in recent years and their Medical Ethics Working Group specifically addressed the issue of the 'doomed embryos' and commented: "The Committee takes seriously the fact that IVF may involve the creation of more fertilised ova than are required for any one treatment and that some may have ethical reservations about this. However it must be remembered that in natural conception many fertilised ova do not implant, and of those that do many do not develop into a successful pregnancy."[137]

The Presbyterian Church argues: "As a church we believe in the sanctity of life from conception. What happens to these spare embryos? Creation of spare embryos creates ethical dilemmas."[138]

All Christian denominations agree that a child must be considered to be a gift from God, not a right to be demanded. According to Wyatt one of the dangers of accepting IVF is that it makes some people view a child as "a commodity at our disposal",[139] or a piece of property that they have a right to own. The Christian attitude should consider the child to be a gift from God who has rights from the moment of conception.

 TASK

Comment on the claim that IVF is not compatible with Christian teaching. Justify your answer.

Secular views on IVF

Secular society generally does not have any concerns regarding the morality of IVF. However, the concept of treating human life as a commodity, as outlined above, is contrary to Kantian ethics. In his practical imperative, Kant argues that it is never acceptable to treat a human being as a means to an end. However, according to Thompson, the "desire for a child implies that the child is being treated as a means (ie to satisfy the desires of the parents) rather than an end in itself."[140]

In contrast there is the idea that all people have the right to a child. This is supported by article 16 of the Universal Declaration of Human Rights that states: "Men and women of full age, without any limitation due to race, nationality or religion, have the right to marry and to found a family."[141]

For many utilitarians IVF is morally acceptable if it promotes the greatest amount of happiness for the greatest number of people, specifically those who suffer from infertility. Jenkins summarises the utilitarian view in the following quote: "Assisted reproduction can bring the pleasure and joy of parenthood to childless couples and to single women, whether they are infertile, post-menopausal or lesbians, or women wanting a dead partner's child."[142]

However, not all utilitarians agree with IVF. Some utilitarians may argue that the low success rate of IVF may lead to greater unhappiness for couples who put their faith in the doctors and the treatment which according to the figures provided above, fails in over 75% of all cases. Another argument against IVF is the issue of the cost involved. Wyatt informs us that in the US a couple will typically spend between $44,000 and $200,000 to achieve a single pregnancy[143] while in the UK the 5,500 births resulting from IVF treatment between January 1995 and March 1996 cost about £75 million.[144] While Singer has no moral objection to the destruction of the foetuses as a consequence of IVF treatment, he does question the "appropriateness of allocating scarce medical resources to this area at a time when the world has a serious problem of overpopulation."[145]

OTHER ASPECTS OF HUMAN EXPERIENCE

Use the internet to research the following cases of pregnancy as a result of IVF treatment. On utilitarian grounds, do you think IVF was morally acceptable in both cases?

(b) The case of Diane Blood

In 1995 Diane Blood asked doctors to freeze sperm from her husband Stephen who was in a coma. After her husband's death, she made a request to use his sperm to become pregnant. She was initially refused by the HFEA but her request was eventually granted and she has since used IVF treatment to have two children.

(c) The case of Patricia Rashbrook

In 2006, 62 year old Patricia Rashbrook became the oldest woman in Britain to give birth to a baby using IVF treatment and the egg of a donor.

Regardless of the rights of parents to have a child, many people from a secular background oppose IVF because of the impact on the children when they grow up. Upon discovering that their biological father was a sperm donor or their mother an egg donor, or even both, they may haves some identity issues. In such circumstances, questions about the children's right to knowledge about the donor and the donor's right to anonymity must be considered. In response, the HFEA initially declared that donors have no parental rights and that information on donors must be kept strictly confidential.[146] However, in April 2005 the HFEA changed the law surrounding donating sperm, eggs or embryos so that people donating after this date would no longer be able to remain anonymous.[147] The intention of this change in policy was to ensure that people conceived from donors could find out about their genetic origins once they reached the age of eighteen.

For many people from both Christian and secular backgrounds, the possibility of IVF enabling them to conceive and carry a child to birth outweighs any of the negative issues associated with the fertility treatment.

 TASK

Create a spider diagram summarising the main ethical issues raised by the treatment of infertility using IVF.

2. Surrogacy

Surrogacy is a form of assisted reproduction which involves implanting a pre-embryo, usually created through IVF, in the womb of a host mother who will carry the child for the duration of the pregnancy. The host then hands the child over to the commissioning couple shortly after it has been born. There are two forms of surrogacy:

- **Partial surrogacy** occurs when the surrogate mother uses her egg and this is fertilised by the sperm from a donor or the sperm from the husband of the commissioning couple.
- **Full surrogacy** occurs when the surrogate is implanted with a fertilised egg which has come from the commissioning couple who may have used their own sperm and ova or those of donors. In the case of full surrogacy, the surrogate will have no genetic connection with the child.

According to the HFEA both types of surrogacy are legal in the UK if carried out for altruistic reasons, for example, where a surrogate simply wants to help a couple to have a child. However, commercial surrogacy, or surrogacy which involves financial gain for the surrogate mother is illegal, although expenses to cover medical treatment or loss of possible earnings from employment can be paid by the commissioning couple to the surrogate mother.

◎ OTHER ASPECTS OF HUMAN EXPERIENCE

The case of the surrogate mother Kim Cotton from 1985 became well known. There was a public outcry at the time because it was claimed that she had received £6,500 for having a baby for an infertile couple. She also sold her story to the media for a further £15,000. In 1988 Kim founded the organisation COTS (Childlessness Overcome Through Surrogacy), which aimed to introduce infertile couples to women who may be willing to act as surrogate mothers for them. It is also reported that she acted as a surrogate to twins for a friend in 1991 and on this occasion there was no financial incentive.[148]

Legally, following the guidelines of the HFEA, the person who gives birth to the child is considered to be the legal mother and she is named on the child's birth certificate. The commissioning couple must then apply to adopt the child within six months of the birth before they can become the legal parents. When this happens, the child's birth certificate will be changed. However, at the age of eighteen the child can request to see the original birth certificate and find out who their surrogate mother was.

Christian views on surrogacy

Christian denominations agree that surrogacy is morally unacceptable. In a document entitled *Personal Origins*, the Church of England comments that surrogacy is unacceptable because the mother who will bring up the child is denied the opportunity to bond with the child during the pregnancy. The document claimed that while the Church of England has no difficulty with adoption, it does believe that it is immoral to create children for adoption.[149] *Personal Origins* also comments that surrogacy will lead to complications because of the bond developed between the surrogate mother and the baby throughout the pregnancy. This bond can be very hard to break once the child has been born.[150] Surrogacy is also condemned by the Roman Catholic Church. The *Catechism of the Catholic Church* states: "Techniques that entail the dissociation of husband and wife, by the intrusion of a person other than the couple (donation of sperm or ovum, surrogate uterus), are gravely immoral."[151] Surrogacy will in most cases involve the use of IVF, therefore for Christians the same ethical issues apply, such as the destruction of embryos.

Secular views on surrogacy

From a secular perspective, there are many advantages to surrogacy. On utilitarian grounds, surrogacy may be considered morally acceptable providing the outcome leads to the greatest amount of happiness for the greatest number. Wilcockson comments: "if three possibly four adults wish to enter freely into a contract to produce a child what possible harm can there be?"[152] Tyler and Reid comment: "where all other attempts at having a child have failed, surrogacy may seem to be a lifeline to infertile couples."[153] Through partial surrogacy, male homosexual couples can also become parents and therefore have the same opportunities as heterosexual couples.

 OTHER ASPECTS OF HUMAN EXPERIENCE

Consider the following case studies in which surrogacy has allowed couples to experience the happiness of having children.

- Alex Patrick was 28 years old when a routine smear discovered a tumour on her cervix. The treatment that she needed to combat the cancer made her infertile. A few years later, after her recovery, she was determined to have a baby with her husband. Alex's twin sister, Charlotte, went through fertility treatment to harvest an egg which was fertilised by Alex's husband's sperm using IVF. Alex's older sister, Helen agreed to act as a surrogate mother and nine months later she gave birth to a baby boy who has since been adopted by Alex and her husband.[154]
- Barrie Drewitt and Tony Barlow are a homosexual couple who were able to become the parents of twins with the assistance of egg donors and a surrogate mother. They have named their children Aspen and Saffron.[155]

From a secular viewpoint there are some concerns about the use of surrogacy:

- Surrogacy may lead to the child having identity issues later in life. There may be up to four people involved in bringing about the birth of a child which includes three mothers: the genetic mother – the source of the egg; a carrying mother – the provider of the uterus; and a social mother – the one providing care after birth.[156] Who will the child regard as being his or her real mother?

- With so many involved in the process of having a baby, there is also the problem of ownership. For example, there have been a number of cases where the surrogate has bonded with the child and when she has given birth has refused to give the child to the commissioning couple. The Baby M case highlights such issues linked to surrogacy.[157] In 1985 an American couple, William and Elizabeth Stern choose Mary Beth Whitehead to act as a surrogate mother for their child. It was a commercial surrogacy, worth $10,000 to Mary Beth and her family. Mary Beth's eggs were fertilised using William's sperm making it a partial surrogacy. Throughout the pregnancy, Mary Beth bonded with the child and when the child was born she hid the baby and claimed that she was suicidal at the thought of having to hand the baby over to the Sterns. The case was taken to court and the Sterns were eventually allowed to have custody of the child. At the end of the trial, Mary Beth's lawyer commented that surrogate mothers "cannot know, until after the child is born, their true feelings about bearing that child."[158] Issues concerning ownership of the child have also arisen in cases when the surrogate discovers that the baby she is carrying has some kind of disability and the commissioning couple no longer want the child and the surrogate is forced to have an abortion. As both the example of Mary Beth and a surrogate forced into an abortion illustrate, surrogacy may also lead to the exploitation of the surrogate mother. Mary Beth and her family were on a low income and she acted as a surrogate to gain some money. According to Wilcockson, feminists regarded this case as "a form of commercial prostitution and a further denigration of women."[159]

- It is also argued that surrogacy treats human life as a commodity, something which can be bought and sold. Wilcockson comments: "Many find the commercialisation of pregnancy deeply repugnant. It reduces human relationships to the market place and turns the baby into a commodity and the mother into a service industry."[160]

PRACTICE ESSAY TITLES

Question adapted from CCEA Summer 2005 AS 6

(a) Examine the central arguments for and against human surrogacy. (35)

Your response could make reference to the following points:
- Biblical views on the sanctity of life
- Views of Christian denominations
- Utilitarian views
- Arguments against surrogacy regarding the identity of the child, ownership issues, exploitation of the surrogate mother, treatment of life as a commodity
- Arguments against surrogacy related to the use of IVF, for example, the doomed embryos

Question adapted from CCEA Summer 2005 AS 6

(b) Explore the view that couples should accept their inability to have children. Justify your answer. (15)

Your response could make reference to the following points:
- Couples should not have to simply accept their inability to have children:
  - Technology has enabled us to overcome other illnesses – why not infertility
  - All people have a right to a child
  - Fertility treatment gives a couple the freedom to have children if they decide to
- However due to the negative effects of IVF and surrogacy, maybe couples should accept their inability to have children:
  - Children are a gift from God, not a right to be demanded – explore
  - The destruction of embryos is a significant problem with fertility treatment and this is contrary to Christian teaching on the sanctity of life
  - There are alternatives to fertility treatment – adoption

3. Pre-implantation Genetic Diagnosis (PGD)

From the moment of conception, our genetic makeup, determined by the DNA inherited from our parents, is fixed. These genes contribute to making each one of us the individual we are today both in terms of our appearance and characteristics. Genetic engineering is a term used to describe a further advance in reproductive technology were doctors can modify or manipulate the genes carried by a pre-embryo in order to eradicate a heredity disease. Once modified, the pre-embryo is implanted into the womb of the mother and in most cases the pregnancy will continue as normal. The proper term for this type of genetic engineering, which is related to human reproduction, is Germ-line gene therapy. Any changes made to the embryo using this process will be passed on to future generations. Vardy and Grosch highlight the implications of such therapy: "Haemophilia or hereditary diseases which are genetically transmitted may thus be capable of being eliminated by altering the genes that carry the disease."[161]

Pre-implantation Genetic Diagnosis (PGD) has been developed as a result of the progress made by scientists in the field of genetics. This technology does not interfere with the genetic makeup of the pre-embryo but it does involve doctors screening the genes of the pre-embryo and only implanting embryos which are free from genetic abnormalities. This practice is legal in the UK and is controlled by the HFEA. PGD has not only enabled embryos to be screened for abnormalities, but it also makes it possible to select the sex of a child and to create saviour siblings – a baby who will save the life of their sick elder brother or sister due to their genetic makeup. It may also be possible to design a baby with the parents requesting the specific characteristics of the child they want.

Elimination of fatal disease

Through the use of PGD, pre-embryos can be screened for diseases such as cystic fibrosis or Down's syndrome and embryos found to be carrying the disease can be destroyed. Only healthy pre-embryos will be implanted, preventing the future suffering of the children and their parents. From a quality of life perspective this technology appears to be morally acceptable. However, there are concerns about the use of reproductive technology in this way. Firstly, if we accept this practice then we accept that the life of a person without any disabilities is of greater value than the life of a person with a disability. Secondly, if we apply the slippery slope argument to this advance in reproductive technology there are additional concerns. As Wyatt comments, it "will enable scientists to detect genetic variants that have a less severe impact on a child's life"[162] for example diabetes or asthma. If this knowledge is available to parents will they have the right to decide not to have a child who will be diabetic or asthmatic and have the embryo destroyed?

However, if regulated, the use of PGD can be very beneficial in the elimination of many illnesses. Clarke comments: "There is widespread approval of this technique, on the grounds that it offers the possibility of removing the causes of later disability and suffering and, significantly, because it is done for the benefit of the embryo itself."[163]

Sex selection

PGD also enables the sex of a child to be chosen by its parents. This allows parents to have the freedom to design their families – if they prefer they could have a balance of boys and girls as opposed to having all boys or all girls. Those from a liberal, secular, background generally have no objection to this practice. However, Wyatt cites findings from a UK HFEA survey carried out in 2003, which suggested that the majority of the UK public were opposed to sex selection, with the exception of selection to avoid sex-linked diseases.[164] As a result of the consultation, sex selection for non-medical reasons remains illegal in the UK. One of the negative implications of sex selection is that the balance between the male-female population may be affected. In India, for example, 50,000 female foetuses are aborted per year due to the preference families have for sons and as a result the ratio of female babies to male babies in India is now 800 girls for every 1,000 boys.[165]

Saviour siblings

PGD has made it possible to screen and select pre-embryos who can become a tissue donor for an existing sibling. Due to the high incidence of rejection of donor tissue, the tissue from a sibling who is a genetic match can be used with greater chances of success.

 OTHER ASPECTS OF HUMAN EXPERIENCE

Zain Hashmi suffered from beta thalassaemia, a rare blood disorder. He needed a bone marrow transplant and neither his parents nor other family members were a suitable match so they could not help. After having been granted permission by the HFEA in 2003, his parents used IVF to produce a number of embryos. The embryos were screened using PGD and one which was genetically suitable for Zain was implanted in the mother's womb. After his sibling was born, cells were taken from its umbilical cord and transplanted into Zain and this procedure saved his life.

After Adam Nash's birth in October 2000, he provided umbilical cord blood stem cells to treat his sister Molly who suffered from fanconi anemia, a bone marrow deficiency.

While the above examples highlight the benefits of PGD, many argue that it creates life which has instrumental value rather than intrinsic value. Using PGD to have a saviour sibling is contrary to Kantian ethics because it treats people as a means to an end, rather than as an end in themselves. Those who oppose PGD claim yet again it is reproductive technology which treats human life as a commodity. However, those who support the use of technology to alleviate suffering argue that the Nash and Hashmi families intended to have other children anyway and using these techniques enabled them to have the best of both worlds – to have both a newborn baby and to save the life of an existing child.

Designer babies

The ability of parents to give birth to saviour siblings is the first step towards designer babies. In the future, it may be possible for parents to ask for children who possess what they feel are the most desirable qualities, for example, high levels of intelligence or outstanding athletic ability. Eugenics is the practice of engineering humans based on what is considered to be the perfect person. There are many ethical issues associated with designer babies. For example, Jenkins speculates that only the rich would have access to such technology and as a result, a group of perfect human beings or "a genetic elect"[166] would be created. Over time, a two tier society may emerge and a new form of discrimination could exist in society, referred to as "geneticism" by Jenkins.

 TASKS

Class debate:

Question adapted from CCEA January 2003 AS 6

"The advent of the designer baby would be a disaster."

Christian views on PGD

Following the sanctity of life principle, PGD is immoral as it results in the destruction of embryos because they possess characteristics which are considered to be undesirable. Christian belief states that every individual has intrinsic value in the eyes of God.

The idea that humans are nothing more than a set of genetic structures which can easily be tampered with is referred to as reductionism.[167] This is contrary to "the religious believer's claim that a human being is far more than simply his or her genetic makeup. To solely concentrate on genetic make-up is a radical impoverishment of what it means to be human."[168]

The Catholic condemnation of the use of PGD to screen and subsequently destroy unsuitable embryos is absolute. In *Evangelium Vitae*, Pope John Paul II declared:

"Prenatal diagnosis, which presents no moral objections if carried out in order to identify the medical treatment which may be needed by the child in the womb, all too often becomes an opportunity for proposing and procuring an abortion. This is eugenic abortion, justified in public opinion on the basis of a mentality...which accepts life only under certain conditions and rejects it when it is affected by any limitation, handicap or illness."[169]

Other Christian denominations are more willing to accept some of the benefits of PGD. For example, *Personal Origins,* produced by the Church of England, argued that parents who remove serious genetic defects from an embryo are acting in a loving and responsible way.[170] Many Christians argue that if surgery is permitted after birth to prevent suffering, why should we not take steps to prevent suffering at an even earlier stage by eliminating the genes that cause this suffering?

Secular views on PGD

People from a secular background, who believe that the quality of life is of greater importance than sanctity of life, will agree that PGD is morally acceptable. Utilitarians, for example, claim that the elimination of fatal diseases and the creation of saviour siblings promote the greatest amount of happiness in society. With regard to sex selection and designer babies, the utilitarian could argue that providing happiness for the greatest number is created and so the use of PGD for such purposes is morally acceptable.

4. Cloning

Cloning refers to the creation of an organism which is genetically identical to one that already exists or which has existed in the past. It is, in effect, making a copy or a replica of a living thing. There are two types of cloning:

- **Reproductive cloning** refers to the creation of a copy of a living thing that is living or has died. While animals have been cloned, there is no evidence that a cloned human has been born yet. Because of the ethical issues surrounding the issue of cloning, it is illegal in the UK to transfer a cloned human embryo into a womb.
- **Therapeutic cloning** refers to the practice of copying cells, which can be then used to replace organs which have failed. While reproductive cloning has the potential to make a copy of a child, therapeutic cloning could, for example, be used to create a replica heart for someone who suffers from heart problems. Therapeutic cloning was made legal in the UK in 1998 by the HFEA.

There are a number of stages involved in the process of cloning:

- A cell is taken from an individual and the nucleus is removed.
- The nucleus is also removed from an ovum and has the nucleus from the individual's cell inserted.
- In a petri dish or test tube, the cell is tricked into growth using chemicals and it begins to develop like any other pre-embryo.
- At this point, the processes for reproductive cloning and therapeutic cloning diverge.

Reproductive cloning	Therapeutic cloning
• The pre-embryo is transferred to the womb of a mother who will carry the baby to birth.	• The pre-embryo is kept in the petri-dish and stem cells are removed. The pre-embryo is then destroyed.

Therapeutic cloning and the use of stem cells

Stem cells removed from the embryo can be used "to cure a range of diseases, produce new organs and rejuvenate almost any part of the human body"[171] and it is because of such benefits that the HFEA has agreed to allow therapeutic cloning. Stem cells appear about one week after fertilisation and can adapt and grow into almost every type of cell in the body. In practical terms, imagine someone has a heart attack. If he or she was cloned for therapeutic reasons, a stem cell from a cardiac muscle cell could be taken from the cloned pre-embryo and could then be injected into the patient's heart and the stem cells would grow to repair the damage caused by the heart attack.[172] One of the most significant aspects of this process is that because the stem cells come from a clone of the individual, they are a genetic match and will not be rejected by his or her immune system. Therefore if therapeutic cloning was fully developed there would be no need for organ donors. However, critics of this technology argue that it is simply growing human beings for spare parts.

Reproductive cloning

The first successful case of reproductive cloning in animals was Dolly the sheep, born in 1996. Dolly was an exact replica of another sheep. As a new reproductive technology, cloning has many advantages. If applied to the cloning of animals, it could prevent the extinction of species of animal and could allow pet lovers to have an identical pet to the one that died. In terms of human reproduction, couples could clone a baby who died shortly after birth, or they could replace a dead child with a new born infant who is genetically identical to the child they lost. Cloning could also allow us to replicate great human beings, such as Albert Einstein, Martin Luther King, John Lennon, etc, provided that we could get one of their cells.

 TASK

Class discussion:

If reproductive cloning was legal and you had the opportunity to clone any figure from the past who would it be and why?

Despite some of the perceived advantages of cloning, it is generally considered to be morally unacceptable from both a religious and secular perspective.

Christian views on cloning

The sanctity of human life principle implies that cloning is contrary to Christian beliefs. Cloning is considered to be disrespectful to God, who alone is the creator of human life. By using technology in this way doctors are playing God and are devaluing the individuality of human life. Using cloning to create another copy of a person implies that human life is replaceable. Despite the benefits of cloning for therapeutic reasons, Christians also consider this to be morally unacceptable as it attacks the human embryo's dignity, because it is simply created for spare parts and then destroyed. If we agree that life begins at conception, then all forms of cloning involve the deliberate destruction of human life.

The Presbyterian Church in Ireland has expressed its concerns over the development of this new reproductive technology. With regard to therapeutic cloning it is concerned with the use of a human embryo "as a 'thing' to be used to benefit another. There is little or no moral status afforded to the embryo."[173] The Presbyterian Church also highlights other concerns related to the issue of reproductive cloning:

- They refer to concerns over the safety of reproductive cloning. Dolly the sheep died at a relatively young age and had developed arthritis before her death. Researchers speculated that Dolly aged prematurely – because she was cloned from a six year old sheep it is believed that Dolly was born with a genetic age of six. On this issue, Professor Richard Gardner, chair of the Royal Society working group on stem cell research and therapeutic cloning, said that this case highlighted "the dangers inherent in reproductive cloning and the irresponsibility of anybody who is trying to extend such work to humans."[174]
- The Presbyterian Church also claims that reproductive cloning could "cause problems within the relationships of the families…[it] may produce more dysfunctional families."[175] Each person has a right to his or her own individual identity. However, the cloned child may feel inferior to the original person and may face an identity crisis as they try to act and live up to the expectations of the person they were created to replicate. This could all lead to psychological problems for the child later in life. As Clarke comments: "Who really wants to be a copy of someone else?"[176]
- Presbyterians also argue: "Reproductive cloning can encourage the tendency to view human life as a product or commodity thus undermining the dignity of each individual."[177]

The Presbyterian Church also comments that reproductive cloning "separates procreation from reproduction."[178] The Catholic Church also considers reproductive cloning and many other forms of reproductive technology as immoral for this reason. Following natural law, reproduction must be a result of the intimate relationship between a married couple and according to Wilcockson: "Cloning confuses and destroys this intimate process of procreation."[179]

In a report on the dangers of cloning, the Catholic Church argues:

"The troubling possibility of the cloning of human beings for 'reproductive' purposes through the technical substitution of responsible procreation is contrary to the dignity of sonship. Even more troubling are the pressing demands of groups of researchers for the legalisation of cloning in order to subject the human embryos 'produced' to manipulation and experimentation, and subsequently to destroy them. This state of affairs highlights a serious deterioration, both in the recognition of the dignity of life and of human procreation and in the knowledge of the irreplaceable and fundamental role and value of the family, not only for the individual but for all humanity."[180]

Secular views on cloning

On utilitarian grounds, therapeutic cloning can be morally justified because of the potential benefits it can bring to those suffering from a range of diseases. For some utilitarians reproductive cloning may also be acceptable. For example, Wyatt considers the implications of reproductive cloning for lesbian couples who could "share biological parentage of a child, and avoid introducing alien genes into their relationship"[181] – the alien genes refer to sperm which is not required for cloning.

However it can be argued that the problems associated with the process of reproductive cloning outweigh any possible benefits. Consider the success rate involved in cloning Dolly the sheep:

- A total of 277 embryos were produced
- Only 23 developed to the point where they could be introduced into the wombs of surrogate sheep
- Dolly was the only one which was successfully carried to term. Of the other 22 many had "severe genetic abnormalities leading to miscarriage."[182]

Thompson continues: "Imagine the scale of physical and emotional suffering involved if this process, in its present form, were used on humans."[183] The abnormalities coupled with the possibility that a cloned child may not lead a happy life due to premature ageing are reasons why utilitarians would not justify the cloning of humans. Cloning is also contrary to Kantian ethics because it treats children as a means to an end, both in therapeutic cloning which creates life to help someone suffering and reproductive cloning which creates a child to replace another one.

 PRACTICE ESSAY TITLES

Question from CCEA Summer 2008 AS 6

i) Explore the view that to overcome problems of human infertility all medical means are morally acceptable. Justify your answer. (15)

Question from CCEA January 2007 AS 6

ii) Explore the claim that such advances are in the long term interest of humankind. Justify your answer. (15)

 CHAPTER SUMMARY

Sanctity of life
- Consideration of biblical teaching which asserts that life is sacred.
- The views of Christian denominations on the sanctity of life.
- Secular views that the quality of life approach is more important than the sanctity of life approach and that the worth of human life varies.

Personhood
- Biblical teaching implies that life in the womb is sacred therefore personhood begins in the womb.
- Christian views that personhood begins at the moment of conception so from this point the unborn child is entitled to moral status.
- The view held by Augustine and Aquinas that ensoulment marked the beginning of personhood.
- The concept that the foetus was not a person but a potential person.
- Other views on when personhood begins such as syngamy, implantation, formation of the primitive streak, brain activity, viability, birth or shortly after birth.

Abortion
- The law on abortion in the UK with reference to the Abortion Act of 1967.
- The implications of biblical teaching on the abortion debate.
- The views of the Roman Catholic Church in opposition to abortion with the exception of abortion which occurs as a side effect of saving the mother's life.
- The view of Protestant denominations who agree that abortion is immoral. However, there are some circumstances in which abortion can be considered the lesser of two evils.
- Consideration of the hard cases in the abortion debate – the case of rape, disability of the foetus and the mother's life at risk.
- The feminist view that the mother's choice is of primary importance in the abortion debate.
- The slippery slope argument in opposition to abortion.
- Application of ethical theory to the abortion debate. Kantian ethics considers abortion to be immoral, while utilitarianism accepts that abortion can be moral if it promotes the greatest amount of happiness for the greatest number.

Human infertility

1. IVF

- Christian views in opposition to IVF, for example, Catholic views that it is contrary to natural law; the destruction of embryos; and selective abortions.
- Views of Protestant Christians who accept that IVF is an acceptable method of treating infertility.
- The secular arguments for and against IVF, for example, the right to a child, identity issues for the child in later life.

2. Surrogacy

- Types of surrogacy and legal issues associated with surrogacy, for example, commercial surrogacy is illegal in the UK.
- Christian views in opposition to surrogacy.
- Secular arguments for and against surrogacy, for example, it can bring the possibility of parenthood to homosexual couples. However, because surrogacy involves so many people there are identity issues for the child involved and ownership issues regarding the bond between the surrogate mother and the child.

3. Pre-implantation Genetic Diagnosis (PGD)

- The purpose of genetic engineering – to eradicate diseases and prevent children from being born into a life of suffering.
- The implications of PGD with regard to disease, sex selection, saviour siblings and designer babies.
- Christian views on the implications of PGD.
- Secular arguments both for and against PGD.

4. Cloning

- The methods used and the types of cloning – therapeutic and reproductive cloning.
- Christian views in opposition to cloning including the view that it is an attack on the dignity of the human person.
- Secular views in opposition to cloning because of the suffering it could impose on humans.

Endnotes

1 Wyatt, J, *Matters of Life and Death*, IVP, Leicester, 1998, p36

2 'Q&A: Hybrid Embryos', BBC News, www.bbc.co.uk, accessed 19 May 2008

3 Singer, P, *Rethinking Life and Death*, Oxford University Press, Oxford, 1994, p131

4 Wyatt, *Matters of Life and Death, op cit*, p51

5 *ibid*, p52

6 'Resolution I 14', Lambeth Conference 1998 Archives, www.lambethconference.org, accessed 4 April 2009

7 'Cloning, Board of Social Witness', p4, Presbyterian Church in Ireland, www.presbyterianireland.org/bsw, accessed 22 January 2009

8 *Catechism of the Catholic Church*, Veritas, Dublin, 1994, 2258

9 Dworkin, R, *Life's Dominion*, Harper Collins, London, 1995, p239

10 Singer, *Rethinking Life and Death, op cit*, p189

11 *ibid*, p190–200

12 Vardy, P & Grosch, P, *Puzzle of Ethics*, Harper Collins, London, 1999, p146

13 Stott, J, *Issues Facing Christians Today*, Fourth Edition, Zondervan, Michigan, 2006, p393

14 Vardy & Grosch, *op cit*, p145

15 Wyatt, *Matters of Life and Death, op cit*, p142

16 Luke 1:41–44

17 Stott, *op cit*, p400

18 Wyatt, *Matters of Life and Death, op cit*, p145–146

19 Wilcockson, M, *Issues of Life and Death*, Hodder & Stoughton, London, 1999, p35

20 Calvin, J, *Commentary on the Last Four Books of Moses*. Quote taken from Wilcockson, *op cit*, p35

21 Stott, *op cit*, p395

22 *Catechism of the Catholic Church*, Veritas, Dublin, 1994, 2270

23 Wyatt, *Matters of Life and Death, op cit*, p147

24 Vardy & Grosch, *op cit*, p149

25 *ibid*, p149

26 Wilcockson claims that for Aquinas, the judgement concerning when ensoulment took place was probably linked to the first movements of the foetus, referred to as 'quickening'. See Wilcockson, *op cit*, p35

27 Wyatt, *Matters of Life and Death, op cit*, p148

28 *ibid*, p147

29 *ibid*, p147

30 Stott, *op cit*, p402

31 Jones, DG, *Brave New People*. Quote taken from Wyatt, *Matters of Life and Death, op cit*, p148

32 Smedes, L, *Mere Morality*. Quote taken from Stott, *op cit*, p402

33 Wilcockson, *op cit*, p39

34 *ibid*, p40

35 Singer, *Practical Ethics, op cit*, p153

36 *ibid*, p153

37 Stott, *op cit*, p402

38 *ibid*, p395

39 Wilcockson, *op cit*, p36–38

40 *op cit*, p36

41 Singer, *Rethinking Life and Death, op cit*, p95

42 Wilcockson, *op cit*, p36

43 *ibid*, p36

44 Stott, *op cit*, p394

45 Singer, *Rethinking Life and Death, op cit*, p94

46 *Comments on the Warnock Report*, The Bishop's Joint Committee on Bioethical Issues, taken from the Appendix

47 *ibid*, taken from p3, 6 & 12

48 Wilcockson, *op cit*, p37

49 Singer, *Practical Ethics, op cit*, p142

50 Stott, *op cit*, p394

51 Singer, *Rethinking Life and Death, op cit*, p102

52 Wilcockson, *op cit*, p38

53 Singer, *Practical Ethics, op cit*, p138

54 Warren, MA, *Abortion*. Quote taken from Vardy & Grosch, *op cit*, p148

55 Stott, *op cit*, p395

56 Singer, *Practical Ethics, op cit*, p139

57 *ibid*, p150

58 *ibid*, p150–151 & 171–172

59 Tooley, M, *Abortion and Infanticide*. Essay in Singer, *Applied Ethics, op cit*, p69

60 Stott, *op cit*, p400

61 'Abortion Statistics: England and Wales 2007', Department of Health Statistical Bulletin.

62 Stott, *op cit*, p391

63 Wyatt, *Matters of Life and Death, op cit*, p126

64 *ibid*, p126

65 *ibid*, p126

66 *ibid*, p126

67 'Abortion Statistics: England and Wales 2007', Department of Health Statistical Bulletin.

68 Wyatt, *Matters of Life and Death, op cit*, p133

69 *ibid*, p127

70 *ibid*, p128

71 'Abortion Statistics: England and Wales 2007', Department of Health Statistical Bulletin.

72 *ibid*

73 Stott, *op cit*, p399

74 *ibid*, p403

75 Wyatt, *Matters of Life and Death, op cit*, p120

76 Wilcockson, *op cit*, p41–47

77 Vardy & Grosch, op cit, p149

78 *ibid*, p150

79 *ibid*, p150

80 *Catechism of the Catholic Church*, Veritas, Dublin, 1994, 2272

81 *Abortion and the Church*. Taken from Wilcockson, *op cit*, p52

82 'Practical Expressions of Methodist Belief', The Methodist Church in Ireland, 2003, p24

83 Wilcockson, *op cit*, p41–47

84 Fletcher, J, *Situation Ethics*. Quote taken from Wilcockson, *op cit*, p53

85 Wilcockson, *op cit*, p42

86 Wyatt comments that the number of adoptions has decreased since abortions have increased under the Abortion Act of 1967. Wyatt, *Matters of Life and Death, op cit*, p132–133

87 Wyatt, *Matters of Life and Death, op cit*, p156

88 *ibid*, p157

89 *ibid*, p157

90 *ibid*, p105–106

91 *ibid*, 1998, p106

92 *ibid*, p106

93 Stott, *op cit*, p405

94 *ibid*, p406

95 *ibid*, p405

96 *ibid*, p405

97 Wyatt, *Matters of Life and Death, op cit*, p156

98 Vardy & Grosch, op cit, p152

99 Thomson, JJ, *A Defence of Abortion* in Singer, *Applied Ethics, op cit*, p38–39

100 Singer, *Practical Ethics, op cit*, p147

101 Thomson, *op cit*, p55

102 *ibid*, p55

103 Wyatt, *Matters of Life and Death, op cit*, p130

104 *ibid*, p130

105 *ibid*, p131

106 Stott, *op cit*, p393

107 Warburton, N, *Thinking From A to Z*, Routledge, Oxon, 2007, p131

108 Wyatt, *Matters of Life and Death, op cit*, p129

109 Singer, *Rethinking Life and Death, op cit*, p92

110 Wyatt, *Matters of Life and Death, op cit*, p120

111 Singer, *Practical Ethics, op cit*, p169

112 *ibid*, p173–174

113 *ibid*, 1993, p183

114 *ibid*, p184

115 *ibid*, p184

116 *ibid*, p191

117 Tooley, M, *Abortion and Infanticide* in Singer, *Applied Ethics, op cit*, p83

118 Singer, *Practical Ethics, op cit*, p143

119 Taken from Singer, *Rethinking Life and Death, op cit*, p132 & 83

120 Stott, *op cit*, p390

121 Wyatt, *Matters of Life and Death, op cit*, p158

122 *ibid*, p157

123 Wilcockson, *op cit*, p141

124 Wyatt, *Matters of Life and Death, op cit*, p78

125 Tyler, S & Reid, G, *Religious Studies*, Philip Allan Updates, Oxfordshire, 2002, p173

126 Wyatt, *Matters of Life and Death, op cit*, p80

127 *ibid*, p80

128 Vardy & Grosch, op cit, p236

129 Wyatt, *Matters of Life and Death, op cit*, p80

130 *ibid*, p80

131 *ibid*, p20–21

132 Wilcockson, *op cit*, p151

133 *Catechism of the Catholic Church*, Veritas, Dublin, 1994, 2377

134 *ibid*, 2379

135 Wyatt, *Matters of Life and Death, op cit*, 1998, p91

136 *Historical Development of the Church of England's Thinking on the Subject*, The Church of England, www.cofe.anglican.org, accessed 31 January 2009

137 Medical Ethical Working Group, Working Paper Number 2, November 1998, Church of Ireland, www.ireland.anglican.org, accessed 15 January 2009

138 'Cloning, Board of Social Witness', Presbyterian Church in Ireland, www.presbyterianireland.org/bsw, accessed 29 January 2009

139 Wyatt, *Matters of Life and Death, op cit*, p90

140 Thompson, M, *An Introduction to Philosophy and Ethics,* Hodder & Stoughton, London, 2003, p189

141 *The Universal Declaration of Human Rights*, United Nations, www.un.org, accessed 15 January 2009

142 Jenkins, J, *Ethics and Religion,* Heinemann, Oxford, 1999, p71

143 Wyatt, *Matters of Life and Death, op cit*, p77

144 *ibid*, p77

145 Singer, *Practical Ethics, op cit*, p163

146 Wyatt, *Matters of Life and Death, op cit*, p79

147 'For donors', HFEA, www.hfea.gov.uk/en/271.html, accessed on 1 April 2009

148 'Now I realise how hopelessly naïve I was to become Britain's first surrogate mother, admits Kim Cotton', Mail Online, www.dailymail.co.uk , accessed on 6 January 2009

149 *Personal Origins: the Report of a Working Party on Human Fertilisation and Embryology*, Board for Social Responsibility [Church of England], 1985, Paragraph 111

150 *ibid*, Paragraph 126

151 *Catechism of the Catholic Church*, Veritas, Dublin, 1994, 2376

152 Wilcockson, *op cit*, p130

153 Tyler & Reid, *op cit*, p174

154 'Sisters make babies with three mums', BBC News, 24 October 2005, www.bbc.co.uk, accessed 10 January 2009

155 'Gay couple become fathers', BBC News, 12 December 1999, www.bbc.co.uk, accessed 10 January 2009

156 Wyatt, J, *The New Biotechnology* in Stott, *op cit*, 2006, p420

157 Wilcockson, *op cit*, p128–129

158 Quote taken from Wilcockson, *op cit*, p133

159 Wilcockson, *op cit*, p133

160 *ibid*, p133

161 Vardy & Grosch, *op cit*, p236

162 Wyatt, *The New Biotechnology* in Stott, *op cit*, 2006, p422

163 Clarke, *Examining Philosophy and Ethics,* Nelson Thornes, Cheltenham, 2002, p152

164 Wyatt, *The New Biotechnology* in Stott, *op cit*, 2006, p421

165 *ibid*, p422

166 Jenkins, *op cit*, p64

167 *ibid*, p65

168 Vardy & Grosch, op cit, p241

169 *Evangelium Vitae*, 14, 25 March 1995, www.vatican.va, accessed 2 January 2009

170 Wilcockson, *op cit*, p149

171 Jenkins, *op cit*, p144

172 *ibid*, p144

173 'Cloning, Board of Social Witness', Presbyterian Church in Ireland, www.presbyterianireland.org/bsw, accessed 20 January 2009

174 'Dolly the sheep clone dies young', BBC News, 14 February 2003, www.bbc.co.uk, accessed 16 January 2009

175 'Cloning, Board of Social Witness', Presbyterian Church in Ireland, www.presbyterianireland.org/bsw, accessed 20 January 2009

176 Clarke, P, *Examining Philosophy and Ethics,* Nelson Thornes, Cheltenham, 2002, p153

177 'Cloning, Board of Social Witness', Presbyterian Church in Ireland, www.presbyterianireland.org/bsw, accessed 20 January 2009

178 *ibid*

179 Wilcockson, *op cit*, p151

180 'Cloning: the disappearance of direct parenthood and denial of the family', Pontifical Council for the Family, www.vatican.va, accessed 16 January 2009

181 Wyatt, *Matters of Life and Death, op cit*, p113

182 Thompson, *op cit*, p193

183 *ibid*, p193

Chapter 4

Sexual Ethics

Chapter overview

This chapter aims to explore the ethical issues surrounding the following topics:
- Marriage and Divorce
- Sex and Relationships
- Sexual Identity
- Contraception

MARRIAGE AND DIVORCE

MARRIAGE IS THE UNION of two people which is acknowledged as a contract in both religious and legal terms. Our religious background will influence our individual views or understanding of marriage and the Bible informs Christians today about the importance of marriage.

In the Old Testament, there are three references that highlight what God considers to be the purpose of marriage:

1. In Genesis 1:28, Adam and Eve are commanded to *"Be fruitful and increase in number; fill the earth"*. Therefore, the initial purpose of a union between male and female in the Old Testament was the procreation of children.

2. In Genesis 2, the second account of creation, God reflects on the fact that *"It is not good for the man to be alone. I will make a helper suitable for him"* (Genesis 2:18). Thus the married relationship has the purpose of providing the couple with intimate companionship.

3. Genesis 2:24 is the third reference which can be understood to highlight the importance of marriage. It states: *"For this reason a man will leave his father and mother and be united to his wife, and they will become one flesh."* In this passage, the strong bond that is created between the couple is very clear – it is a bond

which supersedes even loyalty to one's parents.

From the above references Stott outlines the characteristics of a biblical view of marriage.[1] He claims that marriage must be a heterosexual relationship, between one man and one woman. He continues that God ordains this marriage and the event is marked by a public leaving of one's parents. The married relationship is a supportive partnership, which is consummated in sexual union, with the blessing of children as the product of this loving relationship.

However, the characteristics of marriage set out in scripture are not always respected by key figures in the Old Testament. For example, the Old Testament contains several cases of polygamy where men have multiple wives. Consider the following examples:

- In Genesis 4:19 we are informed that *"Lamech married two women, one named Adah and the other Ziliah."* Lamech was a descendant of Cain, the eldest son of Adam and Eve and his polygamy is not condemned.
- In chapter 29 of Genesis we are told that Jacob, Abraham's grandson, had two wives called Leah and Rachel. As with the previous example, there is no reference to the immoral nature of polygamy.
- 2 Samuel 11:1–4 gives an account of King David's adulterous relationship with Bathsheba. 2 Samuel 3:2–5 informs us that David already had several wives but one evening, as he walked on the roof of his palace he noticed Bathsheba bathing in the distance. Despite the fact that she was married to Uriah, who was one of David's soldiers, David *"sent messengers to get her. She came to him, and he slept with her."*
- In 1 Kings 11:3 we are informed that Solomon *"had seven hundred wives of royal birth and three hundred concubines"*, who were women who lived with and had a sexual relationship with him although they were not married. According to Peter Vardy: "There is no mention at all of this being in any sense morally unacceptable."[2]

Despite references to the contrary, a significant number of biblical references promote monogamy, or faithful marriage to only one partner. For example, Deuteronomy 17:17 states: *"He must not take many wives, or his heart will be led astray."* In the New Testament, Paul taught that marriage was a sacred bond between two people. For example, in 1 Timothy 3:2 and Titus 1:6 he insists that married men must be *"the husband of but one wife."*

Despite the biblical teaching that marriage was a sacred bond between a man and a woman, the book of Deuteronomy in the Old Testament provided grounds for divorce. This right was applicable only to male members of the Jewish faith: Deuteronomy 24:1 states: *"If a man marries a woman who becomes displeasing to him because he finds something indecent about her...he* [can write] *her a certificate of divorce...and* [send] *her from his house"*.

By the first century AD, this passage had been debated and interpreted in many ways according to Wilcockson.[3] In the *Mishnah*, which is a written record of Jewish oral traditions, the Rabbi Shammai interpreted 'something indecent' to mean that divorce was permitted only in the case of adultery. On the other hand the Rabbi Hillel, a contemporary of Shammai, interpreted the phrase 'something indecent' in a more liberal way and claimed that divorce was permissible for *"anything which caused annoyance or embarrassment to a husband"*,[4] for example, if she failed to cook a meal properly or if he simply lost interest in her!

In many instances throughout the synoptic Gospels, Jesus opposes the legalism of the Pharisees. This is evident from his conflict with the Pharisees on the issue of Sabbath observation and religious purity. However, in the case of divorce, Jesus takes an absolutist stance and opposes divorce in all circumstances. Kodell comments: "In case the Pharisees think that Jesus' teaching waters down the law, they should note that his teaching on this point is stricter than that preached by their rabbis."[5] In Mark 10:5–12, Jesus taught that marriage was permanent or indissoluble. He claims that divorce was only permitted by the Mosaic Law because the Jews could not meet the high standards set by God and then adds:

> *"Anyone who divorces his wife and marries another woman commits adultery against her. And if she divorces her husband and marries another man, she commits adultery."*

However, Matthew's Gospel (19:9) adds a unique perspective with regard to Jesus' teaching on divorce. He adds what is referred to as the **exceptive clause** or the **Matthean exception:**[6] *"I tell you that anyone who divorces his wife, except for marital unfaithfulness, and marries another woman commits adultery."*

It is thought by many scholars that Matthew has added this clause to keep his Jewish–Christian audience happy[7] and that Mark's version, which is faithfully reproduced by Luke, is the original.

One final point concerning Jesus' teaching on marriage can be found in Mark 12:18–27 (parallels are Mathew 22:23–33 and Luke 20:27–40) where Jesus implies that the death of a spouse marks the end of a married relationship. In response to a question about the resurrection from the Sadducees, Jesus states: *"When the dead rise, they will neither marry nor be given in marriage; they will be like the angels in heaven."*

The topic of marriage also features in the Pauline epistles. The key ideas of Saint Paul are as follows:

- In 1 Corinthians 7 it is evident that Paul "regards the single state to be superior to the married."[8] He tells the unmarried to remain celibate like Jesus and himself but he continues: *"it is better to marry than to burn with passion"* (1 Corinthians 7:8).
- Paul discusses the exclusive nature of marriage when he informs the Corinthians: *"each man should have his own wife, and each woman her own husband"* (1 Corinthians 7:2).
- Paul also expresses the fact that the bond of marriage is a permanent bond. He states: *"A wife must not separate from her husband. But if she does, she must remain unmarried or else be reconciled to her husband. And a husband must not divorce his*

wife" (1 Corinthians 7:10).

- Paul does however claim that if a Christian is married to a non-Christian and they wish to separate then they may do so: *"But if the unbeliever leaves, let him do so. A believing man or woman is not bound in such circumstances"* (1 Corinthians 7:15).
- In his letter to the Ephesians, Paul further develops his views on the roles within a married relationship. In Ephesians 5:22–24, Paul suggests that similar to the way that Christ has authority over the Church, the husband has authority over his wife:

    "Wives, submit to your husbands as to the Lord. For the husband is the head of the wife as Christ is the head of the church, his body, of which he is the Savior. Now as the church submits to Christ, so also wives should submit to their husbands in everything."

In the next verse, Paul instructs husbands to *"love your wives, just as Christ loved the Church and gave himself up for her."* Rather than translate this as a reference to inequality within a married relationship, Tyler and Reid claim that Paul has a theological point here, not a sociological one: a husband must reflect Christ's example of love, service and sacrifice rather than that of domination and power and that "Such love involves the man in ensuring that the needs of his spouse are met even if it is to his personal detriment."9

 TASK

Class Discussion:

Discuss the relevance of Biblical teaching on the topic of marriage for society today.

 OTHER ASPECTS OF HUMAN EXPERIENCE

Saint Paul was a firm believer that the best way to serve Christ was through living a celibate life. In 1 Corinthians 7:8 he states: *"to the unmarried and the widows I say: It is good for them to stay unmarried, as I am."*

Christian denominations today differ in their approach to the issue of celibate priests and ministers. In the Roman Catholic tradition, priests take a vow of celibacy when they are ordained, whereas ministers from Protestant traditions are allowed to marry because Luther argued that celibacy should not have to be a vocation for everyone.

TASK

Find out more about the reasons given by various Christian denominations for and against married members of the clergy.

Augustine developed the Christian attitude concerning the sacramental nature of marriage. He claimed that Genesis 2:24 is evidence of the fact that marriage was ordained by God.[10] He also agreed with Paul in 1 Corinthians 7:8 in that marriage could help control feelings of lust or sexual urges and therefore through marriage we are able to overcome sin and as a result receive God's grace.

According to Wilcockson, Aquinas agreed with Augustine in that marriage was a way of containing sexual sin.[11] However, Aquinas elaborated on Augustine's teaching and considered marriage in the context of Natural Law. As a result, Aquinas put greater emphasis on the procreative purpose of marriage in line with one of the primary precepts which was to reproduce. This precept was a result of God's instruction to Adam and Eve to *"Be fruitful and increase in number; fill the earth"* in Genesis 1:28.

Heavily influenced by scripture, and the teaching of Augustine and Aquinas, Roman Catholic beliefs concerning marriage are summarised in the *Catechism of the Catholic Church* as follows:

"The matrimonial covenant, by which a man and a woman establish between themselves a partnership of the whole of life, is by its nature ordered toward the good of the spouses and the procreation and education of offspring; this covenant between baptised persons has been raised by Christ the Lord to the dignity of a sacrament."[12]

Therefore, for Roman Catholics, there are a number of beliefs surrounding the topic of marriage:

- The Catholic Church puts emphasis on the **unitive** and **procreative** nature of a married relationship. The purpose of marriage is to unite and to bond the couple as lifelong companions for each other. Within marriage sexual intercourse allows the couple to express this love for each other. In addition to this expression of love, sexual intercourse must always be open to the possibility of procreation – marriage must be life-giving, hence the use of contraception is considered immoral in the eyes of the Catholic Church.
- Marriage is a **sacrament** through which God's grace or favour is granted upon the couple. Church teaching also reflects Paul's teaching from Ephesians 5:25: that the love a couple have for each other must reflect the love Christ has for the Church.
- For Roman Catholics, the marriage bond is **indissoluble**, in other words it is a permanent relationship and cannot be ended through separation or divorce. As far as Catholic teaching is concerned, marriage can only end at the death

of a spouse and only then can remarriage be permitted. This is reflected in the marriage vows, which state: 'till death do us part.' There are no grounds for divorce and the *Catechism of the Catholic Church* claims that "Divorce is a grave offence against the natural law."[13] The Catholic Church does not accept Matthew's exception clause that divorce is permitted on the grounds of adultery, and if one partner has been unfaithful, it is recommended that they should seek to be reconciled with their partner.

The Church permits physical separation of the married couple because "There are some situations in which living together becomes practically impossible for a variety of reasons."[14] The case of domestic violence is one example of such a situation. However, when a couple do separate, neither member is permitted to have another sexual partner nor are they permitted to remarry. The *Catechism of the Catholic Church* continues: "In such cases the Church permits the physical separation of the couple and their living apart. The spouses do not cease to be husband and wife before God and so are not free to contract a new union." As mentioned above in the case of adultery, the Church would again ask the couple to attempt to reconcile their differences: "In this difficult situation, the best solution would be, if possible, reconciliation."[15]

Despite this teaching, many Catholics decide in conscience to divorce and eventually may remarry in a civil ceremony. In this case, the Church considers the new relationship to be an adulterous one because the original marriage is still valid in the eyes of God.

Apart from the death of a spouse, the only other means by which either partner can remarry in the church is if an annulment is granted. According to Roman Catholic teaching, an annulment can invalidate the marriage of a couple. An annulment declares that from the very beginning the marriage was null and void and therefore both people are free to remarry. Grounds for annulment, which will only be granted after thorough investigation, include:

- Refusal or inability to consummate the marriage;
- Duress (being forced or coerced into marriage against one's will or serious external pressure, for example a pregnancy);
- Mental incapacity (considered unable to understand the nature and expectations of marriage).

On the issue of annulment, the *Catechism of the Catholic Church* states:

"The Church, after an examination of the situation by the competent ecclesiastical tribunal, can declare the nullity of a marriage ie that the marriage never existed. In this case the contracting parties are free to marry."[16]

Other Christian denominations have a more liberal approach to marriage and divorce. Many Protestant churches stress the **unitive** purpose of marriage as being of greater importance than the **procreative** – thus they allow the use of contraception. Luther felt that marriage was **not a sacrament** and therefore did not grant us God's grace – he contradicted Augustine's view that marriage could help us overcome sin.

This teaching still continues to influence Protestant Churches today who continue to maintain this view that marriage is not a sacrament. The Methodist Church, for example, recognises only two sacraments: baptism and the Lord's Supper. However, they do accept the "sacred nature of other services, such as marriage."[17]

Luther understood Jesus' teaching in the Sermon on the Mount in Matthew 5:32 to suggest that unfaithfulness was grounds for the marriage bond to be considered broken and therefore for Protestants **divorce is permitted** where adultery has taken place.

On 9 July 2002, the General Synod of the Church of England agreed that those who have been previously divorced could be remarried in their church. The synod recognised that:

- some marriages regrettably do fail and that the Church's care for couples in that situation should be of paramount importance;
- there are exceptional circumstances in which a divorced person may be married in church during the lifetime of a former spouse;
- the decision as to whether or not to solemnise such a marriage in church after divorce rests with the minister.[18]

The Anglican attitude in favour of divorce in certain circumstances is a result of a report from 1966 called 'Putting Asunder', which acknowledged the fact that some married couples experience an 'irretrievable breakdown'[19] and can therefore no longer remain together. Stott claims that this report laid the foundations for the Divorce Reform Act in 1969 which outlines five criteria, one of which must be fulfilled in order for a divorce to be granted:

1. One partner has committed adultery;
2. One partner has committed unreasonable behaviour;
3. One partner had deserted the other for a period of two years;
4. The couple have been living apart for at least two years and both agree to a divorce;
5. The couple have been living apart for at least five years and divorce can be granted whether or not both agree to it.[20]

The Methodist Church in Ireland has a similar attitude towards the issue of divorce and remarriage. On divorce they state:

"Whilst the church upholds the Christian ideal of lifelong marriage, it is recognised that this situation is not always achieved...Where a marriage has broken down irretrievably, and, despite attempts at reconciliation, has demonstrably ceased to exist, divorce should be available."[21]

Concerning remarriage, Methodists also permit remarriage in the Church; however, as is the case in the Anglican Communion, the local minister does not have to take part in the service:

"The re-marriage of divorced persons in Methodist churches is permitted, upon due consideration of the circumstances and with appropriate pastoral care.

Methodist ministers are not required to officiate at such a marriage if they have a conscientious objection."[22]

Many people in society today do not follow any form of religious teaching. Humanists use "reason, experience and respect for others" when considering moral issues and "they do not believe in a god who gives us moral rules."[23] According to the American humanist, Ingersoll, the goal of all humanists is to pursue happiness for oneself and others. In his own words, he stated: "happiness is the only good."[24] On the issue of marriage and divorce, humanists believe that while "marriage is a useful social institution, humanists do not believe that it is 'sacred', [and they] recognise that some relationships fail, and so support liberal divorce laws."[25] The British Humanist Association claims that divorce is "sometimes the best solution, putting an end to conflict, improving the quality of life for everyone in the family."[26]

 TASK

"The dashing young man the lovely young woman marries when she is 23 may turn into the pot-bellied, beer drinking, toe-nail picking, boring, unthinking man of 45 who is obsessed with football, television and pictures of pretty young girls – or into the workaholic whose whole life is devoted to work with no time for his wife or other interests in life.

The lovely young woman may turn into the introverted housewife, totally obsessed with the tidiness and cleanliness of her house, and lacking all sense of individual identity or worth outside the possessions she accumulates – or into the successful career woman for whom home and family are an irrelevance."

The above passage is taken from Peter Vardy's book, *The Puzzle of Sex*, p177.

a) In the passage, what general reasons does Vardy give for marital breakdown?

b) What other reasons are there which cause marriages to end in divorce or separation?

 OTHER ASPECTS OF HUMAN EXPERIENCE

"Marriage is a risky endeavour in which two people commit themselves to each other for life."[27]

As Vardy states, marriage is a 'risky endeavour' and this is supported by evidence which states that there were 144,220 divorces in the UK between 2006 and 2007.[28]

Investigate the support available to couples who are faced with difficulties in their married relationship. You may wish to explore the work of Relate or Accord.

The following websites are useful:
- www.relateni.org
- www.accordni.com

a) Is reconciliation always possible in the case of unfaithfulness?

b) Is reconciliation ever possible in the case of domestic violence?

c) With reference to other aspects of human experience, explore the view that the promise made by a couple on their wedding day to stay together 'until death do you part' must never be broken – no matter what.

 TASK

Question adapted from CCEA Specimen Paper 2009 AS 6

Give an account of the Christian teaching on marriage. (35)

Your response could include the following points:
- Reference to Old Testament (eg Genesis) and New Testament (eg Paul) teaching
- Denominational views of marriage with specific reference to the ideas that marriage is sacramental in nature, that it is both permanent and exclusive
- Reference to the procreative and unitive purposes of marriage
- Denominational views on the issue of marital breakdown; with specific reference to annulment, divorce and remarriage

SEX AND RELATIONSHIPS

Biblical teaching on sex and relationships is quite limited. While there are very few direct references to sex and relationships, biblical teaching generally implies that sexual relationships should take place only within a marriage. For example, Genesis 2:24 states that *"a man will leave his father and mother and be united to his wife, and they will become one flesh."* Paul also refers to the fact that if an unmarried person cannot control their sexual urges, they should marry and have a sexual relationship within this context rather than allow themselves *"to burn with passion"* (1 Corinthians 7:8). He also claims that those who are sexually immoral will not *"inherit the Kingdom of God"* (1 Corinthians 6:10).

The conservative view is that a sexual relationship forms a sacred union between two people and because of that reason, marriage is the only environment for a sexual relationship to take place. Therefore conservative Christians, influenced by the theory of Natural Law would condemn any sexual activity outside marriage (fornication). According to Aquinas: "Matrimony is natural for man, and promiscuous performance of the sexual act, outside matrimony is contrary to man's good. For this reason it must be a sin."[29]

The Catholic Church maintains an absolutist stance on this issue and its views have contributed to the outlook still held today by many that an unmarried couple who live together are considered to be 'living in sin.' On the issue of sex outside marriage, the *Catechism of the Catholic Church* states: "Fornication…is gravely contrary to the dignity of persons and of human sexuality which is naturally ordered to the good of spouses and the generation and education of children."[30]

Cohabitation is therefore frowned upon by the Catholic Church because of an illicit sexual relationship and lack of commitment and trust due to the fact that the couple are not married. The Presbyterian Church in Ireland takes a similar approach to that of the Catholic Church. In a series of booklets produced to give their views on difficult issues faced by Christians today, the Presbyterian Church states: "We affirm that sexual intercourse should take place only within the context of marriage."[31] The Methodist Church in Ireland also agrees:

"Marriage is a relationship, intended as permanent, between one man and one woman within which sexual intercourse establishes a unique intimacy. A loving marriage relationship is seen as the only appropriate relationship within which sexual intercourse may take place."[32]

The Church of England outline its views on the issue of cohabitation in a report entitled 'Something to Celebrate.' On a debate about this issue in 1995, the Archbishop of Canterbury at the time, Dr George Carey, commented: "Cohabitation is not, and cannot be, marriage in all but name…marriage is public and formal whereas… cohabitating relationships…remain private and provisional."[33]

However, other Christians take a more liberal stance on sex outside marriage. Vardy expresses this point very clearly: "If two people are committed to each other, share everything with each other…then it may be morally acceptable to express this intimacy and love in the physical act of lovemaking."[34]

The Catholic psychiatrist, Jack Dominion, agrees with this sentiment and claims that where a relationship is "committed, loving and permanent"[35] then high moral standards are realised regardless of whether the couple are married or not. Wilcockson states: "An unconditional cohabitation based on Christian *agape* love, though unconventional, is nevertheless a Christian 'marriage' in all but name."[36]

Stott[37] agrees that cohabitation may take place for the right reasons, for example the couple may wish to avoid the mistakes made by their married parents; avoid the unnecessary expense of a wedding; or they may refuse to reduce their relationship to a marriage certificate which is simply a 'piece of paper.' He claims that while "some cohabitation may almost be regarded as marriage by another name", two key elements are not present when it is compared to a married relationship:

1. The promise of a lifetime commitment is not present and therefore cohabitation is unstable.

2. The public context in which marriage is undertaken does not exist when a couple 'live together' therefore cohabitation is an informal relationship.[38]

Secular society takes an even more liberal approach towards the issue of sexual ethics. The libertarian approach does not view sexual relationships outside marriage as being immoral providing those involved have consented. Each individual is considered to have personal autonomy and their freedom can not be restricted by religious commands on how to behave.

Feminism is concerned with equal rights and equal roles for women in society. According to Bowie: "Feminists criticise both the traditional Christian approaches to sexuality and the liberal ones."[39] First, Christian attitudes towards sex and relationships are rejected by feminists because they tend to give women an inferior role through the promotion of an androcentric or male dominated outlook. Secondly, the libertarian approach is also criticised by feminists because it assumes men and women have the autonomy to enter a sexual relationship on equal terms, whereas the reality of the situation is that our society is so imbalanced due to years of male domination, that women do not have the sexual equality they may feel they have. Some extreme feminists claim that equality with men (referred to as androgyny) is simply not enough. Bowie outlines the view of an 'extreme feminist', Jill Johnston, who argues for the "separation of men and women and for sex among women, as a political statement to undermine the domination and power of men."[40] This view corresponds with that of Mary Daly who claims that the only way to have a non-exploitative sexual relationship is with another woman.[41]

SEXUAL IDENTITY

Sexual identity refers to a person's perception and expression of their sexuality. It refers to an individual's sexual orientation, whether they are heterosexual, homosexual or bisexual. The word homosexual is derived from the word 'homo' meaning 'same' and describes sexual attraction to a person of the same sex.

Historically, homosexuals have suffered greatly and according to Tyler and Reid, homosexuality "was not removed from the American list of psychiatric disorders until as recently as 1973."[42] Those who were considered to suffer from this 'mental illness' were "locked up in appalling conditions in mental institutions."[43] In December 2005, the first civil partnership ceremonies for gay couples took place in Belfast. The ceremonies were met with opposition from protesters outside the City Hall who referred to homosexual relationships as "an abomination."[44] So what are the ethical issues surrounding the topic of homosexuality?

The Judeo-Christian view does not reflect positively on the issue of homosexuality as material from both the Old and New Testament condemns the practice.

In the Old Testament there are a number of references to the immoral nature of homosexual acts:

- In very general terms, Genesis 2:24 implies that God's plan was for male–female relationships whose offspring would *"fill the earth"* (1:28). Therefore because homosexual relationships do not have the potential to produce offspring they do not form part of God's plan for creation.

- A more specific reference to the immoral nature of homosexuality is contained within the Code of Holiness in Leviticus 18:22: *"Do not lie with a man as one lies with a woman; that is detestable."* Leviticus 20:13 outlines the punishment for such a crime – *"They must be put to death"*.

- Genesis 19:4–11 also refers to the immoral nature of homosexuality, where it appears "that the men of a town wish to rape the male visitors".[45] The men of Sodom arrive and request that the visitors are 'brought out' so that *"we can have sex with them."*[46] As a result of this behaviour, God destroys Sodom. However, according to some scholars, the reason for the punishment is unclear. While some have argued that the punishment is for the "evil of homosexual sex",[47] others have claimed that the punishment was due to lack of hospitality. The reason that some scholars hold this contrasting point of view is due to the different translations of the Old Testament that are available. The above quote from Genesis 19:5 is taken from the New International Version (NIV) of the Bible.[48] However, the New Revised Standard Version (NRSV) does not read *"Bring them out to us so that we can have sex with them"* but instead reads *"Bring them out to us so that we may know them."* According to Tyler and Reid "Although it is possible that the Hebrew verb *yada* ('to know') may allude to sexual knowledge, it could simply mean 'to become acquainted'. If this is the case, then the sin of Sodom was not homosexuality, but lack of hospitality."[49]

Overall, regardless of how we interpret this incident, great care must be taken when attempting to apply moral standards from the Old Testament to modern society. If we condemn homosexuality because of the above references then can we also permit selling our daughters into slavery as sanctioned in Exodus 21:7?

In the New Testament, Jesus does not specifically address the topic of homosexuality. However, his teaching clearly reflected love and mercy for all people, with specific reference to those who were considered outcasts in society at that time. Saint Paul calls Christians to 'imitate Christ' therefore one would imagine that he too would promote love and equality for all people. However, Saint Paul has a very negative attitude towards homosexuals. In 1 Corinthians 6:9–10 he writes:

"Neither the sexually immoral nor idolaters nor adulterers nor male prostitutes nor homosexual offenders nor thieves nor the greedy nor drunkards nor slanderers nor swindlers will inherit the kingdom of God."

In Romans 1:27, Paul again outlines his view on homosexuality: *"Men committed indecent acts with other men, and received in themselves the due penalty for their perversion."*

As with the Old Testament references to homosexuality, scholars have also questioned the relevance of applying Paul's teaching to today's society. Robin Scorggs, for example, argues that Paul's references to homosexuality are "directed against exploitative sex with young boys, which was common in the Graeco-Roman world, and this has nothing to do with voluntary homosexual or lesbian relationships between adults."[50] Peter Vardy continues: "Even if Paul is referring to homosexuality and condemning it this does not mean that this view should be accepted today."[51] Therefore many scholars today claim that it is not appropriate to apply material which is almost 2,000 years old to the issue of homosexuality.

 TASK

Using this information, complete the table below by recording the biblical references relevant to the topic of homosexuality:

Reference	Relevance to the issue of Homosexuality
Gen 2:24	
Lev 18:22	
Gen 19:4–11	
1 Cor 6:9–10	
Rom 1:27	

The references from scripture previously considered have been quoted by many modern Christians in their opposition to homosexuality. For example, the Presbyterian Church in Ireland has outlined the following points:

1. We believe that men and women are created in the image of God and that our sexuality should be recognised as an important part of our personality.
2. We affirm that it is God's will that sexual intercourse should take place in the context of monogamous heterosexual marriage.
3. We believe that people with homosexual tendencies are loved by God, but we also believe that homosexual practice is condemned in both the Old and New Testaments as wrong and against God's design for humankind.
4. We affirm that we are all sinners and all of us are in need of the grace of God. Heterosexual and homosexual sins are equally offensive to our Lord.
5. We believe that in the past many within the Church have discriminated, misunderstood and hurt homosexuals.
6. We call upon all people, whether homosexual or heterosexual, to exercise self restraint and discipline in their sexuality – fidelity within heterosexual

marriage and abstinence outside of it.

7. We urge Christians to offer real support, patience and love to all who struggle with sexual morality and through it all the promise of forgiveness, and hope, in the name of Jesus Christ to all who repent.[52]

This sentiment is also present in the teaching of other Christian denominations. The United Methodist Church, USA, stated in 1996: "We do not condone the practice of homosexuality and consider this practice incompatible with Christian teaching."[53] The Methodist Church in Ireland outline its opinion on this issue in the following statement: "In keeping with New Testament teaching, we are opposed to all debased forms of sexuality and sexual practice, whether heterosexual or homosexual. However, we plead for understanding and tolerance for those whose sexual orientation is towards those of their own gender."[54] Tyler and Reid further develop the Methodist attitude towards the issue of homosexuality: "For homosexual men and women, permanent relationships characterised by love can be an appropriate and Christian way of expressing their sexuality."[55]

In recent years within the Anglican Communion there has been a divided opinion on the issue of homosexuality. Church of England bishops in the 1991 statement 'Issues in Human Sexuality' stated: "homosexual people are in every way as valuable to and as valued by God as heterosexual people." However, when the Anglican community debated the issue of gay members of the clergy and same sex marriages in 1996, they commented that such issues "call into question the authority of Holy Scripture".[56] In 2003, the appointment of Gene Robinson to the position of Bishop of New Hampshire in America caused outrage among many Anglicans because he had been a practicing homosexual for fifteen years. However, it is evident from his appointment that many Anglicans do accept homosexual relationships and homosexual members of the clergy.

Generally, the liberal Christian attitude towards homosexuality is one of acceptance. They put forward the argument that all people are made in the divine image. "If God creates men and women as homosexuals, then that nature and inclination must be good."[57] This point is developed further by Peter Vardy who claims that the key issue in the debate is the depth of love and commitment the couple have for each other. Vardy states that as with any relationship, heterosexual or homosexual, casual sex is destructive:

"Casual homosexual or lesbian sexual activity indulged in solely for the pleasure of the act rather than as a manifestation of a relationship can be as destructive and as meaningless and as damaging to the human integrity of those involved as casual heterosexual sex."[58]

In the Roman Catholic tradition an absolutist approach is taken to the issue of homosexuality. Under all circumstances, homosexual acts are considered immoral. The Catholic view can be summarised as follows:

- It is not sinful to have feelings or an inclination for a person of the same sex. People who have such feelings must be treated with respect and dignity. Such people are called to live a celibate life: "They must be accepted with respect, compassion and sensitivity. These persons are called to fulfil God's will in their lives...Homosexual persons are called to chastity."[59]
- However, the *Catechism of the Catholic Church* also states: "Homosexual acts are intrinsically disordered."[60] It is considered to be morally evil to engage in homosexual sex due to the fact that it is opposed to Natural Law. One of the primary precepts of Aquinas' theory is that the purpose of sex is to reproduce and as "no life can come from the acts"[61] of homosexuals, homosexuality is contrary to God's plan and therefore it is unnatural and immoral.

Stott[62] is keen to point out that the Christian condemnation of homosexual behaviour is not intended to single out homosexuality and homosexuals as being immoral, but that it is important for Christians today to understand that "every kind of sexual relationship and activity which deviates from God's revealed intention is *ipso facto* displeasing to him."

In contrast, Peter Vardy maintains that an attraction to someone of the same sex is very natural for some people. He claims that to deny someone a relationship and tell them to remain celibate because their feelings are unnatural is "tantamount to claiming that a person who has no arms due to a birth defect should not be allowed to write with their feet (as some do) because this is 'unnatural'. Such an argument today verges on the absurd."[63]

The utilitarian, John Stuart Mill, did not consider homosexuality to pose any moral problem. He claims that we are free to act with personal autonomy and make rational choices to promote our own happiness as long as we do not cause harm to others in the process. In his essay, *On Liberty*, Mill comments: "The only purpose for which power can be rightfully exercised over any member of a civilised community, against his own will, is to prevent harm to others."[64]

Australian philosopher, Peter Singer directly applies utilitarian principles to the issue of homosexuality: "If a form of sexual activity brings satisfaction to those who take part in it, and harms no one, what can be immoral about it?"[65]

Austrian psychiatrist, Sigmund Freud (1856–1939) believed that a person's sexuality was determined by their upbringing. He claimed that each person was born bisexual but as our 'super-ego' develops we take on either masculine or feminine traits, depending on how we have been influenced by our parents and others. In terms of ethics, Freud did not consider homosexuality to be immoral. In a letter, written in 1935 to the mother of a homosexual man, Freud reassures the woman: "Homosexuality is assuredly no advantage, but it is nothing to be ashamed of, no vice, no degradation, it cannot be classified as an illness; we consider it to be a variation of the sexual function produced by a certain arrest of sexual development."[66]

The Universal Declaration of Human Rights (UDHR) was adopted by the United Nations in 1948 and while it does not specifically comment on the issue of homosexuality, Article 2 can be interpreted as supporting equal rights for all people regardless of sexual orientation: "Everyone is entitled to all the rights and freedoms set forth therein without distinction of any kind such as race, colour, sex, language, religion, political or other opinion, national or social origin, property, birth or other status."

 ## OTHER ASPECTS OF HUMAN EXPERIENCE

Members of the gay community are persecuted throughout the world today and are therefore denied basic human rights. Archbishop Desmond Tutu refers to examples when "people were frequently hounded...vilified, molested and even killed as targets of homophobia...for something they did not choose – their sexual orientation."[67] In some countries this persecution is state sanctioned.

Try to find examples of such abuses of human rights (the Human Rights Watch website, www.hrw.org, is a good place to start) and discuss whether or not the UDHR needs to be adapted to specifically cater for the rights of homosexuals throughout the world.

CONTRACEPTION

"The use of contraception, whether artificial or natural, means that a couple can have sexual intercourse without the woman becoming pregnant and having a child."[68]

The word contraception refers to any means used to prevent conception. There are many methods of contraception. Barrier methods are used at the time of intercourse eg condoms and diaphragms. Other methods, such as the birth control pill, produce hormones to prevent pregnancy. Surgical methods are also available such as a vasectomy for men and tubal ligation for women. The use of the coil (intrauterine device or IUD) and the morning after pill are more controversial because they work through getting the body to reject the fertilised egg. They are considered by many to be abortifacients because conception has already taken place. According to Wilcockson: "Unlike other methods there is a strong possibility that the IUD and morning after pill are forms of abortion."[69]

There are two references from scripture which are often quoted in the debate on the issue of contraception. The first reference is found in Genesis 1:28 where God commands Adam and Eve to *"Be fruitful and multiply."* As a result of this divine command, many Christians today consider contraception to defy this request. The second Old Testament reference which is considered relevant can be found in Genesis 38:1–11:

> *"Judah said to Onan, 'Lie with your brother's wife and fulfil your duty to her as a brother-in-law to produce offspring for your brother.' But Onan knew that the offspring would not be his; so whenever he lay with his brother's wife, he spilled his semen on the ground to keep from producing offspring for his brother. What he did was wicked in the Lord's sight."*

The Law of Levirate marriage in Deuteronomy 25:5–6 states that the brother of a married man who died without children has an obligation to marry the widow to continue the family line. In the above case, it was the responsibility of Onan to produce a child for his brother. The text describes what is referred to as *coitus interruptus* or the withdrawal method of contraception and this was obviously not pleasing in the eyes of God – Onan was put to death as a result of this incident! Some Christians today use this account to argue against any attempt to prevent pregnancy.

Aquinas' theory of Natural Law states that God's plan for humanity is to "live, to reproduce, to learn, to have an ordered society and to worship God."[70] Today, this teaching is still applied to the issue of contraception by the Roman Catholic Church, who believe that contraception clearly frustrates God's purpose for humanity. The Encyclical *Humanae Vitae*, in 1968 outlined the absolutist view of the Catholic Church on the issue of contraception: "Excluded is any action, which either before, at the moment of, or after sexual intercourse, is specifically intended to prevent procreation."[71]

The *Catechism of the Catholic Church* elaborates:

> "The regulation of births represents one of the aspects of responsible fatherhood and motherhood. Legitimate intentions on the part of the spouses do not justify recourse to morally unacceptable means (for example, direct sterilisation or contraception)."[72]

As the above teaching suggests, artificial methods of contraception are morally unacceptable for Roman Catholics. However, natural methods of birth control, for example the rhythm method, are morally permissible in order to allow for responsible parenthood, for example, to limit family sizes. This method uses the woman's menstrual cycle to predict the most fertile periods and the couple then must abstain from sex at this time. The rhythm method is defined by Michael Wilcockson as follows: "When a woman has a safe period (just before ovulation) when nature provides a moment (or 'rhythm' in nature) when the couple can have sexual intercourse without the probability of having a child."[73]

This absolutist nature of Catholic teaching on the issue of contraception has faced much criticism. Jack Dominion makes the distinction between the unitive and procreative purposes of sex and claims that reproduction is only one purpose of a sexual relationship between a married couple. Other purposes of sex include love, pleasure and the relief of tension.[74]

Many other Christian denominations take a more liberal approach to the issue of contraception. In 1920 for example, the Lambeth Conference of the Anglican Church stated that birth control was immoral: "We utter an emphatic warning against the use of unnatural means for the avoidance of conception, together with the grave dangers – physical, moral and religious – thereby incurred, and against the evils with which the extension of such use threatens the race."[75]

Despite this teaching, ten years later Anglicans were the first church to issue a statement in favour of contraception, which they did at the Lambeth Conference in 1930. In resolution 15 of the Conference, the leadership of the Anglican Communion gave the following advice to married couples:

"Where there is clearly felt moral obligation to limit or avoid parenthood, the method must be decided on Christian principles. The primary and obvious method is complete abstinence from intercourse (as far as may be necessary) in a life of discipline and self-control lived in the power of the Holy Spirit. Nevertheless in those cases where there is such a clearly felt moral obligation to limit or avoid parenthood, and where there is a morally sound reason for avoiding complete abstinence, the Conference agrees that other methods may be used, provided that this is done in the light of the same Christian principles. The Conference records its strong condemnation of the use of any methods of conception control from motives of selfishness, luxury, or mere convenience."[76]

The above resolution from 1930 was the first step towards the view held by most Protestant churches today who agree that every time a couple has sexual intercourse they should not feel threatened by the possibility of having children that they could not support. Many of the Protestant churches today have concluded that the use of birth control can lead to stronger families and better marriages. According to Peter Vardy: "The Anglican, Methodist and Uniting Churches emphasise the 'unitive' aspect of sex within marriage...and therefore allow the use of contraception so that couples can choose when they wish to have children."[77]

The Methodist Church, for example, states on the issue of contraception that "The church advocates responsible family planning, with the use of contraception"[78] and the Presbyterian Church also agrees with this point of view:

"Hence, contraception surely has a place in Christian marriage when it is mutually agreed upon and seen as a method of postponing or spacing or limiting the bearing of children in order to provide opportunities to finish education, develop the personal relationship between spouses and to enable the couple provide better nurture and support to those children they choose to have."[79]

Secular views tend to support the use of contraception. A teleological approach is taken whereby the morality of the use of contraception is assessed by considering the consequences of birth control. Where the use of contraception leads to a positive outcome, it is morally right to use it. From a utilitarian perspective, the use of contraception has many benefits. Within a family situation, contraception can promote happiness as unwanted pregnancies are avoided. Peter Singer considers the benefits of contraception on a greater scale. He holds very strong beliefs about our moral 'obligation to assist' those suffering from poverty (see Chapter 8) and claims that the promotion of the use of contraception can bring demographic benefits and thus assist the plight of those suffering from poverty:

> "We can assist poor countries to raise the living standards of the poorest members of their population. We can encourage the governments of these countries to enact land reform measures, improve education, and liberate women from a purely child-bearing role. We can also help other countries to make contraception and sterilisation widely available."[80]

Humanists, as already mentioned, are people who "seek to live good lives without religious or superstitious beliefs."[81] They have no ethical objections whatsoever to the use birth control. As a consequence, they argue that if contraception "results in every child being a wanted child, and in better, healthier lives for women, it must be a good thing."[82]

Some feminists argue that contraception has many benefits for women. Because of the fact that pregnancy affects women more than men, contraception promotes gender equality. As a result, women can enjoy sexual activity on the same basis as men. It also promotes autonomy for women, giving them the freedom to choose whether or not to have children. However, other feminists argue that contraception has allowed males to further dominate women. Radical feminists such as Mary Daly argue that the pill is literally a poison designed by male scientists to benefit the patriarchy and make it easier to control women. One feminist, S Firestone states that 'women must ensure that they own all the processes of reproduction'.[83]

 PRACTICE ESSAY TITLE

Outline the main features of Christian and secular views on the issue of contraception. (35)

Your response could make reference to the following points:
- Reference to Old Testament (eg Genesis) teaching
- Denominational views with specific reference to the emphasis on the unitive and procreative purposes of sex
- Application of ethical theory to the issue of contraception – both Natural Law and Situation Ethics
- Secular views could include reference to the opinions of utilitarianism, humanists and feminists

OTHER ASPECTS OF HUMAN EXPERIENCE

The AIDS crisis

Almost 39 million people around the world are living with HIV – slightly more than the population of Poland. Nearly two-thirds of them live in Sub-Saharan Africa. The global HIV/Aids epidemic killed 2.8 million people in 2005.[84] However, the use of condoms can prevent the spread of AIDS.

Growth of the world's population

As of June 2008, the world's population is believed to be just under 6.7 billion. This has risen from 2.5 billion in 1950.[85]

a) Discuss the relevance of Christian teaching on the issue of contraception with regard to the extent of human suffering from HIV/AIDS.

b) Discuss the view that the use of contraception must be promoted to reduce population growth and to prevent further environmental damage.

c) Can lessons be learnt from the human experience of people living under China's One Child Policy?

d) With reference to other aspects of human experience, explore the claim that the use of contraception can never be morally justified.

CHAPTER SUMMARY

Marriage and Divorce:

- Biblical Teaching that God is the author of marriage
- Jesus' attitude towards divorce
- Paul's teaching on marriage
- The views of various Christian denominations on marriage
- Emphasis on the unitive and procreative nature of a married relationship
- Denominational views on the issue of marital breakdown, divorce and remarriage

Sex and Relationships:

- Conservative view – sexual relationships are only permitted within marriage
- Libertarian approach – individual autonomy to have a sexual relationship either within or outside of a married relationship
- Feminist attitudes

Sexual Identity:

- Biblical teaching in opposition to homosexuality
- The views of Christian denominations on the issue of homosexuality
- Secular attitudes towards the issue of homosexuality

Contraception:

- Biblical teaching in opposition to contraception
- The views of Christian denominations on the issue of contraception
- Secular attitudes towards the issue of contraception including reference to utilitarian and feminist perspectives

Endnotes

1 Stott, J, *Issues Facing Christians Today*, Fourth Edition, Zondervan, Michigan, 2006, p361

2 Vardy, P, *The Puzzle of Sex*, Harper Collins, London, 1999, p29–30

3 Wilcockson, M, *Sex and Relationships*, Hodder & Stoughton, London, 2001, p100

4 Stott, *op cit*, p368

5 Kodell, J, *Collegeville Bible Commentary, The Gospel According to Luke*, Liturgical Press, 1986, p84

6 Tyler, S & Reid, G, *Religious Studies, Philip Allan Updates*, Oxfordshire, 2002, p182 and Wilcockson, *op cit*, p75

7 Tyler & Reid, *op cit*, p182

8 Wilcockson, *op cit*, p77

9 Tyler & Reid, *op cit*, p183

10 Wilcockson, *op cit*, p78

11 *ibid*, p78

12 *Catechism of the Catholic Church*, Veritas, Dublin, 1994, 1601

13 *ibid*, 2384

14 *ibid*, 1649

15 *ibid*, 1649

16 *ibid*, 1629

17 'Organisation and Worship of the Methodist Church', The Methodist Church in Ireland, www.irishmethodist.org, accessed 27 November 2008

18 'Marriage in Church after divorce', February 2003, Church of England, www.cofe.anglican.org, accessed 28 November 2008

19 Stott, *op cit*, p377

20 *ibid*, p378

21 'Practical Expressions of Methodist Belief', The Methodist Church in Ireland, www.irishmethodist.org, accessed 10 December 2008

22 'Practical Expressions of Methodist Belief', The Methodist Church in Ireland, www.irishmethodist.org, accessed 27 November 2008

23 'A humanist discussion of family matters', British Humanist Association, www.humanismforschools.org, accessed 15 December 2008

24 Bowie, R, *Ethical Studies*, Nelson Thornes, Cheltenham, 2004, p168

25 'A humanist discussion of family matters', British Humanist Association, www.humanismforschools.org, accessed 15 December 2008

26 'A humanist discussion of family matters', British Humanist Association, www.humanismforschools.org, accessed 15 December 2008

27 Vardy, P, *The Puzzle of Sex*, Harper Collins, London, 1999, p186

28 'Divorce', National Statistics Online, www.statistics.gov.uk, accessed 27 November 2008

29 Aquinas, *Summa Contra Gentiles 3.2*, in Wilcockson, *op cit*, p78

30 *Catechism of the Catholic Church, op cit*, 2353

31 'The Family, Social Issues and Resources Committee', Presbyterian Church in Ireland, www.presbyterianireland.org/bsw, accessed 27 November 2008, p9

32 'Practical Expressions of Methodist Belief', The Methodist Church in Ireland, www.irishmethodist.org, accessed 27 November 2008

33 Stott, *op cit*, p366

34 Vardy, *op cit*, p172

35 Bowie, R, *Ethical Studies*, Nelson Thornes, Cheltenham, 2004, p180

36 Wilcockson, *op cit*, p120

37 Stott, *op cit*, p363

38 *ibid*, p363–364

39 Bowie, *op cit*, p182

40 Bowie, *ibid*, p182

41 Wilcockson, *op cit*, p31

42 Tyler & Reid, *op cit*, p184

43 Vardy, *op cit*, p214

44 BBC News, 19 December 2005, www.bbc.co.uk, accessed 10 December 2008

45 Wilcockson, *op cit*, p63

46 Genesis 19:5

47 Wilcockson, *op cit*, p64

48 There are a wide range of translations of the Bible available: I have used the New International Version (NIV) throughout this book, however, other popular translations include the New Revised Standard Version (NRSV), the Jerusalem Bible and The King James Version.

49 Tyler & Reid, *op cit*, p187

50 Scorggs, R, from Vardy, *op cit*, p206

51 Vardy, *op cit*, p211

52 'Homosexuality, Social Issues and Resources Committee', Presbyterian Church in Ireland, www.presbyterianireland.org/bsw, accessed 27 November 2008, p10

53 Bowie, *op cit*, p184

54 'Practical Expressions in Methodist Belief', The Methodist Church in Ireland, www.irishmethodist.org, accessed 27 November 2008

55 Tyler & Reid, *op cit*, p185

56 Bowie, *op cit*, p184

57 *ibid*, p186

58 Vardy, *op cit*, p219

59 *Catechism of the Catholic Church*, Veritas, Dublin, 1994 2358 & 2359

60 *ibid*, 2357

61 Bowie, *op cit*, p185

62 Stott, *op cit*, p458

63 Vardy, *op cit*, p219

64 Mill, JS, *On Liberty*, Cambridge University Press, Cambridge, 1989, p68

65 Singer, P, *The Guardian*, 21 October 2006

66 *American Journal of Psychiatry 107*, 1951, p787

67 Archbishop Tutu, 'OUTSPOKEN Newsletter Spring/Summer 2008', New York, 9 April 2008, www.iglhrc.org, accessed 6 December 2008

68 Wilcockson, *op cit*, p134

69 *ibid*, p139

70 Vardy, P and Grosch, P, *The Puzzle of Ethics*, Harper Collins, London, 1999, p37

71 Flannery, A, *Vatican Council II Volume 2*, Dominican Publications, Dublin, 1998, p404

72 *Catechism of the Catholic Church*, Veritas, Dublin, 1994 2399

73 Wilcockson, *op cit*, p135

74 *ibid*, p135

75 'Resolution 68 – Problems of Marriage and Sexual Morality', The 1920 Lambeth Conference, The Lambeth Conference Official Website, www.lambethconference.org, accessed 28 November 2008

76 'Resolution 15 – The Life and Witness of the Christian Community', The 1930 Lambeth Conference, The Lambeth Conference Official Website, www.lambethconference.org, accessed 28 November 2008

77 Vardy, *op cit*, p180

78 'Practical Expressions in Methodist Belief', The Methodist Church in Ireland, www.irishmethodist.org, accessed 27 November 2008

79 'Contraception, Board of Social Witness', Presbyterian Church in Ireland, www.presbyterianireland.org/bsw, accessed 27 November 2008, p5

80 Singer, P, *Practical Ethics*, Cambridge University Press, Cambridge, 1993, p239

81 British Humanist Association, 'A humanist discussion of family matters', www.humanismforschools.org, accessed 28 November 2008

82 'A humanist discussion of family matters', British Humanist Association, www.humanismforschools.org, accessed 15 December 2008

83 Wilcockson, *op cit*, p29

84 'The Global Spread of HIV', BBC News, www.bbc.co.uk, accessed November 29 2008

85 Population Reference Bureau, www.prb.org, accessed 27 November 2008

Chapter 5
Life and Death Issues

Chapter overview

This chapter aims to explore the ethical issues surrounding the following topics:

- Euthanasia
- Suicide

Note for students and teachers:

This topic will be examined ONLY in Section A of the exam paper and WILL NOT be examined in Section B of the AS paper.

Therefore students are not expected to explore 'other aspects of human experience' as part of their study of this topic at AS Level.

EUTHANASIA

ACCORDING TO PETER SINGER, euthanasia refers to "the killing of those who are incurably ill and in great pain or distress, for the sake of those killed, and in order to spare them further suffering or distress."[1] From Singer's definition, it is easy to understand why euthanasia is quite often referred to as 'mercy killing'. Euthanasia is also referred to as 'assisted suicide' because in many cases, if the people suffering from illness were physically able to, they would end their own life. However, euthanasia raises different ethical issues from suicide because "it involves in some way the direct or indirect use of a third party".[2]

At this stage it is important to note that euthanasia does not refer to:

- the refusal by the patient of extraordinary treatment, which is considered to prolong their life and hence suffering as well.
- the use of pain-killing drugs to treat the patient which have the unintentional

side effect of shortening a person's life. According to Wyatt, "This is the so-called principle of double effect...in the treatment of dying patients, my intention...in giving opiates is to relieve suffering, to bring benefit to these patients. I can foresee that my treatment may shorten life, but that is not my intention."[3]

The act or omissions distinction

In the *New Dictionary of Christian Ethics*, euthanasia is defined as "The intentional killing by act or omission, of one whose life is deemed not worth living."[4] Therefore, we must differentiate between the two methods of euthanasia, active and passive.

1. Active euthanasia

Active euthanasia refers to "a deliberate action to end the life of the patient"[5] to eliminate the suffering that person has to endure. Use of a lethal injection to put someone to death is considered to be a form of active euthanasia. Dr Jack Kevorkian, an American doctor, invented the 'mercitron' which was basically a 'suicide machine' "that allows patients to kill themselves painlessly at the flick of a switch."[6] Dr Kevorkian had to be in attendance to insert the tube in the patient's vein but the patient themselves had to flip the switch. Janet Adkins from Portland in the American state of Oregon, used the machine to prematurely end her life to avoid having to suffer the effects of Alzheimer's disease but after Kevorkian reported her death to the police he was arrested. He was later discharged[7] but his medical licence was suspended. Since then he has been involved in other cases of assisted suicide and as a result he has served eight years in prison for second degree murder. He was released in 2007.

2. Passive euthanasia

Passive euthanasia refers to the situation where treatment is stopped (for example, a feeding tube is removed) and the patient is allowed to die. This is often described as 'allowing nature to take its course'. The case of Terri Schiavo in 2005 caused huge debate in the United States. In 1990 she suffered brain damage after a heart attack which left her in a PVS (persistent vegetative state). She was not considered to be brain dead because she could still breathe without the need of a respirator and could still digest food, although she needed to be fed artificially. Her case went to court on a number of occasions because her husband wanted to allow her to die but her parents refused to allow this to happen. In the end, Terri's husband won the court battle and she was allowed to die through the removal of her feeding tube. As a result, she starved to death. She was 41 years old.

James Rachels claims that the principle of allowing a person to die, through removal of a feeding tube for example, but not being allowed to take direct action designed to kill the patient, is unethical. He states:

"If one simply withholds treatment, it may take the patient longer to die, and so he may suffer more than he would if more direct action were taken and a lethal injection given."[8]

For Rachels and Singer,[9] in terms of morality, active euthanasia is preferable to passive euthanasia because it reduces the extent of suffering that a person must endure. For others, however, the moral distinction between killing and letting die is an important one due to the fact that active euthanasia involves direct action from a doctor to end a patient's life. By way of counter argument, Singer claims that the act of removing a feeding tube is in itself a 'positive act' rather than an omission.[10] In other words, to remove the feeding tube is to actively cause a person's death. In spite of this, however, the law today in England and Wales still makes the distinction between active and passive euthanasia. Passive euthanasia is permitted, for example, in the case of someone who is in a PVS (see notes on the Tony Bland case below) but active euthanasia (use of a lethal injection) is not permitted.

Types of euthanasia:

1. Voluntary euthanasia

This type of euthanasia is at the "request and consent of the dying person." [11] In the eyes of the patient, death is preferable to the suffering that would be involved if they continued to live. Discussions regarding the legalisation of euthanasia usually refer to this type of euthanasia.

2. Involuntary euthanasia

This is euthanasia which has not been requested by the patient, but possibly by their families or their doctors in light of the severe suffering the patient is experiencing. Singer refers to involuntary euthanasia as "when the person killed is capable of consenting to her own death, but does not do so, either because she is not asked, or because she is asked and chooses to go on living."[12]

3. Non-voluntary euthanasia

This type of euthanasia applies to those who are not competent to express their wish to die. Therefore, because of their condition, they are not in a position to ask to live or to die. It could apply to newborn babies or someone in a PVS. According to Wilcockson: "the decision to terminate life is made for someone who is unable to express their will about it."[13]

In the context of non-voluntary euthanasia, the case of Tony Bland, who was badly injured during the Hillsborough football disaster in 1989, is relevant. He was 17 years old at the time of the incident which left him in a PVS. He could breathe and digest food and could possibly live in this condition for decades but his parents requested the right to allow their son to die in 1993. The House of Lords allowed passive, non-voluntary euthanasia: the artificial feeding tube was removed and Tony Bland died a short time later.

The law on euthanasia

The most relevant law in the UK concerning the issue of euthanasia is the 1961 Suicide Act (passed later in Northern Ireland, in 1966, under section 13 of the Criminal Justice Act). This act permits personal autonomy to end one's own life without recrimination (in the case of attempted suicide) but forbids third party involvement. It is illegal therefore to give assistance to a suicide, according to the 1961 Suicide Act.

Since 2002, the high profile cases of Diane Pretty and Reg Crew have highlighted the desire to change this law among the UK population. However, the British government has opposed any reform of the Suicide Act and as the law stands, if someone is convicted of assisting another person in ending their lives, the maximum prison sentence is 14 years. Benevolent motives are not taken into consideration.

- Dianne Pretty was suffering from motor neurone disease. She was paralysed from the neck down and was constantly in pain. However, British courts would not accept her plea to allow her husband to help her die. She continued to fight for her 'right to die' at the European Court of Human Rights claiming that because her husband was not allowed to help her commit suicide, her human rights were being denied. Her case was turned down and she died soon after in May 2002. Her husband stated: "Diane had to go through the one thing she had foreseen and was afraid of – and there was nothing I could do to help".[14]

- Reg Crew, while suffering from the same terminal illness, followed a different path a few months later in January 2003. Before he reached the stage where the pain resulting from his illness became unbearable, he went to Zurich in Switzerland and ended his life at an assisted suicide clinic owned by Dignitas, a Swiss assisted suicide group. On return to Britain, police questioned his wife but the case was dropped.

Many people in society today, who support euthanasia, feel that Diane Pretty should not have had to suffer as she did and Reg Crew should not have needed to go to a foreign country to die with dignity.

 TASK

Using the internet, find out what you can about the cases of Diane Pretty and Reg Crew. Alternatively you could explore the cases of Craig Ewart and Daniel James, who both died in Swiss euthanasia clinics in 2008.

After you have completed your investigation, you could have a class debate on the view that "The law in the UK needs to change to prevent people from suffering in this way."

Religious views on euthanasia

While there is no direct reference to the issue of euthanasia in the Bible, the following passages are relevant to the debate:

- Genesis 1:27 states that human life is created in the image of God (*Imago Dei*) and as a result Christians believe that human life is sacred. This sanctity of life argument is central to Christian attitudes in opposition to euthanasia. Saint Paul elaborates on the idea of the sanctity of life in 1 Corinthians 6:19 when he states: *"your body is a Temple of the Holy Spirit."*

- With reference to the second account of creation in Genesis 2, we are told that God is the author of human life: *"the Lord formed the man from the dust of the ground and breathed into his nostrils the breath of life"* (Genesis 2:7). According to Vardy and Grosch: "If you are a religious believer and consider that life is a gift from God, then you may well argue that your life is not your own. Only God has the right to take life and you have no right to put an end to it early."[15] This concept is reinforced in the Job 1:21: *"Naked I came from my mother's womb, and naked I will depart. The LORD gave and the LORD has taken away"*. Job refuses to take his own life and argues that humans must "accept suffering just as we accept happiness and joy."[16]

- Euthanasia is in direct violation of the commandment: *"You shall not murder"* (Exodus 20:13). This stipulation from the Decalogue is considered to be a moral absolute, which cannot be broken under any circumstances. Wyatt explains the importance of maintaining this respect for life: "When we assist in the killing of another human being, however compassionate and rational our motives might be, we damage our own humanity."[17]

- In Paul's letter to the Romans he writes: *"suffering produces perseverance; perseverance, character; and character, hope"* (Romans 5:3–4). Christians today believe that this and other New Testament references highlight the importance of suffering in the life of a Christian. We can also refer to the suffering of Christ on the cross or the example from 1 Peter: *"… though now for a little while you may have had to suffer grief in all kinds of trials. These have come so that your faith – of greater worth than gold, which perishes even though refined by fire – may be proved genuine"* (1 Peter 1:6–7).

  Suffering can have "spiritual value"[18] by bringing people even closer to God and family members in their final days. According to Wyatt: "Suffering can never be meaningless in a biblical worldview."[19]

- In James' letter, advice is given on how a sick person in the Christian community should be treated: *"Is any one of you sick? He should call the elders of the church to pray over him and anoint him with oil in the name of the Lord. And the prayer offered in faith will make the sick person well"* (James 5:13–15).

In addition to scripture, Natural Law also prohibits euthanasia. The Catholic Church, following Natural Law, consider euthanasia to be morally unacceptable because the direct taking of innocent life is contrary to God's plan. According to Tyler: "An illness which ends in natural death represents a complete life, brought to an end by God within his own timing and purpose, whereas euthanasia represents a challenge to God's divine will."[20]

In 1995, Pope John Paul II outlined the view of the Catholic Church on euthanasia: "Euthanasia is a grave violation of the law of God, since it is the deliberate and morally unacceptable killing of a human person. This doctrine is based upon the Natural Law and upon the written word of God."[21] The *Catechism of the Catholic Church* states: "Those whose lives are diminished or weakened deserve special respect" (2276) but that "Whatever its motives or means, direct euthanasia...is morally unacceptable" (2277). The Church does accept the 'Doctrine of Double Effect', which permits the use of pain-killing drugs to treat the patient, despite the fact that death will be brought closer: "The use of pain killers to alleviate the sufferings of the dying, even at the risk of shortening their days, can be morally in conformity with human dignity if death is not willed" (2279). In addition to this, the 'Principle of Due Proportion' also allows the patient to refuse extraordinary treatment that may prolong suffering: "When inevitable death is imminent it is permitted in conscience to take the decision to refuse forms of treatment that would only secure a precarious and burdensome prolongation of life."[22] Wyatt agrees with this position: "It seems clear that if the burdens of any particular treatment outweigh the benefits, then the treatment should be withdrawn."[23] In the Declaration on Euthanasia, the Catholic Church outlines its support for the Hospice movement: "What a sick person needs is love, the human and supernatural warmth with which the sick person can and ought to be surrounded by all those close to him or her, parents and children, doctors and nurses."[24]

This alternative to euthanasia is acceptable for Christians and non-Christians alike. This is because modern medicine and the use of effective painkillers can reduce some of terminally ill patient's suffering. This, combined with palliative care provided by a hospice, is regarded as an alternative to euthanasia. Wyatt states: "Modern palliative care is a wonderful development in caring...which has taken much of the force out of the euthanasia debate." According to Bowie, palliative care allows a person to die with dignity as "it cultivates respect and sensitivity towards the terminally ill."[25]

The Anglican Communion remains totally opposed to euthanasia. In an article in *The Times*,[26] the leader of the Church of England, Rowan Williams, argued:

"For a believer to say 'the time could come when I find myself in a situation that has no meaning, and I reserve the right to end my life in such a situation,' would be to say that there is some aspect of human life where God cannot break through...an admission that faith had failed."

The Presbyterian Church also opposes euthanasia, regardless of the motives. They claim that the hospice is a viable alternative. The Social Issues and Resources Committee of the Presbyterian Church in Ireland states:

"We believe Christians should urge government and society to adopt the other choices that are available for the alleviation of pain and suffering. Necessary resources should be given to support already successful research into pain relief. Facilities like the Hospice Movement should be encouraged."

Overall, the dignity of the patient at all stages of life is of central importance: "The Christian community should take the lead in showing the prayerful, dignified, respectful care which assures people that they are valued and loved, even in the midst of pain and helplessness."[27]

The Methodist Church agrees with the other Christian denominations with regard to the importance of care for the dying and their ability to refuse treatment which would simply prolong suffering. They state:

"Christian principles insist that we must preserve meaningful life as far as is practicable. However, where a person is clearly terminally ill but conscious, the emphasis must be on maximising the quality of life for that person rather than artificially prolonging it. Where a person is irreversibly comatose there is no moral obligation to prolong medical intervention."

In their statement they conclude with the following message: "We believe that active euthanasia, ie assisting a patient in terminating their life, is contrary to Christian teaching. However, we recognise that this [is] a complex matter and we would encourage further calm, reasoned debate on the issues."[28] This implies that Methodists do not have an absolutist stance on the issue but apply a more situational approach to euthanasia because there may be some situations in which the most loving course of action might demand that "they no longer allow a situation of intolerable suffering to continue."[29]

 TASK

"A patient who is dying of incurable cancer of the throat is in terrible pain, which can no longer be satisfactorily alleviated. He is certain to die within a few days, even if present treatment is continued, but he does not want to go on living for those days since the pain is unbearable. So he asks the doctor for an end to it, and his family joins the request."[30]

Discuss what you think the Christian response to such a request should be.

The Liberal view – arguments for euthanasia

The main arguments in favour of voluntary euthanasia can be summarised as follows:

- Personal autonomy
- Freedom from pain
- A dignified death

Personal autonomy

Autonomy deals with the freedom of the individual to make a choice as to when they end their life. The Voluntary Euthanasia Society (VES) campaign for euthanasia to be legalised in the UK and the issue of personal autonomy is at the centre of their argument, that it is a person's choice whether they live or die: "An adult person suffering from a severe illness, for which no relief is known, should be entitled by law to the mercy of a painless death, if and only if that is their express wish."[31]

Singer argues: "If rational agents should autonomously choose to die, then respect for autonomy will lead us to assist them to do as they choose."[32] This reflects the view of the utilitarian, John Stuart Mill, who stated: "The only purpose for which power can be rightfully exercised over any member of a civilised community, against his own will, is to prevent harm to others."[33]

Freedom from pain

Those who campaign for the legalisation of voluntary euthanasia claim that it is an act of mercy which puts an end to the unbearable pain and suffering endured by the patient. Singer highlights some of the conditions which a terminally ill person may suffer from (and of course, which euthanasia can prevent): "bones so fragile they fracture at sudden movements, uncontrollable nausea and vomiting, slow starvation due to cancerous growth, inability to control one's bladder or bowels, difficulty in breathing, and so on."[34] For many, including Diane Pretty, this kind of existence is a denial of basic human rights. Article 5 of the Universal Declaration of Human Rights (UDHR) states: "No one shall be subjected to torture or to cruel, inhuman or degrading treatment." Many people use the argument that animals are put down to prevent unnecessary suffering, yet the society we live in prevents us from putting an end to unnecessary human suffering.

A dignified death

A person who suffers from an illness such as motor neurone disease will become very dependent on other people to provide for their basic human needs such as feeding, dressing and hygiene. The people who suffer from such conditions argue that they have a very poor quality of life – their life is no longer worth living under these circumstances. Euthanasia allows a person to die with dignity before life reaches this stage. According to Friedrich Nietzchse (1844–1900)[35] it is morally acceptable for a person to end their life when there is no longer any dignity attached to it. He wrote: "In a certain state, it is indecent to live longer...I want to die proudly when it is no longer possible to live proudly."[36]

Euthanasia also allows a person's family to have happier memories of their loved one as they do not have to watch their health and quality of life deteriorate.

By applying the *hedonic calculus* (as defined on page 57) to the issue of euthanasia, it is clear that utilitarians would agree that euthanasia is morally justified. According to

Clarke, there are a number of reasons why utilitarians are in favour of euthanasia.[37]

1. Euthanasia will free the person from pain and will bring happiness in the final days of their life.
2. It will remove the suffering of the relatives as they do not have to watch a loved one suffer.
3. The money spent on medical resources by "keeping alive a 'useless' citizen" who will die anyway, could be put to better use by helping "more deserving cases."
4. Euthanasia is a mark of a liberal society which respects the autonomy of each individual member.

On the other hand, Clarke argues that utilitarianism could view euthanasia as promoting a culture of death, which may devalue life and lead to negative consequences for society.

The Conservative view – arguments against euthanasia

Arguments against voluntary euthanasia can be summarised as follows:

- The 'slippery slope' argument
- Misdiagnosis
- Patient-doctor relationship
- Pressure to die

Slippery slope argument

Many scholars believe that once legislation is passed to allow voluntary euthanasia there would be a gradual decline in moral standards, and society would eventually extend voluntary euthanasia to include those who wish to die but are not terminally ill, and also to the involuntary euthanasia of disabled and others who are considered a burden to society. According to Wyatt: "This is the basis of the 'slippery slope' argument"[38] and this argument was used by the House of Lords in 1993 to justify its refusal to change the law to permit euthanasia. "It would be next to impossible to ensure that all acts of euthanasia were truly voluntary and that any liberalisation of the law was not abused."[39] Wyatt refers to the example of Holland's experience of legalised euthanasia to illustrate the slippery slope. He claims that in Holland, "it seems that this progression down the slippery slope is slowly but inexorably taking place." However, not everyone would agree with this view. According to Kushe: "As of yet, there is no evidence that this has sent Dutch society down a slippery slope."[40]

Euthanasia in Holland

In Holland, guidelines have been in place since 1984 and if they are followed, euthanasia is not considered to be a criminal offence. The guidelines explicitly state that euthanasia can only be a last resort for a patient who is suffering from intolerable pain and for whom there is no hope for improvement. The guidelines also state that the request for euthanasia must be made freely by the patient. Two doctors must be consulted to prevent any misdiagnosis of the patient.

Wyatt identifies the following practices in Holland, which indicate that the slippery slope has taken effect:

- One thousand deaths have occurred without the request of the patients, despite the fact that this is contrary to the official guidelines. Therefore, once voluntary euthanasia has been accepted, involuntary euthanasia occurs.
- Newborn babies whose lives were predicted to be of poor quality were terminated. Older infants with severe birth defects were also allowed to die.[41] Therefore, infanticide is a by-product of this ability of doctors to decide who lives and who dies – further evidence of the slippery slope.

As a result, Wyatt's concludes:

"Once euthanasia is legalised, it seems both logically and practically impossible to prevent the gradual extension to voluntary euthanasia of those who wish to die if they are not terminally ill, and involuntary euthanasia of those whose lives seem futile and pain filled."[42]

Singer disagrees and uses the example of traditional Inuit culture to illustrate the fact that the slippery slope is not a valid argument. Inuits considered it morally and socially acceptable for a man to kill his elderly parents but there was not a gradual extension to the killing of other members of their society.[43]

Misdiagnosis

There have been a number of cases where a patient has been diagnosed as having a terminal illness and it has been found out later that the diagnosis was wrong. According to Wyatt: "Sadly, serious mistakes in diagnosis are not uncommon, even in specialist centres."[44] Even patients in a PVS have been known to recover – doctors cannot predict the future, or know exactly how long a patient has left to live. The counter argument put forward by Singer on this issue is that it is highly unlikely that two doctors, as in the case of Holland, would make a mistake but "against a very small number of unnecessary deaths that might occur if euthanasia is legalised we must place the very large amount of pain and distress that will be suffered if euthanasia is not legalised, by patients who really are terminally ill."[45] Here Singer clearly applies utilitarian theory of the greatest amount of happiness for the greatest number.

Patient–doctor relationship

The patient–doctor relationship would suffer as a result of legalised euthanasia.

According to Bowie: "Killing a patient doesn't fit with what a doctor should do".[46] Jenkins also argues: "mercy killing could destroy the fundamental value of trust between patient and physician."[47] The writings of the Greek philosopher Hippocrates (460–370 BC) have formed what we now refer to as the Hippocratic Oath which is traditionally taken by doctors. It states: "I will use treatment to help the sick according to my ability and judgement, but I will never use it to injure or wrong them."[48] Patients must have the ability to trust in their doctors, whereas legalised euthanasia would also "increase anxieties for elderly and disabled people admitted to hospital";[49] as people going to hospital may feel that they won't come out again. Dr Peggy Norris from the anti-euthanasia group ALERT has claimed that in Holland, elderly people have had to carry what are referred to as 'sanctuary certificates' stating that if they are admitted to hospital they do not want to die. This is an illustration of how the trust has been lost between patients and their doctors. She states:

> "I know of patients in a nursing home who are carrying around what they call sanctuary certificates all the time, stating that they do not want to be helped to die. People are afraid of being sick or of being knocked down in case a doctor takes the decision, without their permission, to stop treatment."[50]

Pressure to die

Those who are opposed to the legalisation of voluntary euthanasia in the UK claim that the sick and elderly may feel pressurised to end their lives because they consider themselves to be a burden on family members. Vardy and Grosch elaborate on this issue: "Imagine that you are being cared for by your daughter and you are incontinent and unable to move easily, you may well feel that you are a burden to others and have a duty to die."[51]

 PRACTICE ESSAY TITLES

Question adaped from CCEA January 2009 AS 6

1) **Give an account of the ethical arguments put forward for and against voluntary euthanasia. (35)**

   Your response could make reference to the following points:
   - Definition and types of euthanasia
   - The act/omissions distinction
   - Arguments for euthanasia including personal autonomy and the right to a dignified death which is free from pain
   - Arguments against euthanasia including the slippery slope argument, misdiagnosis, and the negative impact on the patient-doctor relationship
   - Some reference to Christian views on the sanctity of life

 **...continued**

Question from CCEA January 2004 AS 6

2) Explore the view that for the Christian, the legalisation of euthanasia would be highly undesirable. Justify your answer. (15)

> Your response could make reference to the following points:
>
> • Development of the Christian view of the sanctity of life as opposed to the quality of life principle
> • Discussion of biblical teaching relevant to the issue of euthanasia
> • The Christian view of the role of suffering
> • Discussion of denominational views on euthanasia
> • Possible reference to the experience of the slippery slope effect after the legalisation of euthanasia in Holland

SUICIDE

The word suicide comes from the Latin *sui* meaning 'self' and *cidum* meaning 'murder'. As previously mentioned with regard to the euthanasia debate, under the 1961 Suicide Act, suicide is not illegal, however prior to this it was. According to Vardy and Grosch: "Suicide used to be the only crime you could be punished for if you failed to carry it out."[52]

There are two types of suicide which were identified by Plato (428–348 BC):

1. **Egoistic suicide** refers to taking one's own life because it is felt that life is no longer worth living. This was an immoral act according to Plato because it was regarded as "an act of defiance against the gods."[53]

2. **Altruistic suicide** refers to the selfless act of giving one's life for a greater good. This type of suicide was considered to be morally permissible by Plato.

However, Aristotle (384–322 BC) believed that all forms of suicide were unacceptable because it did not advance the common good of society. He gave two reasons why it was not acceptable. First, it was a rejection of the gods and laws of the city and secondly, society lost a valuable member.[54]

Religious views on suicide

Wyatt comments: "In many ancient cultures, suicide has been glorified as a noble way to die...But in all cultures influenced by the Judaeo-Christian revelation, suicide has been opposed. It is never glorified in the Bible."[55] In the Bible, while suicide is not directly condemned, there are three specific references to the issue:

1. In chapter 16 of the Book of Judges, we learn that Samson's great power had been taken when he was betrayed by Delilah and that he is held captive by the Philistines. The Philistines have already gouged his eyes out and bound him with bronze shackles (v 21) and they have made a request that Samson should 'entertain' them (v 25). As Samson stands between two pillars on which houses rested (in the houses were 3,000 men and women including the lords of the Philistines) he asks God to return his strength so that he can *"with one blow get revenge on the Philistines for my two eyes"*(v 28). As he leans his weight against the pillars, he asks God to *"let me die with the Philistines"* (v 30) and when the houses fall they all die. In this example from the Old Testament, the act of suicide is not condemned.

2. In 1 Samuel 31:3–4, we are informed that Saul was injured in a battle between the Israelites and the Philistines: *"when the archers overtook him, they wounded him critically."* The passage continues: *"Saul took his own sword and fell on it."* As in the case with Samson, the act of suicide is not specifically condemned.

3. The only New Testament reference to suicide is the case of Judas in Matthew 27:3–10. We are simply told the facts – Judas saw that Jesus had been condemned, he repented and returned the thirty pieces of silver and then he hanged himself.

 TASK

Refer back to the biblical references already discussed with regard to the euthanasia debate. Create a spider diagram of the references which are also relevant to the issue of suicide.

The early church made a distinction between the two types of suicide in the same way as Plato did centuries earlier. They claimed that suicide for selfish reasons was immoral, however they promoted altruistic suicide in the form of martyrdom. The reference from John 15:13 has been used to justify altruistic suicide: *"Greater love has no one than this, that he lay down his life for his friends."*

Augustine (AD354–430) proposed that as life is a gift from God it was disrespectful to God to take your own life. He claimed that suicide was always an immoral act even when committed for a greater cause. He was writing in the context of the Donatists who were a group of heretic Christians in North Africa who sought death in any form whether it was martyrdom or suicide. He claimed that suicide was a mortal sin because it broke the commandment, *"You shall not murder"*, in Exodus 20:13.

Aquinas developed the views of Augustine claiming that suicide was contrary to Natural Law – it was a rejection of God's plan for creation. He claimed that suicide was a sin for which we could never repent. Church teaching continued to follow the approach of Augustine and Aquinas for many years. A person who committed suicide was not permitted to be buried at a cemetery and people who attempted suicide and failed were excommunicated. Now, Catholic teaching still reflects the immoral nature of suicide but it has changed to reflect the understanding that many people who commit or attempt suicide suffer from psychological illness or distress. The *Catechism of the Catholic Church* develops the following points on the issue of suicide:

- "Everyone is responsible for his life before God who has given it to him. We are stewards, not owners, of the life God has entrusted to us. It is not ours to dispose of."
- "Suicide contradicts the natural inclination of the human being to preserve his life. Suicide is contrary to love for the living God."
- "Grave psychological disturbances, anguish or grave fear of hardship, suffering or torture can diminish the responsibility of the one committing suicide."
- "We should not despair of the eternal salvation of persons who have taken their own lives. By ways known to Him alone, God can provide the opportunity for repentance. The Church prays for those who have taken their own lives."[56]

Other Christian denominations share this view on the issue of suicide. In general, they recognise the difficult situation that a person who contemplates suicide finds themselves in. They also agree that we must do what we can to support people who have suicidal feelings or people who have suffered as a result of suicide. According to the Methodist Church: "We recognise that suicide is a complex issue, which presents many challenges in developing appropriate responses. We believe that the church's role is to show, in speech and action, the compassion of God for those who are suffering."[57] Due to the high suicide rates in Northern Ireland in recent years,[58] all four of the main Christian denominations here have joined together to voice their concern and to address what needs to be done in order to, firstly, tackle the causes of suicide and secondly, to provide support to the families who continue to suffer as a result of losing a loved one through suicide. In February 2008, the church leaders told the Health Committee at the Northern Ireland Assembly: "churches have a clear role in the managing of this major social problem...Likewise we are committed to reducing the risks by offering a listening ear and a safe place to discuss problems."[59]

The Presbyterian Church, one of the four main denominations in Northern Ireland, has taken steps to do what it can to prevent suicide. In May 2008 it organised a cross denominational conference called 'Suicide and the Church'. Rather than focus on the morality of suicide, the conference was aimed at prevention of suicide and support for families. Mr Lindsay Conway, the Presbyterian director of social services, commented: "Churches have a vital role in the overall management of this major social issue...we now have to think seriously about how we train ministers, youth workers and elders in the whole area of suicide awareness."[60]

The views of Immanuel Kant on suicide

According to Wilcockson, the philosopher Immanuel Kant (17241–804) believed that suicide was wrong "because it would be contrary to the universal duty to preserve life."[61] He asserted that a selfish act such as suicide was immoral because a law permitting suicide cannot be universalised. This refers to the 'categorical imperative' which underpins Kant's ethical theory. Kant wrote: "there is…only one categorical imperative. It is: Act only according to that maxim by which you can at the same time will that it should become a universal law."[62]

Kant considers the moral rule or 'maxim' that would permit suicide: "I make as my principle to shorten my life when its continued duration threatens more evil than it promises satisfaction."[63] After some reflection, he concludes: "such a maxim cannot possibly hold as a universal law of nature and is, consequently, wholly opposed to the supreme principle of all duty."[64] A rule permitting suicide cannot be universalised because suicide does not promote respect for life and it threatens the stability of society through its negative impact on family members and friends.

Effects on others

As well as the religious and moral opposition to the act of suicide, one must take into consideration the effects of suicide on those family members and friends who are left behind to deal with the suffering and grief. According to Wyatt: "Suicide can have devastating effects on others. In fact, it can be one of the most selfish and destructive acts anyone can perform."[65] While people who are suicidal will not in all likelihood think clearly about the consequences of their actions with regard to other people, there is no doubt about the impact the death will have. The support group MIND has the following information on their website:

> "Bereavement following suicide has certain features that may prolong the grieving process. Survivors (the friends and family who have been affected by suicide) may get stuck in an endless and fruitless search for a definitive answer as to why the suicide occurred, or they may believe that they were somehow responsible for the death and may punish themselves by continuing to grieve. Anger and guilt are common reactions to bereavement, but are often more intense and long-lasting among survivors of suicide."[66]

Individual autonomy

A key issue surrounding the topic of suicide is that a person has freedom as an individual to end their life if and when they want. The eighteenth century philosopher, David Hume, claimed that suicide was the one act that allowed the individual to "decisively exercise his autonomy."[67] In *Of Suicide* Hume states:

- "Has not everyone, of consequence, the free disposal of his own life? And may he not lawfully employ that power with which nature has endowed him?"

- "A man who retires from life does no harm to society: he only ceases to do good."
- In relation to Aristotle's point that we cannot take our own lives because society will suffer, Hume states: "I am not obliged to do a small good to society at the expense of a great harm to myself; why then should I prolong a miserable existence, because of some frivolous advantage which the public may perhaps receive from me?"
- "I believe that no man ever threw away a life while it was worth keeping."[68]

The utilitarian principles relevant to the euthanasia debate are also applicable to this discussion on suicide. John Stuart Mill claimed: "Over himself, over his own body and mind the individual is sovereign."[69] If the life of an individual becomes so unbearable that they no longer wish to live, then they have the autonomy to end that life. Wyatt gives a summary of Peter Singer's view on the issue of suicide in the following quote: "The traditional prohibition of suicide should be replaced by the new commandment, respect a person's desire to live or die."[70]

Psychological views on suicide

As already mentioned, Christian attitudes towards suicide have evolved to take psychological factors into consideration rather than condemn suicide outright. Psychologists have made attempts to understand exactly what makes a person want to end his or her life. According to Wilcockson, Freud makes "a genuine attempt to understand the deeper motivations behind suicide."[71]

Freud (1856–1939) claims that our psyche develops in three stages:

1. The **id** is our primitive instinct which seeks to satisfy our basic needs and desires. A newborn baby who cries for food shows the id at work.
2. The **ego** is the next stage of the mind's development where we become more aware of others around us.
3. The **super ego** is the final stage in the development of our psyche. Our conscience develops from social attitudes or past experiences.

He also claimed that we all have a 'death drive' and if we have a negative experience for which we may feel guilt, such as a death in the family, our ego may not be able to cope with this guilt and we self destruct.[72] In terms of morality, suicide is not an act of free will, therefore the person who commits suicide cannot be held accountable for their actions.

The problem of intervention

Another ethical issue surrounding the topic of suicide is the problem of intervention. With regard to issues of life and death, Jonathan Glover highlights two key principles:

1. We must save a person's life when possible
2. We must respect a person's autonomy

With specific reference to suicide, how do we apply these principles? If someone is suicidal, do we attempt to save them by trying to talk them out of it or do we respect their autonomy and allow them to end their life? The problem is developed further when a person makes several attempts to end their life. Glover's solution is that we should try to intervene. It will have been worth it if a life is saved. However, if the person does succeed in ending their lives, our attempt to intervene has not made the situation any worse.[73]

Existentialist views on suicide

Existentialism is a belief that we have personal autonomy and that we exist to enrich our lives and maximise the benefits life brings for ourselves. It is "a philosophy concerned with the nature and meaning of human existence."[74] According to existentialism, there are no religious principles to follow and no God to respect. Kierkegaard (1813–55) believed that, in terms of morality, good is "whatever enables him or her to become a true individual."[75] Sartre (1905–80) took a similar approach as he felt that how we use our personal autonomy shapes our lives. He claimed that "existence precedes essence."[76] In relation to the issue of suicide, one would imagine that existentialists such as Sartre would promote the idea that we have the autonomy to end our lives when we want. However, this is not the case. Sartre claims that suicide is immoral because once we die we are prevented from developing the meaning of our lives. In his 1943 publication, *Being and Nothingness*, Sartre states: "death…can only remove all meaning from life."[77]

 PRACTICE ESSAY TITLES

Question adapted from January 2005 AS 6

1) **Give an account of the Christian view and other views on suicide. (35)**

Your response could make reference to the following points:
- Definition of suicide and reference to different types
- Scripture references regarding the sacredness of human life
- Denominational views on the issue of suicide
- The views of Kant
- The effects of suicide on others
- The issue of autonomy
- Psychological views
- The problem of intervention
- Existentialist views

...continued

Question from Summer 2002 AS 6

2) Explore the view that euthanasia is a form of suicide. Justify your answer. (15)

Your response could make reference to the following points:

- Euthanasia can be considered a form of suicide in a number of ways:
  1. In both cases, personal autonomy is used to decide when a person wants to die. Euthanasia is referred to as assisted suicide.
  2. Religious views consider both to be very similar.
  3. In both cases there is usually a sense of desperation, that there is no other way out of the problem except for death.
- However, there are clearly several differences between euthanasia and suicide:
  1. Suicide requires only one person to act whereas euthanasia requires involvement of another party, usually a doctor. This is reflected in the law.
  2. Suicide does not threaten the patient-doctor relationship. Euthanasia has greater implications regarding how we trust doctors.
  3. Involuntary euthanasia is not a form of suicide because the person does not consent to his/her death.

 CHAPTER SUMMARY

Euthanasia

Definition and methods of euthanasia:

- Active euthanasia is where direct action is taken to end a patient's life.
- Passive euthanasia occurs when treatment is stopped and a patient is allowed to die.

Types of euthanasia:

- Voluntary euthanasia is when a person decides for themselves that they want to put an end to their suffering.
- Involuntary euthanasia is when the patient is able to express their wish to die but does not do so and someone else decides that their quality of life has become so poor that they take steps to hasten their death.
- Non-voluntary euthanasia is when the patient is unable to express their wish to die and the decision to end their life is made for them.

The law on euthanasia

- 1961 Suicide Act permits a person to take their own life. However, because euthanasia involves a third party, it is illegal. Under this act, those who help someone else end their life could face up to fourteen years in prison.

Christian views on euthanasia

- Biblical teaching clearly illustrates the fact that human life is sacred and any attempt to 'play God' by deciding when to end a person's life is immoral.
- The view of the main Christian denominations is that euthanasia is morally unacceptable and palliative care is a viable alternative.

Secular views on euthanasia

- Arguments for euthanasia are based on personal autonomy, freedom from pain and allowing the patient to have a dignified death.
- Arguments against euthanasia are based on the 'slippery slope' argument, misdiagnosis, doctor-patient relationship and pressure on people to die.

Suicide

Definition and types of suicide:

- Egoistic suicide occurs where a person ends their life because they consider it to be no longer worth living.
- Altruistic suicide is a selfless act where someone gives their life for a greater good.

Christian views on suicide:

- Biblical teaching does not specifically condemn suicide, although it does promote the sanctity of life.
- The view of the main Christian denominations is that suicide is a very complex issue and support is needed to address the problem of suicide in our society today.

Secular attitudes towards suicide:

- The views of Kant that suicide is contrary to the categorical imperative
- The negative effect suicide has on others
- Hume on personal autonomy
- Psychological views; Freud
- The problem of intervention
- Existentialist attitudes towards suicide

Endnotes

[1] Singer, P, *Practical Ethics*, Cambridge University Press, Cambridge, 1993, p75

[2] Wilcockson, M, *Issues of Life and Death*, Hodder & Stoughton, London, 1999, p56
A 'third party' in legal terms refers to any person involved other than the principal person. In the case of the euthanasia debate this 'third party' could refer to a doctor or family member who helps the patient die.

[3] Wyatt, J, *Matters of Life and Death*, Leicester, IVP, 1998, p200

[4] Atkison, D & Field, D, *New Dictionary of Christian Ethics and Pastoral Theology*, Leicester, IVP, 1995, p357

[5] Kearon, K, *Medical Ethics – An Introduction*, Columba Press, p34

[6] Vardy, P & Grosch, P, *Puzzle of Ethics*, Harper Collins, London, 1999, p161

[7] Singer, *Practical Ethics, op cit,* p 213
Singer notes that two other people made use of the machine and again Kevorkian was arrested and discharged.

[8] Rachels, J, *Active and Passive Euthanasia* in Singer, P, *Applied Ethics*, Oxford University Press, Oxford, 1986, p30

[9] Singer, *Practical Ethics, op cit,* p213

[10] Singer, P, *Rethinking Life and Death*, Oxford University Press, Oxford, 1994, p76

[11] Jenkins, J, *Ethics and Religion*, Heinemann, Oxford, 1999, p92

[12] Singer, *Practical Ethics, op cit,* p179

[13] Wilcockson, *op cit,* p56

[14] BBC News, 12 May 2002, www.bbc.co.uk, accessed 19 November 2008

[15] Vardy & Grosch, *op cit,* p162

[16] Jenkins, *op cit,* p94

[17] Wyatt, *op cit,* p194

[18] Vardy & Grosch, *op cit,* p162

[19] *ibid,* p195

[20] Tyler, S, K, *Religious Studies*, Philip Allan Updates, Oxfordshire, 2000, p143

[21] *Evangelium Vitae* 65, 1995

[22] 'Declaration on Euthanasia' (Iura et Bona), 1980

[23] Wyatt, *op cit,* p199

[24] Declaration on Euthanasia (Iura et Bona), 1980

[25] Bowie, R, *Ethical Studies*, Nelson Thornes, Cheltenham, 2004, p195

[26] 'Does a right to assisted death entail a responsibility on others to kill?', *The Times,* 20 January 2005

[27] 'Euthanasia, Social Issues and Resources Committee', Presbyterian Church in Ireland, www.presbyterianireland.org/bsw, accessed 19 November 2008

[28] 'Practical Expressions of Methodist Belief', The Methodist Church in Ireland, www.irishmethodist.org, accessed 27 November 2008

[29] Thompson, M, *An Introduction to Philosophy and Ethics*, Hodder & Stoughton, London, 2003, p187

[30] Rachels, *op cit,* p29

[31] Jenkins, *op cit,* p 92

[32] Singer, *Practical Ethics, op cit,* p195

[33] Mill, JS, *On Liberty*, Cambridge University Press, Cambridge, 1989, p68

[34] Singer, *Practical Ethics, op cit,* p198

[35] Nietzchse is described by Thompson as "one of the most fascinating and challenging philosophers of modern times", Thompson, M, *Ethical Theory*, Hodder & Stoughton, London, 1999, p97

[36] Tyler, S & Reid, G, *Religious Studies*, Philip Allen Updates, Oxfordshire, 2002, p79

[37] Clarke, P, *Examining Philosophy and Ethics*, Nelson Thornes, Cheltenham, 2002, p147

[38] Wyatt, *op cit,* p183

[39] Tyler & Reid, *op cit,* p179

[40] Vardy & Grosch, *op cit,* p163

[41] Wyatt, *op cit,* p182 & 183

[42] *ibid,* p183

[43] Singer, *Practical Ethics, op cit,* p217

[44] Wyatt, *op cit,* p183

[45] Singer, *Practical Ethics, op cit,* p197

[46] Bowie, *op cit,* p189

[47] Jenkins, *op cit,* p94

48 Wyatt, *op cit*, p173

49 *ibid*, p184

50 'Involuntary Euthanasia is Out of Control in Holland', *The Times*, 16 February 1999

51 Vardy & Grosch, *op cit*, p162

52 *ibid*, p157

53 Wilcockson, *op cit*, p18

54 *ibid*, p59

55 Wyatt, *op cit*, p193

56 *Catechism of the Catholic Church*, Veritas, Dublin, 1994, 2280–2283

57 'Practical Expressions of Methodist Belief', The Methodist Church in Ireland, www.irishmethodist.org, accessed 27 November 2008

58 According to The Northern Ireland Executive, in 2007 there were 242 deaths by suicide while in 2006 there were 291. Taken from '14 April 2008 – Reduction in suicide figures welcome – McGimpsey', The Northern Ireland Executive, www.northernireland.gov.uk, accessed 15 December 2008

59 'Church Leaders Discuss Suicide With Assembly Health Committee', The Presbyterian Church in Ireland, www.presbyterianireland.org/news, accessed 27 November 2008

60 'Suicide and the Church, Board of Social Witness', The Presbyterian Church in Ireland, www.presbyterianireland.org/bsw/suicide, accessed 27 November 2008

61 Wilcockson, *op cit*, p22

62 Kant, *Groundwork for the Metaphysics of Morals*, 1785, taken from Bowie, R, *Ethical Studies*, Nelson Thornes, Cheltenham, 2004, p58

63 Kant, *Groundwork for the Metaphysics of Morals*, 1785, taken from M Wilcockson, *Issues of Life and Death*, Hodder & Stoughton, London, 1999, p23

64 *ibid*, p23

65 Wyatt, *op cit*, p195

66 Mind, www.mind.org.uk, accessed 27 November 2008

67 Wilcockson, *op cit*, p21

68 Hume, D, 'Of Suicide', taken from Singer, *op cit*, p30

69 Wilcockson, *op cit*, p20

70 Wyatt, *op cit*, p44

71 Wilcockson, *op cit*, p28

72 *ibid*, p28

73 *ibid*, p29

74 Thompson, *op cit*, p105

75 *ibid*, p107

76 *ibid*, p109

77 Sartre, J-P, *Being and Nothingness*, Routledge, 1969, p539

Chapter 6
Ethical Decision Making

Chapter overview

This chapter aims to explore the ethical issues surrounding the following topics:

- Virtue ethics
- Conscience and moral duty
- Ethical relativism and the religious response

VIRTUE ETHICS

THE ETHICAL THEORIES ADDRESSED in previous chapters in this book have included the deontological theories natural law and Kantian ethics, both of which are based on following absolute rules. We have also considered utilitarianism and situation ethics, which are teleological theories promoting a consequentialist approach to morality. Consequentialism is moral decision making which is based on the outcome or the consequences of our actions. Either approach to moral decision making can be referred to as an "act-centred" method and following this approach to moral philosophy we can appeal "to rules, laws, or principles which spell out or give us a method for finding out what is right, or permitted or obligatory."[1]

Virtue ethics follows a different approach to moral philosophy. It does not judge our actions in terms of them being right or wrong nor is it interested in the consequences of our actions. Rather it is concerned with the qualities or virtues we must develop in order to become a better person. As Bowie comments: "virtue theory is interested in defining good people and the qualities that make them good."[2] Virtue ethics is therefore more concerned with 'being' as opposed to 'doing'. The type of person we are is more important than the morality of our actions. Schneewind comments: "It seems to be commonly agreed that a virtue-centred view sees character at the core of morality and supposes that the central moral question is not 'What ought I to do?' but 'What sort of person am I to be?'"[3]

Aristotle and virtue theory

Aristotle (384–322 BC) is the philosopher responsible for the initial development of virtue ethics. Aristotle and two other ancient Greek philosophers, Socrates and Plato, are described by Vardy and Grosch as "the three Greek wise men, as arguably, they laid the foundations for all philosophical inquiry."[4] Aristotle was educated by Plato (428–347 BC) at his academy in Athens from the age of eighteen for almost twenty years. He eventually founded his own school of philosophy in Athens, the Lyceum.

In *Nicomachaen Ethics* (Aristotle's father and son were called Nicomachus), Aristotle claims that everything that exists has a purpose or, to use the Greek term, *telos*. In his attempt to outline the purpose of human life, Aristotle begins by claiming that each and every one of our actions has a purpose or a 'good': "Every art and every investigation and similarly every action and pursuit is considered to aim at some good."[5] This good that we must aim for is not only the good for ourselves but a greater good, the good of all humanity. Aristotle said:

> "If then, our activities have some end which we want for its own sake, and for the sake of which we want all the other ends...it is clear that this must be the Good, that is the supreme Good...while it is desirable to secure what is good in the case of an individual, to do so in the case of a people or a state is something finer and more sublime."[6]

For Aristotle the supreme good is happiness (*eudaimonia* in Greek) which refers to "being happy and living well."[7] Aristotle comments: "what is the highest of all practical goods? Well...there is pretty general agreement. 'It is happiness' say both ordinary and cultured people."[8] Happiness is the ultimate goal in life for Aristotle. While honour, pleasure and understanding are valid goals to have, according to Aristotle they are not the ultimate goal, because we seek only honour, pleasure and understanding to make us happy. However, he claims no one pursues happiness in order to achieve some other goal.

The idea of happiness as the ultimate goal may indicate some parallels between virtue ethics and utilitarianism; however, it must be noted that there are no similarities between the two approaches to ethics. Utilitarianism asserts that our actions must result in consequences that promote the greatest amount of happiness for the greatest number in order for them to be considered moral, and as previously stated, this is not what virtue ethics is about. Aristotle's belief was that in order to achieve this supreme good of happiness for ourselves and others we must develop qualities or characteristics that will make us better people and subsequently help us live good lives. The best life for a human consists of developing and living according to various qualities or virtues. The virtues (from the Greek word *arête*) are central to Aristotelian ethics, hence the name virtue ethics.

Aristotle commented:

> "The virtues therefore are to be understood as those dispositions which will not only sustain practices and enable us to achieve the goods internal to practices, but will also sustain us in the relevant kind of quest for the good, by enabling us to overcome the harms, dangers, temptations and distractions which we encounter."[9]

In *Nicomachaen Ethics* Aristotle claimed that the virtues could be divided into two groups: moral virtues and intellectual virtues.

1. Moral virtues

Moral virtues are the qualities of character we must develop in order to become good people. There are twelve moral virtues which are listed in the centre column of the table below. Aristotle explained that in order to truly live according to these virtues we must avoid acting in a way that overemphasises a virtue or in a way that does not emphasise the virtue enough in our lives. Vardy and Grosch comment: "We must try to ensure that we veer away from either the excess or deficiency, and so hit the 'mean' or midway point."[10] So, as the table illustrates, Aristotle felt that the moral virtues fall between two vices – the vice of excess and the vice of deficiency. Vices refer to qualities which are not acceptable and therefore we must avoid the vices and attempt to find the mean, reflecting the qualities outlined by the virtues. In *Nicomachaen Ethics*, Aristotle uses the example of food and drink to illustrate his point. Too much or too little food and drink will destroy our health while the right amount will ensure that we have a healthier life. The same is true with the virtues, too much or too little will not lead to good behaviour but the right amount is perfect. Consider the following table:[11]

Vice of excess	Virtue	Vice of deficiency
Rashness	Courage	Cowardice
Licentiousness	Temperance	Insensibility
Prodigality	Liberality	Illiberality
Vulgarity	Magnificence	Pettiness
Vanity	Magnanimity	Pusillanimity
Ambition	Proper ambition	Lack of ambition
Irascibility	Patience	Lack of spirit
Boastfulness	Truthfulness	Understatement
Buffoonery	Wittiness	Boorishness
Obsequiousness	Friendliness	Cantankerousness
Shyness	Modesty	Shamelessness
Envy	Righteous indignation	Malicious enjoyment

TASK

Many of the terms in the table are not in regular use today. Compile a glossary which includes a definition of the virtues, the vices of excess and vices of deficiency.

The first virtue outlined by Aristotle is courage. The degree of courage we display in our lives must be balanced because if we have too much courage then we will display the quality of rashness, possibly doing many things without thinking about the effects. However, if we do not have enough courage then we are cowardly and this quality is as unacceptable as being rash. Our behaviour must not be extreme but always proportionate. The doctrine of the mean is concerned with finding the correct level of virtue to live by and it is central to virtue ethics. It is important to note that living according to the mean is not an attempt to have people behave like an average person but tries to have people live according to the virtues and display the characteristics of a perfect person. We can develop the moral virtues by controlling our feelings through habit or practice. Aristotle claims that if we can "have these feelings at the right times on the right grounds towards the right people for the right motive and in the right way…that is, to the best degree; and this is the mark of virtue."[12]

2. Intellectual virtues

While the moral virtues are qualities which are related to our character, intellectual virtues are qualities of the mind which can be developed throughout our lives by the instruction we receive from others. According to Aristotle there are nine intellectual virtues, consisting of five primary virtues and four secondary virtues. Consider the information presented in the following table:[13]

Primary virtues	Secondary virtues
1. Art or technical skill – the ability to be creative and "knowing how to bring something into existence."[14]	1. Resourcefulness – this refers to our ability to be creative or clever about how we do things.
2. Scientific knowledge – knowledge of the universe.	2. Understanding – this refers to more than knowledge about things but about how things work and what they mean.
3. Prudence or practical wisdom – the quality of being careful and not rash or reckless "which helps us to balance our interests with the interests of others."[15]	3. Judgement – our opinions and decisions must be fair, made wisely and "take account of what is right and just for all concerned."[16]

4. Intelligence or intuition – instinctively acting in a way that reflects the intellectual virtues.	4. Cleverness – our ability to learn and understand concepts.
5. Wisdom – knowledge and understanding of all things.	

If we can develop the moral and intellectual virtues in our lives through habit and instruction then we can achieve happiness for ourselves and our community. We must learn the correct way to live according to the virtues from people who are good role models. We ourselves must take responsibility for developing the virtues until the virtues can become for us "an automatic way of living and behaving and part of [our] character, which [we] can exercise without conscious effort."[17] Thompson comments: "developing the virtues is a necessary feature of living alongside others – it is therefore a social, political and moral feature of life, not just a personal one."[18]

For Aristotle, the purpose of developing the virtues is to become a good person. A person who can display the virtues in every aspect of their lives will experience the supreme good of happiness. Aristotle believed that the most important reason or motivation for wanting to live a moral life was to develop friendships. He stated: "Nobody would choose to live without friends even if he had all the other good things."[19]

Aristotle's theory of virtue ethics has faced criticism from modern philosophers. Some of the criticisms of virtue ethics are:

- It is a theory which is aimed solely at the needs of Greek aristocrats who had no real concerns or worries in life and had time to ponder the ways in which they had to behave in order to experience perfect happiness. Greek society was very elitist and the principle "treat equals equally and unequals unequally"[20] is ascribed to Aristotle. This approach to morality was exclusively aimed at the upper class of Greek society and as Vardy and Grosch comment: "It is easy to cultivate the virtues when the mortgage is fully paid up, the children are looked after by a nanny, and one's inheritance pays for the daily needs and wants."[21] Therefore the theory cannot be universalised because not all people can fully experience or appreciate the 'good life' as outlined by Aristotle.
- The theory puts emphasis on behaving according to the virtues and the focus of the theory is on 'being' rather than 'doing'. But the theory does not take the circumstances or consequences of our actions into consideration. What about the negative effects our attempts to be courageous may have on others? Rules are needed to guide our behaviour and to protect all members of society.
- Tyler and Reid comment: "Aristotle's principle of the golden mean is not easy to apply to all virtues…even when there is a mean, how do we identify where it lies? When does courage become foolhardiness?"[22]

Despite such criticisms by modern philosophers, the virtues outlined by Aristotle were accepted and developed in the centuries immediately after him and according to Jenkins: "By the late middle ages, Aristotle's virtue theory was the definitive account of morality."[23] St Ambrose (AD340–397) had already added the theological virtues of love, faith, hope and charity to Aristotle's virtues and in the thirteenth century Aquinas (AD1225–1274), who was heavily influenced by Aristotle, added the natural or cardinal virtues. Aquinas argued that the cardinal virtues should inform our reason and therefore were central to moral decision making. The four cardinal virtues were:

- Prudence, which means that we should be careful and not reckless in how we think or behave.
- Temperance, which refers to doing things in moderation and having self-control.
- Fortitude, which refers to the ability to have courage when bearing pain.
- Justice, which implies that we must be fair to all people. This virtue, according to Jenkins: "enables the individual to direct his will appropriately to relate properly to others."[24]

They are referred to as the cardinal virtues because the word 'cardinal' comes from the Latin word *cardo* meaning hinge. The virtues are the hinges on which our morality depends.[25] Aquinas considered the cardinal virtues to be at the opposite end of the scale from the seven deadly sins (also known as the capital vices) which are pride, avarice (a greed to own things for the sake of it), lust, envy, gluttony (a greed for food), anger and sloth. According to Aquinas, the virtuous person will not allow such vices to influence how he lives his life.

Modern approaches to virtue ethics

While the virtue-based approach to ethics was very popular for centuries, it was generally not accepted from the time of the Enlightenment in the eighteenth century. The Enlightenment was a period during which there was great intellectual development, which included the work of great philosophers throughout Europe. Before the Enlightenment morality had been associated with the virtues and it was believed that "without the necessary qualities of mind and character, a person would be unable to live a moral life."[26] However, during the Enlightenment this way of thinking was rejected in favour of approaches to moral philosophy, which focused on the morality of our actions (Kantian ethics) or the consequences of our actions (utilitarianism). In effect there was a shift in the understanding of ethics from focus on the type of person we should be to a greater concern for the things we do or how we behave. For example, the following quote from the English philosopher John Locke (1632–1704) illustrates how, by the seventeenth century, the idea that the virtues were secondary to moral rules or laws had begun to develop: "By whatever standard soever we frame in our minds the ideas of virtues or vices...their rectitude, or obliquity, consists in the agreement with those patterns prescribed by some law."[27]

However in the twentieth century a number of philosophers rejected the modern approaches to morality and made attempts to revive the importance of a virtue-based approach. Philosophers such as Elizabeth Anscombe (1919–2001) claimed that by following Kantian ethics or utilitarianism a bad person could behave morally and true morality is about much more than this. In 1958, Anscombe, a British philosopher, "launched a scathing attack on both of these traditions"[28] and attempted to renew interest in virtue ethics. In her article entitled *Modern Moral Philosophy*, she questioned the dominance of the deontological and teleological theories and claimed that "virtue ethics might provide a much firmer foundation for reasoning about moral dilemmas."[29] She claimed that concerns about how people behave had replaced Aristotle's focus on the type of person the individual or moral agent actually is and she argued: "actions have replaced persons, behaviour has been separated from people."[30] For Anscombe it was important to return our attention to the character of the person, rather than how successful they were in following rules or principles laid down by philosophers such as Kant or Bentham and Mill.

In *Modern Moral Philosophy* she states: "Anyone who has read Aristotle's *Ethics* and has also read modern moral philosophy must have been struck by the great contrasts between them."[31] She reflects on how this came about and lays the blame firmly with Christianity:

> "The answer is in history: between Aristotle and us came Christianity, with its law conception of ethics…the dominance of Christianity for many centuries, the concepts of being bound, permitted or excused became deeply embedded in our language and thought."[32]

Regarding the "Being vs Doing Debate"[33] or the question of whether moral philosophy should focus on being a good person or simply being obedient to rules or principles, Anscombe felt that our being, or the type of person we should aim to become was far more important than obedience to rules because "good persons do good deeds, but good deeds do not necessarily make good persons."[34] She believed that modern, moral philosophers should abandon the concepts of moral obligation and moral duty and move towards the "meaning in life, and qualities that were worth developing and encouraging",[35] qualities which will ultimately promote *eudaimonia* or the greater good of all people.

Anscombe agreed with Aristotle's idea that "the best life for a human being – *eudaimonia* – consists in the exercise of the virtues."[36] Therefore a "skeletal virtue theory"[37] would consist of the following:

1. An action is right if it is what a virtuous person (or agent) would do in the circumstances.
2. A virtuous person will act according to the virtues as set out by Aristotle.
3. A virtue is a quality or a characteristic a human being must have in order to flourish or to live well.

Another British philosopher, Philippa Foot (born 1920), is a contemporary supporter of virtue ethics. In 1978 she produced *Virtues and Vices and Other Essays in Moral*

Philosophy and argued that the virtues outlined by Aristotle and Aquinas are necessary for a moral society. She comments: "the most systematic account [of the virtues] is found in Aristotle, and in the blending of Aristotelian and Christian philosophy found in St Thomas."[38] She also agreed with Aristotle: "training is the basic groundwork of virtue ethics, which is why the moral virtues need to be nurtured and developed through constant habit, and particularly in early years through enforced habit."[39]

In *Virtues and Vices* Foot asserts that by following a virtue approach to morality, our actions or behaviour is not judged but that "it is primarily by his intentions that a man's moral dispositions are judged."[40] In terms of our behaviour, she felt that if we are living according to the virtues then we will "know and appreciate that there are particular and acceptable means of attaining certain goals, and unacceptable means of attaining the same goals."[41] Put another way, a good action is one which was carried out in accordance with the virtues, as opposed to the vices.

Foot argues that society in general will benefit from a virtue-based approach to ethics. She comments: "Courage, temperance and wisdom benefit both the person who has these dispositions and other people as well; and moral failings such as pride, vanity, worldliness and avarice harm both their possessor and others." She continues: "Nobody can get on well if he lacks courage, and does not have some measure of temperance and wisdom, while communities where justice and charity are lacking are apt to being wretched places to live, as Russia was under the Stalinist terror."[42]

 OTHER ASPECTS OF HUMAN EXPERIENCE

In the conclusion to *Virtues and Vices* Foot comments: "There are some people who do possess all these virtues and who are loved and admired by all the world, as Pope John XXIII was loved and admired."[43]

In groups research the lives of prominent people in society today or in the past and consider how they have lived according to the Aristotelian virtues.

Scottish born philosopher Alasdair MacIntyre (born 1929) also supported an approach to ethics that was based on the Aristotelian virtues and not modern ethical theories, which he considered to put "too much stress on reason, and too little emphasis on people and the contexts in which they live their lives."[44] MacIntyre claimed that the deontological and consequentialist approaches to morality had created a "moral vacuum"[45] or a society in which true morality was absent and morality was nothing more than "the expression of personal preference in a culture which has abandoned the virtues and rejected the sense of community."[46] As a result of this moral vacuum, MacIntyre claims that three archetypal or typical characters that lack the virtues are now present in society: [47]

1. The bureaucratic manager attempts to live in the most efficient manner possible and has no problems with putting profits before principles, for example shutting down factories in order to maximise profits for shareholders. MacIntyre argues: "the manager is generally seen in our culture as morally neutral and…can devise the most efficient means of achieving whatever end is proposed."[48]

2. The rich aesthete is someone who has a sincere appreciation of beauty, for example the arts. This type of person will pursue the more exciting pleasures in life and MacIntyre claims that such people are the focus of media attention and reflect our "celebrity-obsessed culture lacking virtue and meaning."[49]

3. The therapist keeps everything in society in place and charges the bureaucratic manager and rich aesthete vast amounts of money so that they are fit to continue with their pursuits.

MacIntyre supports a virtue-based approach to morality because of the negative impact deontological and teleological approaches to ethics have had. He defines a virtue as follows: "A virtue is an acquired human quality the possession and exercise of which tends to enable us to achieve those goods…and the lack of which effectively prevents us from achieving any such goods."[50] In *After Virtue, A Study of Moral Theory* (1981) he argues that a moral society is one "in which people recognise commonly agreed virtues and aspire to meet them."[51] He also considered the virtues forwarded by Plato and other Greek philosophers such as Protagoras and argued that Aristotle's virtues were the most "coherent and complete" and they "could not be bettered."[52] In *The Nature of the Virtues* MacIntyre specifically focuses on the importance of the Aristotelian virtues of courage and truthfulness. With regard to courage he argues:

"we hold courage to be a virtue because the care and concern for individuals, communities and causes…is so crucial…if someone says that he cares for some individual, community, or cause, but is unwilling to risk harm or danger on his, her, or its own behalf, he puts in question the genuineness of his care and concern."[53]

MacIntyre believed that rather than focus on an approach to ethics which depends on rules or principles, moral philosophy should focus on individuals developing the Aristotelian virtues in their lives, because having a good character will enable people to make the right judgements when it comes to moral decision making. He comments: "The exercise of the virtues is itself a crucial component of the good life for man."[54]

Application of virtue ethics

The discussion so far has focused on virtue theory and the disposition required by individuals in order to behave in a virtuous way. In *Virtue Theory and Abortion*, Rosalind Hursthouse attempts to illustrate how virtue ethics can be applied to moral issues. As has already been established, the assessment of whether abortion is morally acceptable does not depend on our obligation to follow rules or on whether the consequences of the abortion are the most beneficial. According to virtue theory the morality of abortion depends on the motives and thinking of women who have abortions. Hursthouse reflects on the question: "In having an abortion…would the agent be acting virtuously or viciously or neither?"[55] In her discussion, she makes the following points:[56]

- A virtuous person would not take abortion lightly. To think of abortion as killing something that does not matter is callous and light-minded.
- A virtuous person will realise that motherhood and childbearing are intrinsically worthwhile and make a positive contribution to living a full, happy life. A woman who lives her life according to the virtues will not have an abortion for shallow reasons such as wanting to have a good time before starting a family or for issues related to money.
- For women who appreciate the intrinsic value of being a parent, an abortion may be in keeping with a virtuous character. An abortion may be justified for the following reasons:
  i. Those women who already have several children and feel that another child will affect her ability to be a good mother.
  ii. Those women who have already been a good mother and are approaching the age of being a good grandmother.
  iii. Those women who discover that continuation with their pregnancy might kill them.
  iv. Those women who have decided to live a life centred around some other worthwhile activity with which motherhood would compete.
- Hursthouse concludes:
  "Even when the decision to have an abortion is the right decision – one that does not itself fall under a vice-related term and thereby one that the perfectly virtuous could recommend…[due to] the fact that a human life has been cut short, some evil has probably been brought about."[57]

 TASK

Having considered how virtue ethics approaches the issue of abortion, in groups discuss how people who live according to the virtues would treat issues such as euthanasia, capital punishment and sexual ethics.

An evaluation of virtue ethics

Supporters of virtue ethics claim that it is a good approach to moral philosophy because it recognises the importance of the person in moral decision making and "rather than simply looking for rules, it looks at the fundamental issue of what it means to be human."[58] The primary focus of virtue ethics is the people and the quality of their lives, not their discrete actions which are isolated from their character. Following virtue theory, the individual will act from a "direct desire" to behave in a morally acceptable way "without first believing that he or she morally ought to perform that action or have that desire."[59] Therefore virtue ethics encourages people to naturally act in a moral way rather than acting in a particular way because they are obligated to follow rules.

Supporters also argue that if society were to take an approach to moral philosophy which was based on the virtues, then it would be a better place for all people as they strive to develop traits needed to live well, to achieve *eudaimonia*. Virtue ethics is also a practical theory and McDowell comments that by following virtue ethics "Occasion by occasion, one knows what to do…not by applying universal principles but by being a certain kind of person: one who sees situations in a certain distinct way."[60]

It is also argued that virtue ethics is a universal approach to moral philosophy. While contemporary virtue ethics was developed by Foot, an atheist, it is also compatible with Christian thought. Both Anscombe and MacIntyre were converts to Catholicism. Bowie comments that virtue ethics "is an alternative ethical model that fits Christian ethics and also reaches beyond religious ethics."[61]

However a weakness of virtue ethics as an ethical theory is that despite Hursthouse's best efforts, it does not provide us with clear answers to modern moral issues such as euthanasia, contraception and capital punishment in the way that natural law or utilitarianism does. In *On Some Vices of Virtue Ethics* (1984), Robert Louden argues: "people have always expected ethical theory to tell them something about what they ought to do, and it seems to me that virtue ethics is structurally unable to say much of anything about this issue."[62]

In addition to claiming that virtue ethics is weak in terms of casuistry or applied ethics, Louden also argues that virtue ethics does not provide us with a set of rules which prevent intolerable acts such as murder, adultery, stealing, etc. And as every ethical theory should do this, virtue ethics cannot suffice as a fully developed ethical theory. He claims that we need rules and principles to inform our behaviour and the virtues are not adequate as they do not inform society: "there are some acts which are absolutely prohibited. We cannot articulate this sense of absolute prohibition by referring merely to characteristic patterns of behaviour."[63]

Louden concludes by claiming: "no ethics of virtue, pure and unsupplemented, can be satisfactory". However, he does concede that there are benefits to a virtue-based approach to moral philosophy and if supplemented with rules to protect our moral community "the ethics of virtue and the ethics of rules [can be seen] as adding up, rather than as cancelling each other out."[64] This criticism is also developed by Richard Bernstein in *Philosophical Profiles*. According to Vardy and Grosch, Bernstein argues: "MacIntyre has placed too much faith in the wisdom of the 'ancients' (ie Aristotle) and has rejected too quickly the inquiries of the 'moderns' (ie Kant, Bentham, Mill, etc). For Bernstein there are 'truths' to be found in both ancients and moderns."[65]

TASK

Outline and examine the development and principle features of virtue ethics.

CONSCIENCE AND MORAL DUTY

Conscience refers to our innate sense or inner feelings about right and wrong. It is believed by many people that conscience is universal, that it exists in some form for all people from both religious and secular backgrounds. Our conscience has two roles: first, it can help us to decide what the moral thing to do is in certain circumstances. For example, conscientious objectors can refuse to fight in a war because they believe that they have a moral duty to refuse to take part in any act of violence. Doctors can also conscientiously object to perform abortions; for example in 2007 *The Independent on Sunday* reported: "Britain is facing an abortion crisis because an unprecedented number of doctors are refusing to be involved in carrying out the procedure."[66] The role of conscience can therefore be described as legislative because it informs us how to behave.

Second, conscience can be described as judicial in that it judges our actions by making us have feelings of guilt if we have acted immorally. Jenkins comments that conscience "both reflects on and directs behaviour."[67]

 OTHER ASPECTS OF HUMAN EXPERIENCE

Over many years, Amnesty International has campaigned to raise awareness of the plight of 'prisoners of conscience'. Many people throughout the world are held as prisoners of conscience, imprisoned because their beliefs are different to the beliefs held by the state authorities or because they have fought for basic human rights, rights which their ruling authorities do not want the people to have.

One example of a prisoner of conscience is Mordechai Vanunu, an Israeli nuclear technician who gave information to *The Sunday Times* in 1986 regarding the development of Israel's secret nuclear arsenal. He was later abducted by Israeli secret service and was imprisoned for eighteen years. He was released in 2004.

Access the Amnesty International web site (www.amnesty.org) and search for prisoners of conscience in order to find out more about the prisoners of conscience.

Christian views of conscience

In scripture the Greek word *synderessi*[68] is used to refer to conscience. Literally it means 'to know' and the word is used by Paul in the context of knowing the will of

God. In Romans 2:14–15 for example, Paul implies that conscience is universal. He comments that the Gentiles, who have never been taught the Mosaic Law, accept the guidance given by their conscience and therefore naturally follow the moral standards contained within the Mosaic Law:

> *"Indeed when Gentiles, who do not have the law, do by nature things required by the law, they are a law for themselves, even though they do not have the law. Since they show that the requirements of the law are written on their hearts, their consciences also bearing witness…"*

For Paul, conscience is written on the hearts of all humanity and guides or directs all people to behave in a manner which is pleasing to God. In Romans 13:5, Paul gives another example of the purpose of conscience as directing behaviour. He tells his audience that they must obey the state authorities: *"not only because of possible punishment but also because of conscience."* Paul also suggests that our conscience helps us reflect on our moral behaviour. In Romans 9:1, Paul says: *"I speak the truth in Christ – I am not lying, my conscience confirms it in the Holy Spirit."*

In his first letter to the Corinthians, Paul urges the Christians living in Corinth to use their conscience to guide their behaviour on issues such as whether or not they could eat meat which has been sacrificed to false gods. Because of the coexistence of Christians and pagans in Corinth, Christians faced a moral dilemma. They were not sure about the morality of sharing meals during social occasions with their pagan neighbours, especially when the meat the Gentiles served may have been offered to false gods. Paul informs the Christian community in Corinth that they know that *"an idol is nothing at all in the world and that there is no God but one"* (1 Corinthians 8:4) and he then tells them that they could *"eat anything sold in the meat market without raising questions of conscience"* and *"If some unbeliever invites you to a meal and you want to go, eat whatever is put before you without raising questions of conscience"* (1 Corinthians 10:25–27).

In 2 Corinthians 4:2, Paul implies that our conscience sets high standards of behaviour which are acceptable in the eyes of God: *"we commend ourselves to every man's conscience in the sight of God."* Paul is also aware of the guilt conscience can impose on Christians if they fail to live up to these standards: *"let us draw near to God…having our hearts sprinkled to cleanse us from a guilty conscience"* (Hebrews 10:22).

The early Christian church followed Paul's views on the importance of conscience regarding its role in reflecting on and directing moral behaviour. St Jerome (AD147–240) taught that our conscience was the means by which *"we discern that we sin"*.[69] He also acknowledged that conscience had limitations because for some people conscience was not an effective means of directing behaviour: *"in some men we see this conscience overthrown and displaced; they have no sense of guilt or shame for their sins."*[70] Jerome believed that conscience was not a reliable guide to morality for all people as it could be misinformed or misguided.

Augustine (AD354–430) further developed the early Christian understanding of conscience. He believed that conscience was a means of observing God's law; it was "the voice of God speaking to us which we must seek within ourselves."[71] So while he did consider conscience to be universal because all people have the ability to hear this voice of God, like Jerome, he felt that it was not always reliable because some people decide either not to consult or listen to their conscience.

In order for conscience to be an effective means of setting acceptable moral standards, Augustine believed that God's grace was essential. Grace is a gift from God. This refers to the favour that he grants us or the help he gives us to respond to his call. Without this grace we cannot be saved, therefore Augustine believed that only Christians who are aware of God will receive his grace, therefore only Christians will have the ability to act as God intended. Jenkins comments that Augustine believed "God endows each human being with a conscience whereby he or she may know the moral law. However, this knowledge by itself is insufficient...God's grace illuminates the soul by a revelation of God's goodness."[72]

Unlike Augustine, Aquinas (1224–1274) did not believe that conscience was the voice of God or an innate knowledge of right and wrong. Aquinas believed that conscience consisted of the faculty of human reason helping us decide between right and wrong. In his theory of natural law, Aquinas argues that this faculty of reason is central to our ability to make moral decisions. We must use our ability to reason to work out God's plan for us and apply it to ethical decision making. In *Summa Theologica* Aquinas stated: "Conscience is the dictate of reason...he who acts against his conscience always sins."[73] He believed that every individual had the ability to use reason to act morally: "that people basically tended towards the good and away from evil (the '*synderesis* rule')."[73a] Aquinas believed that each individual has this ability to reason, making conscience universal. He agreed that sometimes human reason failed as people pursued an apparent good and that conscience was not infallible as it did not always lead to the right moral decisions being made. He believed that conscience had to be informed and developed in order for it to be adequate as a means for making moral decisions. Our conscience could be developed, according to Aquinas, through reading scripture and developing our relationship with God through prayer.

In contrast to the views of Aquinas, Joseph Butler (1692–1752), an Anglican theologian, believed that conscience was a God-given guide to morality and not human reason making decisions as Aquinas suggested. In *Fifteen Sermons upon Human Nature,* Butler wrote: "Conscience does not only offer itself to show us the way we should walk in, but it likewise carries its own authority with it, that is our natural guide, the guide assigned to us by the Author of our nature."[74] For Butler, because conscience comes from God it must always be obeyed without hesitation: "it is our duty to walk in that path and follow this guide."[75] Butler believed that our conscience was intuitive, that it is in our nature to be able to decide between right and wrong, and guilt or "dissatisfaction with our moral life is the clue that we have acted against our nature."[76] Butler believed that each individual person is motivated by a selfish love of oneself or a genuine love of others (benevolence). Conscience, he believed, directs us to putting others before ourselves and makes us feel guilty with our behaviour if we act selfishly.

John Henry Newman (1801–1890) also developed the view that conscience was comparable to an inner voice – the voice of God. He believed that "the insistent force of conscience suggests that there is someone to whom we feel answerable and responsible, someone who is the personal source of the moral law, God."[77] Newman was an Anglican minister who converted to Catholicism and eventually became a Cardinal in the Catholic Church. His views on conscience are still very influential today. In his novel *Callista* (1855), Newman wrote:

> "My nature feels towards the voice of conscience as towards a person. When I obey it, I feel a satisfaction; when I disobey, a soreness – just like that which I feel in pleasing or offending some revered friend...An echo implies a voice; a voice a speaker. That speaker I love and revere."[78]

While he taught that obedience to our conscience leads "to obedience to the Gospel" he maintained, as did Aquinas, that it is the Christian duty to inform and educate our conscience in order to bring it to maturity and perfection.[79] However, unlike Aquinas, Newman did not accept that conscience was connected to our ability to use reason to work out how to fulfil God's purpose but that conscience is the voice of God.

The idea of conscience as the "voice of God" was further developed by a Protestant theologian Friedrich Schleiermacher (1768–1834) in 1830.[80] However, in more recent years, few theologians would accept the claim that conscience is an infallible voice of God. Many agree with the view that conscience needs to be informed and developed before it can be relied upon as setting acceptable moral standards. The Anglican theologian Joseph Fletcher (1905–1991) believed that there was no such thing as conscience in terms of the voice of God. In *Situation Ethics* he comments: "Situation ethics is interested in conscience as a function not as a faculty. It takes conscience into account only when it is working, practicing and deciding."[81] Therefore he believed that conscience was no more than the thinking process involved in making moral decisions and agreed that "Thomas Aquinas' description is the best: the reason making moral judgments."[82]

The Catholic Church combine both ideas: first, that conscience is the voice of God and second, that it does need to be developed or educated if it is to be a sufficient moral guide. The *Catechism of the Catholic Church* states:

> "Deep within his conscience man discovers a law which he has not laid upon himself but which he must obey...For man has in his heart a law inscribed by God...His conscience is man's most secret core and his sanctuary. There he is alone with God whose voice echoes in his depths."[83]

The *Catechism of the Catholic Church* continues: "Conscience must be informed and moral judgement enlightened."[84]

TASK

Using a spider diagram, summarise the different views of conscience held by Christian theologians.

Secular views of conscience

For many philosophers, conscience and religion are inseparable. For example, in his novel *The Brothers Karamazov*, the Russian philosopher Fyodor Dostoyevsky (1821–1881) claimed: "conscience without God is a horror, it may lose its way to the point of utter immorality."[85] Dostoyevsky believed that without the influence of God in their lives, humans would participate in all sorts of immoral behaviour. This view is expressed by one of the characters in his novel, a Russian monk called Zosima who claims: "for if one has not God, then what crime can there be?"[86] This implies that if our conscience is not influenced by religion we will have no concept of the difference between right and wrong.

However, many people from a secular background believe that proper use of conscience is an important way of ensuring that moral standards are upheld in society. Atheists, for example, do not use scripture or other religious teaching to inform their conscience but still believe that values such as respect for life are very important. Most people, regardless of background or upbringing will value honesty, courage and self control, while few will agree with dishonesty, theft, murder or rape and most people's conscience would prevent them from acting immorally. Secular views on the role of conscience in moral decision making have been developed by Kant.

Kant (1724–1804) believed that we have a moral duty or obligation to do what is right regardless of the consequences. As briefly outlined in chapter 2, Kant believed that in order to fulfil our duty to other people we must follow the categorical and hypothetical imperatives. Kant felt that conscience informed our duty to act morally and to avoid immoral behaviour. Therefore a Kantian conscience "will be one that is sensitive to the fulfilment of duty and the moral law."[87] In *Groundwork to the Metaphysic of Morals*, Kant argued:

"Conscience is not a thing to be acquired, and it is not a duty to acquire it; but every man as a mortal being, has it originally within him. The duty here is only to cultivate our conscience, to quicken our attention to the voice of the internal judge, and to use all means to secure obedience to it."[88]

The Christian and secular view of conscience as an acceptable guide to moral decision making has come under much criticism. There are some difficulties associated with the view that conscience is a universal guide for all people, that it is a guiding voice or set of standards which, to quote Paul, is *"written on our hearts"* (Romans 2:15). For example, those who attacked the twin towers in New York on 11 September 2001 believed that they were doing the will of God and despite the deaths of thousands of people their conscience did not prevent the attacks. It is also argued that conscience can be easily manipulated. For example, many people living in Nazi Germany did not object to the inhumane treatment of many groups of people but instead participated in the brutal treatment of Jewish people, homosexuals and other minority groups.

 ## OTHER ASPECTS OF HUMAN EXPERIENCE

Conscience is supposed to legislate how we behave, yet it has not prevented suffering being inflicted on innocent people. Anscombe, the philosopher responsible for the revival of virtue ethics, commented: "a man's conscience may tell him to do the vilest things."[89] Read the following example from Peter Vardy's *The Puzzle of Evil* and critically reflect on the idea that conscience is not a good starting point for moral decision making.

"In the second world war, the SS guards at Belsen and Treblinka used to save gas by throwing babies and young children into the gas chambers over the heads of the adults before shutting the doors. They would throw children under five, alive, into the bottom of the lime pits before throwing the dead bodies of those who had been gassed down on top of them."[90]

Freud (1856–1939) disagreed with the idea that conscience was an acceptable guide to morality. He believed that conscience was linked to how we were socially conditioned, including how we were brought up by our parents. Therefore he believed that our conscience was simply a product of our upbringing. For Freud, conscience is linked to our super-ego, the part of our mind which stores information from experiences throughout our lives. To Freud, the super-ego acts like a "moral policeman",[91] imposing rules on how we behave. He believed that we must rid ourselves of this storage of guilt because "it does not qualify to be taken seriously in an ethical discussion, since it is no more than an expression of the wishes of one's parents or other significant adults."[92] Bowie explains Freud's views of conscience by using this example: "I may feel guilty about going shopping on a Sunday, because it was instilled in me as a child that this was wrong, although I no longer believe that it's wrong."[93] Freud's view of conscience helps our understanding of the differences in moral values that individuals have. However, he totally undermines the religious view that conscience is a suitable guide to morality.

Nietzsche (1844–1900) believed that there was no God and he famously declared in many of his works that "God is dead."[94] Nietzsche attacked the importance of religious values, claiming that they belonged to societies in the past, which are different to our societies today. In addition, he claimed that these religious values, such as those advanced by Jesus, promoted a form of slave morality, a life of service to others, compassion and sacrifice. He encouraged society to abandon such values and set a new code of morality, which would set standards of what he referred to as master morality. These standards would turn those willing to accept them into the "superman" and ultimately advance humanity by focusing on achieving goals on earth rather than in some non-existent heavenly realm.[95] Nietzsche argued that if we live according to the dictates of our conscience then we are living our lives as slaves to this imposed religious morality. He claimed: "The bite of conscience is indecent"[96] and rather than follow our conscience we must, according to Nietzsche: "overcome...the mark of 'slave morality' and learn to dominate others."[97]

Despite the views of Freud and Nietzsche, for many people in society from both Christian or secular backgrounds, the use of our conscience is an acceptable way of making moral decisions, especially if it has been well informed and educated.

 PRACTICE ESSAY TITLES

Question adapted from CCEA Summer 2006 A2 6

(a) Analyse and discuss the debate about the nature of conscience. (30)

Your response may refer to the following points:
- Definition of conscience.
- Link between conscience and religious belief.
- Compare and contrast the various theories on conscience, for example Aquinas, Butler, Newman, Fletcher, Kant, Freud and Nietzsche.

Question from CCEA Summer 2006 A26

(b) Critically evaluate the view that each person should always follow his/her conscience. (20)

Your response may refer to the following points:
- Conscience can be a good starting point for morality and is used today, for example, conscientious objectors.
- There are problems with using conscience as a guide to morality. It can be manipulated, it is not always well informed and it can create conflict between personal morality and church teaching.

ETHICAL RELATIVISM AND THE RELIGIOUS RESPONSE

Ethical relativism

Ethical relativism refers to an approach to ethics which is not based on absolute or universal laws. Relativism is concerned with the concept that morality is not fixed but will vary for different people and cultures at different times. A relativist approach to morality can help explain why so many people in society today have different standards or values regarding morality. As Tyler and Reid comment, for the relativist "there are no absolute standards, but 'right' is relative to society or the individual."[98]

In society today many people follow a relativist approach to morality and this is evident when people do not always agree on what is considered morally acceptable and what is not. For example, many people do not want the legalisation of abortion in Northern Ireland while for a number of reasons others would prefer to have abortion legalised. The idea that right and wrong can differ between individuals is referred to as **individual relativism.** Those who accept this approach to morality agree that morality is not based on absolute rules or standards but on the values held by an individual who has the autonomy to make his or her own moral decisions.

Cultural relativism is another form of relativism which explains that different cultures, both in the past and in the present have different moral beliefs and standards. For example, in ancient Rome it was considered morally acceptable for gladiators to slaughter wild animals and people (among whom were Christians), as a form of entertainment to an audience of thousands of spectators. Even today, some societies practice traditions that other cultures deplore, such as female circumcision in African cultures. Regardless of how we feel about the customs of different cultures, the cultural relativist is not permitted to pass judgment or condemn practices which are morally acceptable to another culture. Tyler and Reid comment: "no individual culture can claim that their value judgements are better than others, only different."[99]

Relativism appears to promote tolerance and acceptance of different practices and this is considered to be the most important strength that ethical relativism has to offer. Mackie (1917–1981) maintained the relativist view that there are no moral absolutes or objective values and that people live in different ways because they follow different sets of moral values.[100] While the moral values of individuals and cultures do differ, this does not imply that some cultures are totally antinomian or void of any moral standards. It is therefore important to respect diversity within societies and cultures. Rachels (1941–2003) argued that all societies have very similar or common values which are necessary for society to function properly and for all people to live in harmony with each other. For example, all societies tend to care for their children, to promote the importance of telling the truth and promote respect for innocent human life.[101] Jenkins develops the concept of common moral standards and notes that the Golden Rule, given by Jesus during his Sermon on the Mount: *"So in everything, do to others what you would have them do to you"* (Matthew 7:12), is a universal standard of behaviour in many societies and can be found in the religious writings of Jews, Muslims and Buddhists.[102]

Utilitarianism, situation ethics and emotivism are all ethical theories which are relativist. They are not based on rules but on the consequences of our actions and are therefore teleological theories. Relativism accepts and respects the autonomy of individuals and is a flexible approach to morality because it does not limit autonomy by imposing rules which can never be broken. It promotes an approach to ethics which does not focus on the morality of our actions. Therefore an action such as abortion is not seen as intrinsically evil; instead it can be regarded as right or wrong depending on the circumstances.

Utilitarianism supports a relativist approach to morality. When faced with a moral choice a person must decide which course of action will promote the greatest amount of happiness. For example, a utilitarian will not claim that telling lies is intrinsically wrong but they may decide that while in some cases it is unacceptable to lie, in others lying is acceptable if it creates the greatest amount of happiness.

Situation ethics promotes a relativist approach to morality. The situationist will never claim that our actions are intrinsically right or wrong as they are only concerned with consequences of our actions. In *Situation Ethics* Fletcher argues: "The situationist avoids words like 'never' and 'perfect' and 'always' and 'complete' as he avoids the plague, as he avoids 'absolutely.'"[103]

However a criticism of both relativist approaches is that they are based on an absolute principle – happiness in the case of utilitarianism and love in the case of situation ethics. Fletcher comments: "Christian situation ethics has only one norm or principle or law that is binding and unexceptionable, always good and right regardless of circumstances. That is love."[104]

Emotivism is an individualistic approach to morality, which is based on our inner feelings or personal values and not rules. This approach to morality directs us to act in a way that we feel is personally acceptable and avoid acting in a way we disagree with. According to this approach to ethics, morality is subjective, not objective, therefore morality is based on a person's own values and opinions as opposed to rules which are imposed from outside. Following this approach to morality, two people in the same situation can come to different conclusions about what they feel is the right thing to do and neither actions can be judged as being right or wrong by anyone else because "emotivism is a theory that suggests that all moral views are of equal value."[105]

Despite some advantages, there are a number of criticisms of ethical relativism. There are difficulties associated with the view held by cultural relativists that we cannot judge the practices of any culture or society. This is not a realistic principle, especially when one considers the murdering of Jews, homosexuals and the disabled in Nazi Germany. Therefore a weakness of cultural relativism is that it "reduces the meaning of good to that which is socially approved. If a culture endorses wife-beating, then wife-beating is morally acceptable."[106]

Another criticism of a relativist approach to morality is that the rights of minority groups are neither protected nor respected. During the Rwandan genocide in 1994, approximately 800,000 Tutsis were murdered by Hutu militia. Cultural relativists claim that we should not judge the practices of other cultures. However, very few people in our society today would accept or allow such atrocities to take place. Cultural relativism does not protect the rights of all people and therefore obedience to absolute guidelines such as the Universal Declaration of Human Rights (UDHR) is essential in order to protect the rights of all people, and in particular minority groups.

⊚ OTHER ASPECTS OF HUMAN EXPERIENCE

The Ku Klux Klan is a group of white supremacists in America who were active between 1866 and 1869 and re-emerged in 1915. Using the internet investigate the racist activities the group were responsible for, which included racist attacks and lynchings. Use your findings to critically reflect on the idea that according to cultural relativism we should not judge but accept the practices of all cultures and societies.

While some Christians do accept relativism in the form of situation ethics, many Christians are opposed to cultural and individual relativism because of the need for an objective approach to morality. Rather than solve ethical issues by considering how they feel or the values promoted by their community they should be influenced by external factors such as teaching from scripture. For example, according to Genesis 1:27, human life is created in the image of God and Christians therefore maintain that all human life is sacred and this principle must be applied consistently to all ethical issues. Some Christians fear that relativism may lead to nihilism, which is a belief in nothing, no God or objective moral standards. For this reason they reject relativism because God given rules must be respected.

Moral absolutism

Moral absolutism is an approach to ethics dependent on the importance of rules which can never be broken under any circumstances. The rules govern our actions and because our actions are intrinsically good or bad, the rules are absolute regardless of the consequences. The rules are so important that individuals cannot be allowed the freedom to make an exception to the rule. The absolute rules are also considered to be universal and therefore apply to all people at all times.

While a relativist may feel that there are some situations in which abortion is morally acceptable, an absolutist who maintains that all human life is sacred will never allow abortion regardless of the consequences. Absolutist theories include natural law and Kantian ethics. These theories judge our actions on whether or not they follow moral rules and the theories are therefore associated with deontological ethics. As Bowie comments: "Deontologists maintain that acts are right or wrong in themselves (they are intrinsically right or wrong) because of some absolute law perhaps laid down by God, or because they go against some duty or obligation."[107]

Kantian ethics is a deontological approach to morality based on obedience to the categorical imperative, which states that we must "act only according to that maxim by which you can at the same time will that it should become a universal law."[108] Thompson argues that Kant, through developing the categorical imperative, has made an attempt at "getting beneath the cultural diversity and touching some absolute moral standard."[109] For Kant, this absolute moral standard involved acting in a way that is acceptable for everyone to act in and not behaving in ways which cannot be universalised.

Natural law is a deontological theory which insists that morality is based on keeping rules which ensure that we follow God's plan for us. Aquinas stated: "natural law is the same for all"[110] and the rules must be applied universally, by all people, at all times. Following the natural law approach, the Roman Catholic Church maintains an absolutist position and totally opposes ethical relativism. In 1998, Pope John Paul II commented: "Today's ethical relativism, obscuring as it does moral values, leads to modes of behaviour which destroy the dignity of the person."[111] The Catholic view is that Christians must follow an objective approach to morality and have definitive moral standards to inform behaviour. Following this absolutist position the Catholic Church continues to prohibit divorce, homosexuality and the use of contraceptives.

In practical terms absolutism is not an acceptable approach to morality for many people in society. At times rules need to be broken for the greater good and many other Christian denominations such as Methodists, Presbyterians and members of the Church of Ireland permit divorce and the use of contraception. They argue that moral rules are important but in some cases they take second place. To illustrate the point take an example from everyday life. Everyone knows that it is imperative that we respect the rule not to drive through traffic lights when they are red. However, in some circumstances emergency services have to ignore this rule for the greater good. For many Christians the same applies to morality. There are rules which are important but on some occasions it is acceptable to break them. Many Christian denominations agree that a victim of rape, who has become pregnant with the rapist's child, should have the autonomy to have an abortion if she feels that it may assist her in trying to come to terms with what has happened.

 PRACTICE ESSAY TITLES

Question adapted from CCEA Summer 2005 A2 6

(a) Analyse and discuss the challenge of ethical relativism for the Christian. (30)

Your response may refer to the following points:
- Define ethical relativism and outline the key characteristics
- Refer to the challenges that it brings for Christians
  - The rejection of moral absolutes and rules from biblical teaching
  - The need for objectivity, where we are not influenced by personal feelings or opinions in our approach to ethical issues
  - The problems associated with cultural relativism
- Possible advantages that ethical relativism brings to Christians such as flexibility in the cases of abortion and contraception
- Links between ethical relativism and situation ethics

Question adapted from CCEA Summer 2008 A2 6

(b) Critically evaluate the claim that morality is not just a matter of personal preference. (20)

Your response may refer to the following points:

- Explore the view, with reference to egoism and emotivism, that personal preference is an important aspect of moral decision making and is central to the issue of autonomy
- Explore the contrasting view that is about much more than personal preference, that rules should be valued, that we should be faithful to religious teaching and put others before ourselves (altruism) when making moral decisions
- Use examples to develop both sides of the argument

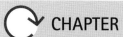 **CHAPTER SUMMARY**

Virtue ethics

- The definition of virtue ethics as an approach to ethics which is not concerned with how we act but is concerned with the character of the people and the qualities they must develop
- The development of virtue ethics by Aristotle, with specific reference to the moral and intellectual virtues
- The views of modern philosophers who have promoted virtue ethics as the most effective approach to morality: Anscombe, Foot and MacIntyre
- Application of virtue ethics to the issue of abortion
- An evaluation of virtue ethics, its strengths and weaknesses, with specific reference to the views of Louden

Conscience and moral duty

- The definition of conscience as our inner sense of right and wrong
- New Testament teaching on conscience, including Paul's idea that conscience is a universal guide for moral living
- Early Christian views on conscience including the views of Jerome and Augustine
- The development of Christian views on conscience including the views of Aquinas, Butler and Newman
- The views of Christian denominations today on the issue of conscience
- Secular views on conscience with specific reference to the views of Kant and Freud

Ethical relativism and the religious response

- The definition of ethical relativism as an approach to morality which will vary for different people at different times
- The distinction between individual relativism and cultural relativism
- Utilitarianism, situation ethics and emotivism are associated with ethical relativism
- An evaluation of the relativist approach to morality with specific reference to Christian views
- An evaluation of moral absolutism as an alternative to relativism.

Endnotes

1 Schneewind, J, 'The Misfortunes of Virtue', in Crisp, R & Slote, M, (Ed), *Virtue Ethics,* Oxford University Press, Oxford, 1997, p180

2 Bowie, R, *Ethical Studies*, Nelson Thornes, Cheltenham, 2004, p112

3 Schneewind, *op cit*, in Crisp & Slote, *op cit*, p179

4 Vardy, P & Grosch, P, *Puzzle of Ethics*, Harper Collins, London, 1999, p19

5 Aristotle, *Nicomachean Ethics.* Quote taken from Vardy & Grosch, *op cit*, p21

6 *ibid*, p22

7 Tyler, S & Reid, G, *Religious Studies*, Philip Allan Updates, Oxfordshire, 2002, p133

8 Aristotle, *op cit.* Quote taken from Vardy & Grosch, *op cit*, p22

9 *ibid*, p105

10 Vardy & Grosch, *op cit*, p29

11 *ibid*, p27

12 Aristotle, *op cit.* Quote taken from Vardy & Grosch, *op cit*, p30

13 Vardy & Grosch, *op cit*, p27–29

14 *ibid*, p27

15 *ibid*, p28

16 *ibid*, p29

17 Tyler & Reid, *op cit*, p133

18 Thompson, M, *An Introduction to Philosophy and Ethics*, Hodder and Stoughton, London, 2003, p157

19 Aristotle, *op cit.* Quote taken from Vardy & Grosch, *op cit*, p31

20 Vardy & Grosch, *op cit*, p200

21 *ibid*, p33

22 Tyler & Reid, *ibid*, p134

23 Jenkins, J, *Ethics and Religion – Second Edition*, Heinemann, Oxford, 2003, p112

24 *ibid*, p112

25 *ibid*, p112

26 Vardy, & Grosch, *op cit*, p101

27 Schneewind, *op cit*, in Crisp & Slote, *op cit*, p181

28 Crisp & Slote, *op cit*, p1

29 Vardy, & Grosch, *op cit*, p109

30 *ibid*, p115

31 Anscombe, GEM, 'Modern Moral Philosophy', in Crisp & Slote, *op cit*, p26

32 Anscombe, *op cit*, in Crisp & Slote, *op cit*, p30

33 Vardy, & Grosch, *op cit*, p112

34 Clarke, P, *Examining Philosophy and Ethics*, Nelson Thornes, Cheltenham, 2002, p 138

35 Thompson, *An Introduction to Philosophy and Ethics*, *op cit*, p159

36 Crisp & Slote, *op cit*, p2

37 Hursthouse, R, 'Virtue Theory and Abortion', in Crisp & Slote, *op cit*, p219

38 Foot, P, 'Virtues and Vices', in Crisp & Slote, *op cit*, p163

39 Vardy, & Grosch, *op cit*, p118

40 Foot, *op cit*, in Crisp & Slote, *op cit*, p165

41 Vardy, & Grosch, *op cit*, p117

42 Foot, *op cit*, in Crisp & Slote, *op cit*, p164–165

43 *ibid*, p177

44 Vardy, & Grosch, *op cit*, p94

45 *ibid*, p103

46 *ibid*, p103

47 *ibid*, p103–104

48 McMylor, P, *Alasdair MacIntyre Critic of Modernity*, Routledge, Oxford, 1994, p129

49 Jenkins, *op cit*, p114

50 MacIntyre, A, 'The Nature of the Virtues', in Crisp & Slote, *op cit*, p128

51 Bowie, *op cit*, p115

52 Vardy, & Grosch, *op cit*, p99

53 MacIntyre, *op cit*, p129

54 *ibid*, p121

55 Hursthouse, *op cit*, in Crisp & Slote, Ed, *op cit*, p228

56 *ibid*, p230–236

57 *ibid*, p234

58 Bowie, *op cit*, p116

59 Louden, R, 'On Some Vices Of Virtue Ethics', in Crisp & Slote, *op cit*, 1997, p203

60 McDowell, J, 'Virtue and Reason', in Crisp & Slote, *op cit*, p162

61 Bowie, *op cit*, p116

62 Louden, *op cit,* Crisp & Slote, *op cit*, 1997, p205

63 *ibid*, p205–208

64 *ibid*, p216

65 Vardy, & Grosch, *op cit*, p107

66 'Abortion crisis as doctors refuse to perform surgery', *The Independent on Sunday*, 16 April 2007, www.independant.co.uk, accessed 1 February 2009

67 Jenkins, *op cit*, p56

68 Bowie, *op cit*, p146

69 *ibid*, p146

70 Hogan, L, *Confronting the Truth*, Paulist Press, New Jersey, 2000, p60

71 Bowie, *op cit*, p146

72 Jenkins, *op cit*, p59

73 Aquinas, *Summa Theologica*. Quote taken from Jenkins, *op cit*, p60

73a Bowie, *op cit*, p146

74 Butler, J, *Fifteen Sermons upon Human Nature*. Quote taken from Jenkins, *op cit*, p60

75 *ibid*, p148

76 Clarke, *op cit*, p 113

77 *ibid*, p 115

78 'Pope's Letter on Newman', *Newman Reader*, 18 June 1990, www.newmanreader.org, accessed 25 January 2009

79 *ibid*

80 Schleiermacher, F, *The Christian Faith*. Quote taken from Thompson, M, *Ethical Theory*, Hodder and Stoughton, London, 1999, p125

81 Fletcher, J, *Situation Ethics – The New Morality*, Westminster John Knox Press, Louisville, 1966, p52

82 *ibid*, p53

83 *Catechism of the Catholic Church*, Veritas, Dublin, 1994, 1776

84 *ibid*, 1783

85 Dostoyevsky, F, *The Brothers Karamazov*, Penguin Books, London, 2003, Introduction pxxviii

86 Dostoyevsky, *op cit*, p408

87 Clarke, *ibid*, p114

88 Kant, I, *Groundwork to the Metaphysic of Morals*. Quote taken from Jenkins, *ibid*, p62

89 Anscombe, *op cit*, in Crisp & Slote, *op cit*, p27

90 Vardy, P, *The Puzzle of Evil*, Harper Collins, London, 1992, p74

91 Tyler & Reid, *op cit*, p156

92 Thompson, *An Introduction to Philosophy and Ethics*, *op cit*, p179

93 Bowie, *op cit*, p149

94 Magee, B, *The Story of Philosophy*, Dorling Kindersley, London, 2001, p172

95 Thompson, *Ethical Theory*, *op cit*, p98–99

96 Magee, *op cit*, p175

97 Jenkins, *op cit*, p65

98 Tyler & Reid, *op cit*, p139

99 *ibid*, p139

100 Bowie, *op cit*, p16

101 Jenkins, *op cit*, p35

102 *ibid*, p38

103 Fletcher, *op cit*, p43

104 *ibid*, p30

105 Thompson, *Ethical Theory*, *ibid*, p34

106 Bowie, *op cit*, p18

107 *ibid*, p7

108 Kant, *Groundwork for the Metaphysics of Morals*. Quote taken from Bowie, *op cit*, p58

109 Thompson, *Ethical Theory*, *op cit*, p93

110 Aquinas, *Summa Theologica*. Quote taken from Gill, R, *A Textbook of Christian Ethics*, T & T Clarke, Edinburgh, 2002, p82

111 Pope John Paul II, 'Message To The World Of Culture And Learning', Vatican: Holy See, 2–4 October 1998, www.vatican.va, accessed 31 January 2009

Chapter 7

Human Rights

Chapter overview

This chapter aims to explore the following topics:

- The nature of human rights
- Christian and secular perspectives on human rights
- Human rights and practice with special reference to women and minority groups

THE NATURE OF HUMAN RIGHTS

IN THE CONTEXT OF HUMAN rights, the word 'right' refers to something that all human beings ought to be allowed or ought to have. According to Stott: "Human rights describe the kind of life a human being should be able to expect by virtue of being human, rather than the rights which people may have by virtue of being citizens of a country or having signed a contract."[1]

The origin of the concept of human rights can be dated back to the time of Plato and Aristotle in the fourth century BC. However, while both Plato and Aristotle developed the ideas of justice and equality they did not believe that all people were equal. It is believed that Aristotle was responsible for the principle "treat equals equally and unequals unequally."[2] For example, in ancient Greece, Athenian males treated each other as equals. However, it was inconceivable that a slave or a barbarian could be treated as their equal. According to Vardy and Grosch: "it would have been improper or plain wrong to treat the slave or the 'foreigner' in the same way that one should treat the Athenian"[3].

In the thirteenth century, Aquinas contributed to the issue of human rights through his development of natural law, an ethical theory which was intended to be universal as it applied to all people at all times. A few centuries later, two English philosophers,

Thomas Hobbes (1588–1679) and John Locke (1632–1704), made a significant contribution to the concept of human rights when they applied Aquinas' "concept of natural law to establish some basic and natural rights of man."[4] The term 'natural rights' refers to rights which all humans are entitled to. They are basic rights which can never be denied because they are "accorded to a being by nature."[5]

Hobbes, for example, argued that it was our natural right not to be harmed by another individual and that it was the responsibility of the governing authorities "to protect the natural rights of the people."[6] In *Leviathan* (1651), he argued that in any society the government must have absolute power in order to ensure that society is ordered and that the rights of all people are protected. Hobbes believed that enabling governments to have "absolute power...is the only way to maximise both the liberty and the security of the individuals who make up the society."[7]

In addition to having the right to life, Locke believed that we also had the right to personal freedom, including freedom of speech, freedom to worship and the right to own property.[8] Locke's teaching was very influential and as a result, by the end of the eighteenth century both America and France had guaranteed basic human rights for their citizens. Magee comments: "the men who drew up the Constitution of the United States had Locke consciously in mind while they were doing so, and referred to him by name in their correspondence with one another. He had a similar influence on French thought throughout the eighteenth century."[9] In the American Declaration of Independence (1776) it is affirmed that "all men are created equal" and that they have the right to "life, liberty and the pursuit of happiness."[10] France's declaration from 1779 uses similar language and highlights the importance of "the natural, inalienable and sacred rights of man."[11]

In 1791, Thomas Paine (1737–1809) developed the concept of natural rights in *The Rights of Man*. He wrote: "all men are born equal, and with equal natural rights." He claimed that such rights were absolute and universal: "Every generation is equal in rights to the generation which preceded it, by the same rule that every individual is born equal in rights with his contemporary."[12]

However, the universal view of human rights is contrasted with the view held by cultural relativists, who believe that it is wrong to claim that one set of human rights can be applied to all people at all times. They argue that human rights will vary for different people depending on their social conditions. Therefore, according to cultural relativists, different cultures will have different moral codes and, as outlined in the previous chapter, the cultural relativist will not judge their practices as being right or wrong. To develop this argument, Michael Ignatieff uses the example of the custom of female circumcision, which is morally acceptable in some cultures despite the terrible suffering young girls and women have to endure as a result of this ritual. He comments that in some societies "rituals of sexual initiation, like genital cutting, for example, are linked to an idea of womanly dignity and worth."[13] However, simply because different cultures or societies have different moral codes, this does not mean that there cannot be universally accepted moral standards which give protection to the basic needs of all people. For example, the vast majority of people will agree that it is always wrong to take an innocent human life and if murder is not condemned then our society could become anarchic. As a result, Stott comments: "we cannot succumb to cultural relativism which may allow a nation to escape its human rights commitments because of its claim to have a different culture."[14]

Due to events within the twentieth century such as the two world wars, the concept of cultural relativism has been largely rejected and the issue of universal human rights has come to the fore. Stott comments that the impact of two world wars, which caused the deaths of sixty million people, including the deaths of six million Jews who were exterminated in the concentration camps and gas chambers during World War Two, once again brought the issue of human rights to "the top of the world's agenda."[15]

As a direct result of the suffering experienced by so many millions of people during the wars, the United Nations (UN) was established in 1945 with the support of fifty-one of the world's countries. Support for the UN has grown and there are now 192 member states.[16] The Charter of the United Nations includes the following points:

- All member states are determined "to save succeeding generations from the scourge of war, which twice in our lifetime has brought untold sorrow to mankind."
- All member states are determined "to reaffirm faith in fundamental human rights, in the dignity and worth of the human person, in the equal rights of men and women and of nations large and small."[17]

Three years after the establishment of the United Nations, on 10 December 1948, the Universal Declaration of Human Rights (UDHR) was published. The declaration has been described as "an inspiring, poetic and visionary document"[18] and its principal author was a French jurist, Rene Cassin, who was honoured by being presented with the Nobel Peace Prize in 1968.

The Preamble to the UDHR states that the rights set out within the declaration are intended to be a:

"common standard of achievement for all peoples and all nations, to the end that every individual and every organ of society, keeping this Declaration constantly in mind, shall strive by teaching and education to promote respect for these rights and freedoms and...to secure their universal and effective recognition and observance."[19]

In addition to the Preamble, which sets the tone of the whole declaration, there are thirty further rights or articles. The first section of the UDHR covers political and civil rights, while the second part covers economic, social and cultural rights.

Political and civil rights are rights which naturally belong to an individual as a citizen of the country in which they live. Civil rights can include the right to own property, to equal protection under the law, and freedom from discrimination, while political rights include the right to participate in the establishment or administration of government and the right to vote. Economic, social and cultural rights, according to Amnesty International, are rights which "relate to the conditions necessary to meet basic human needs such as food, shelter, education, health care, and gainful employment. They include the rights to education, adequate housing, food, water, the highest attainable standard of health, the right to work and rights at work, as well as the cultural rights of minorities and indigenous peoples."[20]

The intention of the United Nations was that the standards contained within the Declaration were universal and absolute and that it was the responsibility of the state authorities, who were the signatories to the Declaration, to ensure that all citizens live according to these basic standards. Some of the human rights include:

- Article 1 – All human beings are born free and equal in dignity and rights
- Article 2 – Everyone is entitled to all the rights and freedoms set forth in this Declaration
- Article 3 – The right to life, liberty and security of person
- Article 4 – The right not to be held in slavery
- Article 5 – The right not to be subjected to torture or degrading treatment or punishment
- Article 6 – The right to recognition everywhere as a person before the law
- Article 11 – The right to be presumed innocent until proved guilty
- Article 14 – The right to seek and to enjoy in other countries asylum from persecution
- Article 15 – The right to a nationality
- Article 16 – The right to marry and found a family
- Article 17 – The right to own property
- Article 18 – The right to freedom of thought, conscience and religion
- Article 23 – The right to work and favourable working conditions
- Article 24 – The right to rest and leisure including holiday pay
- Article 25 – The right to a standard of living adequate for the health and well-being of himself and of his family
- Article 26 – The right to education[21]

 TASK

Visit the United Nations Declaration of Human Rights website at:
www.un.org/overview/rights.html

Print a copy of the UDHR and summarise the contents under the headings shown in the table below:

Political and civil rights	Economic, social and cultural rights

Kofi Annan, former United Nations Secretary General, commented that it is imperative for all people to benefit from the human rights outlined in the UDHR. He stated:

> "Human rights are the foundation of human existence...human rights are universal, indivisible and interdependent...Human rights are what make us human. They are the principles by which we create the sacred home for human dignity...It is the universality of human rights that gives them their strength. It endows them with the power to cross any border, climb any wall, defy any force."[22]

In theory the UDHR presents all people and all governments with a guide to acceptable standards of existence which can be applied to all people to ensure that they are treated with dignity and equality. In reality, however, not all people have such an experience of life. Consider article 25, which states that all people have "the right to a standard of living adequate for...health". However, Vardy and Grosch comment: "there is a vast gap between the rhetoric of rights and the reality of their application. For example, 50 percent of the world's population has no access to clean water and decent sanitation; and a child dies from starvation every two seconds."[23]

 OTHER ASPECTS OF HUMAN EXPERIENCE

In 2004, media attention focused on the abuse by British and American soldiers of the human rights of Iraqi prisoners in a prison near Baghdad. Photographs were published showing the prisoners undergoing torture, humiliation and abuse of their Muslim religious customs. It is also claimed that human rights were also denied to those who were held by the American government in Guantanamo Bay in Cuba. Men held there, who have since been released, have claimed that the interrogation methods used there were the equivalent of torture.[24]

The above examples illustrates the idea that human rights bring responsibilities. If society agrees that all people are entitled to basic human rights then it is the moral duty or responsibility of others in society to ensure that the rights of everyone, especially weaker members of society, are respected and protected. In *The Rights of Man*, Thomas Paine declared: "Whatever is my right as a man is also the right of another and it becomes my duty to guarantee as well as to possess."[25]

PRACTICE ESSAY TITLES

Question adapted from CCEA Summer 2004 AS 6

Examine the central themes of the Universal Declaration of Human Rights. (30)

Your response may refer to the following points:

- The origins and development of the Declaration
- The absolutist nature of human rights
- The issue of cultural relativism
- Reference to civil, political, economic, social and cultural rights enshrined by the Declaration
- Key principles which underpin the Declaration (dignity, equality and responsibility)
- Reference to violations of human rights.

CHRISTIAN AND SECULAR PERSPECTIVES ON HUMAN RIGHTS

Christian teaching supports the idea that each and every person is at the very least entitled to the basic human rights set out in the UDHR. For many Christians, the idea that all people have rights can be found in the creation account in Genesis 1:27. It informs Christians that the life of the first humans and subsequently all life is created in the image of God: *"So God created man in his own image, in the image of God he created him; male and female he created them."*

While Thomas Paine was not an orthodox Christian he was "still Christian enough in his outlook to know that the rights of man go back to the creation of man."[26] Paine stated: "Though I mean not to touch upon any sectarian principle of religion, yet it may be worth observing, that the genealogy of Christ is traced to Adam. Why then not trace the rights of man to the creation of man?"[27] It is in Luke's Gospel that the genealogy or ancestry of Jesus is traced back to Adam, the father of all humanity. According to Kodell: "Luke, writing for Gentiles, wants to show from the beginning that Jesus brings salvation for all the children of Adam."[28] So Christians regard human rights as being universal. In addition, Stott claims that three words summarise the teaching of scripture and therefore the Christian approach to the issue of human rights – dignity, equality and responsibility.[29]

Dignity

The word 'dignity' comes from the Latin word *dignus,* which means worthy. Christians believe that all human life has worth or intrinsic value because it is created by God. The idea that all people deserve to be treated with dignity is reflected in scripture through references such as Psalm 139:13–14, which indicates that all life is unique in the eyes of God:

"For you created my inmost being; You knit me together in my mother's womb. I praise you because I am fearfully and wonderfully made."

Job 10:8–12 is also understood by Christians to imply that God is the author of all life and therefore all life is sacrosanct:

"Your hands shaped me and made me…You moulded me like clay…You gave me life and showed me kindness."

If God is the author of life as the quote suggests then it is immoral to treat human life in an undignified way, as unworthy or invaluable. In Matthew's Gospel the parable of the sheep and the goats also highlights this message. The message of the parable is that if we ignore the rights of those in need – the hungry, the thirsty, etc – then we will face punishment because as Jesus says: *"I tell you the truth, whatever you did not do for one of the least of these, you did not do for me"* (Matthew 25:45). Former Archbishop of Canterbury, William Temple (1881–1944), commented: "There can be no Rights of Man except on the basis of faith in God. But if God is real, and all men are his sons, that is the true worth of every one of them."[30]

Equality

Scripture informs Christians that all people are equal. There are numerous references from both the Old and New Testament which clearly promote equality. St Paul's letter to the Galatians (3:28) is one of the most succinct: *"There is neither Jew nor Greek, slave nor free, male nor female, for you are all one in Christ Jesus."* Another reference which promotes equality can be found in the Acts of the Apostles (10:34) when Peter speaks to Cornelius' household and informs them: *"God does not show favouritism but accepts men from every nation who fear him and do what is right."* In Mark 12:14, some Pharisees said to Jesus: *"Teacher, we know you are a man of integrity. You aren't swayed by men, because you pay no attention to who they are"*. According to Stott, this statement tells us that Jesus "neither deferred to the rich and powerful, nor despised the poor and weak, but gave equal respect to all, whatever their social status. We must do the same."[31] The words of Jesus in the Golden Rule (Matthew 7:12) is central to the Christian understanding of human rights: *"So in everything, do to others what you would have them do to you."*

Responsibility

As previously mentioned, Paine felt that rights brought responsibilities. If Christians see or know of someone who is suffering from poverty and who does not have basic economic rights, as outlined in the UDHR, it is the Christian responsibility to take action on their behalf. For example, in Luke's account of the Rich Man and Lazarus, the rich man is punished because he ignored Lazarus the beggar at his gate, whose poverty was so severe that he *"was covered with sores and longing to eat what fell from the rich man's table. Even the dogs came and licked his sores"* (Luke 16:19–21). James 2:1–9 also informs Christians of their responsibility to those who are denied basic human rights. James informs his audience that as *"believers in our glorious Lord Jesus Christ, don't show favouritism."* The Christian attitude to those who have been denied human rights is that they must take responsibility for putting things right because after all they are their *"brother's keeper"* (Genesis 4:9).

 OTHER ASPECTS OF HUMAN EXPERIENCE

Explore how Christians today carry out their responsibility to ensure that all people are treated with equality and dignity.

You may wish to consider the work of the International Justice Mission, which is a human rights agency that secures justice for victims of slavery, sexual exploitation and other forms of violent oppression. Their website is www.ijm.org

The influence of scripture on the motivation behind their work is evident from the following passage from their website:

"In the tradition of abolitionist William Wilberforce and transformational leaders like Mother Theresa and Martin Luther King Jr, IJM's work is founded on the Christian call to justice articulated in the Bible (Isaiah 1:17): *'Seek justice, protect the oppressed, defend the orphan, plead for the widow.'* IJM's staff members are Christians from a variety of traditions who are motivated by this call to seek justice for the oppressed."[32]

History has shown that Christians have not always taken responsibility for the rights of others. Apartheid, which means separateness, became an official policy of the South African government in 1948. Under this policy the majority black population of South Africa was segregated from the white population and was denied the most basic human rights. Consider the following figures from 1978, which highlight the extent of discrimination in South Africa under the apartheid.

	Blacks	Whites
Population	19 million	4.5 million
Land allocation	13%	87%
Share of national income	<20%	75%
Doctors / population	1 / 44,000	1/400
Infant mortality rate	20% (urban areas)	2.7%
	40% (rural areas)	–
Annual expenditure on education per pupil	$45	$696
Teacher/pupil ratio	1/60	1/22

'The History of Apartheid in South Africa', Stanford Computer Service, www.cs-students.stanford.edu/~cale/cs201/apartheid.hits.html, accessed 12 February 2009

As the figures in the table illustrate, the majority black population of South Africa had less land, income and access to health care and education compared to the minority white population. This inequality in South Africa was a direct result of apartheid, a policy which was supported by the Dutch Reformed Church, a Christian Church formed in Holland during the Protestant Reformation. In 1974, in support of apartheid, the church commented: "a political system based on the autogenous or separate development of various population groups can be justified from the Bible."[33] Despite biblical teaching to the contrary, this group of Christians not only supported but also promoted the oppression of black people in South Africa. However, in 1986, the Dutch Reformed Church changed their attitude towards apartheid and claimed:

"Racism is a grievous sin which no person or church should defend or practice... it deprives a human being of his dignity, his obligations and his rights...the attempt to justify such a prescription as derived from the Bible must be recognised as an error and be denounced."[34]

In many countries today it is the human rights of Christians that are infringed. Stott comments that Christians have become "increasingly oppressed in certain parts of the world and are killed each year by governments or mobs because of their faith."[35] Article 18 of the UDHR states: "Everyone has the right to freedom of thought, conscience and religion". However, in China and Somalia the rights of Christians have been violated. In *Issues Facing Christians Today,* Stott gives the following information:

- In China in 2004, one hundred Protestant church leaders were rounded up and arrested for no reason three times within three months.
- In Somalia being a practising Christian "can lead to death"[36] and entire congregations of Christians have been massacred in recent decades.

 PRACTICE ESSAY TITLES

Question adapted from CCEA January 2002 AS 6

Your response may refer to the following points:
- Relevant teaching from scripture which implies that all people must be treated with dignity and equality
- Teaching from scripture which informs Christians of their duty to take responsibility for those in need: *"you are your brother's keeper"*
- Examples of Christians who have defended the rights of others
- Critical reflection – using examples explore the claim that Christians have not always lived according to this responsibility

Secular views on human rights are similar to the Christian view that it is imperative that all life must be respected and protected. The British Humanist Association, for example, claims: "As Humanists we base our morality on the value of each and every human being."[37] Humanists are faithful to the values of dignity and equality enshrined in the UDHR and are "deeply committed to human rights and campaign to promote a culture of respect for human rights."[38]

As briefly outlined in Chapter 2, Kant's ethical theory consists of both the categorical and practical imperative. The practical imperative states: "So act that you treat humanity, both in your own person and in the person of every other human being, never merely as a means, but always at the same time as an end."[39] In this principle, Kant asserts that it is never acceptable to treat a human being as a means to an end, ie it is immoral to exploit another human being in any way, irrespective of race, religious belief or colour. Vardy and Grosch comment that Kant's practical imperative is "embedded"[40] in the Preamble to the United Nations Charter.

However, for other secular philosophers the concept of natural rights is not acceptable and they reject the idea that each and every human is born with certain rights. Bentham referred to the idea that everyone had natural rights as "nonsense on stilts."[41] While many secular philosophers have rejected the concept of natural rights, the concept of human rights is strongly supported by them. Mill reflected the ideas of Hobbes when he commented: "The only purpose for which power can be rightfully exercised over any member of a civilised community, against his own will, is to prevent harm to others."[42]

Alan Gewirth (1912–2004) believed that human rights are moral rights and are not "dependant on something else, for example, upon someone being white, or being European or American."[43] He argued: "the ultimate purpose of the rights is to secure for each person a fundamental moral status."[44] Gewirth is a philosopher who is best known for rejecting the Golden Rule as the supreme approach to morality. He used the example of how a thief might react to the Golden Rule and claimed that if you always do unto others as you would have them do unto you, a thief might say to the judge: "you wouldn't want to go to prison. How can you send me to prison?"[45] His own supreme moral principle or Golden Rule was: "Agents must act in accord with the generic rights of others as well as their own."[46] Therefore, for Gewirth if members of society are to behave morally, the common rights of all people must be taken into consideration at all times.

HUMAN RIGHTS AND PRACTICE WITH SPECIAL REFERENCE TO WOMEN AND MINORITY GROUPS

Women

According to Stott: "for many thousands of years women have not enjoyed their rights and at the outset of the twenty-first century it is still the case that millions of women are abused and oppressed throughout the world".[47] For example, millions of women continue to be abused and oppressed and in many countries they are still "a low priority when it comes to expenditure on education, employment and health care."[48]

The first significant attempt to secure equal rights for women began in 1792 when Mary Wollstonecraft published *A Vindication of the Rights of Women*. In this work, produced around the same time Paine published *The Rights of Man*, she argued that all women have the right to the same opportunities as men.

Wollstonecraft is believed to be the founder of feminism, the movement which aims to achieve equal rights for women in all spheres of life and to ensure that the voice of women is heard. Throughout the century following her publication, both men and women continued to fight for equal rights for women. For example, in 1869, the utilitarian John Stuart Mill produced an essay entitled *The Subjection of Women*, in which he argued for the emancipation of women. Mill stated: "the principle which regulates...the legal subordination of one sex to the other is wrong itself, and now one of the chief hindrances to human improvement...it ought to be replaced by a principle of perfect equality."[49]

Influenced by the work of Wollstonecraft, the Women's Social and Political Union was founded in 1903 by Emmeline Pankhurst and her daughters Christabel and Sylvia. This union became better known as the Suffragette movement and their campaign throughout the early 1900s attempted to achieve the right for all women to vote. This right was not granted in the UK until the Representation of the People Act was passed in 1928. However, by this time Emmeline Pankhurst had died.

Despite the fact that women were given the right to vote in 1928, feminism, the "movement devoted to the elimination of sex-linked injustice",[50] once again grew dramatically during the 1960s and 70s. This was because many women felt that they did not experience equality with men. Feminists felt that rather than experiencing equality in the workplace, society still considered the role of most women to be the traditional role of housework, looking after children and serving their husbands. This attitude reflects the German phrase: "Kinder, Küche und Kirche", which is translated as "children, kitchen and church". This was obviously unacceptable to feminists and according to Stott was "an example of blatant male chauvinism".[51]

This so-called second-wave feminism is considered to have been started by Betty Friedan (1921–2006) with the publication of her book *The Feminine Mystique* in 1963. Her obituary in the *New York Times* stated that this book "ignited the contemporary women's movement in 1963 and as a result permanently transformed the social fabric of the United States and countries around the world."[52] Friedan argued that the problems that women were experiencing were due to the fact that their image had been created by a patriarchal or male dominated society. In *The Feminine Mystique* she wrote: "It is my thesis that the core of the problem for women today is not sexual but a problem of identity."[53] In *The Female Eunuch* (1970), the Australian born feminist Germaine Greer (born 1939) agreed with Friedan that women's identity had been defined by men and as a result they were the "truly oppressed majority."[54]

Third-wave feminism grew in the 1990s in an attempt to address issues that had not been previously considered by the feminist movement. For example, in *The Beauty Myth*, the American feminist Naomi Wolf (born 1962) accepted that in many ways women were now on a par with men but that because of how women are portrayed through the media, issues such as eating disorders and cosmetic surgery were new forms of oppression of women. She wrote: "More women have more money and power and scope and legal recognition than we have ever had before; but in terms of how we feel about ourselves physically, we may actually be worse off than our unliberated grandmothers."[55]

 TASK

Using the views outlined above and your own research, outline and examine the role of modern feminists in their plight for equal rights for women.

While all modern feminists "share in common the desire to liberate and value women from sexism",[56] there is no unified feminist approach. A number of strands of feminism can be identified: liberal feminism, radical feminism, social feminism and Christian feminism.

Liberal feminism

Liberal feminism is the most mainstream form of feminism, with the primary focus on equality for women. Liberal feminists argue that women must have the same opportunities as men in order to allow them to become equals in society. Unlike radical feminists, liberal feminists do not believe that society needs a major overhaul and they would generally agree that laws such as the Equal Pay Act of 1970 and The Sex Discrimination Act of 1975 have improved the status of women in society. To a liberal feminist, there is evidence of significant progress in recent years with increasing numbers of women filling positions previously occupied by men. However, there is still much room for improvement. For example, Stott comments that in 1970 ninety-nine percent of the managers of top American corporations were male, while twenty-five years later, ninety five percent were men. At this rate it would not be until the year 2270 before "women and men are equally likely to be top managers of major corporations."[57]

Radical feminism

Consider the figures outlined above as an example – it will be the year 2270 before women and men are equal in becoming managers in top American corporations.

Many feminists argue that there is the need for dramatic social change in order to achieve genuine equality for women in all aspects of society. Wilcockson comments: "Many argue that liberal feminism only scratches the surface. True feminism needs to be far more revolutionary if real social justice is to be achieved."[58] Radical feminists are considered to be more revolutionary than liberal feminists. They believe that because society is extremely patriarchal or male dominated, this has led to systematic oppression of women. Until this is addressed on all levels, society will remain unjust. They argue that our society has evolved to become androcentric at heart, centred round men and their opinions, and this must change in order for women to achieve true equality with men.

Radical feminists believe that it is important for women to live as nature intended them to live and not as men have decided they should live. For this reason radical feminism is also often referred to as naturalist feminism. This approach to feminism has parallels with Aristotle's view that everything has a *telos* or purpose and in order to achieve *eudaimonia* or true happiness we must do our best to achieve that purpose. Radical feminists argue that if women are to experience true happiness they must try to fulfil their *telos* or natural purpose and not some purpose which is the product of a patriarchal society.

However, radical feminists differ over what they believe to be a woman's natural purpose. Wilcockson reflects on the difficult questions they face such as "how can we define what is 'natural' and how can we know what characteristics are uniquely female?"[59] For example, is motherhood and reproduction the natural purpose of a woman or have men imposed this purpose? Some radical feminists reject the patriarchal concept that a child needs a mother more than a father and the whole idea of a maternal instinct. Some even go so far as claiming that the only way for women to live a worthwhile life is for men and women to maintain separate institutions and relationships. This branch of radical feminism is referred to as separatist feminism and according to Wilcockson, Mary Daly is the "most influential and certainly one of the most outspoken writers of this kind."[60] Daly has been influenced by Nietzsche, who believed that we should abandon religious values, obedience to which promotes slave morality. Instead he argued that we must set up a new code of morality which is not influenced by religion. Daly agrees and claims that we must abandon the old values, which are the result of patriarchal influence. She takes the idea of separation from male influence literally and claims that for a woman "the only satisfactory non-exploitative sexual relationship has to be with other women."[61]

Other radical feminists agree that when men are in control of reproduction, for example contraception and IVF, then women become nothing more than "a breeder or a prostitute."[62] In *The Dialectic of Sex*, the Jewish feminist, Shulamith Firestone, argued that women must "ensure that they own all the processes of reproduction"[63] such as abortion and contraception, so that they can be liberated from reproduction because in her words "pregnancy is barbaric."[64]

Not all radical feminists take such an approach to the issue of reproduction. Some argue that reproduction is what makes women unique and sets them apart from men. Mary O'Brien, for example, argued that motherhood gave women the opportunity for them "to assert their own identity."[65]

Social feminism

Socialist feminism (sometimes known as Marxist feminism) is similar to radical feminism in emphasising that true equality will not be achieved without major overhauls within society, which in this context specifically refers to economic overhauls.

Karl Marx (1818–1883), known as the founder of communism, believed that society was divided between the minority of people who owned the means of production – the middle class (the bourgeoisie) – and those who work for them – the working class (the proletariat) who form the majority of the population. Because the proletariat did not have the finance to take control of their lives they had to depend on the bourgeoisie and eventually they became like slaves, exploited by the bourgeoisie who made money from their labour. Marx's friend and co-author, Friedrich Engels (1820–1895), applied this concept to the issue of women's rights. He believed that women had become like the proletariat but rather than being exploited by the middle class they were exploited by men.

Socialist feminists argue that there are fundamental inequalities built into a capitalist society because power and capital are distributed unevenly. Thus, it is not enough for women to work individually to rise to powerful positions in society; rather, power needs to be redistributed throughout society. They believe that capitalist societies have devalued the contribution women have made to society. They traditionally remained at home as Europe industrialised, while men worked outside the home to earn the money, making what was perceived to be a more positive contribution to the economy. Therefore, the only way in which women can achieve true equality is when society is free from capitalism and accepts socialism, which will promote equal opportunities for all individuals regardless of sex.

Christian feminism

The three approaches to feminism outlined so far are prominently secular in nature. However, for Christians there is a branch of feminism which seeks to advance and understand the equality of men and women from a biblical perspective. In *What's Right with Feminism*, Elaine Storkey attempts to develop a Christian approach to feminism, which aims to "discern how women are to be treated in God's terms and to move our society from being one which debases and devalues them to one in which they have dignity, equality and freedom to be really human."[66]

Biblical teaching can be used to affirm equality between the sexes. In Genesis 1:27 people are informed:

"So God created man in his own image, in the image of God he created him; male and female he created them."

Peter Vardy states that the Hebrew word for 'man' used in the first line of this text is *adam* and the literal translation of this word is not "specifically gendered" because it refers to a human being in the general sense. He believes it is therefore incorrect "to say that 'God created man' – rather, God created human beings."[67] Stott comments on the significance of this reference in how it promotes equality of the sexes: "From the beginning humanity was 'male and female', and men and women were equal beneficiaries both of the divine image and of the earthly rule."[68] He adds that in this text there is no suggestion that either sex is more God-like or more responsible for the conservation of God's creation than the other – both are equal. Stott argues that the second account of creation in Genesis 2, which was written about four hundred years before the creation account in Genesis 1, also promotes equality between the sexes, although it has been misinterpreted. Genesis 2:18–22 states:

> "The LORD God said, 'It is not good for the man to be alone. I will make a helper suitable for him.' Now the LORD God had formed out of the ground all the beasts of the field and all the birds of the air…But for Adam no suitable helper was found. So the LORD God caused the man to fall into a deep sleep; and while he was sleeping, he took one of the man's ribs and closed up the place with flesh. Then the LORD God made a woman from the rib he had taken out of the man, and he brought her to the man."

Vardy again insists that this reference also promotes equality of the sexes because the Hebrew word *adam* used for man in this reference again refers to a human being and not simply to a male member of the species. He claims that the original *adam* in this account of creation was a "non-gendered earth creature" and "males and females were created simultaneously"[69] by God from this non-gendered creature. Therefore this account of creation promotes the idea that males and females are equal. The idea that women have been created as a helper for man is a misinterpretation of the account because while men and women were different they were still equal. Theologians have made other attempts to explain how this account in Genesis 2 promotes equality of the sexes. For example, in 1157 Peter Lombard, before he became Bishop of Paris, wrote what the passage meant for him: "Eve was not taken from the feet of Adam to be his slave, nor from his head to be his lord, but from his side to be his partner."[70]

A possible reason why this event has been misinterpreted and why the majority of the references throughout the remainder of the Old Testament reflect a patriarchal view, is partly because of the Fall, as described in Genesis 3. Vardy comments: "the idea of male supremacy and female obedience is only introduced…as a result of the disorder brought about by sin."[71] As a result of the Fall, when Eve was deceived by the serpent, ate from the tree of knowledge and *"also gave some to her husband"* (Genesis 3:6), the idea of a woman became one of a temptress[72] and consequently it was believed that she had to be dominated by men. This idea of domination is fairly consistent throughout the Old Testament, although there are a few female characters in the Old Testament such as Ruth, Naomi and Esther who are presented as being worthy of admiration.

However, the New Testament promotes a sense of equality between women and men. It appears to be more consistent with the message presented in Genesis than the rest of the Old Testament. Throughout the Gospel narratives Jesus affirmed equality between the sexes. While the Pharisees at the time of Jesus would not have had women disciples, Luke 8:1–3 informs us that Jesus broke "rules of tradition and convention"[73] as he and the twelve apostles were accompanied by a small group of women disciples who *"were helping to support them out of their own means."* The account of the sinful woman anointing the feet of Jesus in Luke 7:36–38 and the ensuing parable is further evidence of Jesus' equal treatment of women. Stott comments that Jesus "was probably the first man to treat this woman with respect; previously men had only used her."[74]

There are numerous other examples of equality between the sexes throughout the four gospels but it is Paul's words in Galatians 3:28 which make the idea of equality very clear: *"There is neither Jew nor Greek, slave nor free, male nor female, for you are all one in Christ Jesus."* However, Paul's teaching elsewhere in the New Testament does not seem to always support equality between the sexes. Consider the following references from some of the Pauline epistles:

- *"For the husband is the head of the wife as Christ is the head of the church, his body, of which he is the Saviour"* (Ephesians 5:23).
- *"Now I want you to realise that the head of every man is Christ, and the head of the woman is man, and the head of Christ is God"* (1 Corinthians 11:3).
- *"Women should remain silent in the churches. They are not allowed to speak, but must be in submission, as the Law says. If they want to inquire about something, they should ask their own husbands at home; for it is disgraceful for a woman to speak in the church"* (1 Corinthians 14:34–35).
- *"I do not permit a woman to teach or to have authority over a man; she must be silent"* (1 Timothy 2:12).

Some Christian feminists reject this teaching from Saint Paul and argue that because it promotes the idea of male headship it cannot be harmonised with the teaching of equality between the sexes promoted by the account of creation in Genesis and the words and deeds of Jesus in the Gospels. They claim that Paul is simply mistaken or that his teaching is culture bound and although it may have been relevant 2,000 years ago, it is no longer relevant today. This is consistent with other aspects of his teaching, for example, in some of his letters he discusses the topic of slavery without ever condemning it. Elisabeth Schussler Fiorenza (born 1938) is a feminist theologian and a professor at Harvard Divinity School. She believes that Paul's teaching, which suggests a male prejudice or disrespect for the rights of women, reflects a move away from Jesus' message of equality for women, initiated by the male dominated leadership of the early church. In her book, *In Memory of Her*, she argues that within the New Testament there is evidence of conflict between those who followed Jesus' message of equality for men and women and those who had "a male-dominated view of the young Christian church."[75]

However, Stott comments that we must not reject Paul's teaching on this issue and what he has said as outlined in the above references can be reconciled with equality for women. He states: "The husband's headship of his wife…is a liberating mix of care and responsibility rather than control and authority". He adds that Paul's teaching should be understood as meaning that the husband's role is not one of "domination and decision-making" but instead is one of "service and nurture."[76]

The debate concerning the role of women in the church is still pertinent today. Many Christian feminists argue that they would feel that women were truly equal to men if they were permitted to hold positions of responsibility in the Church equal to those held by men. Currently Anglicans, Presbyterians and Methodists allow women ministers, although there have been several controversies surrounding this. For example, in December 2007 a Presbyterian minister in Portadown, Stafford Carson, refused to share a pulpit with a female minister and is reported to have said: "I have difficulties of conscience with the ordination of women, based on the Letters of Saint Paul in the New Testament."[77]

While the ordination of women has caused some divisions in opinion among some Christian denominations, the Roman Catholic Church does not permit the ordination of women to the priesthood at all. The Catholic Church argues that the priest must represent Christ, who was male. They also argue that Jesus appointed twelve apostles who were male and therefore priests must be male. In 1998, Pope John Paul II said: "The Church's teaching that only men may be ordained to the ministerial priesthood is an expression of fidelity to the witness of the New Testament and the constant tradition of the Church." However, he added: "The fact that Jesus himself chose and commissioned men for certain specific tasks did not in any way diminish the human dignity of women…The New Testament makes it clear that women played a vital part in the early Church."[78]

Despite Pope John Paul II's guidance, many Catholics believe that this teaching is urgently in need of reform. They argue that the New Testament not only shows that women played a vital role in the Church but that the New Testament supports the idea of women having equality with men in terms of their roles as leaders in the early Church. Consider the following references:

- It was to women that Jesus first appeared and entrusted the good news of his resurrection (Matthew 28:8–10).
- On the day of Pentecost, as described in Acts of the Apostles 2:17–18, Peter quotes the prophet Joel, who said: "*in the last days…your sons and daughters will prophesy…on my servants, both men and women, I will pour out my spirit.*"
- In Acts 18:3, Paul is reported to have stayed with Aquila and his wife Priscilla, who he refers to in Romans 16:3 as "*my fellow workers in Christ Jesus.*"
- Acts 21: refers to Philip the evangelist who had "*four unmarried daughters who prophesied.*"
- In Romans 16:1, Paul refers to "*our sister Phoebe, a servant of the church in Cenchrea*". However, the word 'servant' can also be translated as a deaconess which implies that she had some position of authority in the early Church.

- In Romans 16:7, Paul also refers to *"Andronicus and Junias, my relatives who have been in prison with me. They are outstanding among the apostles, and they were in Christ before I was."* Stott comments that from the time of all the early Church Fathers it was accepted that Junias was a woman who was more than likely an important missionary worker in the early church.[79]

Many argue that the above references present a strong case for the inclusion of women as ordained priests in the Catholic Church today. Some people argue that Jesus' twelve apostles were all men and if he really wanted women priests he would have had female apostles. However, others reason that he did not have female apostles simply because of the social restrictions at that time. Jewish men would not have listened to women sent to preach the good news to them. Stott concludes that all Christian denominations should permit women ministers because "no biblical principle is infringed" and that the Christian faith would be "enriched by their service."[80]

Rosemary Radford Ruether (born 1936) is an advocate of women's ordination in the Catholic Church. She is a member of Women's Ordination Conference's National Advisory Committee, a group that campaigns for the ordination of women as priests, deacons and bishops into the Catholic Church. In her book, *Sexism and God Talk* (1983), she claims: "women's experience…has been almost entirely shut out of theological reflection in the past" and that feminist theology is "a critical force, exposing classical theology…as based on male experience rather than on universal human experience."[81]

 TASK

Class debate:

"All Christian denominations must accept women as having an equal role to men in all aspects of their church."

Women's rights abused

The human rights of women were violated under the rule of the Taliban, who were a group of Muslims belonging to an ethnic group, the Pashtuns, who ruled Afghanistan between 1996 and 2001. The Taliban enforced the strictest form of Sharia or Islamic religious law and as a result women and girls living under this regime suffered great oppression. According to the Human Rights Watch website: "The Taliban regime succeeded in virtually erasing women from public life".[82] Women were denied rights to work, education and a decent quality of life in general.

For example, Article 23 of the UDHR states that all people have the right to work but in 1996 the Taliban declared that all women should be banned from employment. Educated women have suffered under the regime, who "before the Taliban took power, accounted for 70 percent of all teachers, about 50 percent of civil servants, and 40 percent of medical doctors in the country."[83]

Article 26 of the UDHR states that all people have the right to an education. However, for women who lived under Taliban rule in Afghanistan this right was also violated as girls over eight years old were not permitted to be educated. As a consequence of this policy "the rate of illiteracy among girls in Afghanistan is now over 90 percent."[84] Under Taliban rule in Afghanistan some women organised underground schools. However, if they were caught they faced severe punishments including the possibility of execution for breaking Taliban law.

Article 3 of the UDHR states that all people have the right to "life, liberty and security of person", yet for women under Taliban rule there was no experience of this basic human right. For example, according to the Human Rights Watch:

"Taliban decrees have greatly restricted women's movement, behaviour, and dress, and in fact, virtually all aspects of their lives. In public, women are required under threat of severe punishment to wear the chadari [a head to toe garment that obscures their features, similar to a burqa], and to be accompanied by a close male relative at all times. Violations of the dress code, in particular, can result in public beatings and lashing by the Religious Police, who wield leather batons reinforced with metal studs."[85]

 TASK

Investigate other ways in which the rights of women were abused under Taliban rule in Afghanistan or alternatively investigate how the rights of women are violated in other areas of the world today.

Minority groups

A minority group is a group of people who can be identified by ethnicity, race, religion or gender and whose population is smaller than the controlling majority group in a society. The unfortunate reality for many minority groups throughout the world today is that violations of basic human rights are a daily occurrence. We will consider the following minority groups and how their human rights are violated:

1. Members of the Bahá'í faith in Iran
2. Members of ethnic minority groups in the UK and Ireland

The Bahá'í faith

An Iranian nobleman called Bahá'u'lláh (1817–1892) founded the Bahá'í faith in 1844. Bahá'ís believe that he was the most recent prophet or messenger of God (others have included Moses, Jesus and Muhammad). The Bahá'í faith is a rapidly growing religion "with five million followers in 235 countries and territories throughout the world. There are around 6,000 Bahá'ís in the UK."[86]

In Iran, the majority of the population are Muslims with a minority belonging to the Bahá'í faith. According to one source, of the 69 million Iranians, ninety-nine percent are Muslims and the other one percent are either Jewish, Christian or Bahá'í.[87] The Bahá'í faith promotes peace and the idea that an equal standard of human rights should apply to all people. In Iran, however, the human rights of members of the Bahá'í faith are violated in a number of ways.

Article 3 of the UDHR states: "Everyone has a right to life, liberty and the security of person". However, this right is not experienced by members of the Bahá'í faith in Iran. For example, many families had to flee Iran in 1979 because the country was unsafe for them in the aftermath of the Islamic revolution.[88] Many members of the Bahá'í faith who remained in Iran were executed.[89]

Article 18 of the UDHR states: "Everyone has the right to freedom of thought, conscience and religion", yet members of the Bahá'í faith in Iran do not experience this right. The homes of members of the Bahá'í community are raided, materials related to their faith are destroyed and the leaders of the faith are arrested and imprisoned without any reason other than their faith. In 2006, Dhabihullah Mahrami, a Bahá'í prisoner of conscience who had been detained for ten years solely on account of his faith, died in an Iranian prison.[90]

Article 26 states: "Everyone has the right to education", yet in September 2007, Bahá'í students in Iran reported to Human Rights Watch that Iranian authorities denied 800 of them access to their National Entrance Examination scores in order to prevent them from gaining admission to Iran's universities[91] and therefore refusing them entry into third level education.

The Bahá'í faith continues to face great difficulties in Iran. The Human Rights Watch report for 2008 states that the government in Iran has continued to deny the "Bahá'í community permission to worship publicly or pursue religious activities." For example, on 14 May 2008 "security forces arrested six leading Bahá'í adherents and members of the Bahá'í national coordination group, without informing them of the charges against them, and sent them to Evin prison."[92]

Ethnic minorities

In the UK, members of ethnic minorities also experience human rights abuses. The term 'ethnic minority' refers to a group of people living in a country and who have different race or cultural traditions from the majority of the population. The UDHR asserts: "All human beings are born free and equal in dignity and rights. They are endowed with reason and conscience and should act towards one another in a spirit of brotherhood". However, this spirit of brotherhood is not reflected towards ethnic minorities in many parts of the UK today. Stott comments: "Too many people in Britain have a tendency towards xenophobia",[93] which is a hatred or fear of foreigners or people who are different from the majority population.

In 1993, the racist murder of Stephen Lawrence in London prompted an inquiry into his death because no one had been convicted of his murder and "the unprofessional manner in which the tragedy was handled by the police."[94] The inquiry began in 1997 and was chaired by Sir William Macpherson. The resultant Macpherson report, published in 1999, declared that "institutional racism"[95] within the police force had prevented a proper investigation into the teenager's death.

Article 7 of the UDHR states: "All are equal before the law and are entitled without any discrimination to equal protection of the law." However, this human right was not experienced by either the Lawrence family or many other people from ethnic minorities in the UK. For example, Stott comments that in 2001/2002 "black people were eight times more likely to be stopped and searched [by police] than white people."[96] It is claimed that this institutional racism not only exists in the police force and criminal justice system but also in employment. Stott comments that racism was widespread throughout British society "including health care, housing and social security as well as the private sector. Unemployment…is considerably higher among ethnic minority communities".[97] This is in direct violation of one of the economic rights presented in article 23 of the UDHR, which states: "Everyone has the right to work, to free choice of employment, to just and favourable conditions of work and to protection against unemployment."

Related to the issue of employment in the UK and Ireland is the role of migrant workers in the economy. In 2006, *The Guardian* reported: "Racially motivated attacks, including pipe bombs, bricks hurled through windows and assaults, have risen sharply in Northern Ireland, according to the latest police figures." The article continues:

"Migrant workers, mainly those from new EU states working in meat-packing and food-processing businesses, are being targeted in the latest wave of attacks. Many east Europeans have been driven from their lodgings. In the most recent attack a Polish man suffered multiple fractures to his skull and face after being attacked."[98] This is a further violation of human rights, because Article 13 states: "Everyone has the right to freedom of movement and residence within the borders of each State."

It is feared that migrants are taking jobs from the indigenous population. However, according to Stott the reality of the situation is that they are "filling gaps in the labour market" and are actually contributing to "positive effects on the societies and economies of the host countries."[99]

A further issue related to this topic is the issue of asylum seekers. Asylum seekers are people who seek protection in a host country from persecution in their own country. They have to make an application for asylum and once they receive a positive decision on this they are referred to as a refugee. Article 14 of the UDHR states: "Everyone has the right to seek and to enjoy in other countries asylum from persecution". However, Stott comments: "too many asylum seekers are living on the streets, with little or no financial support. Even when they do have housing, one in five of the places where they live is unfit for human habitation…some have even been killed in racist attacks."[100] Stott claims that the British government has not upheld and respected Article 14 of the UDHR by introducing tough measures in order to prevent asylum seekers entering Britain or accessing the British benefit system.[101]

According to Peter Singer this is morally unacceptable. He argues: "affluent nations should be taking far, far more refugees than they are taking today."[102] This is so important because the majority of the world's refugees today are receiving refuge in the poor less developed countries of the world, putting additional strain on their limited resources. Singer claims: "more than 12 million refugees are in the less developed countries of Africa, Asia and Latin America."[103]

Christian denominations in Northern Ireland follow the teaching of Jesus and argue that we must accept all people into the country. For example, the Methodist Church in Ireland states that they urge "all Methodist people to be open to the diversity and enrichment that can come from people of different cultures, including those who have come to this island as refugees and asylum seekers. We deplore all forms of racism...we encourage local communities to welcome strangers to share in the life of this island."[104]

 TASK

Visit the Human Rights Watch website (www.hrw.org) and explore ways in which the rights of other minority groups are violated throughout the world today.
Students could work in groups, with each group investigating how the rights of a specific minority group are violated. Each group could present their findings to the rest of the class in the form of a PowerPoint presentation.

 OTHER ASPECTS OF HUMAN EXPERIENCE

The rights of children are violated in many countries throughout the world today. Consider the following example from Vardy and Grosch:

"In July 1993 a roving death squad made up of off-duty and retired policemen opened fire on a group of street children who were sleeping rough near a church in Rio de Janeiro, Brazil. Seven children aged between eight and fifteen were killed. According to estimates two children a day are killed by such death squads whose job it is to clear the streets of this 'human debris'."[105]

It was for this reason and many others, for example children being used for prostitution and child labour, that the United Nations produced the Convention on the Rights of the Child (CRC). The CRC outlines a set of "universal norms to which governments and other agencies can be held to account for their treatment of children."[106]

View a copy of the CRC at www.unhchr.ch/html/menu3/b/k2crc.htm

OTHER ASPECTS OF HUMAN EXPERIENCE

Positive discrimination or affirmative action can be defined as the preferential treatment of members of a minority group over a majority group in order to promote equal opportunities for all people by redressing past discrimination against such groups. It is illegal to discriminate in this way. However, many people argue that it is necessary to promote equality in society to make institutional racism a thing of the past. As referred to above, the Macpherson report, commented that there was institutional racism within the police in the UK. In 2007, the BBC reported that Chief constables in England and Wales discussed whether they should attempt to boost the recruitment of black, Asian and women officers using affirmative action.[107] As this is currently illegal it would require changes to the law, but some argue that this would promote the greater good in order to make the police more acceptable to all communities. Affirmative action would occur, for example, when two candidates who have exactly the same qualifications apply for a post but the one whose ethnicity is under-represented would be selected in an attempt to balance the representation of all ethnic groups.

Keith Jarrett, President of the National Black Police Association, told the BBC why he supported the use of affirmative action. He considered the area of Hounslow in London which is predominately inhabited by people from ethic minorities and he claims:

> "Whilst my white colleagues are immensely qualified to do the job, I would put forward that Hounslow would be better served as a borough by a person from an Asian background, who has got culture in common with the local inhabitants, and perhaps speaks the same language."[108]

 PRACTICE ESSAY TITLES

Question adapted from CCEA Summer 2005 AS 6

Critically evaluate the view that discrimination is always immoral. (20)

Your response may refer to the following points:

- An exploration of the negative effects of prejudice and discrimination
- Christian and secular views on the importance of dignity and equality
- Critical reflection – the issue of positive discrimination

 TASK

Research some of the ways in which the human rights of any one minority group are violated in society today.

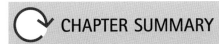 **CHAPTER SUMMARY**

The nature of human rights

- The contribution to the development of the concept of human rights by Aristotle, Aquinas, Hobbes, Locke and Paine.
- The view held by cultural relativists that human rights cannot be universalised.
- The role of the United Nations and the development of the Universal Declaration of Human Rights.
- The contents of the UDHR under the themes of political and civil rights and economic, social and cultural rights.

Christian and secular perspectives on human rights

- Christian teaching on the concepts of dignity, equality and responsibility.
- Secular views on the topic of human rights, with specific reference to the views of humanists, Kant and Gewirth.

Human rights and practice with special reference to women and minority groups

Women

- The development of feminism as a movement to ensure equal rights for women, with specific reference to feminists such as Wollstonecraft, Friedan, Greer and Wolf.
- The different strands of feminism such as liberal, radical and socialist with specific reference to the views of radical feminist Mary Daly.
- Christian feminism and the role of women in the Christian Church today.
- The human rights abuses experienced by women under the Taliban regime in Afghanistan.

Minority groups

- The human rights abuses experienced by members of the Bahá'í faith in Iran.
- The human rights abuses experienced by members of ethnic minorities in the UK today.

Endnotes

1 Stott, J, *Issues Facing Christians Today – Fourth Edition*, Zondervan, Michigan, 2006, p189

2 Vardy, P & Grosch, P, *Puzzle of Ethics*, Harper Collins, London, 1999, p200

3 *ibid*, p201

4 *ibid*, p198

5 *ibid*, p198

6 Thompson, M, *An Introduction to Philosophy and Ethics*, Hodder & Stoughton, London, 2003, p207

7 Magee, B, *The Story of Philosophy*, Dorling Kindersley, London, 2001, p81

8 Vardy & Grosch, *op cit*, p198

9 Magee, *op cit*, p108

10 Stott, *op cit*, p193

11 *ibid*, p193

12 Paine, T, *The Rights of Man*, Kessinger Publishing, Whitefish, 1998, p26

13 Ignatieff, M, *Human Rights as Politics and Idolatry*. Quote taken from Stott, *op cit*, p200

14 Stott, *op cit*, p197

15 *ibid*, p193

16 'Nations Member United States', The United Nations, www.un.org/members/list.shtml, accessed 12 February 2009

17 'Preamble to the Charter of the United Nations', The United Nations, www.un.org/aboutun/charter/preamble.shtml, accessed 12 Feb 2009

18 Jenkins, J, *Ethics and Religion*, Heinemann, Oxford, 1999, p99

19 'Preamble to the UDHR', The United Nations, www.unhchr.ch/udhr/lang/eng.htm, accessed 12 February 2009

20 'Economic, Social and Cultural Rights', Amnesty International USA, www.amnestyusa.org/poverty-and-human-rights/economic-social-cultural-rights, accessed 28 February 2009

21 'The Universal Declaration of Human Rights', United Nations, www.un.org/Overview/rights.html, accessed 12 February 2009

22 'An Agenda For Human Rights', Oxfam Community Aid Abroad, www.oxfam.org.au/campaigns/submissions/humanrights.pdf, accessed 22 February 2009

23 Vardy & Grosch, *op cit*, p197

24 Stott, *op cit*, p192

25 Paine, *op cit*, p55

26 Stott, *op cit*, p195

27 Paine, *op cit*, p26

28 Kodell, J, *The Gospel According to Luke*, Collegeville Bible Commentary, Liturgical Press, Collegeville, 1989, p28

29 Stott, *op cit*, p197

30 Temple, W. Quote taken from Stott, *op cit*, p199

31 Stott, *op cit*, p202

32 International Justice Movement – Frequently Asked Questions, www.ijm.org/faq, accessed 12 February 2009

33 Quote taken from Stott, *op cit*, p275

34 *ibid*, p277

35 Stott, *op cit*, p191

36 *ibid*, p191

37 'A Humanist View of Society', British Humanist Association, www.humanism.org.uk/campaigns/humanist-view-of-society, accessed 12 February 2009

38 'Human Rights', British Humanist Association, www.humanism.org.uk/campaigns/human-rights, accessed 12 February 2009

39 Kant, *The Metaphysics of Morals*. Quote taken from Bowie, R, *Ethical Studies*, Nelson Thornes, Cheltenham, 2004, p58

40 Vardy & Grosch, *op cit*, p196

41 *ibid*, p199

42 Mill, JS, *On Liberty*, Cambridge University Press, Cambridge, 1989, p68

43 Vardy & Grosch, *op cit*, p206

44 Gewirth, A. Quote taken from Vardy & Grosch, *op cit*, p206

45 'Alan Gewirth, 1912–2004, rational ethicist who challenged Golden Rule', University of Chicago News Office, www-news.uchicago.edu/releases/04/040517.gewirth.shtml, accessed 13 February 2009

46 *ibid*

47 Stott, *op cit*, p209

[48] Stott, *ibid*, p210

[49] Mill, JS, *The Subjection of Women*, republished 2008 by Forgotten Books, www.forgottonbooks. org, accessed 22 February 2009

[50] Radcliffe Richards, J, *The Sceptical Feminist,* Routledge, Oxford, 1980, p90

[51] Stott, *op cit*, p333

[52] 'Betty Friedan, Who Ignited Cause in Feminine Mystique, Dies at 85', *New York Times*, 05 February 2006, www.nytimes.com/2006/02/05/ national/05friedan.html, accessed 03 March 2009

[53] Friedan, B, *The Feminine Mystique*, Penguin Books, London, 1992, p68

[54] Greer, G, *The Female Eunuch.* Quote taken from Stott, *op cit*, p325

[55] Wolf, N, *The Beauty Myth,* Random House, Canada, 1997, p10

[56] Wilcockson, M, *Sex and Relationships*, Hodder & Stoughton, London, 2001, p20

[57] Stott, *op cit*, p326

[58] Wilcockson, *op cit*, p23

[59] *ibid*, p28

[60] *ibid*, p30

[61] *ibid*, p31

[62] *ibid*, p29

[63] *ibid*, p29

[64] Firestone, S, *The Dialectic of Sex,* Morrow, New York, 1970, p226

[65] Wilcockson, *op cit*, p29

[66] Storkey, E, *What's Right With Feminism.* Quote taken from Stott, *op cit*, p327

[67] Vardy, P, *The Puzzle of Sex*, Harper Collins, London, 1999, p5

[68] Stott, *op cit*, p328

[69] Vardy, *op cit*, p8

[70] Quote taken from Stott, *op cit*, p334

[71] Vardy, *op cit*, p9

[72] *ibid*, p10

[73] Stott, *op cit*, p331

[74] *ibid*, p331

[75] Vardy, *op cit*, p45

[76] Stott, *op cit*, p344

[77] 'No room for lady minister at Christmas service', *Portadown Times*, 20 December 2007, www. portadowntimes.co.uk/news/No-room-for-lady-minister, accessed 03 March 2009

[78] 'Address of Pope John Paul II to the Bishops from the States of Michigan and Ohio', 21 May 1998, Vatican: Holy See, www.vatican.va/holy_father/john_paul_ii/speeches/1998/may, accessed 03 March 2009

[79] Stott, *op cit*, p347–348

[80] *ibid*, p352 & 354

[81] Radford Ruether, R, *Sexism and God-talk*, SCM Press, London, 2002, p13

[82] 'Out go the Taliban, but will Afghan women be excluded', Human Rights Watch, 3 November 2001, www.hrw.org/en/news/2001/11/03/out-go-taliban-will-afghan-women-be-excluded, accessed 07 March 2009

[83] 'Afghanistan Humanity Denied – Systematic Violations of Women's Rights in Afghanistan', Human Rights Watch, www.hrw.org/legacy/ reports/2001/afghan3, accessed 7 March 2009

[84] *ibid*

[85] *ibid*

[86] 'The Baha'I Faith – Basic Facts', Baha'I Community of the United Kingdom, www.bahai. org.uk/gi/intro.htm, accessed 13 February 2009

[87] 'The Current Population of Iran', Kwintessential, www.kwintessential.co.uk/country/iran/ population.html, accessed 28 February 2009

[88] The Islamic Revolution in 1979 transformed Iran from a monarchy into a republic.

[89] 'Persecution of Baha'is in Iran', Baha'I Faith US, http://iran.bahai.us/overview/, accessed 1 May 2009

[90] 'Iran: Inquiry needed in the death of Baha'i prisoner of conscience', Amnesty International, www.amnestyusa.org/document.php?lang=e&id= ENGMDE130042006, accessed 13 February 2009

[91] 'Iran: Allow Baha'i Students Access to Higher Education', Human Rights Watch, www.hrw.org/ en/news/2007/09/19/iran-allow-baha-i-students-access-higher-education, accessed 13 Feb 2009

[92] 'January 2009, Country Summary, Iran', Human

Rights Watch, www.hrw.org/sites/default/files/ related_material/iran.pdf, accessed 22 February 2009

[93] Stott, *op cit*, p280

[94] *ibid*, p283

[95] 'Met's incompetence in Lawrence investigation', BBC News 24 March 1999, http://news.bbc.co.uk, accessed 13 February 2009

[96] Stott, *op cit*, p284

[97] *ibid*, p285

[98] 'Loyalists blamed as racist attacks on migrants double in Ulster', *The Guardian*, 30 May 2006, www.guardian.co.uk/uk/2006/may/30/race. northernireland, accessed 13 February 2009

[99] Stott, *op cit*, p280

[100] *ibid*, p281

[101] *ibid*, p281

[102] Singer, P, *Practical Ethics*, Cambridge University Press, Cambridge, 1993, p263

[103] *ibid*, p249

[104] 'Practical Expressions of Methodist Belief', The Methodist Church in Ireland, 2003, p23

[105] Vardy & Grosch, *op cit*, p193

[106] Stott, *op cit*, p209

[107] 'Police heads debate ethnic quotas', BBC News, 19 April 2007, www.bbc.co.uk, accessed 07 March 2009

[108] *ibid*

Chapter 8
Environmental Ethics

Chapter overview

This chapter aims to explore the ethical issues surrounding the following topics:

- Poverty and the just distribution of the world's resources
- The ecological debate including the religious contribution
- Religious and secular views on the welfare and rights of animals

POVERTY AND THE JUST DISTRIBUTION OF THE WORLD'S RESOURCES

ACCORDING TO TYLER AND REID: "in its simplest form, poverty could be defined as a lack of financial resources rendering an individual, community or nation unable to meet the needs basic for survival."[1] However, within this broad definition of poverty we can differentiate between two specific types of poverty – **relative** poverty and **absolute** poverty.

Relative poverty is the type of poverty that many people are familiar with in Northern Ireland today. Some members of our community are very well off and live a lifestyle which reflects their financial situation. Their neighbours, however, may not be as well off and cannot afford to buy the luxury items or to take the family holidays that others can enjoy. Singer defines relative poverty as "meaning that some citizens are poor, relative to the wealth enjoyed by their neighbours."[2]

Absolute poverty, on the other hand, is defined by Robert McNamara, former president of the World Bank as "a condition of life so characterised by malnutrition, illiteracy, disease, squalid surroundings, high infant mortality and low life expectancy as to be beneath any reasonable definition of human decency."[3] This can be contrasted with absolute affluence which refers to a situation where people "have more income than they need to provide themselves adequately with all the basic necessities of life."[4]

Singer contrasts the lifestyles of those who live in absolute affluence with those who live in absolute poverty. He claims that after having paid for food, shelter, clothing, health care and education, those who have absolute affluence still have money left over to spend on luxury items such as:

- food which is bought for the 'pleasure of the palate', not to prevent hunger;
- new clothes which are bought to 'look good', not to keep warm;
- a new house which is bought to have a playroom for the kids, not to keep off the rain;
- "And after all this, there is still money to spend on stereo systems, video cameras, and overseas holidays."[5]

From the above definitions of absolute poverty and absolute affluence, it is obvious that the world's resources are unequally distributed. The Make Poverty History campaign in 2007 made this point very clear when it stated: "80% of the world's population share 20% of the world's resources while 20% of the world's population share 80% of the resources." Another similar statistic is presented by Bellamy and Quayle who state: "two thirds of the world are starving while the other third is slimming."[6] Both pieces of evidence clearly highlight the fact that the world's resources are not equally distributed. Singer agrees and claims that the most significant contributor to world poverty is not the fact that we cannot produce enough food to feed everyone but the unequal distribution of the world's resources. He claims: "The problem is essentially one of distribution rather that production…only by transferring some of the wealth of the rich nations to the poor can the situation be changed."[7] This division which exists between developed and developing countries is often referred to as the 'north – south divide' with the developed countries located in the northern hemisphere (with the exception of Australia) and the developing countries in the southern hemisphere. However, during the 1990s and the economic growth of some countries in Asia, Stott claims: "global poverty was now more complex than a simple north – south divide."[8]

There are various reasons why nations suffer from absolute poverty. Some of the main causes of poverty can be outlined as follows:

- The place where you live will determine whether or not you suffer from poverty and the extent of such poverty. In the UK and Ireland, people who have no means of income due to unemployment, for example, are still entitled to benefits such as income support and free health care which secure a minimum standard of living. There are generally no such provisions in developing countries.
- Not having the 'means of production' is another factor which contributes to the level of poverty in a country. Poor countries may not be able to use their natural resources to help develop their economy because they cannot afford to buy the industrial machinery and other means of production which are needed to exploit their natural resources. As Walker states: "there's little advantage in sitting on a gold mine if you don't own mining equipment."[8a] One solution to this problem is that the poor countries can borrow from wealthy countries in order to finance

the purchase of such capital; however, this has drawbacks due to the high levels of interest which the loans accumulate. The knock-on effect of this is that less money is then available for the country to invest in infrastructure. For example, Stott informs us that Malawi spends more on debt repayments than health care, despite the fact that one in five people are HIV positive there.[9] One quote which highlights the overall extent of the problem of debt is from the Jubilee 2000 campaign, which continues to make attempts to cancel world debt: "In 1997, Comic Relief raised £26 million. This was paid back by Africa in debt repayments in just over a day."[10]

- In developing countries, the emphasis is often on increasing military strength, which reduces the amount of gross national product (GNP) that can be invested in infrastructure, health and education, areas which would obviously assist development. Also, in many developing countries, natural disasters will have a negative impact on any attempt to develop. The hurricanes, tsunamis, earthquakes, and flooding of recent years contribute to the level of poverty faced by such countries.

Regardless of the actual causes, there is no doubt about the negative impact poverty has on human experience in the developing world. In his book, *Practical Ethics*, Peter Singer clearly outlines some of the effects of poverty:

- 400 million people do not have access to adequate food supplies to ensure that they "sustain their bodies and minds in a healthy state."
- Millions of people across the world are constantly hungry and suffer from infections and diseases which could be prevented by a better diet;
- As a result of the infections and diseases which are related to malnutrition: "14 million children under five die every year."[11]

Other effects of poverty include the fact that people are forced into poor working conditions because they simply have no alternative. Children are often sent into this type of work and do not receive any form of education. Another issue is that of bonded labour, which in many ways is a form of slavery. Many people in the developing world are forced to borrow money from local lenders in an attempt to improve their chances of survival. As a result they are forced to work for the lenders as bonded labourers in order to repay the loan. The money lenders exploit the labourers in many ways. For example, the value of the hours worked is usually more than required to repay the loan but quite often a number of generations must work for the lender before they consider the loan to be fully repaid. People also "have to engage in de-humanising activities which ensure survival, for example, prostitution, or the selling or abandoning of children."[12]

Do we have a moral responsibility to assist those affected by absolute poverty, and attempt in some way to tackle the problem of the unequal distribution of the world's resources?

Religious views on poverty

In the Old Testament, there are many references which promote a sense of responsibility towards the poor. Tyler and Reid sum up the teaching of the Old Testament on the issue of poverty as follows: "In the Old Testament, the people of Israel were instructed to be compassionate and generous in providing for the indigent poor."[13] Outlined below are some passages from the Old Testament about their obligation to help those in need of aid.

- Genesis 1:26–9 indicates that human life is created in the image of God. It also informs us that God gave us *"every tree that has fruit with seed in it. They will be yours for food."* This verse implies that as stewards of God's creation we have a moral obligation to ensure that all people are treated with respect and dignity and that they have enough food and other basic requirements for life.
- Genesis 4:9–10 refers to the incident where Cain murdered his brother Abel. God asked Cain: *"Where is your brother Abel?"* and Cain's reply was: *"I do not know. Am I my brother's keeper?"* This reference can be applied to the issue of poverty because the Christian attitude is that we are responsible for the wellbeing of our fellow human beings.
- Leviticus 19:9–11 prohibited farmers from reaping the edges of their fields at harvest time and the Israelites were also told that they were not permitted to *"reap to the very edges of your field or gather the gleanings of your harvest. Do not go over your vineyard a second time or pick up the grapes that have fallen"* because they had to leave this for the poor people and aliens (foreigners).
- Deuteronomy 24:17–22 repeats the above prohibition from Leviticus; however it also adds that the remnants of the farmer's crop are for the benefit of orphans and widows in addition to aliens. Aquinas developed this point of view and claimed: *"whatever a man has in superabundance is owed, of natural right, to the poor for their sustenance."*[14]
- Psalm 82:3–4 also promotes a sense of social justice for the poor. It states: *"Defend the cause of the weak and fatherless; maintain the rights of the poor and oppressed. Rescue the weak and needy; deliver them from the hand of the wicked."*
- Isaiah 58:6–9 develops this concern for the poor. It requests that people *"share your food with the hungry"* and *"provide the poor wanderer with shelter."*
- According to Tyler and Reid: "The prophets are harsh in their condemnation of the selfish, idle rich, who ignore the needs of the poor."[15] This is reflected in Amos 5:21–4 which states: *"But let justice roll on like a river, righteousness like a never-failing stream!"* Micah 6:8 is also relevant to this issue of social justice for the poor: *"And what does the LORD require of you? To act justly and to love mercy and to walk humbly with your God."*

In the New Testament, Jesus' teaching reflects a great sense of empathy with the poor.

- Matthew 25:31–46 gives an account of the parable of the Sheep and Goats in which the Son of Man is responsible for the judgement of all the nations of the world. Those who have helped the following groups of people are told by Jesus that they will have eternal life because *"whatever you did for one of the least of these brothers of mine, you did for me"*:

  i. Feed the hungry

  ii. Give drinks to the thirsty

  iii. Welcome the stranger

  iv. Clothed the naked

  v. Take care of the sick

  vi. Visit the prisoners

However, those who have not fed the hungry and ignored the other groups of suffering people will be *"cursed, into the eternal fire prepared for the devil and his angels"*, because in addition to ignoring these people they have ignored Jesus. According to Harrington: "At the final judgement all humanity is to be judged according to acts of kindness done to poor and suffering people."[16]

- Mark's account of the Rich Young Man (Mark 10:17–31) gives another example of the duty of a Christian to assist those in need. In order to *"inherit eternal life,"* the man is told that he must *"go, sell everything you have and give to the poor"*, in addition to his observance of the commandments.

- In Luke 4:18–19, we are informed that Jesus was in the synagogue at Nazareth on the Sabbath and he read an extract from the prophet Isaiah which said that someone would be anointed to *"preach good news to the poor."* The passage implies that this has been fulfilled through Jesus. Tyler and Reid claim: "Jesus conspicuously adopted the Old Testament principle of care and compassion for the poor and destitute."[17]

- Luke's version of the Beatitudes in 6:20–22 refers to the *"poor"* as being blessed rather than the *"poor in spirit"* who are referred to in Matthew's version. According to Barrell: "Luke's version is more simple and straightforward than the more spiritual version of Matthew."[18] In Luke's Beatitudes, it is the poor and hungry *now* whom Jesus is concerned about.

- Two of Luke's unique parables – The Good Samaritan, and The Rich Man and Lazarus – again highlight the importance of helping those who are less fortunate than ourselves. In the parable of the Good Samaritan (Luke 10:25–37), we learn that in order to truly show love of neighbour, Christians must help anyone in need. Kodell claims that this account highlights the fact that Jesus' understanding of neighbour is: "there is no one who is not my neighbour…it is not a matter of blood bonds or nationality or religious communion."[19] This message can apply to an obligation to help all people suffering from poverty, despite the fact that they are not immediate neighbours. In the parable of The Rich Man and Lazarus (Luke 16:19–31), the message once again is that the poor cannot be ignored. Lazarus is a wealthy man and each day he passes and ignores the poor beggar who lies at the gates to his house. As a result of his failure to help the beggar, when Lazarus dies, he is punished in the afterlife and is, in his own words: *"in agony in this fire."* According to Guy, this parable is concerned with the dangers from selfishness and "disregard of one's unfortunate fellow man."[20] Overall, because of the above references and many others found in the third Gospel, Barclay states: "Luke's Gospel has a very special place for the poor."[21]

- Saint Paul highlights the importance of the equal distribution of resources in his first letter to the Corinthians. In 1 Corinthians 11:21 he is angry with the members of the Corinthian community who ignore the needs of the poor at the celebration of the Lord's Supper. He states: *"for as you eat, each of you goes ahead without waiting for anybody else. One remains hungry, another gets drunk."* In chapter 12, Paul emphasises the fact that all members of the Church make up one body: *"The body is a unit, though it is made up of many parts; and though all its parts are many, they form one body. So it is with Christ…If one part suffers, every part suffers with it"* (1 Corinthians 12:12–26). This reference can be applied to the issue of poverty in the world. Paul's use of the phrase 'one body' in this context can be understood to refer to the "unity and diversity of the community"[22] at Corinth. Paul implies that Christians have a responsibility to care for any member of the community who suffers. Even on a global scale, if someone is suffering as a result of poverty there is an obligation on Christians to do what they can to relieve that suffering.
- Paul does not claim that as a result of helping others we make life more difficult for ourselves. In 2 Corinthians 8:13 he states: *"Our desire is not that others might be relieved while you are hard pressed, but that there might be equality."*

 TASKS

The above reference from 2 Corinthians, in addition to many others from the Old and New Testaments, leads Stott to conclude: "two fundamental biblical principles apply to the issue"[23] of world poverty – the principles of unity and equality. The principle of unity refers to the fact that "the earth is one and the human race is one" while equality refers to the fact that we are "equally God's children."[24]

To complete the following table, decide whether the biblical references discussed above promote a sense of unity, equality or both. Explain your decision.

Theme of Unity	Theme of Equality

OTHER ASPECTS OF HUMAN EXPERIENCE

Liberation Theology is concerned with the liberation of the poor and oppressed throughout the world. It became very influential in Latin America in the late 1960s and views Christ's ministry in the context of setting people free from any form of oppression. It is based on references such as Luke 4:18–19, where Jesus quotes the prophet Isaiah:

> *"The Spirit of the Lord is on me, because he has anointed me to preach good news to the poor. He has sent me to proclaim freedom for the prisoners and recovery of sight for the blind, to release the oppressed, to proclaim the year of the Lord's favour."*

Walker claims that Liberation Theology "has been instrumental in challenging the world structures which maintain divisions between rich and poor."[25]

Investigate the following:

- key figures associated with Liberation Theology
- the impact it has had on human experience in Latin America
- the reasons why it has faced so much opposition from within the Christian faith

All Christian denominations use the above references to encourage their congregations to act responsibility towards the poor. Methodists highlight the importance of long term development in the following quote:

> "The Methodist conference recognises the obligation laid upon Christians to go to the relief of those in need, to ensure rehabilitation after natural or man made disasters, and to assist in fundamental development – so as to enable people to become responsible for their own futures."[26]

Methodist belief, therefore, aims to promote "action to address poverty and promote sustainable development worldwide." Members of the Methodist Church in Ireland are requested to take practical steps to make a positive contribution to the quest for equal distribution of the world's resources: "Members of the Methodist Church are encouraged to donate at least 1% of their income to the work of world development. In keeping with this principle, 1% of all church income is directed to world development funds."[27]

The Church of Ireland also promotes a moral responsibility to those in need throughout the world. Through its 'Bishops' Appeal' it aims to:

- educate the Church at home about the needs and concerns of people in the less developed world and the causes of poverty
- encourage Church members to examine the reasons for the problems facing the less fortunate in the world and to consider what we can do to change conditions

- encourage informed prayer and prayerful action aimed at strengthening the poor
- raise the funds needed to allow Bishops' Appeal to support development projects and alleviate the suffering caused by disasters, both natural and man-made[28]

Catholic teaching on the Christian response to the issue of world poverty is outlined in the *Catechism of the Catholic Church*: "God blesses those who come to the aid of the poor and rebukes those who turn away from them. It is by what they have done for the poor that Jesus will recognise his chosen ones."[29] Another quote from the *Catechism of the Catholic Church* highlights the importance of taking action necessary to help the poor and those who do not must take some responsibility: "St John Chrysostom recalls this: 'Not to enable the poor to share in our goods is to steal from them and deprive them of life. We must perform works of mercy towards the poor.'"[30] The 'works of mercy' refer to the feeding of the hungry, giving drinks to the thirsty etc, as outlined above in the parable of the sheep and goats from Matthew's Gospel. The *Catechism of the Catholic Church* also states:

"How can we not recognise Lazarus, the hungry beggar in the parable, in the multitude of human beings without bread, a roof or a place to stay? How can we fail to hear Jesus: As you did it not to the least of these, you did it not to me?"[31]

◎ OTHER ASPECTS OF HUMAN EXPERIENCE

Investigate how aid agencies in Northern Ireland fulfil their responsibilities to help people in need in the developing world today. The following websites may be useful, but you may investigate others also:

- Christian Aid – www.christianaid.org
- Trocaire – www.trocaire.org
- Tearfund – www.tearfund.org

Consider the following points:

- The specific problems faced by developing countries across the world
- The assistance given by the aid agencies in both the short term and long term
- The impact of such help on the human experience of those suffering from poverty

Peter Singer and the utilitarian approach

The primary concern for a utilitarian is to promote the greatest amount of happiness for the greatest number of people. In terms of the distribution of the world's resources, utilitarians would "want to support programmes which distributed wealth more fairly."[32] As a utilitarian, Peter Singer fully supports such programmes. In chapter five, Life and Death Issues, it was noted that Singer (and James Rachels) believed that in terms of morality, we cannot differentiate between taking active steps to kill someone and doing nothing, which allows someone to die. On the issue of poverty, Singer applies this principle and says that it is as wrong to allow a person to die as it is to kill them and as a result he claims: "people in rich countries are allowing those in poor countries to suffer from absolute poverty…if allowing someone to die is not intrinsically different from killing someone, it would seem that we are all murderers."[33] He does agree that spending money on luxury items is not as bad as pulling a trigger and deliberately shooting someone;[34] however, he does say that ignoring the poor could be "on a par with killing someone as a result of reckless driving."[35] To illustrate the 'obligation to assist' those in need he uses the example of a child who is drowning in a pond. Singer claims that when we ignore the needs of those suffering from poverty by spending money on luxury items, we act like someone who ignores a child drowning in a pond because they might get their clothes muddy. In other words, we are more concerned with our own material well being than we are with other people's lives. In an article in the *New York Times* Magazine, Singer claimed that if we decided not to spend money on eating at fancy restaurants and new designer clothes and instead donated the money to aid agencies, it "could mean the difference between life and death for children in need."[36] He estimates that $200 in donations to an organisation such as Oxfam "would help a sickly 2-year-old transform into a healthy 6-year-old – offering safe passage through childhood's most dangerous years."[37]

Singer's moral principle to help combat world poverty is this: "If it is in our power to prevent something very bad from happening, without sacrificing anything of comparable moral significance, we ought to do it."[38] He continues: "we have an obligation to help those in absolute poverty that is no less strong than our obligation to rescue a drowning child from a pond. Not to help would be wrong, whether or not it is intrinsically equivalent to killing."[39] Singer himself lives by this principle as he donates 20% of his income (mostly to Oxfam) to help those suffering from poverty to have a better quality of life. He recommends that all members of developed countries should donate at least 10% of their income to tackle the problem of the unequal distribution of the world's resources. He claims: "the conventionally accepted standard – a few coins in a collection tin when one is waved under your nose – is obviously too low."[40] While Singer does agree that every family in the developed world may not be able to afford 10% of their income, he claims that all families who do not have a large number of dependants, who are on average or above average incomes "ought to give a tenth of their income to reducing absolute poverty. By any reasonable ethical standards this is the minimum we ought to do, and we do wrong if we do less."[41]

TASK

Discuss the arguments for and against Singer's proposal that everyone who can afford to should donate 10% of their income to assist those suffering from poverty.

Is the standard he sets too high?

Not everyone would agree with Singer's principle that we have a moral obligation to assist those in need. Some may claim that it is up to the government, not each individual to address the issue of distribution of the world's resources. The United Nations recommended that developed countries should donate a minimum of 0.7% of GNP to developing countries. Only five countries[42] even reach this minimal target however, and sometimes when money is given to developing countries it is in the form of 'tied aid' whereby conditions are attached to it. For example, the money must be spent buying goods from the country which donated the money. This argument says that it is clear that we cannot rely on the government alone and it is important that we give privately and encourage our governments to fulfil their responsibility as well.

Others may claim that we should aim to tackle poverty in our own country before we attempt to help other countries. Singer himself comments on the fact that few people could stand by and watch a child drown; however many can ignore a famine in Africa. This argument – of taking care of our own – is not valid when, through the media, we witness the absolute poverty suffered by those in developing countries in comparison to the issue of relative poverty in our own society. Stott agrees and claims: "we cannot evade our responsibility to the world's poor people on the grounds that they belong to other nations and are no concern of ours."[43]

Egoism and intuitionism

Egoism refers to the idea of putting our own personal interests above the interests of anyone else. On the issue of poverty, an egoist will not feel that he or she is responsible for sacrificing their own wealth and happiness in order to save the lives of others. At an extreme level, an egoist may consider debt of a developing country to be good because it "subsidises his own life at others' expense."[44]

Consider this situation that a utilitarian may face: Imagine that you have £20 in your pocket and intend to use it to go to the cinema. However, outside the cinema someone is collecting for Oxfam because millions of people face a crisis due to a recent natural disaster in some foreign country. You weigh up the pleasure created for yourself by attending the cinema compared to the benefit the £20 will bring to those facing death. As a utilitarian you must promote the greatest amount of happiness for the greatest number, so you give the money to Oxfam. A week later you are in the same situation and again because of your moral obligation to assist those in need, you give the money to Oxfam. And so on. From an egoist perspective, this outcome is an unacceptable one and we must put ourselves and our experiences of life first.

Susan Wolf wrote an article in 1982 called 'Moral Saints'[45] and in this article she argues that if we forget about our self, like the utilitarian not going to the cinema, then we will do without things that make our life satisfying. She defines a moral saint as a person "whose every action is as morally good as possible" and uses the example that the moral saint will always attempt to promote the welfare of others rather than their own needs. She states: "If the moral saint is devoting all his time to feeding the hungry or healing the sick or raising money for Oxfam, then necessarily he is not reading Victorian novels, playing the oboe or improving his backhand." She continues: "An interest in gourmet cooking will be difficult for a moral saint because the use of resources cannot be justified." Despite the fact that we may not want to read Victorian novels, or play the oboe etc, the point Wolf makes is very clear – we have our own personal ways to make our lives more satisfying and if we become a moral saint then we will fail to develop this aspect of our lives to its full potential. Therefore, according to Wolf: "it is good not to be a moral saint." She argues for a more balanced approach to caring for the needs of others and promotes a "form of intuitionism" whereby our intuition informs us of how exactly we should strike this balance between giving to charity and helping ourselves, for the benefit of our own well-being as well as the benefit of those in need.

Humanism

Bowie claims: "Humanists believe that we should pursue happiness and the happiness of others."[46] For humanists, there are no religious values or principles to follow but instead they consider secular ideas concerning morality. In general terms, humanists will want to consider the consequences that their actions will have on other people and they will want to promote respect for all people at all times. With regard to the issue of equal distribution of the world's resources, humanists would agree that we have a responsibility to assist those suffering from poverty. Humanists will, according to Bowie: "believe in shared values, as expressed in documents such as the Universal Declaration of Human Rights" (UDHR).[47] For example, Article 25 of the Universal Declaration of Human Rights states:

"Everyone has the right to a standard of living adequate for the health and well being of himself and of his family, including food, clothing, housing and medical care and necessary social services, and the right to security in the event of unemployment, sickness, disability, widowhood, old age or other lack of livelihood in circumstances beyond his control."

For millions of people today, this basic human right describes a situation they will never see. Because of poverty, other human rights are also denied. For example, Article 23 states: "Everyone has the right to work, to free choice of employment, to just and favourable conditions of work and to protection against unemployment." Just and favourable conditions of work do not exist for many, for example those who work as bonded labourers.

 OTHER ASPECTS OF HUMAN EXPERIENCE

The UDHR declares that all people should have "favourable conditions of work."

Explore how a decision to pay a small amount extra to purchase 'FAIRTRADE' products can give Third World producers better working conditions.

Critically reflect on the idea that ethical consumerism has made a positive impact on the human experience of producers in developing countries.

The Fairtrade website, www.fairtrade.org, may be of some use for this activity.

Side effects of development

Some commentators claim that poor countries should not be assisted with their development. Two main reasons can be suggested for holding this attitude.

1. Environmental damage

One concern about the attempts to evenly distribute the world's resources and to enable the economies of developing countries to grow is the impact this will have on the environment. Walker states: "The issue is quite clear. Economic development brings environmental challenge."[48] A direct result of industrialisation is greater environmental pollution. Another effect of industrialisation is the changes it brings to society in general. People have more income and will demand more luxury items. Walker uses the example of China's economic development to make his point clear. As China develops and its population, which is in excess of one billion people, begin to make more demands for refrigerators and other electrical goods, it is obvious that the environmental impact will be disastrous, not only in the production of such goods but also in how to manage the waste created by this consumerist society. However, Walker suggests one possible solution. He claims that with the knowledge and experience that the developed countries have gained in recent years: "poorer countries should be helped to ensure that their development does not have a harmful environmental impact."[49] Therefore, it is the duty of developed nations to assist poor countries to develop in an environmentally friendly way.

2. Increased population

Singer refers to this as the most serious objection to the argument that there is an obligation to assist because if we help those living in poverty, we ensure that more people are born to live in poverty in the future. [50] It is argued by some commentators that because their situation is so futile aid should not be given to certain countries and instead allow famine, disease and natural disasters to reduce the countries' populations to a level that they can cope with. Garrett Hardin[51] uses the imagery of a lifeboat which is already full to capacity, in an ocean of drowning people. The people in the lifeboat have a choice: they can save some people by taking them on board, but the result will be that the boat cannot cope with so many people and it will sink and everyone on board will drown. Alternatively they can refuse to allow anyone else on board and let the others drown so that those in the boat survive. Hardin refers to this situation as 'lifeboat ethics' and claims that as it is better to have some survivors than none, we should "leave the poor to starve, for otherwise the poor will drag the rich down with them."[52]

However, the reason why so many of the world's population are starving is not because there is not enough food to feed everyone – there is more than enough food in the world to adequately feed all of the earth's inhabitants. Therefore allowing so many people to die to reduce the demand on the world's limited resources, as suggested by Hardin, is not the solution to world poverty. People are hungry not because of limited production but because the rich nations demand a disproportionate share of what is produced. Walker uses the example that during the famine in Ethiopia, which influenced the first Band Aid record in 1984, Ethiopia was still exporting huge amounts of food to other, richer countries.[53]

Singer suggests two alternatives to the "very great evil" of population control by famine and disease:

1. Assist countries to increase the standard of living and include, as part of this aid, education on contraception. As standards rise, people will realise that they do not need to have as many children as their parents did to provide economic support, and the birth rate will fall. Singer claims that developed countries have already reached this stage "and their populations are growing only very slowly, if at all."[54]

2. Singer is a renowned animal rights campaigner and he claims that if we were to stop producing food to feed animals for human consumption, the food saved could eradicate world hunger. He claims: "If we stopped feeding animals on grains and soybeans, the amount of food saved would – if distributed to those who need it – be more than enough to end hunger throughout the world."[55]

In conclusion, it can be argued that there is a moral obligation to assist those suffering from poverty. Whether we take a utilitarian approach or have a Christian outlook, there are strong reasons to suggest that if we do not help, we are not behaving morally. Stott's advice, that we must attempt to live a 'simpler lifestyle' and to 'grow in generosity' while being happy and thankful for all that we have in our lives is very relevant.[56]

PRACTICE ESSAY TITLE

Question adapted from CCEA Summer 2006 A2 6

Identify and consider the moral issues raised by world poverty. (30)

Your response could make reference to the following points:

- Definition and types of poverty eg absolute and relative
- A discussion of the unjust distribution of the world's resources with reference to the 'north-south divide'
- Religious views – reference to scripture and teaching of various Christian denominations
- Secular views – utilitarian views with specific reference to Peter Singer, egoist views and humanitarian views

THE ECOLOGICAL DEBATE INCLUDING THE RELIGIOUS CONTRIBUTION

According to Jenkins, environmental ethics "examines the moral basis of environmental responsibility"[57] and enables us to evaluate our own personal attitudes and behaviour regarding environmental issues. Recent media attention has focused on the environmental crisis we now face due to the effects of global warming, for example, melting ice caps and rising sea levels. As a result, Walker claims: "The apparently precarious state of our home planet is a regular feature of scientific and ethical discussion."[58]

When exploring the issue of environmental ethics, it is important to differentiate between intrinsic value and instrumental value.

- In the context of environmental ethics, **instrumental value** refers to the idea that things have value for human use – to further some other ends. Many people today have an anthropocentric (human centered) attitude towards the environment and claim that the environment should only be respected because of the benefit it brings to humans. For example, one could argue that a rainforest has instrumental value in that it can provide us with raw materials and land for farming, or that we should avoid pollution to water so that it will be safe to drink.
- **Intrinsic value**, on the other hand, means that things have a value in their own right – they are an end in themselves. For example, the rainforest has its own "value in itself independently of its prospects for furthering some other ends",[59] in other words, the needs of humans.

Environmental issues

John Stott identifies five main areas of widespread environmental concern in relation to the current environmental crisis. [60]

1. Population growth

Increasing population, especially over the last two centuries has had a detrimental impact on the environment. Stott outlines this dramatic expansion in the world's population using the following figures:[61]

Year	Approximate Population
1800	1,000,000,000
1900	2,000,000,000
1974	4,000,000,000
2006	6,100,000,000
Predicted population in 2050	11,000,000,000

On the issue of environmental ethics, this rise in population leads to increased demands for energy, increased need for space to live and increased waste. Walker claims that population growth is a real cause for concern. Like any other system, the environment can only sustain so much of any particular activity.[62]

2. Resource depletion

The earth's natural resources are finite and unless we restrict their use we will soon run out. Stocks of coal, oil and gas, which have formed over millions of years, will not last forever. Our use of other resources such as organic materials, for example wood, and food resources such as fish, must be assessed and action taken to reduce our consumption. Stott claims: "If the current rate continues, the world's rainforests are predicted to disappear within 100 years, causing an incalculable impact on climate and on plant and animal species"[63] He also discusses the fact that water is a scarce resource and he even claims: "it has long been said that water will be even more important than oil as a threatened scarce resource in the next fifty years."[64]

3. Reduction in biodiversity

The Planet Earth contains a wide range of species of living organisms. However, because human interference with the environment has led not only to the destruction of these organisms' natural environment, but also to climate change, many of these species face extinction or have already become extinct. This is a problem not simply because we do not want species to become extinct but moreover because of the far reaching environmental impact that occurs when the fine balance of an ecosystem is disrupted. As an example, Stott uses the effect of the significant decline of sea otters off the west coast of the United States. The sea otters lived primarily on a diet of sea urchins. As the numbers of otters fell, the sea urchins multiplied and as a result they "decimated the kelp forests leading to biologically impoverished, desert-like stretches of sea floor"[65] where no other life, such as fish and squid, could exist.

4. Waste disposal

The phrase 'Reduce, Reuse and Recycle' has become very popular in recent years because of the fact that our planet can no longer cope with the waste produced by the ever increasing population. In the UK, the Economic and Social Research Council found that, in 2004, the UK population produced 335 million tonnes of waste. Stott puts it this way: "The average person in the UK throws out his or her body weight in rubbish every three months"[66] and we must add to this average, the waste produced by industry. The Economic and Social Research Council informs us of what happens to this waste:

> "The majority of waste goes into landfill sites (74 percent) while 8 percent is incinerated and 18 percent is recycled or composted. It is estimated that 600 million batteries are landfilled every year, representing 20,000–40,000 tonnes, with each battery requiring 50 times more energy to produce it than they generated. Every year over 1 million computers are landfilled with only 20 percent recycled. On average, every household in the UK uses, and then throws away, one two-litre plastic bottle every day – with plastic taking hundreds of years to biodegrade."[67]

5. Climate change

Climate change generally refers to long term changes in the weather such as increasing or decreasing temperature, rainfall, and wind patterns. It is believed that our climate is currently undergoing change and this has been referred to as global warming. Walker claims that, as humans, we must take responsibility for the consequences of our lack of respect for the environment: "The activities of humans in the recent past have had a serious negative effect on the earth's climate. If these activities go on unchecked, then the implications for life on earth as we know it could be serious."[68]

The cause of global warming is linked to the 'greenhouse effect'. The greenhouse gases in the earth's atmosphere absorb and store some of the heat produced by the Sun's radiation. It is necessary to store some of this heat but too much is not good. However, the problem is that we have produced too many greenhouse gases, for example carbon dioxide, and as a result our atmosphere now absorbs too much of the Sun's radiation. As a direct result of having too much solar radiation in our atmosphere, global warming has taken place. There are a number of negative effects of global warming:

- Walker refers to 'freak' weather conditions which result in climatic imbalance which can have a negative effect on agriculture.[69] Stott agrees and claims: "2005 saw hurricanes added to the list of indications that climate change was taking place."[70]
- Any rise in temperature, no matter how insignificant it may seem, will have a major impact on the environment. As ice caps melt and oceans expand, small

islands and coastal regions may well disappear.

- Stott adds 'ocean acidification' as another consequence of global warming.[71] He claims that oceans have absorbed excess amounts of carbon dioxide to attempt to maintain the status quo but as a result their ability to sustain ocean life has been affected.

Some commentators have claimed that global warming is not a cause for concern, that the earth is experiencing a natural climate change, similar to the way in which ice ages have come and gone in the past. However, it does seem more than a coincidence that this trend in rising global temperature began in the nineteenth century, when humans began to burn fossil fuels in order to industrialise. Walker claims: "It is widely agreed that human contributions to a possible greenhouse effect are significant and do require our attention."[72] The issue of global warming received the attention of the world's leaders in December 1997 in Kyoto, Japan, when they met to discuss ways in which our 'carbon footprint' could be reduced. From 2005, the Kyoto Protocol bound nations to reduce carbon emissions to between six and eight percent below 1990 levels by 2012. Developing countries were treated with greater flexibility, due to the fact that they have to balance economic development alongside care for the environment.

The main source of carbon dioxide emissions is the burning of fossil fuels, which is necessary for industrialisation. As fossil fuels are burned, they release carbon dioxide (CO_2) which they have held for millions of years. Added to this problem is the fact that there is widespread destruction of forest areas (referred to as the 'lungs of the world' by Stott[73]) which are no longer able to absorb carbon dioxide from the atmosphere.

In addition to carbon dioxide, chlorofluorocarbons (CFCs) are another form of greenhouse gas which contribute to global warming. CFCs are also, however, responsible for the depletion of the ozone layer – the layer around the earth's atmosphere which protects us from the Sun's harmful radiation. As a result of this ozone depletion, humans are now more exposed to ultraviolet rays from the Sun, which are a cause of skin cancer. A hole in the ozone layer was discovered in 1985 over the Antarctic and by 1991 it was 21,000,000 square kilometres in size. By the mid 1990s, neighbouring countries reported harmful effects for plants, animals and humans.[74] Walker notes that the UV radiation causes damage to the DNA of all living matter and it will lead to genetic mutation among future generations of life on earth.[75] CFCs are found in aerosols and fridges, so yet again, as is the case with global warming, human activity is responsible for the depletion of the ozone layer. Steps have been taken to reduce the use of CFCs and to prevent further damage to the ozone layer. The Montreal Protocol in September 1987 made attempts to phase out the use of CFCs by 1996 for developed countries and 2006 for developing countries. As a result, most, if not all of our aerosols and fridges are CFC free. However not all countries have achieved this target.

Although unrelated to climate change, another side effect of pollution is acid rain. Its negative impact on the environment is beyond all doubt as the following quote from S Gordon highlights: "Some southern German states have lost over 90% of their silver fir (trees)...in Sweden, at least 18,000 lakes are completely acidified – dead. In Norway, 5,000 square miles of lakes are devoid of fish."[76] Industry and car exhaust fumes produce sulphur and nitrogen oxide which form an acid when they come into contact with water. When it falls as rain, it makes the sea, rivers and the soil more acidic which has a negative effect on plants and animals.

All five areas of concern, when viewed together, allow us to fully appreciate the crisis that the environment now faces.

 TASK

Use the internet to explore some of the issues mentioned above in greater detail. You could present your findings to your class using a PowerPoint presentation.

According to Vardy and Grosch "three broad ethical approaches have been adopted over the past twenty years or so"[77] with regard to the study of environmental ethics. The three approaches are as follows:

1. The Libertarian Extension
2. The Ecological Extension (also referred to as eco-centrism)
3. Conservation Ethics

1. The libertarian extension

This attitude towards the environment is based on the idea that all living entities have intrinsic value and should therefore be allowed to exist without human interference. Vardy and Grosch explain that this approach is concerned with the idea that "the human race has extended its own concept of individual rights to non-human animals and, occasionally, to inanimate entities."[78] The inanimate entities refer to non-living parts of our environment. Andrew Brennan, for example, argues that all ontological entities (anything that actually exists) deserve to be treated as having intrinsic value by humans simply because they exist. In this context, even rivers and mountains are considered to have intrinsic value and therefore it is immoral for humans to do anything which would interfere with nature, for example, to pollute a river or to tunnel into the side of a mountain.

Paul Taylor is another key figure in this area of environmental ethics. In his book, *Respect for Nature*, written in 1986, he argued that animals, insects and plants have intrinsic value or a good of their own, "which human beings have a duty to respect."[79] He applies the principle used by Kant that we can never treat the environment as a means to an end for human beings and therefore claims that it is immoral to value plants and animals simply for the benefit they bring to humans. According to Vardy and Grosch, Taylor does not claim that we must extend duty to protect a pile of sand because it is "a non–living entity" and does not have a 'good of its own'.[80]

Peter Singer can also be described as a libertarian with regard to his views on the environment. The key ideas presented by Singer can be summarised as follows:

- Humans must extend the concept of individual rights to include 'non-human animals'. If we claim that animals do not have intrinsic value, then we are guilty of 'speciesism' – a prejudice in favour of our own species at the expense of another species.

- Singer disagrees with Brennan and Taylor in that he finds the issue of plants and other non-life forms having intrinsic value as being problematic. He states: "the life of a being that has no conscious experience is of no intrinsic value"[81] and "ecological ethics might be more plausible if applied at a higher level, perhaps at the level of species and ecosystems."[82] He claims that only sentient creatures have wants and desires and therefore only sentient creatures should be treated as having intrinsic value. He argues: "It is significant that none of the grounds we have for believing that animals feel pain hold for plants."[83]

- As a utilitarian, Singer is concerned with minimising the suffering that we leave for future generations. He outlines his environmental ethic and claims that such an ethic "would find virtue in saving and recycling resources...to throw out material that can be recycled is a form of vandalism or theft."[84] Singer also claims that our current choices regarding recreation are not 'ethically neutral' in terms of the negative impact they have on the environment. For example, he is critical of the popularity of sports such as motor car racing and claims that this is unethical due to the "consumption of fossil fuels and the discharge of carbon dioxide into the atmosphere."[85]

- Singer's 'environmental ethic' is largely related to his views on animal rights which will be explored towards the end of this chapter. He claims that our eating habits and in particular, our preference for a meat–based diet have contributed to the current ecological crisis:

"energy intensive factory farming methods...are responsible for the consumption of huge amounts of fossil fuels. Then there is the loss of forests...so that cattle can graze. All of this amounts to a compelling reason for a largely plant based diet."[86]

2. The ecological extension (eco–centrism)

Eco-centrism does not focus on the individual rights of every living and non-living entity as the Libertarian Extension does, but instead focuses on the overall importance of interrelationships between all things that exist on the planet.

Aldo Leopold wrote an essay in 1949 called 'The Land Ethic' which outlined his view that humans are not in control of land but are simply equal members of the community which includes soil, water, plants and animals, which he collectively refers to as 'the land'. In terms of our moral duty towards the environment, Leopold wrote: "A thing is right when it tends to preserve the integrity, stability and beauty of the biotic community. It is wrong when it tends otherwise."[87] The biotic community Leopold refers to is a community which includes groups of interdependent organisms such as plants and animals who live in the same area as each other and interact together.

Arne Naess, a Norwegian philosopher, developed this idea in the 1970s. He used the phrase 'deep ecology' to explain that humans cannot be separated from the natural environment, that the world is not a collection of isolated objects but a network of interrelated beings. He claimed that we must try to preserve the earth for its own sake, because of its intrinsic value and not for the instrumental value it has for humans. Naess contrasted 'deep ecology' with the anthropocentric 'shallow ecology' which considers the environment to have instrumental value for humans. According to Jenkins: "Deep ecology recognises the intrinsic value of all living beings and views human beings as just one particular strand on the web of life."[88]

Similar to the views held by Brennan, some deep ecologists apply their ethic beyond living things to include everything that exists in the biosphere. In their book, Deep Ecology, Devall and Sessions claim: "all organisms and entities in the ecosphere, as parts of the interrelated whole, are equal in intrinsic worth."[89]

In 1977, James Lovelock put forward the 'Gaia Hypothesis', which considers the planet to be a living entity with its own in-built sense of rationale. He claims that the earth is "in a sense alive and that we are in the process of killing it".[90]

However, the earth fights back to maintain itself against destruction and it "gradually alters its own geophysical structure so that the whole human race is obliterated or massively reduced in order to halt the human engineered environmental damage which threatens the survival of the planet itself."[91]

In terms of our responsibility towards the environment, Lovelock attempts to convince us: "it is in our interest to convince our planetary host that we are worth keeping on as environmentally conscientious house-guests."[92]

3. Conservation ethics

Conservation ethics refers to an anthropocentric approach to environmental ethics in that we must conserve the environment because of the benefits that this will bring to humans. The environment is there for our use and pleasure – it has instrumental or extrinsic value and the means by which humans can gain both pleasure and profit.

An egoist, for example, may wish to conserve the environment. An egoist is someone who behaves in a way that they feel will benefit them personally, and their moral choices will vary depending on the individual involved. Generally, they may not care too much about the environment unless it directly affects them. However, some might take a long term view of environmental issues and wish to do what they can to protect the environment. For example: "an egoist with children might believe that it is in his best interests to lessen pollution because it might have consequences for his children after his death."[93]

Religious views on the ecological debate

In the context of conservation ethics it is also relevant to discuss the Christian attitude towards the environment. Christians generally fit into this category as they would not consider it right for humans created in the image of God to offer equal rights to plants and animals (libertarian extension) nor would they consider themselves to be on a par with plants and animals (eco-centrism).

The Old Testament sends out a mixed message as far as our responsibility to the environment is concerned. Two themes are present: dominion and stewardship.

1. Dominion

In chapter one of the Book of Genesis we are told that God gave mankind dominion and control over the natural world. *"Then God said, 'Let us make man in our image, in our likeness, and let them rule over the fish of the sea and the birds of the air, over the livestock, over all the earth, and over all the creatures that move along the ground'"* (1:26). He then told them to *"Be fruitful and increase in number; fill the earth and subdue it. Rule over the fish of the sea and the birds of the air and over every living creature that moves on the ground"* (1:28). This view clearly suggests that non-human things have only instrumental value. According to this teaching, nature exists for human benefit and for no other reason. Psalm 115:16 develops this idea of dominion: *"The highest heavens belong to the Lord, but the earth he has given to man."*

This biblical teaching has come under great criticism and has been held responsible for the current environmental crisis. Peter Singer, for example, argues that for centuries this teaching has sent out the following message: "Nature itself is of no intrinsic value, and the destruction of plants and animals cannot be sinful, unless by this destruction we harm human beings." He continues that the above passage from Genesis implies: "to act in a way that causes fear and dread to everything that moves on the earth is not improper; it is, in fact, part of a God-given decree."[94] Stott refers to critics of Christianity who also claim, like Singer: "these verses are to blame for contemporary ecological irresponsibility."[95] He cites the example of Ian McHarg who claims that the references from Genesis quoted above, encourage "the most exploitative and destructive instincts in man" and that God's words were "a declaration of war on nature."[96]

Stott, however, claims that this dominion referred to in Genesis is "a cooperative dominion,"[97] and that the earth belongs to both God and humans. As a result, humans have a responsibility to look after and maintain the earth, not to dominate it. Stott claims: "it would be ludicrous to suppose that God first created the earth and then handed it over to us to destroy it."[98]

2. Stewardship

Many would agree with Stott's point of view and claim that God intended humans to be stewards of his creation. In other words, it is the duty of people to be the caretaker of this property which God has entrusted to them. A number of scriptural references support this point:

- The second account of creation in Genesis 2 states: *"The LORD God took the man and put him in the Garden of Eden to work it and take care of it"* (2:15).
- Psalm 24:1 states: *"The earth is the Lord's and everything in it."*
- Leviticus 25:23 supports this view: *"the land is mine [God's] and you are but aliens and my tenants."*

In this role – as stewards of God's creation – it is a Christian responsibility to try to prevent further damage to the planet.

⊚ OTHER ASPECTS OF HUMAN EXPERIENCE

The focus of the annual Trocaire campaign during 2008 was 'Tackling Climate Injustice.' Trocaire claim that climate change is already having a negative impact on the human experience of people in the developing world. The report, 'Tackling Climate Injustice' highlighted the fact that developing countries have experienced extreme changes in climate and that because people in these countries depend so heavily on the land: "Even the smallest changes in the weather, brought about by changes to the climate, can make poor people more vulnerable due to the impact this has on these basic resources."[99]

The report includes a range of information on the impact the ecological crisis has had on developing countries. For example, Minister Monyane Moleleki, Minister of Natural Resources, Lesotho, has this to say about the extreme weather conditions they experience:

"The farmers are suffering because nothing happens when it is supposed to – traditional rainy seasons are no longer predictable. The numbers of droughts have doubled since the late 1970s and when the rains come, they come in torrents."

Visit the Trocaire website (www.trocaire.org) and access the report 'Tackling Climate Change'. Investigate the impact global warming has already had on the human experience of people in the developing world.

In light of the environmental crisis we face and the suffering humans have already encountered because of this crisis, what can be done? There are a number of options. I have already discussed Singer's 'environmental ethic' in that he promotes recycling, ethically neutral recreation, limited consumption of fossil fuels and a vegetarian diet! We can take our own practical steps to limit the damage that we as individuals inflict on the environment:

- We can attempt to become more energy efficient, for example getting the bus to school rather than asking for a lift in the family car. We can switch electrical items off when they are not being used.

- We must try to avoid leading a materialistic lifestyle. According to Stott: "At the root of the ecological crisis is human greed."[100] It is therefore our responsibility to avoid extravagance and wanting things for the sake of having them rather than needing them.
- We can investigate ways in which to invest in renewable resources such as solar power or wind power and many students throughout Northern Ireland do this as part of their science related extra-curricular work, eg The Young Scientist competition.
- We must follow the 3 Rs – Reduce, Reuse and Recycle.

In the same way that Christians feel they have an obligation to do what they can to assist those suffering from world poverty, they also have a moral obligation to respect the environment and do what they can to 'leave it as they found it' for future generations without adding to its destruction.

 OTHER ASPECTS OF HUMAN EXPERIENCE

Many people today suggest that nuclear power is an environmentally friendly alternative to fossil fuels and is the primary resource that can meet our increasing demand for energy.

Many consider nuclear power to be a clean and green source of energy in comparison with fossil fuels. However, the most significant objection to nuclear energy is the radioactive by-product which needs to be carefully stored for a very long period of time. Coupled with this is the likelihood of an accident occurring, such as the Chernobyl disaster in 1986 when a nuclear reactor exploded, causing birth deformities 20 years after the event.

Using the internet, investigate the advantages and disadvantages of using nuclear power as an alternative to fossil fuels and answer the following questions:

1) Critically evaluate the claim that nuclear power is a possible solution to the problem of our energy needs.

2) Critically reflect on the impact using nuclear power may have on human experience.

PRACTICE ESSAY TITLES

Question adpated from CCEA Summer 2002 A2 6

a) Identify and consider the main ethical issues concerning the environment. (30)

Your response could make reference to the following points:
- A brief overview of some environmental issues
- Refer to the distinction between intrinsic and instrumental value
- Consider various approaches to the debate, eg Libertarian extension, eco-centrism and conservation ethics
- Christian perspectives – dominion and stewardship

Question adapted from CCEA Summer 2002 A2 6

b) Critically evaluate the claim that care of the planet is a human responsibility. (20)

Your response could make reference to the following points:
- The ways in which humans have damaged the environment and therefore must take responsibility
- The Christian responsibility as a 'caretaker' of God's creation
- The utilitarian attitude that we must preserve the environment for the benefit of future generations
- The egoist attitude that if pollution does not affect an individual in a negative way, then there is no need to feel responsible
- The opinion that humans have not contributed to global warming – it is simply part of nature's cycle, much like previous ice ages
- This responsibility is not difficult – simple steps can be taken in our everyday lives such as recycling, using public transport, etc

ANIMAL RIGHTS

This section aims to explore one last issue surrounding the general theme of environmental ethics, which is animal rights. Jeremy Bentham (1748–1832), the founder of utilitarianism, was the first philosopher to focus on the need for equal treatment of animals. For Bentham, the issue was primarily about the suffering humans imposed on animals. In 1789, he wrote:

"But a full grown horse or dog is beyond comparison a more rational, as well as a more conversable animal, than an infant of a day, or a week, or even a month, old. But suppose they were otherwise, what would it avail? The question is not, Can they reason? Nor can they talk? But, can they suffer?"[101]

Before considering the ethical responses to the issue of equality for animals, it is necessary to firstly consider how animals suffer at the hands of humans.

Examples of poor treatment of animals

According to Vardy and Grosch: "the moral debate about animals generally revolves around five controversial areas".[102]

1. **Animals being bred and killed for food** often involves animals living their entire life in a very cramped and quite often dirty space where they cannot move adequately or even turn around. They are not given a chance to behave in the way that nature intends. Animals are often factory farmed with an emphasis on profit rather than the welfare of the animal. Is this morally acceptable?

   Some argue that humans are carnivorous and that meat provides us with nutrition that cannot be found in vegetables. However, Singer argues that the slaughter of animals for food is immoral because of the suffering sentient beings endure and furthermore, eating meat is not essential to our nutritional needs.[103] As already noted, Singer also claims that the farming of animals as a source of food is wasteful with regard to the world's resources – he implies that a 'plant based diet' can contribute to the solution to environmental crises and world poverty. He writes: "it may be best to make it a simple principle to avoid killing [animals] for food."[104]

 TASK

Class discussion: Comment on the claim that "animals eat each other, so why shouldn't we eat them?"

2. **Animals being used for medical experiments** begs the questions: is the suffering and death of animals such as mice justified if a cure for cancer may be found as a result of it? What about injecting chimps with AIDS? It is not ethical to use humans in such experiments, and so animals are the next best alternative because they share so much of our DNA. According to some philosophers, whose views will be considered later, the death of a human is much worse than the death of an animal. Without the results from research on animals we would not currently have a cure for the measles or treatments which prolong the lives of people with HIV. However, Singer, who believes that animals and humans should be treated equally, argues: "If the experimenter is not prepared to use an orphaned human infant, then his readiness to use non-humans is simple discrimination."[105]

Those who oppose animal experimentation, refer to the practice of vivisection (which is the dissection of, or any cutting or surgery upon, a living animal for the purpose of scientific investigation) and the obvious pain that the animal has to endure throughout this process. Opponents of animal experimentation also argue that the results gained from such experimentation may not necessarily apply to humans. Singer claims: "the benefits to humans are either non–existent or uncertain, while the losses to members of other species are certain and real."[106] Many also claim that there are alternative computer based techniques which are ignored by researchers because of the costs involved. Jenkins refers to computer modelling, the use of human cell cultures, test tube techniques and the use of synthetic membranes as possible alternatives to animal experimentation.[107]

 PRACTICE ESSAY TITLES

Question adapted from CCEA Summer 2004 A2 6

Critically assess the view that the use of animals in medical experimentation is wrong. (20)

 OTHER ASPECTS OF HUMAN EXPERIENCE

Xenotransplantation is the use of animal organs to replace failing human organs.

Investigate some of the advantages and problems associated with this type of medical procedure.

What implications does this have for the rights of animals? Are there any other ethical issues involved in using this advance in technology?

3. Animals are used in testing cosmetics to ensure that when products are made available for human use they are safe and have no unwanted side effects. For example, producers of shampoos and other personal care products test the safety of their products by dripping concentrated solutions of them into the eyes of animals. However, in recent years alternatives have been developed and as a result many products now clearly indicate that they have not been tested on animals.

4. Breeding and killing animals for fur is another controversial issue. Vardy and Grosch claim that while "it would be difficult to object to an Eskimo killing a seal for clothing…the range of alternative textiles available to the average westerner makes the slaughter of minks and rabbits unnecessary."[108] This attitude, that the use of animal fur is unnecessary, has become prevalent in many countries in recent years due to the ethical issues and also to the availability of alternative products.

5. Hunting and killing animals for sport has caused controversy in recent years with specific reference to the issue of foxhunting. Those who wish to maintain the practice of foxhunting claim that it allows farmers to control the population of foxes who kill their stock of animals; that it has been an important country tradition; and that it provides people with a form of entertainment. For many, however, the above reasons do not justify the cruelty inflicted on the fox and a ban has been imposed on the practice of foxhunting in Scotland since 2002 and in England and Wales since 2005. Other sports are also considered to be immoral because they exploit or cause unnecessary suffering to animals, for example, bull fighting in Spain.

 TASKS

Investigate and evaluate each example of the poor treatment of animals given above. Are any of the examples of the suffering of animals morally acceptable?

What about the abuse of animal rights when we keep animals as pets, or when we pay to watch performing animals at the circus or animals kept in zoos? Is this morally right?

There are three general approaches to the issue of animal rights:
1. Equal rights for animals
2. The absolute dismissal argument
3. The pragmatic dismissal argument

Equal rights for animals

Many would claim that all living things have an intrinsic value and deserve to be protected from cruelty. As discussed, some philosophers have attempted to apply this sense of value to plants and other non-living entities. However, applying equal rights for animals has been a more popular concept in recent years. Not to give equal rights to animals has been referred to as 'speciesism' by R Ryder, which is explained by Vardy and Grosch in the following way: "an expression of stubborn preference for beings of one's own kind and a clear prejudice against members of another kind."[109] Since the publication of his book, *Animal Liberation,* in 1975, Peter Singer is considered by many to be the founder of the modern animal rights movement. Singer claims, much like the way society today finds racism and sexism morally unacceptable, we must also treat speciesism as being equally unacceptable. In an article, 'All Animals Are Equals', Singer argues that we must change our attitudes and accept the fact that 'human animals' and 'non-human animals' must be treated with equality. He wrote: "I am urging that we extend to other species the basic principle of equality that most of us recognise should be extended to all members of our own species."[110] Singer refers to the practices of using animals for food and experimentation, as referred to above, as evidence of speciesism in society today.

According to Singer, what makes humans and many 'non-human animals' equal – and therefore using animals for food and experiments immoral – is the concept of personhood. Singer claims that in order to exist and have rights as a person, a being must possess two qualities:

- They must be **rational**, in other words, they can reason and understand;
- They must be **self-conscious** beings, in that they are aware of themselves and others around them.

In *Practical Ethics*, Singer uses numerous examples to illustrate how non-human animals display the characteristics of a person. He also argues, as already discussed in chapter 3, that human infants and humans with severe mental disabilities are not persons. One such example of a non-human animal who displayed the characteristics of a person is 'Washoe', a chimpanzee who was taught to use sign language. Washoe was rational in that she learned to understand and use hundreds of signs and could use them to form simple sentences. As far as self-consciousness was concerned, Washoe, when shown an image of herself and asked 'Who is that?' would reply 'Me, Washoe' using sign language. When living with other chimpanzees, she adopted an infant chimp and taught it how to sign as well.[111] Singer develops his argument that animals should be treated with equal consideration: "killing a chimpanzee is worse than the killing of a human being who, because of a congenital intellectual disability, is not and never can be a person."[112] In addition to apes, Singer claims that whales, dolphins, cats, dogs and pigs (he reflects – "are we turning persons into bacon?"), to name a few, are rational and self-conscious, and therefore persons. He concludes his list of non-human persons with the claim that it could be extended "to the point at which it may include all mammals."[113]

Singer, however, does not consider all animals to display the qualities of a person. For example, he states: "fish appear to be the clearest case of animals who are conscious but not persons."[114] He continues: "When we come to animals who are not rational and self-conscious beings, the case against killing is weaker."[115]

Tom Regan is another philosopher who claims that animals should have equal rights. In his 1984 publication, *The Case for Animal Rights*, he argued: "The fundamental wrong is the system that allows us to view animals as our resources, here for us – to be eaten, or surgically manipulated, or exploited for sport or money."[116] He also comments: "Reason compels us to recognise the equal inherent value of these animals and, with this, their equal right to be treated with respect."[117]

Stephen Clarke also argues that animals should have respect but not necessarily because they have so much in common with us. According to Vardy and Grosch: "animals are simply different creatures sharing the same planet as ourselves and, as such, are deserving of respect."[118]

The absolute dismissal argument

The absolute dismissal argument refers to the traditionally held view that animals do not have ethical significance. According to Vardy and Grosch: "Traditionally, philosophy has not been effective at defending the moral status of animals."

It was the Greek philosopher Aristotle (384–322 BC) who was initially responsible for the view that humans were superior to animals. Unlike the modern views of Singer, he claimed that animals did not have the ability to reason. He claimed: "brute beasts [exist] for the sake of man – domestic animals for his use and food, wild ones for food and other accessories of life."[119]

Descartes, the seventeenth century French philosopher, believed that animals were not capable of experiencing pain and he experimented on them without anaesthetic.[120]

Kant (1724–1804) also believed that animals did not deserve to be treated as having moral status. He denied the fact that animals were self-conscious beings and he claimed that we could treat animals as a means to an end, in other words, treat animals for our own purposes because they do not have intrinsic value. He stated: "So far as animals are concerned, we have no direct duties. Animals are not self-conscious, and are there merely as a means to an end. That end is man."[121]

Michael Fox argued in his book *The Case for Animal Experimentation* (1986) that because animals do not appreciate their lives and because they are not rational or self-conscious they do not have intrinsic value. He disagreed with the view of Descartes who felt that animals could not experience pain, but claimed instead that animals are not entitled to moral status simply because they suffer and feel pain. He later changed his mind, however, and claimed that our duty not to cause harm to humans should also be extended to animals.

Pragmatic dismissal argument

The absolute dismissal argument is problematic in that it can be used to justify animal suffering on a grand scale, whereas this approach – the pragmatic dismissal argument – promotes the idea that while animals are not considered to be in any way equal to humans, they do deserve to be treated with a degree of respect. Vardy and Grosch use the example: "if there was a question of saving Lassie or her owner then the animal takes second place." [122] They continue: "on the face of it the ethics of pragmatism appears attractive" and they claim that this is what most people do in practice today – they respect the rights of animals to a certain point but human need takes priority at all times.

Religious views on animal rights

As with the discussion on environmental ethics, the Christian attitude towards the issue of animal rights depends on our interpretation of the two accounts of creation in

Genesis 1 and 2. The first account of creation gives the impression that animals were created for the benefit of humans, that humans have **dominion** *"over all the earth, and over all the creatures that move along the ground"* (1:26). This implies that animals can be used as humans deem necessary, whether for food or work. The second account of creation implies that humans have a responsibility to act as **stewards** over the animal kingdom because Genesis informs us that we are to *"work it and take care of"* the animals brought into the Garden of Eden (2:15).

We can consider other references from scripture. For example, before the flood at the time of Noah, which is recorded in Genesis 6, God instructed Noah to bring animals into the ark: *"You are to bring into the ark two of all living creatures, male and female, to keep them alive with you."* This could suggest that by including two of every species God shows that he is concerned for the welfare of animals. However, one could be critical and claim that God has no real concern for animals because he drowns almost every animal on the earth to punish humans.

In the Old Testament, animals are allowed to rest on the Sabbath according to Exodus 20:10, and in Proverbs 12:10 we are informed: *"A righteous man cares for the needs of his animal."* However, the New Testament also stipulates that animal sacrifice is compulsory: Luke's Gospel gives the example of Mary's sacrifice of two turtledoves when Jesus is presented in the Temple (Luke 2:22–24). In Luke 8:26–39 we also learn of Jesus' apparent lack of concern for animal life when he sends the evil spirits who possessed Legion into a herd of pigs, which then drown in a nearby lake.

In the early Church, Augustine (AD350–430) developed the view of Aristotle and claimed that because animals have no sense of reason they cannot be treated on a par with humans. Aquinas (1225–1274) further developed this view and claimed: "It matters not how man behaves to animals, because God has subjected all things to man's power."[123] Stott claims: "Aquinas taught that animals exist entirely for human pleasure and profit."[124] However, Aquinas did argue that if we allow ourselves to mistreat animals in any way, we are a step closer to disrespecting humans. In *Summa Contra Gentiles*, (1260), Aquinas argued: "Through being cruel to animals one becomes cruel to human beings."[125] However, one exceptional figure at around this time did treat animals with respect and equality. St Francis of Assisi (1181–1226), the patron saint of animals and the environment, treated animals "as his equals, his brothers and sisters."[126]

Andrew Linzey is a modern Christian theologian who has written widely on the issue of animal rights. He claims that nowhere does the Bible specifically say that animals were simply made for us to treat as we like. He does claim that what is promoted in scripture is the idea of "kindness, responsibility, even communion, with animals."[127] He argues that one theme which emerges from reading scripture is that it is the duty of the strong to protect the weak. Animals, according to Linzey, are weak and therefore deserve respect from humans: "I suggest that the weak and defenceless should be given not equal, but greater, consideration. The weak should have moral priority."[128] He refers to animals as "fellow creatures" and tells us that we need to "move away from the idea that animals are things, machines, tools, commodities, here for our use or means-to-human-ends, to the idea that animals as God given, sentient beings have their own intrinsic value, dignity and rights."[129]

Many Christians today would agree that while human beings, created in the image of God, have much greater importance than animals, it is the Christian duty to respect all aspects of God's creation. Christians agree that giving equal consideration to animals is a step too far, few would disagree with the following words of John Stott: "Christians should protest against all perceived cruelty to animals, and campaign for their humane treatment in all circumstances."[130] Vardy and Grosch promote the concept of 'proportionalism' and claim: "animals should be accorded moral rights unless there is a proportionate reason which would justify these being waived".[131] For example, at the time of a natural disaster, if a choice had to be made between saving the life of a human and the life of an animal, the human must come first.

 PRACTICE ESSAY TITLES

Question adapted from CCEA Summer 2008 A2 6

Outline and examine the various religious and moral viewpoints in the Animal Welfare debate. (30)

Your response could make reference to the following points:
- The use of animals for food, experimentation, cosmetic testing, clothing, sport, etc.
- The issue of equal rights of animals including the views of Singer, Regan and Clarke.
- The absolute dismissal argument with reference to the views of Aristotle, Descartes, Kant and Fox.
- The pragmatic dismissal argument.
- Christian views on dominion and stewardship with specific reference to scripture, Augustine, Aquinas and Linzey.

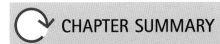 CHAPTER SUMMARY

Poverty and the just distribution of the world's resources

- Types of poverty – absolute and relative.
- Absolute affluence.
- Causes and effects of poverty.
- Biblical teaching on the issue of poverty.
- Denominational views.
- Secular views – utilitarian, egoist, intuitionalist, humanist.
- Consideration of some side effects of development.

The ecological debate

- The terms intrinsic and instrumental value.
- Awareness of environmental issues such as climate change, population growth and disposal of waste.
- The Libertarian extension – humans should extend rights to animals and even plants.
- Eco-centrism or the Ecological extension – humans are on a par with all other parts of our environment.
- Conservation ethics – a human centred approach to the environment, which supports respect of the environment because of the benefit it brings to humans.
- Biblical Teaching and the Christian response to environmental issues including reference to the debate regarding dominion or stewardship.

Animal rights

- Examples of the poor treatment of animals such as using animals for food and medical experimentation.
- Equal rights for animals and the views of key figures such as Peter Singer.
- The Absolute dismissal argument which claims that animals have no moral status.
- The Pragmatic dismissal argument is a compromise in that animals deserve to be treated with some respect, however, humans are more important.
- Christian attitudes towards the issue of animal rights with specific reference to scripture and the views of Andrew Linzey.

Endnotes

1 Tyler, S, & Reid, G, *Religious Studies, Philip Allen Updates*, Oxfordshire, 2002, p200

2 Singer, P, *Practical Ethics*, Cambridge University Press, Cambridge, 1993, p218

3 *ibid, p219*

4 *ibid, p221*

5 *ibid, p221*

6 Walker, J, *Environmental Ethics*, Hodder & Stoughton, London, 2000, p87

7 Singer, *Practical Ethics, op cit*, p220-1

8 Stott, J, *Issues Facing Christians Today – Fourth Edition*, Zondervan, Michigan, 2006, p162

8a Walker, *op cit*, p91

9 *ibid*, p167

10 Walker, *op cit*, p93

11 Singer, *Practical Ethics, op cit*, p219

12 Walker, *op cit*, p93

13 Tyler, S, & Reid, G, *op cit*, p200

14 Quoted in Singer, *Practical Ethics, op cit*, p234

15 Tyler, S, & Reid, G, *op cit*, p200

16 Harrington, D, *Collegeville Bible Commentary, The Gospel According to Matthew*, Liturgical Press, 1991, p102

17 Tyler, S, & Reid, G, *op cit*, p201

18 Barrell, EV & KG, *St Luke's Gospel – An Introductory Study*, John Murray Publishers, London, 1982, p52

19 Kodell, J, *Collegeville Bible Commentary, The Gospel According to Luke*, Liturgical Press, 1991, p61

20 Guy, HA, *The Gospel of Luke*, Macmillan Education Limited, London, 1972, p117

21 Barclay, W, *The Gospels and Acts Vol. 1*, SCM, London, 1966, p217

22 Getty, MA, *Collegeville Bible Commentary, First and Second Corinthians*, Liturgical Press, 1991, p57

23 Stott, *op cit*, p178

24 *ibid*, p178–182

25 Walker, *op cit*, p108

26 Methodist Statement in 'What the Churches say on Moral Issues.' Quote taken from Elson, M & Watton, VW, *Catholic Christianity Today*, Hodder & Stoughton, London, 2000

27 'Practical Expressions of Methodist Belief', The Methodist Church in Ireland, accessed 26 November 2008

28 'The Church of Ireland World Aid and Development Programme', Church of Ireland, www.bishopsappeal.ireland.anglican.org, accessed 27 November 2008

29 *Catechism of the Catholic Church*, Veritas, Dublin, 1994, 2443

30 *ibid*, 2446

31 *ibid*, 2463

32 Walker, *op cit*, p104

33 Singer, *Practical Ethics, op cit*, p222

34 *ibid*, p223

35 *ibid*, p228

36 'The Singer Solution To World Poverty', *New York Times Magazine*, 5 September 1999

37 *ibid*

38 Singer, *Practical Ethics, op cit*, p229

39 *ibid*, p230

40 *ibid*, p246

41 *ibid*, p246

42 Only Norway, Denmark, Sweden, Luxembourg and the Netherlands meet this target according to Stott. Scott, *op cit*, p166

43 Stott, *op cit*, p179

44 Walker, *op cit*, p104

45 Wolf, S, *Moral Saints*, Journal of Philosophy, Number 8, August 1982

46 Bowie, R, *Ethical Studies*, Nelson Thornes, Cheltenham, 2004, p168

47 Bowie, *op cit*, p168

48 Walker, *op cit*, p98

49 *ibid*, p97

50 Singer, *Practical Ethics, op cit*, p235

51 Harding, G, 'Living on a Lifeboat', reprinted from *BioScience*, October, 1974, www.garretthardinsociety.org, accessed 12 Dec 2008

52 Singer, *Practical Ethics, op cit*, p236

53 Walker, *op cit*, p100

54 Singer, *Practical Ethics, op cit*, p239

55 *ibid*, p220

56 Stott, *op cit*, p186 & 318

57 Jenkins, J, *Ethics and Religion – Second Edition*, Heinemann, Oxford, 2003, p150

58 Walker, *op cit*, p2

59 Jenkins, *op cit*, p150

60 Stott, *op cit*, p136

61 *ibid*, p136

62 Walker, *op cit*, p36

63 Stott, *op cit*, p139

64 *ibid*, p138

65 *ibid*, p141

66 *ibid*, p141

67 Economic and Social Research Council, www.esrc.ac.uk/ESRCInfoCentre, accessed 27 November 2008

68 Walker, *op cit*, p29

69 *ibid*, p31

70 Stott, *op cit*, p144

71 *ibid*, p144

72 Walker, *op cit*, p32

73 Stott, *op cit*, p139

74 *ibid*, p142

75 Walker, *op cit*, p34

76 *ibid*, p37

77 Vardy, P & Grosch, P, *Puzzle of Ethics*, Harper Collins, London, 1999, p222

78 *ibid*, p222

79 Jenkins, *op cit*, p156

80 Vardy & Grosch, *op cit*, p226

81 Quote taken from Vardy & Grosch, *op cit*, p222

82 Singer, *Practical Ethics*, *op cit*, p282

83 *ibid*, p70

84 *ibid*, p285–286

85 *ibid*, p285

86 *ibid*, p288

87 Jenkins, *op cit*, p157

88 *ibid*, p158

89 Singer, *Practical Ethics*, *op cit*, p281

90 Jenkins, *op cit*, p157

91 Vardy & Grosch, *op cit*, p232

92 Jenkins, *op cit*, p157

93 Walker, *op cit*, p45

94 Singer, *Practical Ethics*, *op cit*, p266–268

95 Stott, *op cit*, p152

96 *ibid*, p153

97 *ibid*, p148

98 *ibid*, p154

99 'Tackling Climate Injustice', Trocaire, March 2008, www.trocaire.org, accessed Nov 26 2008

100 Stott, *op cit*, p156

101 Quoted in Singer, P, *Applied Ethics*, Oxford University Press, Oxford, 1986, p221

102 Vardy & Grosch, *op cit*, p208

103 Singer, P, *Applied Ethics*, Oxford University Press, Oxford, 1986, p222

104 Singer, *Practical Ethics*, *op cit*, p134

105 Singer, *Applied Ethics*, *op cit*, p224

106 Singer, *Practical Ethics*, *op cit*, p66

107 Jenkins, *op cit*, p151

108 Vardy & Grosch, *op cit*, p209

109 *ibid*, p214

110 Singer, *Applied Ethics*, *op cit*, p216

111 Singer, *Practical Ethics*, *op cit*, p111–112

112 *ibid*, p118

113 *ibid*, p132

114 *ibid*, p119

115 *ibid*, p132

116 Jenkins, *op cit*, p155

117 Regan, T, 'In Defence of Animals', Quoted in Walker, *op cit*, p55

118 Vardy & Grosch, *op cit*, p219

119 *ibid*, p209

120 *ibid*, p211

121 *ibid*, p211

122 *ibid*, p214

123 *ibid*, p210

124 Stott, *op cit*, p151

125 Jenkins, *op cit*, p153

126 Stott, *op cit*, p151

127 Linzey, A, 'Animal Theology', Dialogue Magazine, Issue 26, April 2006

128 Linzey, 'Animal Theology'. Quoted in Walker, *op cit*, p56

129 Linzey, 'Animal Theology', Dialogue Magazine, Issue 26, April 2006

130 Stott, *op cit*, p152

131 Vardy & Grosch, *op cit*, p28

Chapter 9

War and Peace

Chapter overview

This chapter aims to explore the ethical issues surrounding the following topics:

- The Just War tradition in Christianity
- Ethics of contemporary warfare
- Pacifism

THE JUST WAR TRADITION IN CHRISTIANITY

WAR REFERS TO A PERIOD of fighting between two groups of people because of a conflict that has arisen between them. Jenkins defines war as "armed hostilities between peoples, frequently different nations, sometimes between different parties within a nation, as in a civil war, or between one small group and the state, as in a guerrilla war."[1]

1. Old Testament references

In the Old Testament the act of war is not specifically condemned; in fact there are a significant number of examples where war was considered to be necessary and where Israel was required to fight against its enemies. According to Tyler and Reid: "God is presented as a God of action and his activity is frequently seen in his engagement in conflict with those who oppose him and his will for his covenantal people."[2] War was considered to be a part of Israel's "fight for survival and existence"[3] and it was considered morally acceptable for the Israelites to go to war to acquire and protect their land. Therefore, war was permitted both as an act of offence and defence. The following Old Testament references are relevant to the topic of war:

- In Joshua 6 we learn that Joshua attacks Jericho as part of his attempt to invade

Canaan. We are informed: *"They devoted the city to the LORD and destroyed with the sword every living thing in it—men and women, young and old, cattle, sheep and donkeys"* (Joshua 6:21).

- In Joshua 10:40 we are told that on another occasion *"Joshua subdued the whole region...with all their kings. He left no survivors. He totally destroyed all who breathed, just as the LORD, the God of Israel, had commanded."* By today's standards, this unmerciful act of indiscriminate slaughter cannot be referred to as a 'just' act of war.

- Deuteronomy 2:34 highlights an additional example of mass murder during war: *"At that time we took all his towns and completely destroyed them—men, women and children. We left no survivors."*

- The Old Testament informs us that war was to be conducted under the guidance of God, who was personally involved in the victories experienced by the Hebrews: *"The LORD your God, who is going before you, will fight for you, as he did for you in Egypt, before your very eyes"* (Deuteronomy 1:30). This is also reflected in Deuteronomy 20:4: *"For the LORD your God is the one who goes with you to fight for you against your enemies to give you victory."*

- However, the writings of the prophets in the Old Testament look forward to a time where there are no wars but instead a time of peace. Micah 4:1–4 reflects on a time when *"Nation will not take up sword against nation, nor will they train for war anymore. Every man will sit under his own vine and under his own fig tree, and no one will make them afraid"*. Isaiah 40:2 also reflects: "prophets had grown war-weary"[4] when he comments: *"Speak tenderly to Jerusalem, and proclaim to her that her hard service has been completed, that her sin has been paid for"*.

2. New Testament references

The New Testament reflects a total antithesis of the Old Testament teaching considered above. According to Tyler and Reid: "Jesus refused to take the way of military power to achieve his goal, and challenged his disciples when they attempted to do so themselves"[5]. The latter part of this statement is an obvious reference to the account of Jesus' arrest in the Garden of Gethsemane, when Peter strikes out at the High Priest's servant, cutting off his ear and Jesus responds: *"Put your sword back into its place; for those who live by the sword will die by the sword"* (Matthew 26:52–53). This non-violent attitude held by Jesus is clearly illustrated in the Sermon on the Mount in Matthew 5–7. A number of specific references from this sermon are relevant:

- One of the Beatitudes states: *"Blessed are the peacemakers, for they will be called sons of God."* Therefore, a blessing is given to those who avoid war and work to promote peace.

- In Matthew 5:43, Jesus refers to teaching from the Old Testament about our attitude towards our enemies and rather than simply *"love your neighbour"* as the Old Testament commands in Leviticus 19:18, we are informed by Jesus that we must show love and mercy towards all people, even our enemies. Jesus said: *"You have heard that it was said 'You shall love your neighbour and hate your enemy'. But I say tell you: love your enemies and pray for those who persecute you."* Jesus' teaching implies that we must approach any situation with *agape* love and in terms of the topic of war, many commentators believe that *agape* love would not allow it.

- In Matthew 5:39, Jesus teaches on the issue of revenge. He rejected the Old Testament concept of *lex talionis* (as defined previously on p24), *"an eye for an eye and a tooth for a tooth"* and said: *"If someone strikes you on the right cheek, turn to him the other also."* Here, Jesus' teaching implies that we should accept and put up with injustice rather than fight against it.

 TASK

Using the above references from scripture, complete two spider diagrams: one outlining biblical references which justify war and the other outlining references opposing war or violence.

Early Christian thought and the development of Just War Theory

Based on the teachings of Jesus, the early church opposed all forms of violence or retaliation to the extent that the first generation of Christians did not defend themselves, even when faced with the prospect of being fed to the lions, which took place under persecutions initiated by Nero in AD64. This attitude, however, did not last any longer than the first few hundred years of the existence of Christianity. In AD313, the process which made Christianity the official religion of the Roman Empire began. The 'Edict of Milan' was a formal law or decree issued by the Roman emperors Constantine and Licinius in AD313, which declared that the Christian faith must be tolerated within the Roman Empire.[6] As a result, persecution of Christians became illegal. In AD380, the emperor Theodosius took the next step and made Christianity the official religion of the Roman Empire. He stated: "It is our desire that all the various nations...should continue in the profession of that religion which was delivered to the Romans by the divine Apostle Peter."[7] Within a short period of time it was believed that the reluctance of Christians to fight was creating a weakness in the Roman Empire.[8]

To combat this perceived weakness, Augustine (AD354–430) used biblical teaching to support the view that in some situations, war could be considered morally acceptable for Christians. To illustrate his point, he referred to Moses' killing of the Egyptian, which was justified on the grounds that there was "a desire for justice not revenge, or cruelty or lust for power."[9] Wilcockson also proposes: "Augustine makes much of Jesus' argument from silence", as when Jesus cures the Roman centurion's servant in Matthew 8:8–0, he does not condemn the man for being a soldier, he praises his faith: *"I have not found anyone in Israel with such great faith."* Also, John the Baptist's

265

request in Luke 3:14, that soldiers do not intimidate or extort – rather than completely renouncing violence – is further evidence that military force was not condemned.

Augustine was, therefore, the first Christian to contribute to the justification of violence concept. Vardy and Grosch inform us: "Augustine put forward two conditions under which a war could justifiably be waged:"[10]

1. It had to have a legitimate authority.

2. There had to be a just cause.

With regard to the legitimate authority, Augustine felt: "it was right for Christians to go to war in the interests of the state."[11] This reflects Paul's teaching in his letter to the Romans, when he claims: "Let every person be subject to the governing authorities. For there is no authority except from God."[12] Paul felt that God had delegated authority to the state and as a result Christians were obligated to obey the wishes of the state, even if they were requested to fight.

For Augustine, the concept of a just cause meant that there had to be a justified reason for war. It should attempt to prevent harm being caused to innocent human life or to avenge wrongdoing, in order to prevent it from happening again. Therefore, just cause could not simply refer to wanton acts of violence or revenge.

At the time of the Crusades (1095–1291) the issue of war was considered to be acceptable in order to capture places of religious importance in the Holy Land from the hands of Muslims. Pope Urban II, who began the Crusades in 1095, felt that God gave his support to the atrocities committed by the Christian invaders. He stated: "When an armed attack is made upon the enemy, let this one cry be raised by all the soldiers of God: 'It is the will of God!' 'It is the will of God!'"[13]

In the thirteenth century, Aquinas (1224–1274) added another condition to the two already put in place by Augustine. He claimed that the intention behind the declaration of war had to be just and stated: "It is necessary that the belligerents should have a rightful intention, so that they intend the advancement of good, or the avoidance of evil."[14] Aquinas agreed with Augustine that a war should be declared by a legitimate authority and should have a just cause, as it can stop human suffering. However, he also insisted that the motive for going to war must be pure, rather than a lust for power, a just war should attempt to end suffering and promote a lasting peace. Thus, the third condition added to the 'just' war theory in the twelfth century was:

3. Right intention.

Luther (1483–1546) agreed with the fact that, in some cases, acts of war can be morally justified. He claimed that war "is the will of God" because if it was wrong, Moses, Joshua and David would have been condemned by God, rather than praised by him.[15] Luther, like Augustine, also felt that we have a duty to be obedient to "the earthly authorities through whom God operates"[16]. 1 Peter 2:13–14 offers evidence to support this: *"Submit yourselves for the Lord's sake to every authority instituted among men: whether to the king, as the supreme authority, or to governors, who are sent by him to punish those who do wrong and to commend those who do right."* According to Vardy and

Grosch, both Luther and Augustine "said that Jesus ruled out malitia (hatred) not militia (fighting)."[17] Therefore, violence was permitted in order to enable people to stand up for the greater good of humanity, but it was not permitted if it was simply out of hatred for an enemy.

In the sixteenth century, the Spanish theologians, Francisco de Vitoria (1492–1546) and Francisco Suarez (1548–1617) added three further conditions to further develop the Just War Theory:

4. Entering into war must be a last resort.
5. One must only go to war if there is a reasonable chance of success.
6. Proportionality is necessary during the conduct of war. Unnecessary and indiscriminate violence must not be used during war but the minimum amount of force must be used to secure victory.[18]

The next significant development of the Just War Theory in the Christian tradition was "one of the most comprehensive statements on just war conditions",[19] which came from Catholic bishops in America in 1983, entitled 'The Promise of Peace: God's Promise and Our Response.' Their findings provide us with what we now accept as the Just War Theory. Their principles, influenced by the outcome of the Nuremberg trial held after the end of the World War Two, made a clear distinction between the conditions surrounding the declaration of a 'just' war (*Jus ad Bellum*) and how a 'just' war should be fought (*Jus in Bello*). Stott comments that the Just War Theory is "held by a majority of Roman Catholics and Protestants today."[20]

The Just War Theory

As it now stands, the Just War Theory consists of a total of nine principles which include:

- Seven principles concerning the **beginning** of war, which must be satisfied before a just war can be declared. These are referred to as *Jus ad Bellum*.
- Two principles concerning conduct **during** war, which are referred to as *Jus in Bello*.

JUS AD BELLUM – When it is right to go to war

1. Just cause

In order for it to be considered just, the war's primary intention must be the protection of innocent life and human rights. War must only confront "a real and certain danger", according to the statement published by the Catholic bishops.[21] War cannot be declared because one country wants revenge or to 'get even' with another country. There is some debate among commentators about what exactly makes a cause 'just'. The United Nations attempts to clarify the issue and state that at any time countries can take: "such action as it deems necessary in order to maintain or restore international peace and security."[22]

OTHER ASPECTS OF HUMAN EXPERIENCE

Saddam Hussein was accused of violating the human rights of the Kurdish people living in Iraq. According to reports, thousands of Kurds were killed by Saddam Hussein's regime in the 1980s.[23]

In one attack in March 1988, chemical weapons were used against Kurds living in the town of Halabja which left 5,000 dead and 7,000 injured or with long-term illnesses.[24]

Based on this information alone, do you think the declaration of the first war on Iraq by the British and Americans in 1990, was morally justified. In other words, was there a just cause?

2. Competent or legitimate authority

The Just War Theory insists that a just war can only be declared by a legitimate authority, a legally-appointed or democratically-elected government. Thus, a just war cannot be declared by "private individuals or private armies."[25] This condition has the potential to limit acts of war. However, how do we define a 'legitimate authority'? For example, Robert Mugabe's leadership of the government in Zimbabwe is legitimate as he is officially the president of the country. However, since controversy surrounding recent elections, the G8 countries have issued a statement in July 2008, which insists: "We do not accept the legitimacy of any government that does not reflect the will of the Zimbabwean people."[26] Clearly this condition is flawed, as on some occasions a government may not be representative or competent.

3. Comparison of justice

According to Vardy and Grosch: "This involves comparing the justices of the claims of both sides in a conflict."[27] The case of both sides must be equally considered before a war can be considered to be a just one. In reality, however, this will be very difficult, if not impossible, as it is likely that both sides will insist that they have a just cause worth fighting for and they will be reluctant to attempt to understand the other's point of view.

4. Right intention

The intentions behind the declaration of war must not be due to revenge or hatred but have justice and lasting peace as its motive. This is similar in many ways to the concept of a just cause because the war must be fought for the right reasons;

as Aquinas said: "for the advancement of good, or the avoidance of evil."[28] Vardy and Grosch criticise this theory, claiming that having the right intention "is difficult to justify."[29] They use the example of Mussolini, who thought he had the right intention in bringing the Catholic faith and civilisation to Ethiopia when he invaded it. Hitler thought he had the right intention of creating 'living space' for the Aryan race when he gave the orders for the USSR to be invaded. However, the right intention must be for reasons such as lasting peace and justice for all people, not land, greed or revenge.

5. Last resort

The Just War Theory insists that in order for a war to be considered just, it must only be fought as a last resort, and that before war has been declared, all possible alternatives have been explored and exhausted. War cannot be the result of an immediate reaction to events. For example, negotiations between diplomats representing both parties must have taken place and despite the best efforts of all involved, have failed. Even if diplomacy fails, other sanctions can be imposed such as trade sanctions. In February 2003, when the British government was considering whether or not to join the US in the war against Iraq, Rowan Williams, Archbishop of Canterbury and the leader of the Church of England, referred to this principle of 'last resort' when he commented: "I think Christians generally would hold that unless other means of resolution had been exhausted, it would be hard to justify pre-emptive action. It does not look as if we have exhausted all the possibilities yet."[30] However, one difficulty with this approach is the fact that if countries wait too long to ensure that all other options have failed, it gives the enemy a chance to increase strength, for example, to reinforce their army.

6. Likelihood of success

A country should not go to war unless it is fairly certain that it will be victorious. The reason that this condition is enshrined in the Just War Theory is because it would be immoral to lead an army to their slaughter for no apparent gain. According to Vardy and Grosch, the Catholic bishops include this criterion to "prevent irrational resort to force or hopeless resistance when the outcome of either will clearly be disproportionate or futile."[31] Stott comments that it is foolhardy to go to war when one does not expect to succeed because thousands will have died without establishing the cause for which they sacrificed their lives.[32]

7. Proportionality

The injustice being fought and the suffering inflicted by war must be in reasonable proportion. The injustice which we want to put an end to must be serious enough to outweigh the loss of life and the destruction which will obviously occur as a result of the war. In other words, the war must be considered as the lesser of two evils as it is not acceptable to cause vast amounts of suffering over a minor injustice. Bowie supports this: "a state should not wage a war that causes substantially more suffering and destruction than the actual wrong done by the enemy."[33]

JUS IN BELLO – How a war should be fought

1. Proportionality

This condition not only applies to the decision of whether war is acceptable but also how a war must be fought in order for it to be a just war. The use of violence in a war must be proportional to the threat of the enemy and minimum force should be used at all times. Therefore, excessive or unnecessary violence is prohibited by the Just War Theory. Vardy and Grosch give the following example of the disproportionate use of violence: "It would, for instance, have been unacceptable for Britain to drop a nuclear bomb on the capital of Argentina after Argentina invaded the Falklands."[34]

2. War must discriminate

A just war must discriminate between those involved in fighting the war and those who are not involved. Non-combatant immunity is an essential component of the Just War Theory. Innocent civilians must not be the direct targets of an attack. Indiscriminate acts of war, such as carpet bombing, used by the Nazis or the Allies during World War Two when they attempted to destroy entire cities, are considered morally unacceptable. For example, the bombing of Hamburg killed 40,000 innocent civilians in a single night[35] and 135,000 people died in Dresdon during two days of bombing in 1945.[36] Such attacks by the Allies on German cities may have helped bring an end to World War Two, but can this loss of life ever be justified? According to the Just War Theory, the answer is no, because the attacks did not discriminate against innocent people.

However, it is very difficult to differentiate between combatants and non-combatants. Many may consider civilians who support the war effort by working in a munitions factory to be legitimate targets. The Catholic bishops claim that the following groups cannot be classified as combatants: "school children, hospital patients, the elderly, the ill, the average industrial worker producing goods not directly related to military purposes, and farmers."[37] According to this criterion, prisoners-of-war must also have a guarantee that they will have protection from attacks.

TASK

According to the Just War Theory, which groups of people from the following list should be considered innocent and therefore immune from attack during a war?

- Politicians and generals who direct wars
- Soldiers who fight in the war
- Medics who attend wounded soldiers
- Munitions workers whose work directly supports the war effort
- Non-military workers who support the war effort through production of food and other necessary resources
- Civilians who do not support the war, but who pay taxes which finance the war
- Civilians who support the war but do not contribute to it in any way

OTHER ASPECTS OF HUMAN EXPERIENCE

Explore the causes and effects of a modern day war. You could consider the war in Iraq, the conflict in Gaza or any war you wish to investigate. Apply the Just War Theory to this conflict. Critically reflect on the following points:

1) Was the war you have considered a 'just' war? Explain using each of the conditions outlined in this section.

2) Is the Just War Theory adequate in its provision of clear guidelines regarding the conflict you have considered?

Evaluation of the Just War Theory

There are a number of advantages to having the Just War Theory:

- The Just War Theory makes it morally acceptable to fight in self-defence or to protect human rights as it provides a "framework to permit the use of violence in controlled circumstances and against certain targets."[38] In this regard, the Just War Theory is consistent with the theory of Natural Law (as defined on page 45). One of the primary precepts of Natural Law is to 'live harmoniously in society' and Natural Law would "support the idea of self-defence as a natural and rational justification for war."[39]
- The Just War Theory sets out strict guidelines which must be adhered to before a war can be declared and it therefore limits acts of war because if the conditions are not met then war cannot be declared. According to Jenkins the Just War Theory does not promote the idea of wars but is intended to "prevent them by showing that going to war except in certain limited circumstances is

wrong, thus motivating states to find other ways of resolving conflicts."[40]

- The Just War Theory also limits excessive use of violence during a war through promoting the use of minimal force, thus minimising the cost of human life lost throughout the conflict.
- The Just War Theory recognises that the need may exist to overthrow a tyrannical aggressor such as Adolf Hitler, who will continue to abuse human rights until something is done to stop him. In such cases, war is the lesser of two evils and the Just War Theory will support war in such necessary circumstances. However, the theory of tyrannicide, which refers to the murder of a tyrant for the greater good of society, could be considered as an alternative to any form of war for this reason. Vardy and Grosch claim that if Hitler or Saddam Hussein had been assassinated, great suffering could have been avoided: "If the death of one man who is held to be wicked would be likely to save the lives of millions, can it be justified?"[41]

 OTHER ASPECTS OF HUMAN EXPERIENCE

Dietrich Bonhoeffer was a German Lutheran theologian who was involved in a plot to assassinate Hitler in 1944.

Investigate the events surrounding this assassination attempt and the death of Bonhoeffer.

Despite some of the obvious strengths, the Just War Theory has faced some serious criticisms:

- The Just War Theory is only a theory and one cannot guarantee that the conditions set out will be followed or applied in all cases. This is the opinion of realists, who, according to Bowie "argue that the just war conditions are... too simplistic and impractical."[42] For example, it is acceptable to say that, in theory, the use of violence must be proportional to the threat soldiers are under. However, as is very often the case, "the conduct of soldiers in the heat of war is difficult to control – to expect men who have been ordered to kill, to keep their heads and hearts free of hatred towards the 'enemy' is an almost impossible task."[43]
- Some of the conditions set out by the Just War Theory are useless unless we have the benefit of hindsight – they cannot be fulfilled unless we possess the ability to predict what will happen in the future. For example, we will never know if lasting peace will be the outcome of a war or if thousands of people will have died in vain. We can never know if the country declaring war will be successful or not. Bowie uses the example of the war in Vietnam. The Americans felt that it was very likely that they would be successful but

"America lost the war despite its overwhelming military superiority."[44]

- Any theory which supports the use of violence under any circumstances is wrong because ultimately innocent human life will be lost and the principle 'Do not kill' violated. Some commentators have argued that the age of 'smart weapons' (weapons which are guided to their target and therefore cause little or no damage to surrounding people and buildings[45]) has reduced this problem. However, despite this, innocent people still suffer. For example, Vardy and Grosch comment that when such weapons were used during The Gulf War in 1991 "sometimes things went wrong as when…one of the missiles went out of control and hit a residential area."[46] As Jenkins puts it, when this happens it "straightaway violates the principles of proportionality and discrimination."[47]

 TASK

Chapter 7 deals with the topic of Human Rights. Revisit the Universal Declaration of Human Rights and discuss which specific Human Rights are violated during times of war.

Other criticisms of the Just War Theory include:

- The theory can be applied by both sides involved in the conflict to make both appear to be just. Tyler and Reid claim: "both sides will apply it in such a way that their claim to justice is legitimate, and yet both claims cannot surely be equally valid."[48]
- War for any reason is contrary to the teachings of Jesus, especially those found in the Sermon on the Mount, which has already been outlined and will be discussed further in the section on pacifism.
- In general, weapons of mass destruction violate the principles of proportionality and discrimination. Therefore, as Jenkins comments, weapons of mass destruction "make a nonsense of the theory."[49] The use of nuclear weapons will be discussed in greater depth in the following section.

PRACTICE ESSAY TITLES

Question adapted from CCEA Summer 2004 A2 6

(a) Explain and consider the origins and development of the Just War Theory. (30)

Your response could make reference to the following points:

- An account of the historical development of the Just War Theory
- The input of key figures such as Augustine and Aquinas
- The criteria for a Just War with reference to the specific conditions for *Jus ad Bellum* and *Jus in Bello*
- Examples of application of the Just War Theory, eg World War Two, etc
- A discussion of the strengths and weaknesses of the theory

Question adapted from CCEA Summer 2002 A2 6

(b) Critically assess the view that war is a necessary evil. (20)

Your response could make reference to the following points:

- Conflicts where war may have been a necessary evil, eg World War Two, Iraq, Afghanistan
- Development of the realist view of war
- Criticisms of the pacifist views of war
- The suffering of innocent people renders all war immoral
- Modern weapons have led to a situation where war must be avoided at all costs

ETHICS OF CONTEMPORARY WARFARE

There are a number of ethical issues involved concerning modern warfare. These include the following four issues:

- The impact of war on human experience
- Weapons of Mass Destruction (WMD)
- The rise of terrorism
- The problem of militarism

1. The impact of war on human experience

War inflicts unnecessary suffering on millions of humans throughout the world. All humans are created in the image and likeness of God (Genesis 1:27) and therefore war, which destroys human life, is immoral.

Conventional warfare (ie war which does not involve the use of nuclear weapons) causes human suffering in a variety of ways, for example the use of child soldiers, the creation of refugees, the use of barbaric weapons and genocide.

- The use of **child soldiers** in modern conflict is a major cause of concern. Young children living in war torn countries are quite often abducted from their parents and forced to follow orders or die. Stott[50] comments that there may be as many as 300,000 child soldiers involved in conflicts throughout the world today.

The following quotation from the Human Rights Watch website highlights the extent of this problem:

"Child soldiers perform a range of tasks including: participation in combat; laying mines and explosives; scouting, spying, acting as decoys, couriers or guards; training, drill or other preparations; logistics and support functions, portering, cooking and domestic labour. Child soldiers may also be subjected to sexual slavery or other forms of sexual abuse."[51]

 TASK

Visit the Human Rights Watch website and search for 'The Voices of Child Soldiers'.

Read some of the accounts of the experiences of children as a result of their direct involvement in war.

- Another effect of war on human experience is that it causes suffering through the creation of **refugees**. Because of the effects of war, people are forced to flee their home country and seek refuge in other countries where they feel safer. Singer[52] argues that there are 15 million refugees in the world today who take refuge in the developing areas of the world and this puts an even greater strain on their limited resources. Therefore the knock-on effect of war in this respect has a much greater negative impact on human experience.
- War also causes human suffering through the use of **barbaric weapons** such as **landmines**, which according to Stott claim between 15 and 20,000 new casualties every year.[53] Land mines were first used during World War Two and are still used today in a number of conflicts.[54] They are designed to maim rather than kill, so that a greater amount of resources are used caring for an injured soldier in comparison to dealing with a dead soldier. The International Campaign to Ban Landmines claims that landmines laid during times of war are immoral for a number of reasons:
  1. They are indiscriminate, as they cannot be aimed and can kill or injure soldiers, children, civilians, peacekeepers and aid workers alike.
  2. They are inhumane and those who survive the effects of the immediate blast often require amputations and extensive rehabilitation.

3. They are counterproductive in terms of a country's economic development as they deprive people of land and often kill livestock.

- War can also lead to **mass murder** of groups of people, with the intention of destroying the existence of the entire group or race. This is referred to as **genocide**, a word formed by a Jewish refugee Raphael Lemkin in 1944 to describe the Nazi policy, which sought to destroy the Jewish race. The word comes from the Greek word for race, *geno* and the Latin word for murder, *cide*. More recently, genocide has taken place in Rwanda in 1994, when the Hutus killed 800,000 people from another group, the Tutsis, over a period of one hundred days. This 'ethnic cleansing' is considered to be an international crime. However, it still remains a feature of war today. For example, in Sudan, the government and their militia, known as the Janjaweed, are fighting rebel groups in the Darfur region of west Sudan. They indiscriminately attack civilians from the same ethnic group as the rebels. According to an article produced by the United States Holocaust Memorial Museum, as a result of this genocide in Darfur, "hundreds of thousands of civilians have died from violence, disease, and starvation, and thousands of women have been raped. More than 2.5 million civilians have been driven from their homes, their villages torched and property stolen."[55]

◎ OTHER ASPECTS OF HUMAN EXPERIENCE

The suffering experienced by such a multitude of people during times of war has led many to doubt the existence of God. They claim that if God really existed and if he is omniscient, omnipotent and benevolent why would he allow such suffering to take place? Elie Wiesel's book *Night* is a written account of the suffering endured by Jews in concentration camps during World War Two. Wiesel is a Holocaust survivor and was held in Auschwitz and Buchenwald. As a result of his experiences during the Holocaust he lost faith in the existence of God and this is expressed in the following lines which describe how he felt during his time in Auschwitz:

"Never shall I forget that night, the first night in camp...

Never shall I forget that smoke.

Never shall I forget the small faces of the children whose bodies I saw transformed into smoke under a silent sky.

Never shall I forget those flames that consumed my faith forever...

Never shall I forget those moments that murdered my God."[56]

He also describes the execution of three prisoners in the camp for possession of arms – one was a small boy. As he was executed, one of the thousands of onlookers shouted: "Where is merciful God? Where is he?" As they watched the boy die, the same onlooker again cried in despair: "For God's sake, where is God?" Wiesel, in response replied: "This is where – hanging here from the gallows."[57] As his response suggests, the Holocaust destroyed Wiesel's faith as he felt that a God who would allow such suffering and not intervene in any way was not worthy of worship.

The counter-argument used by those who justify the existence of God in light of so much evil is referred to as the 'free will defence' which asserts that God has given humanity free will and people who commit evil acts, such as those committed during war as described earlier, do so because they abuse their God-given freedom. Harold Kushner comments that because we have free will "some bad people choose evil...some have the ability to do harm to millions."[58] For many Christians today, hardship and suffering encountered during times of war can have the effect of strengthening their religious faith. They feel that God is not detached from human suffering, as Wiesel felt, but that he is present and endures suffering alongside humanity. As Kushner comments, God "was with the victims, and not with the murderers",[59] but, having created humans as autonomous beings, there was nothing he could do to prevent this suffering.

2. Weapons of Mass Destruction (WMD)

Conventional warfare inflicts human suffering on a massive scale. However, this suffering is relatively limited in comparison to the suffering inflicted if Weapons of Mass Destruction were used. WMD have the potential to destroy the existence of human life as we know it and on this issue Stott comments: "of all the global problems which confront us today, none is graver than the threat of the self-destruction of the human race."[60]

WMD are divided into three separate groups and are referred to by Stott as 'ABC' weapons, which he claims: *"challenge the relevance of the 'just war' theory"*:

a) Atomic (or Nuclear) weapons
b) Biological weapons
c) Chemical weapons[61]

a) Atomic (or Nuclear) weapons

One of the problems with war in our modern society is the availability and destructive capability of nuclear weapons. Nuclear weapons are currently held by at least seven countries, according to Stott, including the United States, Britain, France, Russia and China.[62]

The dangers of using nuclear weapons were made clear in August 1945 when the US dropped nuclear bombs on Hiroshima and Nagasaki in Japan. Over 140,000 people died in the immediate aftermath of the explosion and even more suffered death soon afterwards due to the effects of radiation. Stott refers to the immediate effects of the atomic bombs as experienced by victims:

> "Within a few seconds the thousands of people in the streets in the centre of the town were scorched by a wave of searing heat. Many were killed instantly, others lay writhing on the ground screaming in agony from the intolerable pain of their burns...Hiroshima had ceased to exist."[63]

Many claim that the use of the atomic bomb was morally justified because they brought an end to the war and in this case the end justifies the means. However, the long term effects are just as horrific as the immediate effects of the bomb. Babies continue to be born with severe abnormalities due to the effects of radiation and there is still a high incidence of cancer in these areas over sixty years later. This high incidence of cancer will continue long into the future and Stott comments that the long-term negative impact that such weapons have on the environment is incalculable.[64]

During the Cold War it was also believed that it was an advantage for a country to increase its arsenal of nuclear weapons so that it would not be attacked by another country. It was believed that the possession of nuclear weapons acted as a deterrent. For example, Britain would not strike first and thus avoid a nuclear attack from another country in retaliation. According to Measor, the concept of mutually assured destruction (MAD) refers to the idea that if one country launches a nuclear attack on another country which also possess nuclear weapons, then they will reciprocate by returning fire at the aggressor. He claims: "if MAD exists its presence will serve as an extremely effective nuclear deterrent."[65] Stott claims that it is morally defensible to possess weapons which will never be used in order to prevent other countries from using their nuclear weapons. However, he claims: "a deterrent lacks credibility if the enemy knows we would never use it, and if it lacks credibility it loses its power to deter."[66]

Another advantage of having a stockpile of nuclear weapons is that they can be used in self defence in the event of an enemy takeover. The reality of domination by another country may be a greater evil than a nuclear war because we could never allow our country to be subjugated. For many people, subjugation would be intolerable, even worse than nuclear war. However, Stott reflects on what he believed to be the greater evil in such a scenario and concludes that it would be better to live under an oppressive regime than have to bear responsibility for the destruction of humanity – to suffer injustice ourselves rather than inflict injustice on others.[67]

Despite any advantages that the possession of nuclear weapons may have, many people in society today are involved in campaigns which they hope will lead to nuclear disarmament. Those who support CND (Campaign for Nuclear Disarmament), for example, aim to achieve unilateral disarmament. This will occur only when one country takes the initiative and disarms all of its nuclear weapons. It is then hoped that other countries will follow their example. As an alternative to unilateral disarmament, countries could engage in multilateral disarmament, whereby they would agree with a number of other countries to reduce their stockpile of nuclear weapons by a certain amount within a specific time.

Christian denominations are unequivocal in their condemnation of nuclear weapons and also call for nuclear disarmament. The Church of England reported in 1948 that "the use of nuclear weapons cannot be justified"[68] because they are inconsistent with the concept of a just war. The Catholic Church also made clear at the Second Vatican Council: "Any act of war aimed indiscriminately at the destruction of entire cities or of extensive areas along with their population is a crime against God and man himself."[69] According to Stott: "Christians everywhere, together with all those who want peace, should therefore campaign for the abolition of weapons of mass destruction."[70]

b) Biological weapons

Biological weapons spread diseases such as anthrax and smallpox, causing maximum suffering to those receiving the attack. Such weapons are relatively inexpensive in comparison to nuclear weapons and this has created tension among the leaders of the world as poorer rogue countries are able to afford them. One of the reasons for the invasion of Iraq in 2003 was because it was believed that Iraq was stockpiling such weapons. This caused panic due to its links with Al Quaida and the threat of possible terrorist attacks. No weapons were ever found.

c) Chemical weapons

The use of mustard gas during World War One was the first time chemical weapons were used during war and as already mentioned, chemical weapons have been used by Saddam Hussein's regime against the Kurds in more recent times.

The greatest fear with regard to the use of biological and chemical weapons today is that because they are so inexpensive to develop they could be easily used by terrorist groups. During the attacks on London on 7 July 2005, suicide bombers detonated four bombs within seconds of each other. Many were killed and hundreds injured, but if, as was feared, biological or chemical weapons had been used, the consequences would have been much more severe.

 TASKS

1. Nuclear weapons were used at the end of World War Two and it is believed that they brought an end to the war. Do you think it is ever acceptable to use any form of weapon of mass destruction – nuclear, chemical or biological?

2. Comment on the claim that a nuclear war could never be a just war. Refer to the conditions outlined in the Just War Theory to justify your answer.

3. The rise of terrorism

Stott argues: "the human conflict with which we are grappling at the outset of the twenty-first century is not the threat of nuclear exchange between nation states, but the rise of terrorism."[71] Reference has already been made to the attacks on London in July 2005 which have been blamed on Muslim extremists. In Islam, the concept of *Jihad* or a 'holy war' derives from the Qur'an and refers to the responsibility of a practising Muslim to defend Islam using force, if necessary, when Islam is under threat or oppression. This idea of *Jihad* is used by extremist groups to justify attacks, such as those in London or on the Twin Towers on 11 September 2001. In fact, some Muslims believe that this practice of suicide bombing is the ultimate way of serving Allah. It is their key to Paradise, despite the fact that the attacks do not discriminate in any way against men, women and children who may simply be on a crowded bus or in a busy restaurant.

The topic of suicide bombing raises many ethical issues. However, in the context of the present discussion, if groups such as Al Quaida acquire or develop WMD, this would be a major concern because they would not hesitate to use them to further their own cause. The named reason for the invasion of Iraq was a war on terror because it was felt that Iraq had developed weapons of mass destruction and would allow them to fall into the hands of terrorists. On the other hand, the debate about this war on terror has raised questions about the legitimacy of war. The media has provided several examples of American and British troops involved in the abuse of prisoners-of-war in Iraq. There is also the issue of the denial of basic human rights to internees held at Guantanamo Bay, where it is alleged that sleep deprivation and torture are used on detainees. It is also claimed that when this war was declared it was not a last resort. The attack on Iraq was pre-emptive and it was not legitimised by the United Nations.

4. The problem of militarism

Militarism refers to the glorification of war[72] and in many societies today a military spirit is prevalent. Jenkins[73] highlights some of the values of militarism:

- Militarism makes people have a blind obedience to their leaders, where they follow whatever the authoritarian regime instructs them to do. This blind obedience was evident from the control the Nazis had over the German population through propaganda and fear prior to World War Two.
- Militarism creates an elitist society which reflects the hierarchy of authority in the military. As a result, divisions are created in the class system.
- Militarism dehumanises society because soldiers are trained to be aggressive through brutal training regimes and, as a result, they no longer have "respect for human life or feeling."[74]

PACIFISM

A person is referred to as a pacifist if they oppose war and violence. Pacifists will generally believe that war causes too much destruction and loss of human life and is therefore morally unacceptable. There are two types of pacifism:

- Total pacifism
- Relative pacifism

Total pacifism

Total pacifism prohibits any form of violence or participation in military activity regardless of the motives. Many Christians today are total pacifists due to the absolute prohibition of killing in the Decalogue (Exodus 20:13) and the teachings of Jesus, in the Sermon on the Mount, where he totally rejected any form of resistance. They also refer to the actions of Jesus in the Garden of Gethsemane when he did not retaliate against his opponents. Jesus taught that we must love our enemies and exemplified this when he forgave those who were responsible for his death (Luke 23:34). Absolute or total pacifism follows the example and teaching of Jesus and therefore does not allow people to engage in military activity. Jesus and the entire tradition of the early church up to the time of Constantine (AD272–337) practised non-violence. In Romans 12:14–21, Paul supports the pacifist stance: *"Bless those who persecute you; bless and do not curse...Rejoice with those who rejoice; mourn with those who mourn. Live in harmony with one another...Do not be overcome by evil, but overcome evil with good."*

Tertullian (AD160–220), one of the Early Church Fathers, outlined the standard Christian attitude in opposition to war in the second century. Tertullian believed that Christians had to avoid bloodshed at all costs and therefore, Christianity and military service were incompatible. Tertullian referred to the incident in the Garden of Gethsemane and commented: "But how will a Christian man war without a sword which the Lord has taken away? The Lord, in disarming Peter, unbelted every soldier."[75]

The Quakers and Amish communities still follow this teaching, that violence is intrinsically wrong. George Fox (1624–91), the founder of Quakerism, believed that war was incompatible with the teachings of Jesus and, as a result, the Quakers declare that the Spirit of Christ will "never move us to fight and war against any man with outward weapons, neither for the kingdom of Christ, nor for the kingdoms of the world."[76]

Those who are pacifists have the ability to refuse to fight if a war is declared and conscription imposed. They can become 'conscientious objectors' and rather than directly fighting in a war they can work as civilians or as non-combatants who care for injured or dying soldiers. Alternatively, a pacifist can oppose injustice using non-violent protests to highlight the cause. There have been many examples of people who have applied pacifist principles of non-violence to their quest for lasting peace. Gandhi and Martin Luther King both refused to use violence, but protested instead using other non-violent methods.

OTHER ASPECTS OF HUMAN EXPERIENCE

- Mahatma Gandhi (1869–1948) promoted a non-violent struggle in India in order to gain freedom from British rule. Jenkins[77] comments that Gandhi and his followers were attacked and beaten time after time, yet they did not retaliate nor were they defeated. Like Jesus, Ghandi rejected any form of revenge or retribution and in relation to the concept of an eye for an eye, he famously commented "an eye for an eye makes the whole world blind."
- Martin Luther King (1929–68) was also involved in non-violent action such as strikes and peaceful protests to oppose racism in America during the 1960s. He envisaged a society where all people would be treated equally and in his famous speech made on 28 August 1963, he said: "I have a dream that my four little children will one day live in a nation where they will not be judged by the colour of their skin but by the content of their character."

Research the life and work of either Gandhi or Martin Luther King. What impact did their protests have on their own human experience and the human experience of others?

Critics of absolute pacifism, however, such as the Protestant theologian Reinhold Niebuhr claim that the concept of pacifism is naïve and that pacifists are guilty of accepting evil instead of fighting against it.[78] For example, it would be immoral to allow Hitler and Nazism to spread unchecked throughout Europe. Pacifists would argue that you cannot defeat evil by killing innocent people, yet force was required to stop the Nazis. Vardy and Grosch comment: "if all warfare is rejected, this also means rejecting the possibility of taking up arms to protect innocent people against a cruel and vicious government."[79]

Relative pacifism

The above criticisms lead some to justify the use of force in certain circumstances. Relative or nuclear[80] pacifism claims that we should strive to solve problems using peaceful methods. However, as a last resort, the use of violence in the struggle for justice is sometimes legitimate. Many claim that total pacifism is too idealistic and they feel that a realist approach is necessary. This considers the fact that the consequences of war can sometimes be justified. According to Bowie: "Realism argues that special moral rules apply...this means that war that serves the national interest is morally acceptable."[81]

Biblical teaching can also be used to justify this point of view. In Genesis 9:6 we are informed: *"Whoever sheds the blood of man, by man shall his blood be shed; for in the image of God has God made man."* In the context of this, we should not stand by and allow innocent blood to be shed, as Stott claims: "to shed the blood of the innocent is, therefore, the gravest social sin."[82] For Christians, it is their moral responsibility to protect innocent life. This is the view of the main Christian denominations today, which are of the opinion that the idea of justice is of central importance to the issue. In order for justice to exist there must be harmony between all groups in society and the rights of all individuals must be preserved. The importance of justice is promoted in Amos 5:21–4 which states: *"But let justice roll down like a river, righteousness like an never-failing stream!"* and Micah 6:8 asks: *"And what does the LORD require of you? To act justly and to love mercy and to walk humbly with your God."* In the absence of justice for all people, it is acceptable to go to war so that they achieve equality.

Methodist teaching reflects this approach to war. Methodists believe:

"the principles of pacifism are clearly in keeping with the message of Jesus. We believe that both the creation and the use of weapons of mass destruction are immoral…however, we recognise that in practice, there may be circumstances in which limited military action is a necessary evil in order to reduce or remove an even greater evil."[83]

The Catholic Church also comments: "All citizens and all governments are obliged to work for the avoidance of war. However…governments cannot be denied the right of lawful self-defence, once all peace efforts have failed."[84]

 PRACTICE ESSAY TITLES

Question from CCEA Specimen Paper 2009 A2 6

(a) Present a case for and discuss the central ethical issues surrounding pacifism. (30)

Question from CCEA Specimen Paper 2009 A2 6

(b) Critically assess the view that all Christians should be pacifists. (20)

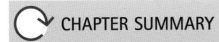 **CHAPTER SUMMARY**

The Just War tradition in Christianity

- Old Testament references which generally support the concept of war.
- New Testament teaching which promotes the concept of pacifism.
- Development of the Just War Theory by Augustine, Aquinas, de Vitoria, Suarez and the Catholic bishops.
- The conditions of the Just war Theory under the headings *Jus ad Bellum* and *Jus in Bello*.
- An evaluation of the Just War Theory.

Ethics of contemporary warfare

- The negative impact of war on human experience with reference to child soldiers, refugees, use of barbaric weapons and the issue of genocide.
- The effects of weapons of mass destruction with specific reference to the debate about the use of nuclear weapons.
- The rise of terrorism.
- The problem of militarism.

Pacifism

- Total pacifism with relation to the teachings of Jesus and the problems associated with this approach.
- Relative pacifism and the claim that war can be justified as the lesser of two evils to ensure that all people are treated with justice and equality.

Endnotes

1 Jenkins, J, *Ethics and Religion*, Heinemann, Oxford, 1999, p118

2 Tyler, S & Reid, G, *Religious Studies, Philip Allen Updates*, Oxfordshire, 2002, p193

3 Wilcockson, M, *Issues of Life and Death*, Hodder & Stoughton, London, 1999, p111

4 *ibid*, p111

5 Tyler & Reid, *op cit*, p194

6 Bettenson, H, *Documents of the Christian Church*, Oxford University Press, Oxford, 1986, p16

7 Quote taken from Bettenson, H, *Documents of the Christian Church*, Oxford University Press, Oxford, 1986, p22

8 Vardy, P & Grosch, P, *Puzzle of Ethics*, Harper Collins, London, 1999, p168

9 Wilcockson, *op cit*, p112

10 Vardy & Grosch, *op cit*, p168

11 *ibid*, p168

12 Romans 13:1

13 Pope Urban II. Quote taken from Jenkins, J, *Ethics and Religion* – Second Edition, Heinemann, Oxford, 2003, p170

14 Aquinas, *Summa Theologica*, 1273. Quote taken from Bowie, R, *Ethical Studies*, Nelson Thornes, Cheltenham, 2004, p207

15 Wilcockson, *op cit*, p113

16 *ibid*, p113

17 Vardy & Grosch, *op cit*, p176

18 Bowie, *op cit*, p200

19 Vardy & Grosch, *op cit*, p169

20 Stott, J, *Issues Facing Christians Today* – Fourth Edition, Zondervan, Michigan, 2006, p106

21 Bowie, *op cit*, p200

22 United Nations Article 51. Quote taken from Wilcockson, *op cit*, p107

23 'Killing of Iraq Kurds Genocide', BBC News, 13 December 2005, www.bbc.co.uk, accessed 12 November 2008

24 'Iraqi Kurds Recall Chemical Attack', BBC News, 17 March 2002, www.bbc.co.uk, accessed 12 November 2008

25 Vardy & Grosch, *op cit*, p170

26 'G8's Zimbabwe Statement', BBC News, 8 July 2008, www.bbc.co.uk, accessed 12 November 2008

27 Vardy & Grosch, *op cit*, p171

28 Bowie, *op cit*, p200

29 Vardy & Grosch, *op cit*, p171

30 Thompson, M, *An Introduction to Philosophy and Ethics*, Hodder & Stoughton, London, 2003, p214

31 Vardy & Grosch, *op cit*, p171

32 Stott, *op cit*, p107

33 Bowie, *op cit*, p201

34 Vardy & Grosch, *op cit*, p173

35 Wilcockson, *op cit*, p110

36 Stott, *op cit*, p97

37 Bowie, *op cit*, p202

38 *ibid*, p202

39 Thompson, *op cit*, p213

40 Jenkins, *op cit*, p172

41 Vardy & Grosch, *op cit*, p176

42 Bowie, *op cit*, p202

43 Jenkins, *op cit*, p174

44 Bowie, *op cit*, p203

45 Thompson, *op cit*, p212

46 Vardy & Grosch, *op cit*, p175

47 Jenkins, *op cit*, p123

48 Tyler & Reid, *op cit*, p197

49 Jenkins, *op cit*, p122

50 Stott, *op cit*, p98

51 'Child Soldiers Global Report 2008 – Summary, Coalition To Stop The Use Of Child Soldiers', Human Rights Watch, www.hrw.org, accessed 12 January 2009

52 Singer, P, *Practical Ethics*, Cambridge University Press, Cambridge, 1993, p249

53 Stott, *op cit*, p97–8

54 International Campaign to Ban Landmines, www.icbl.org, accessed 2 January 2009

55 'Genocide Emergency: Darfur', United States Holocaust Museum, www.ushmm.org, accessed 5 January 2009

56 NIGHT by Elie Wiesel. Copyright © 1972, 1985 by Elie Wiesel.

57 *ibid*, p65

58 Kushner, H, *When Bad Things Happen To Good People*, Anchor Books, New York, 2004, p92

59 *ibid*, p94

60 Stott, *op cit*, p97

61 *ibid*, p105

62 *ibid*, p101

63 *ibid*, p101

64 *ibid*, p102

65 Measor, N, 'Games Theory and the Nuclear Arms Race', in Singer, P, *Applied Ethics*, Oxford University Press, Oxford, 1986, p238

66 Stott, *op cit*, p119

67 *ibid* p122

68 The Church and the Atom, 1948, Quote taken from Tyler & Reid, *op cit*, p198

69 The Catholic Church. Quote taken from Stott, *op cit*, p115

70 Stott, *op cit*, p115

71 Stott, *op cit*, p122

72 *ibid*, p166

73 Jenkins, *op cit*, p166

74 *ibid*, p124

75 Kelly, J, *The World of the Early Christians*, Liturgical Press, 1997, p162

76 The Quakers. Quote taken from Wilcockson, *op cit*, p104

77 Jenkins, *op cit*, p127

78 Tyler & Reid, *op cit*, p198

79 Vardy & Grosch, *op cit*, p178

80 Nuclear pacifism refers to the belief that war which makes use of nuclear weapons can never be considered 'just' because of the devastating consequences which result from using such weapons. Nuclear pacifists agree that war which uses conventional weapons is acceptable in certain limited circumstances and this belief is similar to that held by relative pacifists.

81 Bowie, *op cit*, p206

82 Stott, *op cit*, p113

83 'Practical Expressions of Methodist Belief', The Methodist Church in Ireland, accessed 26 November 2008

84 *Catechism of the Catholic Church*, Veritas, Dublin, 1994, 2308

Chapter 10

Ethics of Justice and Punishment

Chapter overview

This chapter aims to explore the ethical issues surrounding the following topics:
- Methods and purpose of punishment: the ethical debate
- Ethical and religious perspectives on punishment
- Capital punishment

T HE CONCEPT OF JUSTICE has been developed from the time of Plato to more modern philosophers such as Nozick and Rawls. According to Horner and Westacott, justice includes "fairness" and "equal opportunities for all to make something of their lives."[1]

The various theories concerning justice can be divided into two general groups:

1. Theories which focus on the importance of the individual, promoting the idea that the individual comes first, are generally referred to as 'individualistic' theories of justice.

2. In contrast, theories of justice which focus on the importance of the community are referred to as 'communitarian' theories, "which are based on the assumption that the good of the community must come before the good of any single individual within it."[2]

In *The Republic*, the ancient Greek philosopher Plato (428–347 BC) outlined a communitarian approach to justice "where the good of the city-state is placed above the good of any single individual."[3] Plato argued that justice was concerned with the protection of all people from suffering at the hands of others who may wish to exploit them. Thompson comments that for Plato, justice "is a matter of achieving harmony between the different parts of society."[4]

Thomas Hobbes (1588–1679) was an English philosopher who developed the concept of a just society from an individualistic perspective. In his book *The Leviathan*, published in 1651, he argued that the leader of a society should establish just laws to preserve the freedom and to protect the rights of the people under his authority. In return, the members of society must respect the laws and the authority of the ruler. Hobbes' idea of a 'social contract' therefore aims to "ensure maximum freedom combined with personal security."[5]

John Locke (1632–1704), another influential English philosopher, believed that individuals should have rights, but these rights must be governed by the laws of the society in which we live. He argued that it was the responsibility of the state authorities to ensure that rights are upheld and that laws are respected. Locke followed an individualistic approach to the concept of justice. He considered that each individual had "a moral right not to harm another"[6] but that we should not have to worry about the needs of anyone else; we should simply concern ourselves with our own personal or individual needs.

The Swiss philosopher, Jean-Jacques Rousseau (1712–1778) argued in favour of a 'social contract' based on communitarian principles. He believed that in order to create a just society, people should have individual liberty but they must also move away from a "self-focused lifestyle to one that took account of others."[7] Rousseau believed that laws should be created by members of society coming together and voting to express the general will or what is best for society as a whole. Once laws are made by all members of society acting together, everyone is legally bound to keep the laws without exception. Unlike the views held by Locke, Rousseau believed that the rights and the needs of the individual were secondary to the general needs of society.

John Rawls (1921–2002) produced *A Theory of Justice* in 1971, in which he expressed his belief that not only are we morally obliged to ensure that we do not harm another person, but that we also have an obligation "to assist those who are worse off than ourselves."[8] His approach to justice is communitarian in nature. Rawls claimed that in order to have a truly just society, we must imagine a situation whereby we put aside all personal bias. If we were able to do this then we would establish two principles.

1. Each person has the equal right to the maximum amount of liberty.
2. Inequalities are only permitted if they will benefit the less well-off members of society.[9]

If we accept Rawls' approach to justice then in our society today we must view "the law, the court and the judges as the protectors of the weak."[10]

Robert Nozick (1938–2002) approached the concept of justice from a more individualistic perspective than Rawls. Rather than view justice as helping those in need, Nozick, in his book *Anarchy, State and Utopia* (1974), claimed that justice was about entitlement. According to Nozick, as individuals we are entitled to all of our earnings and possessions providing that we remain within the boundaries of the law. Therefore, we do not have a moral obligation to assist those who are less well off than ourselves but we must not exploit others in order to acquire wealth.

TASK

Using the above views of justice, complete two spider diagrams highlighting the views of the philosophers mentioned:

1. An outline of the individualistic theories of justice

2. An outline of the communitarian theories of justice

METHODS AND PURPOSE OF PUNISHMENT: THE ETHICAL DEBATE

In order to ensure that justice is promoted in society, rules or laws are created by the governing authorities so that individual members of society are aware of what is considered to be acceptable and unacceptable behaviour. To vindicate these rules, punishments are enforced to deal with instances when the rules governing society are broken. Tyler and Reid claim: "Justice...will have little meaning if the governing body of society...cannot ensure that its laws are respected by its citizens."[11]

The purpose of punishment

According to Tyler and Reid, punishment refers to "The intentional infliction of pain by a legal authority on those who have breached its standards of behaviour."[12] There are five key aims of punishment:

1. Protection
2. Retribution
3. Rehabilitation
4. Deterrence
5. Vindication

1. Protection

Criminals threaten the safety of the individuals who live in their community and they also threaten the stability of society in general. Therefore punishment, such as sending criminals to prison, is necessary to protect society and allow those living in it to feel safer. The utilitarian John Stuart Mill comments: "The only purpose for which power can rightfully be exercised over any member of a civilised community against his will is to prevent harm to others. His own good is not a sufficient warrant."[13] On utilitarian grounds, punishment can therefore be justified due to the greater good that results from the protection of the whole community. In some cases, prison can also protect the criminal from society, for example, from vigilantes who want to take the law into their own hands because of the repulsive nature of the offender's crime.

2. Retribution

The aim of using punishment as a form of retribution or revenge is based on the Old Testament concept of *lex talionis*, *"eye for eye, tooth for tooth"*[14] which implies that those who have done wrong must bear the consequences of doing so. The criminal is individually responsible for the crime and must pay for what they have done wrong. Society is entitled to some sort of revenge because of the behaviour of the criminal. Consequently the purpose of punishment is not to reduce crime but simply to satisfy the need for something to be done to compensate the victims of crime. Wilcockson[15] notes that this aim of punishment is referred to as being 'backward looking' because it does not aim to reduce crime, but simply to give criminals what they deserve. This idea of 'just deserts' is a key principle related to the aim of retribution.

A number of philosophers agree with this purpose of punishment.

- Kant, for example, agreed that it is important that criminals get what they deserve, for no reason other than the positive impact this has on society: "When someone who delights in annoying and vexing peace–loving folk receives at last a right good beating, it is certainly an ill, but everyone approves of it and considers it as good in itself."[16]
- Rachels also agrees that it is acceptable to treat criminals "in the same way that they have treated others...those who have treated others badly deserve to be treated badly in return."[17] With reference to the concept of justice, Rachels believes that in order for the victims of crime to receive justice, the criminals must be adequately punished.

However, the concept of *lex talionis* is relevant only if the crime was intended. Those who commit crime accidentally cannot be punished in the same way as those who have intentionally committed a crime. For example, Vardy and Grosch[18] contrast the case of a wife who has been the victim of domestic violence and who kills her husband in self defence with the case of armed robbers killing a bank guard. Of course the punishment cannot be the same in both cases because it would be wrong to think of punishment in terms of revenge for the victim of domestic violence who has acted in self defence. The problem with retribution is that it does not take into account the mental state of the person who has committed the crime or factors which can mitigate a crime. Wilcockson comments that retributivism is "barbaric and void of any human compassion or benevolence."[19] The other problem with the concept of *lex talionis* is that it cannot be applied consistently. For example, it can be applied to cases of murder whereby someone who takes a life has their own taken from them, but how do we apply it in the case of punishment for stealing or sex offences, etc.

An alternative to retribution is restorative justice, which aims to "repair the harm caused or revealed by criminal behaviour."[20] This form of punishment aims to restore or give something back to those who have been injured and quite often it will impose a punishment or burden on the criminal, so that their victim is satisfied that they have realised the extent of the harm they have caused. Restorative justice programmes promote key values which include:

1. Encounter: the offenders and their victims may meet to discuss the crime and its effects
2. Amends: offenders must take steps to atone for the harm they have caused
3. Reintegration: restorative justice aims to fully restore victims and offenders to the community[21]

The offenders do not literally have to replace the stolen or damaged goods, as the concept of *lex talionis* promotes, but they must provide some sort of satisfaction for the suffering they have caused the victim. Bowie[22] comments that restorative justice may lead on to the rehabilitation or reformation of the criminal, because if they realise the suffering they have caused the victim, they will not commit crime again.

3. Rehabilitation

This aims to reform or change the character of the criminal or their values so that they will not re-offend. It attempts to address and remove the causes of crime. Unlike retribution, rehabilitation is forward looking. It is considered to be an effective way of reinforcing to the criminal important values, attempting to give them a second chance, an opportunity to "return the offender back into society as a useful member."[23] In practical terms, this system sometimes brings criminals face to face with the victims of their crimes to make them aware of the effects their actions have had on other people. This approach is mainly used for young offenders as explained by Vardy and Grosch: "Junior offenders are sometimes confronted with those individuals whose property they have damaged in order for them to see the effects of their action, with the aim that once they see this they will not re-offend."[24]

In reality, however, prisons are not places which can easily reform people and their experience may actually harden their criminal disposition[25]. As Vardy and Grosch put it, prisons are "schools of crime in which contacts are made and techniques are learnt."[26] To illustrate the negative impact prisons have on human experience, they use the example of a young man who was imprisoned in the US for one year for the possession of marihuana. He was put in a room with twelve other men who sexually assaulted him every hour for forty-eight hours. Vardy and Grosch conclude: "This is hardly the atmosphere conducive to reform."[27] The view that prison is not effective at rehabilitating offenders is shared by Bowie, who argues: "half of all prisoners re-offend within two years."[28] Another concern is the difficulty in knowing if they are actually rehabilitated. For example, a person could be imprisoned for sex offences and through good behaviour, putting on an act and saying the right things to the right people, he could be released and offend again. A third concern is that the victims of the crime may feel that justice has not been served because the crime committed to them or to a family member has gone relatively unpunished because so much attention has been directed at reforming the offender.

4. Deterrence

This purpose of punishment aims to discourage people from committing crimes, either through preventing criminals from re-offending or by putting off would-be criminals as they may decide that the crime is not worth the risk of being punished in the same way as others who have committed the crime. Vardy and Grosch use the words of Sir Thomas Burnet, an eighteenth-century judge, who said to a man he had sentenced to death for stealing a horse: "You are not being hanged for stealing a horse, but so that horses may not be stolen."[29] Therefore the suffering and in some societies, the death of the criminal, is an example to others of what will happen to them if they are involved in criminal activity. This is also a forward looking aim of punishment as it attempts to make society a better place.

However, it is not clear from available evidence if punishment does actually deter. In the heat of the moment many criminals do not consider the consequences of their actions and therefore do not think rationally about the punishment they are likely to receive if they are caught.

5. Vindication

This aim of punishment considers the punishment of the criminal as necessary or justified in order to inform society that laws must be respected and that law breaking will not be tolerated. Therefore, this aim of punishment sends a message to society that those in authority intend to uphold justice and while the law may been broken, it is imperative that others keep this law.

The methods of punishment

Tyler and Reid[30] outline the common methods of punishment used today, all of which intend in some way to meet the five aims of punishment as described above.

- Harm to the body. Corporal punishment, for example, the loss of a hand for a thief. Capital punishment, the execution of a criminal for the most serious crimes.
- Harm to property, such as taking goods away from criminals who have accumulated wealth through drug dealing or imposing fines as a quick and effective punishment.
- Restriction of movement, for example, the removal of freedom through imprisonment, curfew or electronic tagging. This could also refer to the imposition of community service, whereby the criminal must do something positive for society to compensate for his wrongdoing.
- Harm to reputation refers to the public shaming of the criminal. In some cases this is to protect society, for example, the publication of the sex offenders list makes people aware if anyone who has been convicted of sex offences lives in a certain area.

ETHICAL AND RELIGIOUS PERSPECTIVES ON PUNISHMENT

Before moving on to the capital punishment debate, there are five additional ethical perspectives to consider on the issue of punishment.

1. Utilitarian views on punishment
2. The views of Kant
3. The issue of moral responsibility
4. Human Rights Issues
5. Christian attitudes towards punishment

Utilitarian views on punishment

The utilitarian ideal, which aims to promote the greatest amount of happiness for the greatest number, implies that punishment can be morally justified if it benefits society. We have already noted the comment made by John Stuart Mill, which argued that punishment and the subsequent removal of the criminal's freedom is essential to ensure that harm does not come to other people. Utilitarians also argue that if punishment has the effect of deterring people from committing crime, then it is worthwhile because society will be a better and safer place in which to live, achieving happiness.

Vardy and Grosch[31] comment that one problem with the utilitarian view is that it could justify punishment of an innocent person if it had the effect of promoting greater happiness in society. For example, if a large crowd of people living in a community are about to riot due to the inability of the police to convict a murderer or a rapist, the punishment of someone who is innocent could appease the crowd and "diffuse the tension in the community."[32] However, one could argue that if it was discovered that the innocent person was punished, the effect of knowing the state was responsible for this miscarriage of justice would create a greater amount of unhappiness. Vardy and Grosch conclude: "Whatever the short term benefit that might come from the punishment of an innocent person, the harm that would result if and when the truth came out would more than outweigh any such benefits."[33]

On utilitarian grounds, the cost of punishment must also be taken into consideration. Sending criminals to prison is a very expensive method of protecting society and it is often not good value. For a utilitarian, a more cost effective approach is necessary and the money saved could be put to better use, to promote greater happiness through, for example, a better health care system or better schools to give young people a brighter future.

PRACTICE ESSAY TITLE

Question adapted from CCEA Summer 2008 A2 6

Critically assess the view that in the utilitarian approach to punishment, the innocent will always suffer. (20)

The views of Kant

As previously mentioned, the German philosopher Immanuel Kant (1724–1804) agreed with punishment on the grounds of retribution and claimed that it is important that the criminal receives punishment because he deserves it. Kant believed that each individual has personal autonomy to act how he or she pleases, however, with this freedom comes moral responsibility. In *Philosophy of Law* Kant argues: "the last murderer lying in prison ought to be executed...this ought to be done in order that every one may realise the desert of his deeds."[34] Kant's 'categorical imperative' states that we must act according to rules which can be applied universally. Because a rule permitting murder can never be universalised, murder is immoral and if we allow a murderer to live, we reduce the value of human life. Therefore Kant believed that capital punishment was justified and Wilcockson sums up Kant's view by stating: "in permitting a murderer to live one is undermining the essential values on which society is founded."[35]

The issue of moral responsibility

In order for punishment to be morally acceptable, the offender must have committed his or her crime as an autonomous moral agent. If the freedom of an offender is limited due to mental illness, coercion or other restrictions then it is acceptable to claim that they cannot be punished in the same way as someone whose freedom was not restricted by other factors. The concept of 'diminished responsibility' states that some factors diminish the extent to which we are to blame for our actions. Jenkins[36] outlines some factors which limit our freedom and diminish the responsibility we must take for our actions.

- If someone is under the influence of powerful medication which produces psychological side effects they may not be fully responsible for their actions.
- If a person who is very young commits a crime and it was believed that they did not have the ability or maturity to think rationally about the consequences, they could not be held accountable for their actions.
- People who are forced to do something, for example, if a gun is held to their head they are obviously not morally accountable for their actions.

Vardy and Grosch consider the idea that criminal tendencies may in fact be inherited. The implication of this suggestion is that if our genetic make-up, over which we have no control, is responsible for criminal behaviour, criminals do not act freely and therefore cannot be punished. Vardy and Grosch comment: "If it can be established that criminal tendencies are based on genetic factors, then the whole arena of the debate about crime and punishment will be changed."[37] If humans are not free when they act, but have been determined by background, they cannot be punished for what they have done because freedom and moral responsibility are related.

Determinism is the belief that we have no freedom whatsoever and that all of our actions are determined by prior events or experiences. If this is the case – according to Bowie – then "humans can't be morally blameworthy for their actions"[38]. Two of the most influential determinist thinkers were Sigmund Freud (1856–1939) and Burrhus Frederic Skinner (1904–1990).

- Freud claimed that we are not free but that we act according to our upbringing because our brain has been conditioned by what we have learnt from our life experience. Therefore, as our ego and superego develop from our experiences as we progress through life, our sense of right and wrong is determined. If we are not free, as Freud suggests, we cannot be punished. As Bowie comments: "If human actions are caused by external influences, the people can't be morally responsible for those actions."[39]

- Skinner was an American psychologist who argued that the notion that humans are free is merely an illusion. His major work was called *Beyond Freedom and Dignity* and was published in 1971. In his work, he argues that every human action is the result of two things: the genetic blueprint passed on to the embryo at the moment of conception and the experiences of events which took place during our childhood. Skinner insists that belief in free will is not based on reason but is a primitive superstition and it is only because we do not fully understand the causes of our behaviour that we consider ourselves to be free. For Skinner, we are simply the products of our environment. In relation to the issue of crime, he stated: "It is the environment which is responsible for the objectionable behaviour, and it is the environment, not some attribute of the individual, which must be changed."[40]

Clarence Darrow (1857–1938), the famous American lawyer, related the views of determinist thinkers to the issue of punishment. In order to avoid the death penalty for his clients he argued that they were not morally responsible for their actions. He claimed: "The principle thing to remember is that we are all the products of heredity and environment; that we have little or no control, as individuals, over ourselves, and that criminals are like the rest of us in that regard."[41] Darrow did not argue that criminals should not be sent to prison. In fact he claimed that this was necessary to protect society, however, he did assert that they may not be morally responsible for their actions.

In one specific case in 1924, Darrow defended two teenagers who were on trial for the kidnapping and murder of a 14 year old, Bobby Franks. The teenagers were wealthy and intelligent graduates. He argued that they boys were a product of their upper class upbringing and could not be held responsible for their actions. He argued that they must be locked up to protect society but that they should not be executed for their crimes. His summation to the jury included the following statement: "If there is a responsibility anywhere, it is…somewhere in the infinite number of his ancestors, or in his surroundings, or in both…he should not be held responsible for the acts of someone else."[42] On this occasion, his plea was successful and the two killers were punished with life in prison as opposed to execution.

Vardy and Grosch agree that our actions may be influenced by our 'nature and nurture', ie, our genes and the environment which we grow up in. However, they also claim that these factors may only "influence rather than determine behaviour."[43] So it would be wrong to maintain the view of hard determinists such as Freud and Skinner who insist that we are not free, therefore we cannot be held morally responsible for our actions and cannot be punished. It is more realistic to accept the view of soft determinism, that we have free will and that while some of our actions may be conditioned, we are still responsible and blameworthy for immoral actions. As Clarke comments: "Full blown determinism would therefore undercut a basic premise of both the Christian faith and our common understanding as human beings, that we possess enough freedom to be held responsible for what we do."[44]

 PRACTICE ESSAY TITLES

Question adapted from CCEA Summer 2005 A2 6

Critically assess the view that right moral behaviour demands personal responsibility. (20)

Your response could make reference to the following points:
- The concept of determinism: the influence of genetics and environment on behaviour
- The views of determinists such as Freud and Skinner
- The idea of diminished responsibility
- Use of examples such as Clarence Darrow
- The concept of free will
- The idea that personal autonomy brings responsibility
- Views of Aquinas, Kant and Mill who agree with the idea of free will

OTHER ASPECTS OF HUMAN EXPERIENCE

After the brutal murder of three year old Jamie Bulger in Liverpool in 1993, two ten year olds – Robert Thompson and Jon Venables – were convicted of his abduction, torture and murder. At their trial it was argued that their poor upbringing was a factor which contributed to their behaviour on that day. The boys were released in 2001, after a process of rehabilitation and were moved to secret locations having been provided with new identities.

Explore the Jamie Bulger case and discuss the claim that if an impressionable child is brought up knowing only violence, foul language and selfish adult behaviour, they cannot be held responsible for their behaviour. Considering the fact that Jamie's parents will always suffer as a result of their loss, was the release of Jamie's two killers with new identities morally acceptable?

Human Rights Issues

It is of vital importance that human rights are not abused when punishment is inflicted on a criminal. Punishment must be proportional, humane and respect the equality and dignity of all people. Article 5 of the Universal Declaration states that all people have "the right not to be subjected to torture or to cruel, inhuman or degrading punishment" and the punishment inflicted on criminals must reflect this.

Christian Attitudes towards punishment

On the issue of punishment, the Old Testament puts emphasis on the need for revenge. As previously mentioned, the acceptance of retaliation was emphasised in Leviticus 24:19–20: *"If anyone injures his neighbour, whatever he has done must be done to him: fracture for fracture, eye for eye, tooth for tooth. As he has injured the other, so he is to be injured."* This concept of *lex talionis* was "the common procedure in ancient criminal cases"[45] and was actually intended to limit punishment in that it prevented excessive punishment from being inflicted. TD Alexander comments that the *lex talionis* principle ensures: "the punishment should be no less, or no worse, than the crime demands."[46]

The Old Testament also refers to the importance of punishment in the context of bringing up a family. In Proverbs 13:24 it states: *"He who spares the rod hates his son, but he who loves him is careful to discipline him."* Proverbs 23:13 also states: *"Do not withhold discipline from a child; if you punish him with the rod, he will not die."* The book of Deuteronomy goes even further on the use of punishment to discipline one's children: *"If a man has a stubborn and rebellious son who does not obey his father and mother and will not listen to them when they discipline him…Then all the men of his town shall stone him to death"* (Deuteronomy 21:18-21).

OTHER ASPECTS OF HUMAN EXPERIENCE

Some fundamentalist Christians today take the teaching from Proverbs literally and use it to justify their use of a wooden 'rod' or stick to discipline their children. One Christian writes:

> "The purpose of a spanking is not to cause any lasting bodily harm, but to cause spiritual correction...Parents should not fear that spanking will hurt or cause them to die, although some scream loud enough that it sounds that way. On the contrary, it is a kindness to a child, as they will respect authority, if it is done properly."[47]

With regards to the punishment of children, debate whether this method of discipline is morally acceptable in society today.

The Christian approach to crime and punishment reflects Jesus' teachings because it stresses the importance of forgiveness as opposed to retribution. The following New Testament references are relevant:

- On the issue of *lex talionis*, *"eye for eye"*, Jesus comments: *"If someone strikes you on the right cheek, turn to him the other also"* (Matthew 5:39).
- In the Sermon on the Mount Jesus informs his followers that they must not judge others *"or you too will be judged"* (Matthew 7:1). According to McKenzie[48] this teaching implies that we should not judge harshly or condemn anyone, although according to Harrington, it "does not rule out the practice of correction within the community".[49]
- On the issue of forgiveness we can consider the account in Matthew 18:21, when Peter asked Jesus how many times he should forgive someone who has wronged him and Jesus replied that we must forgive someone *"seventy times seven"*, not seven times as Peter suggested. This number is significant in suggesting that forgiveness for a Christian does not have any limits and Harrington comments: "The new number is not to be taken literally. The point is that Christians have no right to place any limit on forgiveness."[50]
- The need for a Christian to forgive those who have harmed them was exemplified by Jesus when he forgave his killers before he died on the cross: *"Father, forgive them, for they do not know what they are doing"* (Luke 23:34).

Despite this teaching, Jesus never explicitly states that punishment is wrong. Therefore Aquinas had no reservations in saying that punishment could take place if it was to prevent evil. In *Summa Theologica* (1273) he argued that when a criminal does something immoral through abuse of their God-given freedom, they lose their human dignity and they have "the subject state of animals...so it becomes justifiable to kill a malefactor as one would kill an animal."[51] He considered it more beneficial for society to remove the evildoers. Bernard Hoose summarises the views of Aquinas on the issue of punishment. He claims that Aquinas permitted the execution of a man for major faults and the removal of one of his limbs for less serious offences: "Suppose, then, that a limb is removed as a penalty to restrain him from sinning...the community as a whole will benefit."[52]

While Aquinas' teachings on Natural Law and other issues such as the Just War Theory and conscience are still very influential among Christians today, his views on punishment are not. Christian denominations today generally agree that both punishment and forgiveness are important. In addition to the references from the New Testament already considered, Christians use other references such as the teaching contained within the Lord's Prayer (Matthew 6:12) and the parable of the Unmerciful Servant (Matthew 18:23–35):

- In the Lord's Prayer, which is used by virtually all Christian denominations, the words *"Forgive us our debts, as we also have forgiven our debtors"* are used. They imply that forgiveness must be an essential component of the Christian approach to punishment because God forgives us only on the condition that we have forgiven others.

- In the Parable of the Unmerciful Servant we are also informed that, in order for Christians to receive God's forgiveness, we must be prepared to forgive others. In the parable, the master is angry with his servant who has not forgiven a fellow servant and says: "Shouldn't you have had mercy on your fellow servant just as I had on you?" (v33) The servant was then handed over to be tortured and Jesus comments: *"This is how my heavenly Father will treat each of you unless you forgive your brother from your heart"* (v35). McKenzie comments that the meaning of this parable is: "the forgiveness of God knows no limit and neither should man's forgiveness."[53] This is a further example of Christians having a duty to forgive those who offend them in any way, rather than seeking revenge.

On the issue of punishment, the Catholic Church teaches that the protection of innocent people is the primary purpose of punishment and if necessary, as the *Catechism of the Catholic Church* states, the death penalty may be required:

"Preserving the common good of society requires rendering the aggressor unable to inflict harm. For this reason the traditional teaching of the Church has acknowledged as well founded the right and duty of legitimate public authority to punish malefactors by means of penalties commensurate with the gravity of the crime, not excluding, in cases of extreme gravity, the death penalty."[54]

However, despite this official teaching contained within the *Catechism of the Catholic Church*, the leadership of the Catholic Church have commented that capital punishment is not necessary in modern society, that alternatives such as life in prison can protect society from the aggressor as well as capital punishment may do. However, it is important that the offender does provide satisfaction to society for his or her crime. They must make up for their wrong-doing and as Bowie states, this involves "satisfaction being made to the individuals affected, to society and to God."[55]

CAPITAL PUNISHMENT

While the death penalty is still legal in many states in The United States of America, in most other countries throughout the world today it has been abolished as it is considered to be a cruel and inhumane form of punishment, regardless of the seriousness of the crime committed. To highlight how cruel and inhumane capital punishment actually is, consider an article which appeared in a Kuwait newspaper, *The Arab Times*, which informs us that on the 20 January 2004 a 35 year old man was hanged for drug trafficking. It adds that the man took "19 minutes and fifty-six seconds to die."[56] This demonstrates the torture many people have to endure as they are put to death. Other methods of capital punishment include electrocution and the lethal injection which, according to many is a more humane method of execution. According to Amnesty International, however, this "can cause excruciating pain"[57] although the mixture of chemicals injected into the criminal causes paralysis and the witnesses to the execution will not be aware of the pain he has to endure.

In Northern Ireland, the last execution took place at the Crumlin Road Gaol in 1961 while in England, the death penalty was last used in 1964 and was then abolished for a trial period in 1965 which then resulted in permanent abolition in December 1969, except for a small number of crimes which included treason and piracy. These were removed in 1998.

 TASK

Using the internet, find out which countries throughout the world still use the death penalty as a form of punishment. Investigate the crimes for which people can be sentenced to death and the methods various countries use to execute criminals.

 TASK

Class debate:

"There would be significantly less serious crime in Northern Ireland if the death penalty was reintroduced as a form of punishment."

There are many arguments in favour of capital punishment. For example, many Christians maintain that the biblical concept of *Lex Talionis* gives moral justification for the use of the death penalty for people who have taken the lives of other human beings. Human life is sacred and the murderer must pay for what he or she has done to another person with their own life. In Genesis 9:6 the right to seek retribution is further expressed: *"Whoever sheds the blood of man, by man shall his blood be shed; for in the image of God has God made man."* The criminal's death may also give the family of the victim the satisfaction of knowing that justice has been served, in that the criminal got what they deserved. The utilitarian, John Stuart Mill, agreed with the principle that we must show total "regard for human life" and in his speech in favour of capital punishment, delivered in 1868, he claimed that in order to do this we must adopt a rule "that he who violates that right of another forfeits it for himself, and that while no other crime that he can commit deprives him of his right to life, this shall."[58] He firmly believed that capital punishment was acceptable on the grounds of retribution. Mill commented: "it appears to me that to deprive the criminal of the life of which he has proven himself to be unworthy…is the most appropriate, as it is certainly the most impressive, mode which society can attach to so great a crime the penal consequences."[59]

Those who argue in favour of the reintroduction of the death penalty, claim that capital punishment is the only threat that may deter some criminals. A Victorian lawyer, Sir James Fitzjames Stephen, commented in 1864: "No other punishment deters men so effectually from committing crimes as the punishment of death."[60]

Consider the following information from America during the period 1960 to 1976 which is provided by Wilcockson in his book *Issues of Life and Death*.[61]

Year	Executions	Number of murders
1960	56	9,140
1975	None – capital punishment was suspended.	20,510
1976	Capital punishment reintroduced.	12% drop in the number of murders.

As the figures indicate, there were over nine thousand murders in America during 1960. In the same year, 56 death row inmates were executed. However, when capital punishment was suspended in 1975, the murder rate more than doubled. When capital punishment was reintroduced, the murder rate fell. While this evidence suggests that capital punishment does deter murderers not everyone would agree. Some scholars argue that such evidence may simply be coincidental. Vardy and Grosch, for example, comment that not only is there little clear evidence that the death penalty does deter but that "few murders are committed by people who weigh up the likely consequences"[62] of their action. Vardy and Grosch continue that a life sentence in prison can be as effective a deterrent as the death penalty. An alternative set of statistics provided by Wilcockson suggest that there is no conclusive relationship between the death penalty and a lower murder rate. Wilcockson uses the example of Canada, where

"17 years after abolition, the murder rate is 27% lower."[63] Therefore the answer to whether capital punishment is an effective deterrent or not is inconclusive. In 1988, a United Nations report concluded: "The research has failed to provide scientific proof that executions have a greater deterrent effect than life imprisonment."[64] However as recently as 2003, David Davis the conservative MP, argued for the reintroduction of the death penalty in the UK. He said: "If somebody plans to carry out a series of murders... then this is obviously an evil and pre-meditated attack and in that case, there could be a deterrent effect."[65]

It is also argued that capital punishment is the best way to protect society from rapists, child abusers and murderers, and because life in prison rarely means life, repeat offenders should be sentenced to death. According to Wilcockson the "finality of capital punishment secures peace of mind"[66] because otherwise there is a chance that the criminal could escape from their prison cell, could organise crime from prison or be released on parole and re-offend. Another argument is that lengthy prison sentences are a waste of taxpayer's money. Capital punishment is relatively cheaper than keeping a person behind bars for the rest of his or her life. This argument may seem very harsh because it considers human life in terms of monetary value. Supporters of capital punishment, however, claim that the murderers or rapists who have shown no remorse for what they have done do not deserve to live and the money saved by their immediate death could be spent on health care – helping people who actually deserve to live.

 TASK

In December 2003, Ian Huntley was convicted of the murder of Holly Wells and Jessica Chapman and was sentenced to serve two life sentences in prison.

In your opinion, should the death penalty be reinstated for such criminals if they show no remorse for what they have done?

Christians who oppose the death penalty would argue that while the Mosaic Law permits the use of capital punishment for eighteen different crimes, such as adultery (Deuteronomy 22:22), homosexuality (Leviticus 20:13), disobedience to one's parents (Exodus 21:15) and magic (Leviticus 20:27), to name but a few, it is not appropriate to apply all laws from the Old Testament to issues in our society today. The death penalty contradicts the teaching of Jesus which promotes the concepts of love, compassion and forgiveness. In addition to references already cited, there are other references from scripture which insist that the sinner is treated with mercy.

- In Luke's Gospel, the Parables of the Lost imply that all sinners will be forgiven if they are sorry for their sins. In the Lost Son for example, we learn that God is willing to forgive our sins as long as we are sorry for our actions

(Luke 15:11–32). With regard to the capital punishment debate, the Christian responsibility is to give offenders a chance to repent and reform rather than sentence them to death.

- With specific reference to the capital punishment debate, the case of the woman who committed adultery as recorded in John 8:3–11 implies that Jesus does not support this form of punishment: Jesus comments: *"If any one of you is without sin, let him be the first to throw a stone at her."* According to Vawter: "The lesson of the story is not that sin is no longer of importance nor that God does not punish sin, but that God extends mercy to the sinner."[67]

- This theme is also evident in one of Matthew's Beatitudes: *"Blessed are the merciful, for they will be shown mercy"* (Matthew 5:7). The message is clear – if we are unmerciful or unforgiving in relation to those who have sinned against us, we in return will be excluded from God's mercy.

The position of the Catholic Church on the issue of capital punishment has previously been outlined in the quote from the *Catechism of the Catholic Church*, on page 299, which states that capital punishment is permissible "in cases of extreme gravity." Pope John Paul II clarified this position in 1995, in an encyclical *Evangelium Vitae*. In this he stated that capital punishment was only to be administered: "in cases of absolute necessity, in other words, when it would not be possible otherwise to defend society. Today, however, as a result of steady improvement in the organisation of the penal system, such cases are very rare, if not practically non-existent."

From this quote it is evident that Catholic teaching is concerned with protection of society and this reflects a natural law approach, as one of Aquinas' primary precepts was to 'live harmoniously in society'. Wilcockson claims that the reason why the Catholic Church will not totally exclude capital punishment is because it "would weaken the Church's view of war and the possibility of killing the wicked in this context."[68] Despite this official teaching, the experience of many Catholics is that capital punishment can never be justified under any circumstances. Sister Helen Prejean, for example, has written a book, *Dead Man Walking*, outlining her experience as a spiritual adviser to death row inmate Patrick Sonnier. As a result of her experiences, she believes that capital punishment is never permissible. Those who oppose capital punishment claim: *"You shall not murder"* (Exodus 20:13) must be regarded as a moral absolute and as capital punishment is contrary to this divine command it should not be permitted under any circumstances. However, a problem is encountered when applying this stipulation to capital punishment because originally it was never intended to rule out capital punishment. Huesman comments that the commandment intends to "protect the very sacredness of human life by forbidding murder. Killing in battle or by capital punishment is not an issue here."[69]

Other Christian denominations totally oppose the death penalty. The Church of England last discussed the issue of capital punishment in 1983. They stated at their General Synod in 1983: "this Synod would deplore the reintroduction of capital punishment into the United Kingdom sentencing policy." The subject has not been debated since.[70] Because the death penalty is not a relevant issue in Northern Ireland today, nor likely to become one in the future, many of the Christian denominations here do not have specific teaching on the issue of capital punishment. The ongoing debate on capital punishment in many of the American states, however, means that Christian churches there have much more to say on the issue. For example, the United Methodist Church in America "declares its opposition to the retention and use of capital punishment and urges its abolition." Several reasons are given which include:

- The death penalty falls unfairly and unequally upon marginalised persons including the poor, the uneducated, ethnic and religious minorities, and persons with mental and emotional illnesses.
- There can be no assertion that human life can be taken humanely by the state.
- In the long run, the use of the death penalty by the state will increase the acceptance of revenge in society and will give official sanction to a climate of violence.[71]

On the other hand, the Wesleyan Church, which has its roots in Methodism, states that capital punishment "should be reserved for those crimes committed in serious circumstances which are clearly defined by law and administered by justice."[72]

One major issue regarding capital punishment is that it does not give the criminal a second chance or an opportunity to reform. It ignores what should be the Christian purpose of punishment which aims to rehabilitate the criminal so that they may return to society and attempt to make a positive contribution to it. Wilcockson comments: "The reformist position inevitably leads to a broadly anti-death penalty position."[73] During the lengthy time that perpetrators spend on death row, many have genuinely reformed but still have been executed. For example, Stanley Tookie Williams spent 24 years on death row for murder and for his role in leading a violent American street gang. During his time on death row he became a totally reformed character, writing children's books warning them about the dangers of gang involvement. He even received a letter from President Bush commending him for his work.[74] Despite seeming to fully reform his character, Stanley Tookie Williams was executed on 13 December 2005.

 TASK

Using the internet research the case of Stanley Tookie Williams, or other criminals who were sentenced to death but who had reformed in prison. Find out the following information:

- What crime did they commit?
- What evidence was there that they had reformed in prison?
- In your opinion was capital punishment necessary in this case or would life in prison have been adequate?

You could present your findings to the class.

Abolitionists claim that the use of the death penalty is hypocritical because the state authorities murder a criminal to prove that it is wrong to murder. Vardy and Grosch argue that the practice of capital punishment "forces the state down to a low moral level,"[75] to the same level as the criminal. In 1935, the leader of the Church of England, William Temple, argued that capital punishment was immoral because "its action in taking life where murder is proved will do more to undermine regard for life, and therefore even to encourage murder, than the terrible nature of the punishment could do to check murderous impulse."[76]

Amnesty International campaign for the abolition of the death penalty and their website states that they oppose "the death penalty in all cases without exception regardless of the nature of the crime, the characteristics of the offender, or the method used by the state to kill the prisoner" because "this cruel, inhuman and degrading punishment...violates the right to life as proclaimed in the Universal Declaration of Human Rights." [77]

Capital punishment is a denial of the basic right to life as stated in Article 3 of the Declaration and it also violates Article 5: "No one shall be subjected to torture or to cruel, inhuman or degrading treatment or punishment."

One of the most significant arguments in opposition to capital punishment is the fact that an innocent person may be put to death. This has happened on many occasions and continues to happen in countries where capital punishment is still used. For example, according to statistics, February 2006 saw the 123rd person released from death row because his innocence was proven. However, in twenty cases there is overwhelming evidence that the executed defendant was innocent.[78] At least if someone is sent to prison by error there is some possibility that the error can be rectified. Consider, for example, innocent people who have been jailed and later released such as the Birmingham six and the Guildford four, who spent over 15 years in prison for crimes they did not commit. If the death penalty had been legal in Britain at that time these men would never have received justice. As previously mentioned, John Stuart Mill was an advocate of the death penalty. However, he did concede that the case of an innocent person being put to death by mistake was a significant argument against the death penalty:

"There is one argument against capital punishment which I cannot deny to have weight...that if by an error of justice an innocent person is put to death, the mistake can never be corrected; all compensation, all reparation for the wrong is impossible."[79]

One of the reasons why the British public campaigned for the abolition of the death penalty was because an innocent person was put to death. In 1953, Derek Bentley was executed because a police officer was shot. However, Bentley did not shoot the officer because he was being held by other police officers at the time. His accomplice in the burglary, who did shoot the officer, was too young to face the death penalty so Bentley was executed instead which "sparked off widespread abolitionist feeling amongst the general public" in Britain.[80] Bentley was granted a posthumous pardon in 1993.

There are a number of ethical issues related to the experience of capital punishment in the American states where the death penalty is used. Many abolitionists claim that the death penalty discriminates, that it does not take the mental state of the criminal into consideration and it does not save money compared to the alternative punishment of life in prison.

1. It has been claimed that in the USA, capital punishment discriminates against certain groups of people. For example, many abolitionists argue that poor people who cannot afford proper legal representation, black people and members of ethnic minorities are more likely to face the death penalty. The Death Penalty Information Centre states that there is a "continuing injustice of racism in the application of the death penalty."[81] The United States has an approximate population of 300,000,000 people, 80% of whom are white and 12% black according to the US Census Bureau.[82] However, since 1976, 57% of those who were executed were white and 34% black and of those currently on death row, 45% are white and 41% black.[83] Many use this evidence to justify the conclusion that black people are being sentenced to death far in excess of white defendants for similar crimes. In other words, race is a factor in deciding who lives and who dies, therefore it is argued that capital punishment in America is immoral.

   If capital punishment was still an available method of punishment in the UK, one could speculate that here too, ethnic minorities would be more likely to receive the death sentence. The MacPhearson Report, produced after the inquiry into the racist murder of black teenager Stephen Lawrence in 1993, concluded that racism existed within the British police force.

   In the United States, women are at the other end of the scale in that they are less likely to be sentenced to death, despite being convicted of the same horrific crimes as men who are sentenced to death. As of the end of December 2007, 51 women were on death row in America but execution is very rare. There have been only eleven executions of women since 1976, around 1% of all executions, although women commit more than 1% of crimes which deserve the death penalty. The last woman sentenced to death in America was Frances Newton in 2005, for the murder of her husband and two children.

2. The concept of diminished responsibility highlights the fact that the offenders are not fully responsible for their actions and therefore should not be punished on a par with someone who is fully aware of and responsible for his or her actions. Despite this, in America there have been numerous cases of people who have been put to death despite suffering from mental illness at the time they committed the crime and did not possessed the extreme culpability or blameworthiness needed before the death sentence can be imposed.

   In an article entitled 'The Execution of Mentally Ill Offenders', Amnesty International USA claims that at least one hundred of the people put to death since 1976 "suffered from some form of serious mental illness or mental impairment."[84] The report concludes that Amnesty's long term aim is to totally abolish the death penalty in America, but: "As a minimum first step…perhaps the USA can be persuaded to rid itself of one of the most shameful aspects of this indecent punishment – the execution of people with serious mental illness."[85]

 TASK

Visit the Amnesty International USA website (www.amnestyusa.org) and read the report 'The Execution of Mentally Ill Offenders.'
Give particular attention to Appendix 1, which lists one hundred executed prisoners and discusses their mental state at the time they committed their crimes.

In your opinion, is the fact that these offenders were executed moral?

3. The issue of money was mentioned above as a reason in support of the death penalty. It is less expensive to put someone to death than to keep them imprisoned for the rest of his or her life. However, capital cases are very expensive and some defendants are on death row for 15 years or more. This is inhumane in itself but necessary to ensure that appeals are carried out and the evidence fully investigated. Abolitionists argue that capital cases which result in the death of a defendant actually cost significantly more than cases which do not involve the death penalty. Consider the following information from the Death Penalty Information Centre:

   "A new study released by the Urban Institute on March 6, 2008 found that…the average cost to Maryland taxpayers for reaching a single death sentence is $3 million–$1.9 million more than the cost of a non-death penalty case."[86]

   This is only one example from one of the American states. However the website (www.deathpenaltyinfo.org) provides evidence that this is also the case in other states where the death penalty is used as a method of punishment.

In conclusion, retribution seems the only valid argument in favour of capital punishment. However, from a Christian perspective, this argument is morally unacceptable because it is a Christian's responsibility to forgive the offender and offer rehabilitation (a second chance). In addition to this, there is no certainty that the death penalty does actually deter criminals or that it offers society more protection than imprisoning the criminal for life. While those who support capital punishment may argue that a murderer or a rapist deserves to be punished severely, those who oppose capital punishment feel that the death penalty creates more problems than it attempts to solve – the possibility that innocent people may be sentenced to death and that capital punishment is unfairly used against minority groups.

 PRACTICE ESSAY TITLES

Question adapted from CCEA Summer 2003 A2 6

(a) Outline and examine the ethical issues raised by the debate on crime and punishment. (30)

Your response could make reference to the following points:

- Aims of punishment – protection, retribution, rehabilitation, deterrence and vindication
- Ethical issues such as utilitarian views, moral responsibility and human rights
- Christian values on punishment

Question adapted from CCEA 2003 A2 6

(b) Critically assess the claim that capital punishment is morally justified. (20)

Your response could make reference to the following points:

- The extent to which capital punishment fulfils the aims of punishment for example, protection, retribution, rehabilitation and deterrence
- Christian teaching with specific reference to the concept of reformation and rehabilitation
- Discuss other ethical issues such as the problem of the execution of innocent people and discrimination

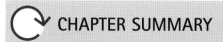 CHAPTER SUMMARY

Introduction

- Various views on the concept of justice:
  1. Individualistic theories of justice – Hobbes, Locke and Nozick
  2. Communitarian theories of justice – Plato, Rousseau and Rawls

Methods and purpose of punishment: the ethical debate

- The purpose of punishment:
  1. Protection
  2. Retribution
  3. Rehabilitation
  4 Deterrence
  5. Vindication

- Methods of punishment:
  1. Harm to the body
  2. Harm to property
  3. Restriction of movement
  4. Harm to reputation

Ethical and religious perspectives on punishment

- Utilitarian views that punishment must maximise happiness in society.

- The views of Kant that punishment is morally acceptable in order for society to have retribution.

- The issue of moral responsibility with specific reference to:
  1. The concept of free will and moral responsibility
  2. The idea of diminished responsibility
  3. The implications of determinism in the debate concerning crime and punishment

- Human rights issues

- Christian attitudes with specific reference to teaching from:
  1. Teaching from the Old Testament
  2. Teaching from the New Testament
  3. Views of various Christian denominations

Capital punishment

- Arguments in favour of capital punishment:
  1. The issue of retribution
  2. Capital punishment is an effective deterrent
  3. Capital punishment protects society from murderers

- Arguments against capital punishment:
  1. The impact of Jesus' teaching on the capital punishment debate and the Christian ideal of reformation
  2. Capital punishment is a moral contradiction – using killing to teach that it is wrong to kill
  3. Capital punishment is a violation of human rights
  4. The possibility than an innocent person may be put to death by error
  5. Other issues such as discrimination and economic issues

Endnotes

1 Quote taken from Tyler, S & Reid, G, *Religious Studies, Philip Allen Updates*, Oxfordshire, 2002, p205

2 Vardy, P & Grosch, P, *Puzzle of Ethics*, Harper Collins, London, 1999, p133

3 Vardy & Grosch, *op cit*, p135

4 Thompson, M, *An Introduction to Philosophy and Ethics*, Hodder & Stoughton, London, 2003, p207

5 Vardy & Grosch, *op cit*, p134–5

6 *ibid*, p135

7 Bowie, R, *Ethical Studies*, Nelson Thornes, Cheltenham, 2004, p259

8 Vardy & Grosch, *op cit*, p136

9 Thompson, *op cit*, p208

10 Bowie, *op cit*, p261

11 Tyler & Reid, *op cit*, p209

12 *ibid*, p210

13 Mill, JS, *On Liberty*, Cambridge University Press, Cambridge, 1989, p68

14 Leviticus 24:19–20.

15 Wilcockson, M, *Issues of Life and Death*, Hodder & Stoughton, London, 1999, p76

16 Kant, I. Quote taken from Bowie, *op cit*, p266

17 Rachels. Quote taken from *ibid*, p266

18 Vardy & Grosch, *op cit*, p187

19 Wilcockson, *op cit*, p77

20 Restorative Justice Online, www.restorativejustice.org, accessed 26 November 2008

21 *ibid*

22 Bowie, *op cit*, p267

23 Wilcockson, *op cit*, p80

24 Vardy & Grosch, *op cit*, p183

25 Tyler & Reid, *op cit*, p212

26 Vardy & Grosch, *op cit*, p. 184

27 *ibid*, p188

28 Bowie, *op cit*, p266

29 Vardy & Grosch, *op cit*, p184

30 Tyler & Reid, *op cit*, p211

31 Vardy & Grosch, *op cit*, p184

32 *ibid*, p184

33 *ibid*, p184

34 Kant, I. Quote taken from Wilcockson, *op cit*, p84

35 Wilcockson, *op cit*, p84

36 Jenkins, J, *Ethics and Religion – Second Edition*, Heinemann, Oxford, 2003, p24

37 Vardy & Grosch, *op cit*, p189

38 Bowie, *op cit*, p266

39 *ibid*, p89

40 Skinner, BF, *Beyond Freedom and Dignity*, Hacket Publishing Co, 1972, p76–77

41 Jenkins, *op cit*, p25

42 Darrow, C, *Attorney for the Damned*. Quote taken from Minton, A, (ed), *Philosophy: Paradox and Discovery*, McGraw-Hill, New York, 1976, p304

43 Vardy & Grosch, *op cit*, p190

44 Clarke, P, *Examining Philosophy and Ethics*, Nelson Thornes, Cheltenham, 2002, p108

45 Faley, R, 'Leviticus', *The Jerome Biblical Commentary*, Geoffrey Chapman, London, 1970, p83

46 Alexander, TD, *From Paradise to Promised Land: An Introduction to the Main Themes of the Pentateuch*, Paternoster Press, Carlisle, 1995, p88

47 'What exactly is the rod mentioned in Proverbs', Religious Tolerance.Org, www.religioustolerance.org, accessed 26 November 2008

48 McKenzie, J, *The Gospel According to Matthew, The Jerome Biblical Commentary*, Geoffrey Chapman, London, 1970, p75

49 Harrington, D, *Collegeville Bible Commentary, The Gospel According to Matthew*, Liturgical Press, 1991, p36

50 *ibid*, p78

51 Aquinas. Quote taken from Wilcockson, *op cit*, p85

52 Hoose, B, *Received Wisdom*, 1994, quote taken from Vardy & Grosch, *op cit*, p181

53 McKenzie, *op cit*, p96

54 *Catechism of the Catholic Church*, Veritas, Dublin, 1994, 2266

55 Bowie, *op cit*, p266

56 Taken from an article in the *Arab Times*, 21 January 2004

57 '57 'Lethal Injection', Amnesty International USA, www.amnestyusa.org, accessed 26 November 2008

58 Mill, JS, 'Speech in Favour of Capital Punishment', in Singer, P, Applied Ethics, Oxford University Press, Oxford, 1986, p102

59 *ibid*, p98

60 Wilcockson, *op cit*, p87

61 ibid, p88

62 Vardy & Grosch, *op cit*, p187

63 Wilcockson, *op cit*, p88

64 ibid, p88

65 'Tories' Davis Backs Death Penalty', BBC News 16 November 2003, www.bbc.co.uk, accessed 12 November 2008

66 Wilcockson, *op cit*, p89

67 Vawter, B, *The Gospel According to John, The Jerome Biblical Commentary*, Geoffrey Chapman, London, 1970, p441

68 Wilcockson, *op cit*, p94

69 Huesman, J, Exodus, The Jerome Biblical Commentary, Geoffrey Chapman, London, 1970, p57

70 'Legal and Criminal Justice', The Church of England, www.cofe.anglican.org, accessed 27 November 2008

71 'The Book of Resolutions 2004', The People of the United Methodist Church, www.umc.org, accessed 8 January 2009

72 'Contemporary Issues – Sanctity of Life', The Northwest District of the Wesleyan Church, www.nwwesleyan.org, accessed 10 December 2008

73 Wilcockson, *op cit*, p90

74 'Stanley Williams', Wikipedia, www.wikipedia.org, accessed 26 November 2008

75 Vardy & Grosch, op cit, p187

76 Wilcockson, *op cit*, p92

77 'Abolish The Death Penalty', Amnesty International, www.amnesty.org, accessed 6 December 2009

78 'Execution of Innocents', Dead Man Walking Update, www.deadmanwalkingupdate.org, accessed 26 November 2008

79 Mill, 'Speech in Favour of Capital Punishment', Singer, *op cit*, p102

80 Wilcockson, *op cit*, p82

81 'The Death Penalty in Black and White', Death Penalty Information Centre, www.deathpenaltyinfo.org, accessed 28 November 2008

82 Cencus.org, www.quickfacts.census.org, accessed 28 November 2008

83 'The Death Penalty in Black and White', Death Penalty Information Centre, www.deathpenaltyinfo.org, accessed 28 November 2008

84 'The Execution of Mentally Ill Offenders', Amnesty International USA, www.amnestyusa.org, accessed 28 November 2008

85 ibid

86 'Costs of the Death Penalty', Death Penalty Information Centre, www.deathpenaltyinfo.org, accessed 28 November 2008

Glossary

Abortion – the removal of an embryo or foetus from the uterus in order to end a pregnancy.

Abortifacient – a substance that induces abortion.

Absolute affluence – a standard of living where people have more income than they need to adequately provide them with all the basic necessities of life.

Absolute dismissal argument – the view that animals do not have moral status and are not entitled to the rights or protection from humans.

Absolute poverty – poverty is so extreme that people do not have enough money or resources to secure the necessities required for a basic standard of living.

Absolutism – an approach to ethics which stresses the importance of rules which can never be broken under any circumstances.

Act or omissions distinction – the moral distinction between taking action to end a person's life or passively allowing them to die by, for example, the removal of a feeding tube.

Affirmative action – or positive discrimination refers to the preferential treatment of members of a minority group over a majority group in order to promote equal opportunities for all people by redressing past discrimination against such groups.

Almsgiving – the act of making a financial contribution to help those suffering from poverty.

Amoral – an action which cannot be considered to be good or bad in terms of morality because it is committed by someone who does not know the difference between good and bad.

Androcentric – focused on or dominated by males or masculine interests.

Annulment – the formal declaration by the Catholic Church that a marriage has been invalidated.

Antinomian – an approach to morality which does not consider rules to be important and can be considered to be the opposite of legalism.

Apartheid – means separateness and was the term used to describe the official policy of separating white and black people by the South African government.

Apodictic – direct rules such as the Ten Commandments which follow the pattern 'You shall not ...' and do not have punishments listed alongside them.

Apparent goods – a concept related to natural law which refers to the belief that humans do wrong because they believe that they are doing right. In such a case people are in pursuit of an apparent good.

Asylum seekers – people who seek protection in a host country from persecution in their own country.

Autonomy – the idea that humans are free to make their own moral choices.

Bioethics – the analysis of the ethical issues surrounding advances in biological sciences such as new reproductive technologies.

Cardinal virtues – the virtues that Aquinas felt should influence human reason and moral decision making. They are prudence, temperance, fortitude and justice.

Casuistry – the process of beginning with fixed moral principles and applying them to individual situations.

Categorical imperative – Kant's principle that in order to live moral lives we must only act in a way which can be universalised.

Cloning – to make a copy of something or to replicate it. Reproductive cloning refers to making a copy of a human or an animal while therapeutic cloning refers to making a copy of cells which can be then used to replace organs which have failed.

Conscience – our innate sense or inner feelings about right and wrong.

Conservation ethics – a human centred approach to environmental ethics which supports respect of the environment because of the benefit it brings to humans.

Contraception – methods used to prevent conception.

Covenant – an agreement or promise.

Cultural relativism – the concept that the beliefs and practices of an individual or community should only be considered in terms of the culture of that individual or community.

Decalogue – Greek name for the Ten Commandments, literally translated as ten words.

Deontological – an approach to ethics which is based on the morality of our actions in terms of our duty towards other people or our obedience to rules.

Descriptive ethics – a simple description of the way in which people behave.

Determinism – the idea that every action or aspect of behaviour is determined by a previous event. Hard determinism asserts that humans are not free in any way while soft determinism accepts that free will and determinism are compatible.

Deterrence – an aim of punishment which has the intention of using punishment in order to prevent people from committing crime.

Diminished responsibility – the idea that some factors diminish the extent to which individuals are to blame for their actions.

Discrimination – negative behaviour against a person or a group due to their race, sex or religion which results in them being treated unfairly.

Divine Command Theory – the view that something is good because God has commanded it and that something is immoral if God has informed us through scripture.

Dominion – the biblical concept that humans have been given the authority from God to rule over the earth.

Double effect – the idea that people should only focus only on the primary intention of our actions, rather than any secondary side effects their actions may have.

Ecological Extension / Eco-centrism – an approach to environmental ethics which focuses on the overall importance of interrelationships between all things that exist on the planet.

Egoism – an approach to ethics which asserts that individuals should behave in a way that promotes their self interest above the interests of others.

Emotivism – an approach to ethics which rejects rules or moral principles and asserts that moral statements are simply expressions of what the speaker believes about the issue.

Ethic – a set of principles or moral values which help us distinguish between what is considered to be right or wrong behaviour.

Ethics – also referred to as moral philosophy, is a branch of philosophy which is concerned with the morality of our actions and whether they are right or wrong.

Ethnic minorities – groups of people living in a country that have different race or cultural traditions from the majority of the population.

Euthanasia – the practice of ending a person's life in order to prevent them from having to endure additional suffering.

Euthyphro dilemma – the question of whether or not God is the source of morality.

Existentialism – a belief that all humans have personal autonomy and exist to enrich their lives.

Feminism – a movement which aims to achieve equality for women. Different strands of feminism include liberal feminism, radical feminism, social feminism and Christian feminism.

Fornication – a term used to refer to sexual intercourse between a couple who are not married to each other.

Gaia Hypothesis – the theory held by James Lovelock which outlined the idea that the planet earth was alive and possesses its own in built sense of rationale which is used to maintain conditions necessary for its survival.

Genocide – murder of or violent crimes against specific groups of people with the intention of destroying the very existence of that group.

Hedonic calculus – Bentham's method of measuring the amount of happiness an action could produce in order to decide on the most acceptable way for utilitarians to behave.

Humanism – a secular approach to morality which believes that all humans are equal in dignity and worth.

Immoral – an action which is considered wrong or bad.

Individual relativism – the concept that right and wrong can differ between individuals.

Infanticide – intentionally causing the death of an infant.

Institutional racism – racism which is widespread throughout society and occurs with public institutions such as the government and criminal justice system.

Instrumental value – the value of an object, not in itself, but for some other purpose. In environmental ethics instrumental value refers to the concept that things such as forests have value because of the benefit they bring to humans.

Intrinsic value – the value of something in itself and not because of the benefits it can bring to others.

In vitro fertilisation – a procedure used to help an infertile couple conceive when the egg from a female is fertilised by sperm from her partner or a donor in a Petri dish or in a 'test tube'.

Just war theory – a theory initiated by Augustine and Aquinas which permits war under certain conditions.

Justice – the idea of fairness and equal opportunities for all people.

Ku Klux Klan – a white supremacist group who violated the human rights of black people living in America.

Legalism – a legalistic approach to ethics or morality is one which considers obedience to rules and regulations as being of primary importance.

Liberation theology – a school of theology which is concerned with the liberation of the poor and oppressed throughout the world.

Libertarian Extension – an attitude towards the environment which is based on the idea that all living entities have intrinsic value and therefore should be allowed to exist free from human interference.

Matthean exception – a reference unique to Matthew's Gospel which suggests that Jesus permitted divorce on the grounds of unfaithfulness.

Moral – an action which is considered right or good.

Morality – a study of the right or wrong actions or behaviour of an individual.

Natural law – an ethical theory developed by Thomas Aquinas which is based on the principle that moral behaviour consists of following God's plan for creation.

Natural rights – basic rights which all human beings are entitled to regardless of any other factors.

Normative ethics – the branch of ethics which is concerned with the examination of right and wrong or moral and immoral behaviour.

North-south divide – a term used to refer to the geographical division which exists between developed and developing countries in the world.

Pacifism – opposition to violence or war.

Parousia – the second coming of Christ.

Practical imperative – Kant's principle that people must not be treated as a means to an end, but always as an end in themselves.

Pragmatic dismissal argument – the idea that while animals are not considered to be in any way equal to humans, they do deserve to be protected from unnecessary suffering and treated with respect.

Pre-implantation Genetic Diagnosis (PGD) – an advance in reproductive technology which allows doctors to screen the genes of the pre-embryo and only implant embryos which are free from genetic abnormalities into the womb of the mother.

Primary precepts – a term which refers to Aquinas' views on the overall purpose of human life which is to live, reproduce, learn, have an ordered society and worship God. The secondary precepts are rules that follow from obedience to the primary precepts.

Primitive streak – forms on the embryonic cells about fourteen days after conception and it acts like a line of symmetry ensuring that the pre-embryo fully develops. According to the HFEA, research is not permitted on embryos after this stage.

Principle of Due Proportion – a principle which allows a terminally ill patient to refuse extraordinary treatment that may have the effect of prolonging their suffering.

Proportionalism – the approach to morality which asserts that there are certain moral rules and that it can never be right to go against these rules unless there is a proportionate reason which would justify it.

Racism – a belief that one race of people is better than others which often leads to prejudice or discrimination against the race who are perceived to be inferior.

Reason – the innate ability of humans to reflect on and direct their moral behaviour.

Refugees – people who flee their home country in order to seek refuge or protection in another country. They are referred to as asylum seekers until they receive a positive decision on their application to stay in a host country.

Rehabilitation – an aim of punishment which has the intention of using punishment in order to reform the offender so that they can return to society and make a positive contribution to it.

Relative poverty – some members of society are poor in comparison to the wealth enjoyed by their neighbours but do not suffer from extreme or absolute poverty.

Relativism – an approach to ethics which is concerned with the idea that morality is not fixed but will vary for different people and cultures at different times. It is therefore not based on absolute or universal laws.

Sacrosanct – sacred.

Sanctity of life – the concept that human life is sacred or sacrosanct as it is created in the image of God.

Shallow ecology – an approach to environmental ethics which considers the environment to simply have instrumental value for humans.

Situation Ethics – an ethical theory developed by Joseph Fletcher which is based on the principle that moral behaviour consists of following the most loving course of action.

Slippery slope argument – states that a relatively small first step will inevitably lead to a chain of related events which have a much greater negative impact on society.

Speciesism – discrimination by humans against non-human animals because they are from a different species than humans. Using animals for medical experimentation and for food could be considered to be a form of speciesism.

Stewardship – the biblical concept that it is the responsibility of humans to act as the caretakers of the environment as property which God has entrusted to us.

Suffragettes – an early twentieth century movement which aimed to achieve the right for women to vote.

Surrogacy – a form of assisted reproduction which involves implanting a pre-embryo in the womb of a host mother who will carry the child for the duration of the pregnancy and who will then hand the child over to a commissioning couple shortly after it has been born.

Syngamy – the name for the process which takes place in the immediate 24 hours after conception during which time the genetic material from the father and mother are conjoined.

Teleological – a branch of ethics which states that morality is based on the consequences of our actions.

Utilitarianism – an ethical theory developed by Bentham and Mill which is based on the principle that moral behaviour consists of acting in a way that promotes the greatest amount of happiness for the greatest number of people.

Viability – the point from which a foetus can live outside the mother's womb.

Virtue ethics – an ethical theory which emphasises the importance of living according to the Aristotelian virtues, in contrast to the approaches which focus on obedience to our moral duty, rules (deontology) or theories which emphasise the importance of the consequences of actions (teleology).

Xenophobia – An unreasonable fear, distrust, or hatred of strangers, foreigners, or anything perceived as foreign or different.

Index

St. Patricks Grammar School DOWNPATRICK BT30 6NJ	Book Number		

This book is the property of St. Patricks. Pupils should maintain this book in good condition and should not write notes on it or deface it in any way. A charge will be made if it is lost or has been badly treated.

Write your Name, Teacher's Initials, Form and Year on the top available space.

UPON REQUEST THIS BOOK MUST BE RETURNED TO YOUR CLASS TEACHER.

Issue	Name	T/Init.	Form	Year
1				
2				
3				
4				
5				
6				
7				
8				